GAMES WE PLAY

GAMES WE PLAY

SPORTS IN SOUTH ASIA

EDITED BY

RONOJOY SEN
OMITA GOYAL

India International Centre

OXFORD
UNIVERSITY PRESS

Oxford University Press is a department of the University of Oxford.
It furthers the University's objective of excellence in research, scholarship,
and education by publishing worldwide. Oxford is a registered trademark of
Oxford University Press in the UK and in certain other countries.

Reprint published by
Oxford University Press
22 Workspace, 2nd Floor, 1/22 Asaf Ali Road, New Delhi 110002, India

© India International Centre 2018

First Edition published by India International Centre in 2018
Reprint published by Oxford University Press in 2020

South Asia's Sporting Mosaic was originally published in *IIC Quarterly*
(Winter 2017–Spring 2018). This reprint is published by arrangement with
India International Centre for sale/distribution throughout the world.

The moral rights of the authors have been asserted.

ISBN-13: 978-0-19-012681-0
ISBN-10: 0-19-012681-7

Typeset in ITC Berkeley Oldstyle Std 10.5/12
by Tranistics Data Technologies, Kolkata 700091
Printed in India by Rakmo Press, New Delhi 110 020

CONTENTS

ix: Preface
OMITA GOYAL

xi: Foreword
KARAN SINGH

xiii: Introduction: The Landscape of Sport in South Asia
RONOJOY SEN

ARTICLES

I DEVELOPMENT OF CRICKET

3: The Mercurials: The Nature of Pakistani Cricket
ALI KHAN

17: Cricket in Bangladesh
HABIBUL HAQUE KHONDKER

30: The Journey of Indian Women's Cricket from the 1970s
SHANTHA RANGASWAMY

39: Indian Premier League: The Great Indian Story
MIHIR BOSE

II NATIONALISM COMMUNALISM RACE CLASS AND GENDER

53: Innocence and Indian Cricket
SATADRU SEN

67: Cricket in Abstemious Times
SANKARAN KRISHNA

76: Sports, Radio and Memory: Looking Back at the 1970s
AVIJIT GHOSH

87: When Politics Ran Riot at Eden Gardens
SOUVIK NAHA

98: 'Indians Make Us Angry!': Australian Perceptions of Touring
Indian Cricket Teams, 1947–2017
IAN SIMPSON

111: India's Sporting Frontier: Race, Integration and Discontent
in the North-east
DUNCAN MCDUIE-RA

126: Reinforcing Difference: The History of Women's Involvement
in Physical Activity in India
PAYOSHNI MITRA

PHOTO ESSAY

135: Focus Sport

ARTICLES

III BEYOND CRICKET

157: The Decline of Hockey in Pakistan
SHAHARYAR M. KHAN

163: A Story of Two Different Worlds: Indian Hockey's Glory Run
and the Unending Struggle
SUNDEEP MISRA

174: The Future of Indian Football
NOVY KAPADIA

189: Football in Post-Independence Bangladesh
KAUSIK BANDYOPADHYAY

202: India's Shuttle Story: Breaking through Barriers to Take Flight
ABHIJEET KULKARNI

212: A Well-Kept Secret: The History of Rugby in Sri Lanka
SHANAKA AMARASINGHE

IV ANCIENT PURSUITS AND MODERNITY

227: The Great Gama and His Legacy
RUDRANEIL SENGUPTA

240: Wrestling with the History of Yoga as Sport in Modern India
JOSEPH S. ALTER

254: Bodybuilding in India: Bollywood Bodies
and Middle-Class Lifestyles
MICHIEL BAAS

266: Racing on Water: A Short History of *Vallam Kali* in Kerala
AMRITH LAL

V SPORTS ADMINISTRATION

281: Guru Dutt Sondhi: Indian IOC Member and Visionary of
Asian Integration through Sport
STEFAN HUEBNER

294: See You in Court: The Legal Challenge Against
India's Sports Bosses
SHARDA UGRA

VI SPORT IN FILM AND LITERATURE

307: Sport in Indian Film
AMY J. RANSOM

319: 'I Won't Let You Down'
MOTI NANDI (TRANSLATED BY ARUNAVA SINHA)

329: About the Editors and Contributors

PREFACE

Sport is as important in our everyday lives as is education, for instance, and is integral to any society. History, culture and arts have defined India, and sport has been a part of it, dating back to pre-colonial times. As Ronojoy Sen aptly writes in his Introduction, there was life before cricket.

The list of contemporary sports played in the country is long. Besides cricket, hockey, tennis, football and badminton, Indian sportspersons have made a mark in wrestling, shooting, boxing, among many others. What is even more encouraging is that the number of women in sports, even unconventional ones like these, has increased. And this despite the discrimination women continue to face in their private and professional lives. Mary Kom made history over a decade ago in boxing, more recently, Navjot Kaur did India proud by winning the gold in wrestling. And as I write, the amazing Manu Bhaker, all of 16 years old, who just won her second gold in shooting. Hopefully the story of her journey to the top will inspire the youth of today.

Kabaddi, the age-old but forgotten sport that we all played as children, has made a comeback with the Pro Kabaddi League. It is perhaps the first time that a sport was promoted with as much fanfare as cricket, and in 2017, television viewership came a close second. Let's hope that one day all sports will get the place they deserve.

Despite this, however, sport in India still has a long way to go. The articles in this volume touch on the problems that confront the sports scenario in the region as a whole, be it corruption, faulty policies, lack of adequate financing, among several other challenges. The most significant obstacle is lack of state support. Most sportspersons survive on determination and passion for the game, without even basic infrastructure, leave alone financial backing. Sport, therefore, remains largely the domain of the elite. Sport is not all about professional sport; it is about play, not winning, it is about enjoying a game. In fact, the word 'Sport' derives from the French *desport*, meaning leisure. What we lack is a sporting culture, and we have to patronise sport as much as we do art. Perhaps the place to start is with the youth.

It is unfortunate that sport is not a priority at home since parents are more concerned about their children's grades and future prospects. In fact this is true of most schools as well. There might be opportunities to try out for teams, but what happens to the majority of students who don't want to or who are not encouraged to? What happened to sport as an activity in school? Not everyone can or needs to be a champion, or even consider sport as a career. What is important to recognise is that without sport, a child's health is at risk, especially as our lives are becoming increasingly sedentary. The core principle of yoga, for example, is that the mind and body must be in unison for overall well-being. Further, sport teaches us to work as a team, and this is the best lesson that will hold us in good stead in life.

This volume does not claim to be a definitive account of sport in South Asia. Its uniqueness lies in the fact that along with papers on professional sport, it includes personal narratives that make the game come alive. We are grateful to the contributors who readily agreed to be part of this effort.

◆

OMITA GOYAL

FOREWORD

Sport remains one of the few activities which effectively cut across national, linguistic, religious and other barriers. India has a long tradition of indigenous sports such as wrestling, archery and kabaddi. With the advent of Western influence, of course, we have taken in a huge way to cricket—where we now excel—hockey, football, tennis, badminton and boxing. If we add chess, this is another area where we are producing grandmasters. These sports are, of course, not confined to India but are spread widely over the region.

This special issue on sports in South Asia brings together a number of interesting essays from around the region which clearly show the universal significance of sports. The South Asian participation in the Olympic Games goes back almost a century, and although we are still not able to match the performance of other Asian countries, such as China and Japan, our sportspersons are beginning to make a significant impact on the world scene.

A special word needs to be said about yoga, which is perhaps not a sport in the classical sense, but can play a major role in developing physical fitness and mental agility, thus helping sportspersons reach their full capacity. Despite our obsession with cricket, this issue deals with a wide spectrum of other sports and, I am sure, will be read with great interest by sports lovers everywhere. Women are also making an increasing contribution to sports in many spheres, especially badminton and wrestling. This is a good sign because if we are to catch up with other nations, Indian sportspersons will need to make a major contribution.

KARAN SINGH

◆

INTRODUCTION
The Landscape of Sport in South Asia

RONOJOY
SEN

ong before the British conquered the Indian subcontinent, South Asians were involved in sport. It is not entirely by accident that the premier awards for sportspersons in India are named Arjuna awards and those for coaches named after Dronacharya, both central figures from the great Indian epic, Mahabharata. In a civilisation where the epics still have a greater hold on the imagination than cut-and-dried historical narratives, this is perhaps not unnatural. But the nomenclature of the awards is also a clue to the ancient origins of organised sport in South Asia. Difficult as it might be to imagine, there was life before cricket and the various games introduced to the Indian subcontinent by the British. Not all the ancient sports have survived, and some of them are perhaps lost forever. But there are many extant sports, such as wrestling, whose origins go back several centuries. And there are others like cricket, introduced along with other sports by the British in the long 19th century, which South Asians have made their own.[1]

This book looks at the different sports played and watched in South Asia and situates them in the region's history, society and economy. The activities covered span sports like cricket, which enjoys a religion-like status across South Asia, to more local ones such as boat racing in Kerala. As recently as 20 years ago, the entry on India in a handbook of sports studies could claim, though not entirely accurately, that the sociological study of sport in India essentially remains virgin territory (McDonald, 2000: 540). The same could be said for the rest of South Asia. There are of course several fine books on the history of cricket in South Asia, with Shapoorjee Sorabjee's book going back as far as 1897. However, the other sports are woefully under-represented, with some notable exceptions. South Asia's tryst with the Olympic Games, which goes back to 1920, has been documented in a few books. There are of course several autobiographies and biographies of South Asian sportspersons, again mostly of cricketers. In recent times, there have been many more books on and by non-cricketers. While cricket figures prominently in this issue, we have made every effort to look at the diverse elements of South Asia's sporting mosaic.

The idea of a collection on sport in South Asia is not entirely a novel one. There have been at least three published volumes, with the first one being published in 2005. Indeed, some of the contributors to this volume—Joseph Alter, Satadru Sen and Kausik Bandyopadhyay—have written for the earlier books. There are, however, significant differences between the earlier publications and this book. For one, this volume looks at some sports, such as badminton, wrestling, boat racing and rugby, which did not find a place in the earlier books. Second, innovations, such as the Indian Premier League (IPL), which has changed the way cricket as well as other sports are played and watched, really took off only after the earlier books were published. Third, this collection arguably brings together academic (anthropologists, historians and political scientists), journalistic and autobiographical genres in a way the other volumes have not.

The idea was to bring together a collection of essays which contributes to a better and more nuanced understanding of sport in South Asia, but is also readable. Much of the academic writing on sport has been constrained by the goal of laying a claim to putting sports studies on the same pedestal as other more mainstream disciplines. This collection is not encumbered by such lofty aims. It seeks to understand and contextualise the different sports played in South Asia without, hopefully, taking away the joy and passion that accompany sport.

Then, again, there is really no justification needed for another collection on sport in South Asia. The most obvious is the ubiquity of sport, as in most other societies. We take inspiration from what Joseph Strutt wrote in the late 18th century: 'In order to form a just estimate of the character of any particular people it is absolutely necessary to investigate the sports and pastimes most prevalent amongst them' (Birley, 1993: 1). If one were to add up the number of hours the average person spends (or wastes, depending on one's perspective) playing, watching or discussing sport, we would be very surprised. Besides, there are huge sums of money and sponsorship riding on sport in South Asia, particularly cricket. Indeed, 2020 is an apposite year to be bringing out a collection of essays on sport in South Asia since the Olympic Games returns to Asia and to Tokyo. India, which has traditionally been a poor performer in the Olympics, would be looking to reap a bigger medal harvest than before in sports like shooting, badminton, wrestling and boxing. But the more compelling reason is that sport is inherently worthy of study for what it reveals about human nature and societies. As Johan Huizinga (1980) puts it: 'All play means something,' going on to add, 'Play cannot be denied. You can deny, if you like, nearly all abstractions: justice, beauty, truth, goodness, mind, God. You can deny seriousness, but not play.' It is also true in the South Asian context, as Dipesh Chakrabarty (2005: 3) points out, 'Social historians of India have paid more attention to riots than to sports, to street-battles with the police than to rivalries on the soccer field.'

DEVELOPMENT OF CRICKET

Cricket is undoubtedly the most popular sport in South Asia and is flourishing in unlikely corners of the region, such as Nepal and Afghanistan. India is also the financial nerve centre of the game, generating over 70 per cent of revenues associated with the sport. This issue contains several essays that examine, both frontally as well as through other prisms such as nationalism, race and class, the development of cricket in Bangladesh, Pakistan and India.

Among the essays that look directly at the development of cricket in South Asia is Ali Khan's analysis of the nature of Pakistani cricket. Khan explores why Pakistani cricket has often been described as 'mercurial'—terrible on the field one day and world champion on another. He offers several reasons for this, including the lack of a well-defined domestic structure for cricket. This has led to a cricketing culture which has, in turn, led to 'high-risk match winners', rather than 'consistent performers'. As the game has modernised, other nations have adopted rigid training schedules. Pakistan has resisted this trend which helped it, according to Khan, produce brilliant but sometimes inconsistent players. Khan also questions whether the 'mercurial' tag is in reality a stereotype, just as West Indian cricketers were once called 'calypso' cricketers.

Habibul Haque Khondker explores the history of cricket in Bangladesh going back to colonial times. During the period from 1947 to 1971, when Bangladesh was still East Pakistan, non-Bengalis dominated cricket, and the Bengalis who were involved in playing cricket usually came from the upper classes. Cricket was then marked by social exclusion and was dominated by West Pakistan. Cricket in independent Bangladesh gave Bengali-speaking players a chance to prove themselves. The sport also became more democratic and inclusive. A number of top Bangladeshi players now hail from rural areas and are from the lower-middle classes and poor backgrounds. The democratisation of cricket, according to Khondker, has also become a source of national pride in Bangladesh and heightened a sense of national belonging.

Shantha Rangaswamy's essay is the only one by an author who played a sport at the highest level. Rangaswamy, who captained India in the 1970s, chronicles the early days of women's cricket in India where she played a pioneering role. From the first women's national championship in 1973, where only three states participated, to the heady win against the West Indies in Patna in 1976, watched by over 40,000 spectators, Rangaswamy's paper is an invaluable personal account of the formative years of women's cricket. Her essay is most timely, as women's cricket in India has now reached an all-time high in popularity after the Indian team was runners-up in the 2017 women's World Cup.

Finally, Mihir Bose analyses the transformation wrought by the IPL which completes 10 years in 2018. According to Bose, the IPL lies at the centre of India's financial and administrative dominance of world cricket. At one time, English and Australian cricketers avoided touring India, but now they cannot keep away. As he puts it, 'Two centuries ago, the British came to India to make money and founded an empire. Now their cricketers come to India to make the sort of money they could never make anywhere else.' Besides its alliance with big business and Bollywood, Bose also alludes to the dark underbelly of corruption associated with the IPL.

NATIONALISM, COMMUNALISM, RACE, CLASS AND GENDER

Yet another set of essays in this issue uses sport to focus on the themes of nationalism, communalism, race, class and gender in India. Satadru Sen, who tragically passed away in 2018, turns the gaze away from cricketers to spectators or consumers. He does so by looking at the idea of 'innocence', which he believes has been a persistent ideal in cricket and the sporting community at large. He traces the trajectory of innocence of a small, modernising class in India, which was isolated from the world, to a very different model of 'innocent isolation', which characterises contemporary consumers of cricket. From the 1950s to the 1980s, while cricket provided Indians a window to the outside world, the sport was also limited to the urban and middle class. From the 1990s, with the ushering in of liberalisation, things changed dramatically. For Sen, the IPL was 'the perfect symptom of the Indian version of globalised capitalism, monopolistic privilege and the "gold-rush" culture of liberalisation'. The IPL also created a new kind of fan who was 'newly moneyed and brashly confident'. Sen proceeds to argue that the 'monkey gestures' in 2007 by Indian fans at the mixed-race Australian cricketer, Andrew Symonds, was a sign of 'innocence having arrived'.

Sankaran Krishna expresses vividly what it was like to be a schoolboy cricketer and a cricket fan in India in the 1960s and 1970s. He focuses on the materiality of the cricketing equipment with which middle-class children played and how they interwove with the larger political economy of an import-substituting postcolonial society, where foreign goods were 'imbued with class, scarcity and a whiff of the illicit'. He also singles out radio commentary as the most important marker of that era, and writes that being a cricket fan was an 'active work of imagination'. He concludes by noting that the abstemiousness of the middle class also came with a sense of being a 'privileged oasis'. This was in contrast to the easy availability of things in contemporary India, which manages to erase the less fortunate.

Avijit Ghosh's essay, which is also a personal take on the 1970s, has parallels with Krishna's paper. Radio commentary and devouring sports books and magazines were an inextricable part of Ghosh's middle-class childhood. Ghosh, however, writes from the perspective of someone who grew up in the smaller towns of Ranchi and Arrah. While Ranchi might have been a backwater compared to the bigger metros, such as Kolkata and Mumbai, Arrah, the headquarters of Bhojpur, was a 'counter narrative'. As Ghosh puts it, 'In Ranchi, it was easy to get hold of a copy of *Sportsweek*. In Arrah…to buy any readable stuff on sports in English, you took the local train to Patna, about 50 km away.' While Ghosh provides insights into what nourished a middle-class schoolboy in India's hinterland, it is also about memory and nostalgia which are integral to any sports fan's engagement with sport.

Just as India–Pakistan relations play a major role in the politics of South Asia, the India–Pakistan rivalry is one of the defining features of sport in South Asia. Souvik Naha examines the violence that occurred during an India–Pakistan cricket match at Eden Gardens, Kolkata, in 1999. The series marked the return of India–Pakistan cricket to India after 13 years and was held in the backdrop of several confidence-building measures between the two countries. Naha analyses the violence by looking at media coverage, both in English and Bengali, of the incident. His paper explores spectatorship as a complex and highly subjective form of behaviour, structured around communal tension and nationalism. He contends that the media's mediation of the riot exhibited the often-overlooked facet of journalists both participating in, and representing, the sporting public.

Ian Simpson, too, looks at media representations: the Australian press' response to the Indian cricket team's tours of Australia from 1948 onwards. He seeks to resolve questions about the nature of Australian perceptions of Indian cricketers—and, by extension, of India itself—through a survey of the accounts of Indian cricket tours in the popular press and the writings of sports journalists and cricketers. Australian commentaries on the early tours initially borrowed heavily from an orientalist rhetoric of racial stereotypes which constructed Indian cricketers in terms of artistry, magic and inspired brilliance, on the one hand, and as lethargic and lacking in physical strength and endurance, on the other. These images were challenged, though not entirely displaced, during the latter decades of the 20th century as the Australian media registered a growing awareness that a new type of Indian cricketer had emerged, one driven by a ruthlessly competitive, 'win-at-all-cost' mentality.

North-east India, which is increasingly the nursery for India's sporting talent and for stars like Mary Kom, is the subject of Duncan Mcduie-Ra's essay. He explores the ways by which the North-east is located within and beyond the nation through sport. He makes three arguments. First, sport has become a means to integrate India's troubled frontier into the national imaginary. Second, for many people in the North-east, sport is the passport to a job, and sporting aspirations are not necessarily linked to any nationalist sentiment. Third, while sporting success offers the opportunity for acceptance in mainstream India, it compounds rather than challenges racial stereotypes for North-east communities. According to McDuie-Ra, 'For those who cannot run, punch, or kick a ball, the experience of India remains complex and has altered little with the rise of sporting heroes from the region.'

The last essay in this section is a historical paper by Payoshni Mitra on women's involvement in sport and physical activity, particularly in Bengal. She begins with the iconic victory of Mohun Bagan over the East Yorkshire Regiment in the final of the 1911 IFA (International Football Association) Shield tournament, but then adds a twist to the story. A report in the *Manchester Guardian*, in 1911, stated that a 'Miss Tagore' was responsible for Mohun Bagan's win. The person in question was in reality Sarala Devi Chaudhurani, a relative of Rabindranath Tagore, who was deeply involved in physical education in Bengal in the early 20th century. After marriage, she shifted her focus to women's education and wrote *A Scheme for an Indian Girls' School*. However, the educational curriculum for girls did not emphasise physical education. Analysing other movements, such as the Girl Guides Movement set up in 1911, Mitra argues that they 'failed to forge a new identity for the girls in early or mid-20th century India, and certainly did not liberate them from their gendered destinies'.

BEYOND CRICKET

While cricket might be the most popular and written-about sport in South Asia, hockey and football have sizeable constituencies in the region. Indeed, hockey is the 'national' game of both Pakistan and India, but has suffered a decline in popularity over the past several decades. Then there are other sports, such as badminton in India and rugby in Sri Lanka, which have built up a sizeable following over the years.

The essays in this section by Shaharyar Khan and Sundeep Misra document the decline of hockey in Pakistan and India, respectively, from the time when both countries were the best in the world. Shaharyar Khan begins his account, which is interspersed with personal recollections, from the 1948 Olympics when Pakistan first played in the Olympics as an independent nation. Khan recalls how he watched the 1960 Rome Olympics final, where Pakistan won its first gold medal beating arch-rival India, at a stranger's home in Oxford. As a Pakistani diplomat, Khan was able to meet the Pakistani Olympic team when it stopped in London. His association with hockey continued when he raised an amateur team in Islamabad. Khan identifies the growing popularity of cricket from the late 1970s, and the introduction of AstroTurf and changes in rules as some of the factors that led to the decline of hockey in Pakistan.

Misra's essay mirrors Shaharyar Khan's account, though India's decline started earlier than Pakistan's. He identifies the Indian team at the 1964 Tokyo Olympic Games, which had the likes of Prithipal Singh, as the last of the great teams. He describes in detail India's Olympic campaign that culminated in a tense, one-goal victory over Pakistan in the final. Since then it has been a downhill journey, except for India's win at the 1975 World Cup. Like Khan, Misra points to India's inability to have a say in the dramatic changes in rules for hockey as one of the reasons for its decline. But he also believes tactical deficiencies, lack of consistency and a rapid turnover of coaches have hurt India.

Unlike hockey, no South Asian country has had a great record in football. But football continues to have a large fan base, particularly in certain parts of the region such as Bengal, North-east India, Kerala and Goa. Novy Kapadia focuses on the future of Indian football, following the staging of the Under–17 World Cup in India in 2017, which saw record crowds and made members of the Indian Under–17 team household names. Kapadia asks whether the World Cup will help in improving football standards in the country. He also examines the impact of the Indian Super League (ISL), which exists alongside the older I–League. Legacy clubs, such as Mohun Bagan and East Bengal, however, remain outside the fold of the ISL. While the ISL clubs offer better professional structure, coaching and support staff, its impact on grassroots development is still minimal.

When Bangladesh became independent in 1971, football was undoubtedly the most popular spectator sport there. Kausik Bandyopadhyay traces the evolution of football in Bangladesh from 1971. In the early days, Bangladeshi clubs, such as Dhaka Mohammedan Sporting and Abahani Krira Chakra, performed well in foreign tournaments and Bangladeshi players became popular in the Calcutta League. However, the Bangladeshi national team always performed poorly. From the 1990s, football began declining in popularity. One of the reasons was poor administration and the other was the popularity of international football. During this period, cricket came to replace football in popularity and the domestic game witnessed a steady decline. While football World Cup fever grips Bangladesh every four years, its dream of playing in the tournament remains unattainable.

The story of badminton, one of the few success stories of Indian sport in recent times, has been documented by Abhijeet Kulkarni. The sport is believed to have originated in the British military barracks at Poona in 1860, and by the 1940s India was producing international stars like Prakash Nath. Although badminton has always been a popular sport with the Indian middle class, it was not till Prakash Padukone's win at the 1980 All England Championship that India produced a world champion. Since then, another veritable revolution has taken place with Hyderabad's Gopichand—winner of the All England in 2001—being a central figure. Currently, India is bristling with world-class talent, with P.V. Sindhu, who won the world championship in 2019 and the Olympic silver medal in 2016, and B. Sai Praneeth, Kidambi Srikanth and Parupalli Kashyap having become world beaters.

Rugby is probably not the first sport that comes to mind when one thinks of South Asia. But, as Shanaka Amarasinghe notes, rugby was introduced by the British to Sri Lanka (then Ceylon) in 1879. The first club, the Colombo Football Club, was formed the same year before the sport moved upcountry to the plantations. However, it was the schools set up by missionaries that became the nurseries of rugby. The most-watched rugby match in Sri Lanka remains the annual encounter between Trinity College and Royal College. It began in 1920 and regularly draws 20,000 spectators at the ground, and several million on television. A national side of sorts has been around from 1907, when an All Ceylon team played the New Zealand's All Blacks in Colombo. Subsequently, Colombo has hosted several foreign teams and international tournaments. While Sri Lanka is the second-largest rugby-playing country in Asia behind Japan, its current low ranking in world rugby does not do justice to the sport's rich history.

ANCIENT PURSUITS AND MODERNITY

Wrestling is possibly South Asia's oldest documented sport. And Ghulam Mohammad, better known as Gama Pehlwan, can lay claim to being India's first sporting superstar. Gama went to England in 1910, just another poor subject of the British Raj, and came back as Rustom-e-Zamana—the champion of the world—striking a telling blow for India at the very heart of the empire. Rudraneil Sengupta writes about Gama's incredible tour to England and the media coverage there. He also describes a modern-day *dangal* (wrestling tournament) and how little things have changed over the last two centuries. While physically there is little that remains of Gama's legacy (he died in penury in Pakistan, where he migrated after Partition, in 1960), his story and the legends around him continue to live in the hearts and minds of India's wrestlers.

Joseph Alter links wrestling and yoga, which has ancient origins, but is now being marketed as India's greatest export. He argues that underlying what appears to be radical discontinuity, gross appropriation and multifarious claims made about the meaning of yoga, is a theory of embodied self-development that has much greater continuity than might appear to be the case. Although Alter admits that there are obvious differences between wrestling and yoga, he believes there is also deep 'continuity in terms of the relationship between gross and subtle physiology in general and the embodied dynamics of sex, power and self-control in particular'. He points out that the conceptualisation of yoga as an athletic sport began in the 1930s in the aftermath of Eugen Sandow's travels in British India, concluding that 'wrestling as yoga anticipates yoga as sport in 20th century Indian history'.

While Sengupta looks at the continuities in wrestling in India and Alter analyses the subtle connections between *kushti* and yoga, Michiel Baas examines the growth of bodybuilding as a popular sport. While bodybuilding has a long history in India—Alter mentions figures like Bishnu Ghosh who, in the early 20th century, combined yogic postures with forms of bodybuilding—Baas looks at the increase in the last decade or so of the number of bodybuilding competitions. He argues that this is connected to the emergence of a new bodily ideal among middle-class men which, fuelled by its popularity in Bollywood movies, has also had a marked effect on the growth of gyms in urban India. His essay discusses the popularity of bodybuilding in India, its connections to older forms of working out, as well as the manner in which it relates to the changing way middle-class men reflect on their bodies in terms of aesthetics, assumed masculinity and sexuality. Baas notes that while bodybuilding remains a lower-middle-class preoccupation, the upper-middle-class clientele of gyms desires an 'ideal-type lean, muscular' body made popular by Bollywood heroes.

The final essay in this section by Amrith Lal is on *vallam kali*. Vallam may be translated from the Malayalam as boat, whereas kali has a host of meanings that range from sport, to performance, and spectacle. As Lal explains, vallam kali can be seen as a competitive sport but, occasionally, it signifies a ritual spectacle and even a temple pageant. According to one view, the tradition dates back to early 17th century. However, vallam kali as a competitive sport is of recent origin. When Prime Minister Jawaharlal Nehru visited Kerala for the first time after its formation as a state, he was deeply impressed by snake boats competing on the Vembanad Lake. Since then, the Nehru Trophy boat race is held every year on the second Sunday of August. It attracts thousands of spectators, and is broadcast live on radio and television. Now, competitive boat races are held all over Kerala. Lal traces the history of vallam kali and locates it in the political, social and economic context of Kerala.

SPORTS ADMINISTRATION

Sports administrators are generally reviled figures in South Asia. Stefan Huebner provides a corrective with his essay on Guru Dutt Sondhi, who was a central figure in the founding of the first Asian Games, in New Delhi, in 1951. Huebner focuses on Sondhi as a visionary of Asian cooperation and integration, and the criticism he faced for his lack of organisational abilities. As an Indian member of the International Olympic Committee (IOC), Sondhi promoted amateurism and low-cost sports events. Sondhi also rejected attempts to link sports events to nationalism, since this undermined his aim of encouraging internationalism and egalitarianism. Viewed against the background of Western and Japanese imperialism, and later decolonisation and the Cold War, Huebner emphasises Sondhi's vision of social improvement and pan-Asian cooperation.

In a far cry from Sondhi's time, global sport and sporting bodies, such as Fédération Internationale de Football Association

(FIFA) and the IOC, are under intense scrutiny over issues concerning governance, accountability and transparency. As Sharda Ugra writes, the 2010 Delhi Commonwealth Games, marred by corruption, highlighted a deep malaise in the administration of Indian sport. The 2011 Sports Development Bill, meant to inject transparency in sport administration, was shot down. A National Sports Code has remained a mere set of guidelines. In 2016, the Supreme Court accepted the recommendations of the Lodha Committee intended to radically reform the functioning of the most powerful sports body in India—the BCCI—and subsequently appointed a committee to run cricket. There have been demands that the Lodha recommendations be implemented in the other sports' bodies. While Ugra is optimistic about reform, she also notes that arguments always centre on age-limits, tenure restrictions and voting rights of officials, rather than what is best for Indian sport or its athletes.

SPORT IN FILM AND LITERATURE

In 2001, *Lagaan*, which revolved around a cricket match set in colonial India, brought Bollywood film to the attention of international critics and audiences. Since then, we have witnessed a spate of successful sports films, featuring the nation's most popular stars. However, as Amy Ransom points out in her essay, a tradition of sport-themed films in India dates back to at least the 1970s, when films like the Bengali-language *Mohun Baganer Meye* were made. She argues that the Indian sports film borrows some conventions from Hollywood sports film, but is infused with locally specific themes and aesthetics, and represents a unique, hybrid subgenre. However, like sports film in other modern, pluralistic nations, Indian sports film also frequently contributes to the construction of a common national identity built on the playing field.

There is no essay in this collection on the place of sport in literature. Indeed, South Asia does not have a great tradition of sports literature. One exception is Moti Nandi (1931–2010), journalist and writer, who wrote a series of novels in Bengali centred on sport ranging from football to swimming. Some of his best-known novels are *Striker*, *Stopper* and *Koni*, which was also made into a film. The final piece in this collection is, fittingly, a translation by Arunava Sinha of one of Nandi's more difficult novels, *Aparajito Ananda*

(Undefeated Ananda), published in 1984. The excerpt that we carry is on the fevered imagination of the teenaged Ananda—whether it is playing against Jimmy Connors at Wimbledon, or smashing a century against the West Indies—as he lies on a sickbed. It is also about the place of fantasy in every sports fan—be it imagining oneself, like Ananda, in extraordinary situations, or willing one's favourite team or hero to victory in improbable circumstances.

We also have a photo essay by Pal Pillai and Ali Bharmal. The pictures, which cover a range of sports, including those like kabaddi that have not been covered in this collection, capture the timelessness and beauty of sporting action. The visuals have a universality which contrasts with the South Asian focus of the essays.

There are, of course, absences in this collection, some due to the inability to get contributions on particular sports or countries, and others because of space or time constraints. Despite the gaps, we hope that this bouquet of essays will not only prove to be intellectually stimulating, but also entertaining.

◆

NOTE

1.   Parts of this Introduction are drawn from Ronojoy Sen (2015).

REFERENCES

Birley, Derek. 1993. *Sport and the Making of Britain*. Manchester: Manchester University Press.

Chakrabarty, Dipesh. 2005. 'Introduction: The Fall and Rise of Indian Sports History', in Boria Majumdar and J.A. Mangan (eds.), *Sport in South Asian Society: Past and Present*. London: Routledge.

Huizinga, J. 1980. *Homo Ludens: A Study in the Play-Element in Culture*. London: Routledge and Kegan Paul, Ltd.

McDonald, Ian. 2000. 'India', in Jay Coakley and Eric Dunning (eds.), *Handbook of Sports Studies*. London: Sage Publications.

Sen, Ronojoy. 2015. *Nation at Play: A History of Sport in South Asia*. New York/New Delhi: Columbia University Press/Penguin.

Sorabjee, Shapoorjee. 1897. *Chronicle of Cricket among Parsees and the Struggle: European Polo versus Native Cricket*. Bombay.

◆◆

DEVELOPMENT OF CRICKET

THE MERCURIALS
The Nature of Pakistani Cricket

ALI KHAN

Mercurial—(of a person) subject to sudden or unpredictable changes of mood or mind.

4 June 2017: The outdoor spaces across Pakistan, where large screens had been mounted for the highly anticipated clash between Pakistan and India, had emptied out hours before Pakistan succumbed feebly to India. Another loss to their great rivals in an international tournament had left a pall of gloom hanging over the country. Pakistan had been at its worst—poor fielding, wayward bowling and inept batting. Such had been the scale of defeat in their first match of the Champions Trophy in England that Pakistan faced elimination, unless they won every subsequent match. Disappointed fans back in Pakistan did not break TV sets or burn effigies. Of late, Pakistan has only rarely defeated India and, realistically, few expected Pakistan to win the match. But the manner of the defeat—the one-sidedness of it—left even the staunchest fans shaken. In fact, there was disappointment throughout the cricketing community, as neutral observers and even Indian supporters mourned how one of cricket's greatest rivalries was now almost irrelevant.

18 June 2017: Exactly two weeks later Pakistan stood as champions, having comprehensively defeated India in the final—out-bowling, out-batting and out-fielding the favourites. En route, they had beaten number-one ranked South Africa, Sri Lanka, home-favourites England, and then the tournament-favourites, India. It was a turnaround of gargantuan proportions and one that only Pakistan could have achieved. Cricket lovers immediately cast their minds back 25 years when a similar scenario emerged during

the 1992 World Cup in Australia. Then, Pakistan had also almost been eliminated, being saved only by the weather and an abandoned match. Following that, every subsequent game they played was a knockout. At the conclusion of the tournament, Pakistan had won the World Cup, defeating England in Melbourne.

Pakistan has taken on the reputation of a team so mercurial that it redefines the meaning of an unpredictable nature. One is reminded of Henry Wadsworth Longfellow's famous poem about the little girl who had a curl in the middle of her forehead: 'When she was good, she was very good indeed, but when she was bad, she was horrid.'

This article looks at the reasons for Pakistan's inconsistency in cricket, examining social and cultural factors, the domestic structure, coaching and leadership to try and understand the phenomenon.

THE LEARNING ENVIRONMENT

The learning environment, whether it be the home, the school, or the sports field, has an enormous impact on the subsequent development of an individual. In this section, I trace the manner in which the culture of the setting, leading up to involvement in international cricket, impacted the character of Pakistani cricketers and, therefore, of Pakistani cricket.

Pakistan's early cricket teams were dominated by those who came from relatively well-off backgrounds. The main nurseries for the sport, following Partition in 1947, were the universities in Lahore, particularly Government College, Islamia College and Punjab University, with the annual fixture between Government College and Islamia College attracting crowds of over 6,000.

The game was largely the preserve of the wealthy elite, belonging to the network of college alumni steeped in the traditions of British education, language and culture. Cricket in the 1950s has been described as a 'social outing' for the college and university alumni of both Lahore and Karachi, who often attended matches 'to be seen' and to network. Few players from lower- to lower-middle-class backgrounds had the opportunity to play first-class cricket, and the sport only had limited popular following (Little and Valiotis 2012: 214).

Even in the major urban centres of Lahore and Karachi, cricket did not spread to the urban poor. It was unknown amongst the rural peasantry, nor (with a handful of examples) was it taken up by the aristocracy and the landowning class (Oborne, 2014: 43).

This changed from the late 1970s, as the game began to reach out beyond the urban confines of Lahore and Karachi. Much of this was prompted by developments in media and communication, with television, in particular, displacing radio as the primary form of coverage. Complementing the growth in media and communication was the fact that the cricket team met with increasing success and, by the 1980s, a new generation of Pakistani cricketers emerged, playing the game with captivating and intuitive talent. Many of these players came not from Lahore and Karachi but from the smaller centres in Punjab: Mushtaq Ahmed was from Sahiwal; Inzamamul Haq from Multan; Shoaib Malik from Sialkot; Aaqib Javed from Sheikhupura; and Waqar Younis from Burewala. Several were from humble backgrounds: Yousuf Youhana was the son of a sweeper; Shoaib Akhtar's father was a night watchman; and Mushtaq Ahmed's father was a daily-wage labourer.

This new generation of cricketers was not sourced from the universities, nor from the elite or middle classes. Most had learnt their cricket on dusty *maidans* (open spaces) or the under-funded state schools. They learnt the game by copying the heroes they saw on television, rather than through coaching at school or university. The success of the team, and the fact that it was increasingly beamed across Pakistan on television, meant that there was a burgeoning enthusiasm for the game, and a very large and youthful population of talented individuals were always likely to be thrown up. These individuals played the game with a natural flair and intuitiveness which brought a fearlessness to their game. The fact that few of the players had received any early coaching meant that their untamed talent would remain explosive and unpredictable; this lesser dependence on preparation and meticulousness meant a reliance on instinct, rather than forethought and planning. The consistency that could have complemented their natural talent would need greater coaching and structure than cricket in the maidan could provide.

There was another innovation during the early 1980s that had a major impact on the nature of Pakistani cricket. Tape-ball cricket has played a crucial role in moulding the character of generations of Pakistani cricketers from the 1980s onwards. Yet its influence on cricket in Pakistan has rarely been recognised.

For two decades after Partition, cricket was played in clubs, schools and universities. This was formal, organised cricket, with proper equipment and grounds. But from the 1970s, Pakistan and its cities saw an explosive urban growth and Karachi, in particular, expanded rapidly.

As Pakistan's urban population increased, driven by rural–urban migration and natural increases, space began to run short. Schools built additional classrooms over their sports grounds and public grounds became scarcer. This led to a decline in club and school cricket and, in conjunction with the high cost of cricket equipment, necessity became the mother of invention. In Karachi, it was new residential areas, including, for example, the middle-class locality of Nazimabad that had vast empty spaces and wide, sparsely populated avenues which became the venues. It is rumoured[1] that it was in Nazimabad that electrical tape was first stretched across a tennis ball, allowing fast bowlers to propel the ball at high speed without getting loopy 'tennis ball' bounce. As the tape frayed, the ball mimicked swing. Spinners dispensed with flight and began producing the 'doosra' (or the mystery ball). It produced some of Pakistan's most legendary fast bowlers: Wasim Akram, Waqar Younis, Shoaib Akhtar and Mohammad Amir. Actions and techniques changed as tape-ball players emerged onto the 'conventional' cricket scene. The bowlers flourished, even though it also led to the proliferation of illegal bowling actions. Batsmen emerged less often. Matches were played at a frenetic pace, typically 4 to 15 overs in duration, with 20 runs per over being achievable, and this rarely prepared the batsmen for the 'occupation of the crease'.

According to Hussain (2015), the emergence of tape-ball cricket was given further impetus by the broadcasting of day–night cricket from Australia, in 1979, by Pakistan Television. Inspired by the massive lights that international cricketers played under in Adelaide, Sydney and Melbourne, Karachi began using street lights and coloured clothing to start their own version of night cricket.

A typical street game might be played in a narrow lane, not more than 15 feet wide, with houses on both sides. If you are lucky, there will be a vacant plot on one side. Lighting for night matches is provided by 1000-watt, hanger-lights: yellow tubes that are hung overhead (and one of the players almost always has to be a makeshift electrician). Often, there is only enough light to cover the pitch, the bowler ghosting in from the darkness into the batsman's view. Matches are four to six overs long, but usually between eight and 15 overs in tournaments (ibid.).

By the 1990s, tape-ball cricket, aided by the demise of both school and club cricket, had spread so wide that 'virtually every modern Pakistani Test cricketer has played tapeball before regular cricket' (Heller and Oborne, 2016: 324). Pakistan's older generation may have learnt their cricket at school, but the modern ones mostly picked it up off the streets.

But while tape-ball cricket expanded the game enormously, it did so in an unfettered and unbridled manner. It was a game of high intensity, innovation and energy, and those who played it, did so with a rare passion. The laws of the game were simplified: there was no room for the leg before wicket, and umpires had a minimal role to play. Those who played this form of cricket had rarely received any formal coaching. As with their earlier maidan counterparts, they saw their heroes on television and tried to emulate them in their local matches.

With both—players from the maidan and street-based, tape-ball cricketers—the role of coaching is minimal. This contrasts with the older style of cricket where players emerged from a more structured environment, mainly through school and university where coaches would hone the talent of their pupils before they progressed to playing at the club and domestic levels. This more conventional route certainly has its advantages, one of which is a more consistent level of performance based, as it were, on mentorship, drills, practice sessions and refining techniques. But there are disadvantages as well.

In the 1970s and 1980s, English cricket was seen as suffering from 'over-coaching'. Pakistan's flamboyance, vivacity and haphazardness contrasted with rigidity and the stolidity of English cricket where coaching had strangled any natural flair. This was typified by the great English opening batsman, Geoffrey Boycott—known for his practice regime, his technical correctness, his consistency as a batsman, and for being dropped from the team after scoring a painfully slow double-hundred against India in 1967. Pakistan's cricketers took the opposite route, often depending on their minimally-coached, hyper-talented match winners who played a high-risk, low-percentage game which, while it produced spectacular wins, was, by definition, unpredictable.

Waqar Younis, one of Pakistan's greatest fast bowlers, as quoted in Samiuddin, embodies the spirit perfectly:

> We've never given importance to coaching. We were never analytical or scientific. Actually, in the 1990s, we never did analyse anyone. 'He plays well here, don't put him there.' It's not how long do you bowl at him there, what kind of field, what lengths, what is the B plan, what is the C plan, after that goes wrong, what happens? We had a one-game plan. Go out there, get a wicket. We had resources. We sensed it and said, okay, bring Waqar back. Not even the captain decided. Sometimes, I would go to the captain and say, give me two overs, let me do it. It was a kind of teamwork, within the team, but not like we'd have a plan from the beginning (2014: 467).

But where instinctual responses failed, they were unable to fall back on a store of knowledge that might come from coaching. The result was inconsistency in performance. The lack of coaching was exacerbated by the fact that from the 1990s onwards, in particular, Pakistan's cricketers often lacked even a basic education. Most developed countries have players with a basic educational background, and even developing countries have players who have completed a basic education. Sri Lanka draws its talent from a healthy, extensive school programme. India's cricketers have also been drawn from a more educated pool. In the long run, this lack of basic education is a negative factor in developing a cricketer's outlook and maturity.

For cricketers who have the benefit of consistent coaching, the advantage lies in the passing on of experience and the knowledge of just how particular situations may be dealt with. Pakistani youngsters, emerging from street or maidan cricket, usually receive their first genuine coaching when selected at the club or even first-class level. By that time, most are already 19 years old and set in their techniques. They have not received any coaching in the formative 11 to 15 age bracket.

The nature of street and maidan cricket, as well as the mindset these forms engender, allows for an unfettered and exuberant type of player, but, along with the absence of coaching and, to a lesser extent, a basic level of education, also leads to greater inconsistency, as bursts of instinctive brilliance are followed by periods of complete blankness. In fact, Heller (2016) quotes two former international cricketers—wicket keepers Rashid Latif and Moin Khan—who now run cricket academies in Karachi, on the need to introduce the basic skills of conventional cricket into the armoury of their teenage pupils who have only played tape-ball cricket, while trying to maintain the natural flair and élan of their own version of the game.

MODELS OF INCONSISTENCY

While inconsistency has been a characteristic outcome, Pakistan has also been a highly effective team,[2] and the fact that this success has often been driven by the brilliantly inconsistent has prompted more players to follow this route. This has often resulted in Pakistan picking players from the wilderness, based simply on spotting raw talent. Amongst the most famous examples are one of Pakistan's greatest batsmen, Inzamam-ul-Haq; arguably the finest-ever left-arm fast bowler, Wasim Akram; and one of Pakistan's most explosive and popular all-rounders, Shahid Afridi. Inzamam and Akram were picked up after Imran Khan saw them at a practice session and found them to be far more talented than some of the players already in the national team. Afridi debuted at the age of 16 and in his first innings shattered the record for the fastest century in one-day cricket.

The team's success, driven by the type of players earlier mentioned, did mean a continued focus on talent and instinct, rather than coaching and method. This has been Pakistan's strength, and its weakness. But it did mean that the penchant for talent was reinforced, leading to a constant replication of the system. Therefore, the continued emphasis on talent and the disparagement of the less flamboyant, coached player who might be less naturally talented, but whose dedication in practice allows him to often surpass his more talented counterparts. Pakistan's most successful batsman—Younis Khan—is a typical example. Lacking the extravagance of his fellow Pathan, Afridi, Younis Khan's work ethic and dedication saw him become Pakistan's leading run scorer in Test cricket. Similarly, Misbah-ul-Haq, Pakistan's most successful Test Match captain, tolerated, throughout his career, taunts from local fans of 'tuktuk', a derogatory reference to his sober and measured style of play.

This has led to a situation where talent is disproportionately valued over other aspects that together make for a successful cricketer. These would include fitness, mental strength and the need for hours of practice. Yet, while young boys overwhelmingly want to be Shahid Afridi, few will say they want to be Misbah-ul-Haq or Younis Khan. In Pakistan, the spectacular match winner is in far greater demand than the solid, steady workhorse.

The result is the continued emergence of players characterised by inconsistency—the ability to win matches with spectacular performances, but also the tendency to snatch defeat from the jaws of victory.

The late Bob Woolmer, who in 2004 became one of Pakistan's first foreign coaches, brought with him the new-found emphasis on modern coaching—fitness, biomechanics, mental conditioning— and these complemented the skill, talent and passion of Pakistani cricketers. Under this regime, Pakistan gained a consistency that they had lacked in the past. It was also a period of relative stability, with few changes in captainship and management. Woolmer's first impressions of the team he was going to coach were that he had never supervised such a talented group of cricketers; but he was highly critical of the team's fitness levels. But, for Woolmer and other coaches who came after him, there was a recognition that this inconsistency would remain in place until the players and the administration themselves realised that consistent success in modern sport requires both talent and, increasingly, a commitment to structured practice sessions, fitness and mental conditioning—areas that Pakistan has only fitfully addressed in the past and has, only recently and reluctantly, begun to institute on a more regular basis.

This brings me to another important element in the unpredictable nature of Pakistani cricket, and which is alluded to earlier: Pakistan's inconsistency has always been exacerbated by the lack of stability in administration and leadership.

LEADERSHIP

Leading a team in a sport is always an important position to hold, but the captain in cricket has a particularly critical role. The length of the game—three hours, at the least, and five days, at the most— means that on-field decisions are particularly important, as strategy unfolds like a game of chess. A cricket captain is not only required to be a leader but must also be a man manager, and be tactically adept at making bowling changes, deciding on the field, declarations, batting orders and team selection.

It is also true that Pakistan has historically been a difficult team to lead: rebellions against captains, tensions between Karachi and Lahore lobbies, and strong individualistic characters have seen a large number of players taking over captaincy. From the early 1950s, Pakistan's players were seen as 11 individuals unable to play as a team. Throughout the 1970s, a squad of superstars failed cohesively as a team and it was only in the 1980s, under Imran Khan—an authoritarian, all-powerful captain, who ruled on the basis of his charisma and character—that the Pakistani team played as a unit, bringing a degree of stability. As Samiuddin points out:

> Between 1995 and 1998, six different men captained Pakistan. Across 2009 and 2010, four different men captained the Test side. Sixteen different men have led Pakistan (in Tests) since Imran and Javed Miandad left. Between these sixteen, the leadership has changed a staggering twenty-six times (2014: 438).

Imran Khan was able to groom a young team, inculcating qualities of professionalism and discipline that had been lacking in the past. However, since Imran's retirement in 1992, Pakistan has had 17 captains—in contrast, Australia has had five, and England and India, eight.[3] Pakistan's 17 captains also include two periods of six years at a stretch for Misbah-ul-Haq (46 Test Matches, between 2011 and 2017) and Inzamam-ul-Haq (31 Test Matches, between 2000 and 2006). But, for most of Pakistan's cricket history, captains, players, coaches, selectors and administrators have changed repeatedly, and amidst this chaos any sense of order and consistency was lost.

Instability at the top leads also to instability below, as each new regime change brings a new set of selectors, coaches, captains and players. Stability, so that players can be identified and then given the confidence to become permanent members of the team, has been rare. The constant chopping and changing at all levels has meant that a great deal of inconsistency had been built into the system. One player that I spoke to had been dropped five times in a career that had lasted only 11 matches!

Australian cricket's policies have been in stark contrast to Pakistan's. In the early 1980s, Australia went through a period of decline. Rebuilding began in 1984 when they appointed Allan Border as captain and Bob Simpson as coach. The two remained together at the helm of the Australian cricket team for an entire decade. Following Border's retirement, Mark Taylor captained for another five years, and his successors Steve Waugh and Ricky Ponting for six years and eight years, respectively. Individual players also benefited from the stability in leadership, as they found their respective niches in the team—each knowing his role intimately. It is therefore unsurprising that Australia have been the most consistently dominant team from the late 1980s onwards. In their case, a period of decline led to Australian cricket developing a plan and executing it meticulously. Structure and preparation brought consistency to their cricket.

As for Pakistan, during periods of stability—i.e., during the captaincies of Imran, Inzamam and Misbah—Pakistan produced more consistent results. They reached the number one Test ranking in 1988 under Imran, and in 2016 under Misbah. But every time an era of stability ended, it was replaced by a turbulent one where continuous change restored the conditions that bred inconsistency. Thus, instability stemmed not only from the players—their character and temperament—but also from the game's administrators who rarely promoted stability and sound leadership, and failed to implement long-term plans that would have put in place institutions and structures to strengthen Pakistani cricket.

The failure of cricket administrators is most obvious in the manner in which the domestic game in Pakistan has regressed. The importance of domestic cricket to the national team cannot be overstated, as this is the arena where budding cricketers are incubated for international competition. Unfortunately, even here the seeds of inconsistency are nurtured, rather than addressed.

At the most basic level, even the format of domestic tournaments appears to constantly be in flux. The number of teams in the domestic game has varied from as little as eight (in 1989) to 24 (in 2004) to 16 (in 2016 and 2017). It has been rare for the number to remain unchanged for more than a couple of years at a stretch.

In addition, most first-class teams do not have qualified staff in terms of coaches, trainers, physiotherapists and analysts.

In other cricketing countries, domestic teams have support staff that work all year round with their players and are often as competent as their international counterparts. Over the last decade, the quality of pitches and cricket balls has also declined, impacting the overall quality of both batsmen and bowlers. Part of this is related to Pakistan losing its right to host foreign teams in Pakistan, following the terrorist attack on the Sri Lankan cricket team in 2009 in Lahore. This has placed an enormous financial strain on the Pakistan Cricket Board, as all international matches are now played in the United Arab Emirates. It has also meant that facilities and grounds in Pakistan are falling into disrepair, and ancillary staff is difficult to afford, thereby further weakening the domestic system.

The increasing mediocrity of the domestic game means that cricketers are unable to hone their skills at this level and are often ill-equipped to take on the challenge of international cricket. Some will survive through their talent and luck, which is an essential part of any sport. But failure at the international level often leads to a return to domestic cricket, where the player is meant to iron out shortcomings. But the absence of an enabling environment usually means that remedial work is not possible, as the domestic programme does not provide a competitive challenge to its players. Pakistan's famous opening batsman of the 1970s, Majid Khan, spoke to me about his experience of playing in Australia, stating that he felt that inter-state Sheffield Shield matches often had the intensity of a Test Match. Pakistan's Quaid-e-Azam matches, in contrast, hardly attract any spectators and are devoid of the challenge of competitive matches. Those trying to rectify their faults and inconsistencies then do not find the environment to make the required improvements, leading to players repeatedly making the same mistakes. At the same time, aspiring cricketers also do not have their physical or mental mettle tested. Inconsistencies remain endemic and are difficult to eradicate, so that players go in and out of the international team and are only rarely able to overcome their shortcomings. And when they do, it is usually through an atypical extended run at the international level.

I have spoken of the largely structural and social issues that have promoted inconsistency in Pakistani cricket. The background of the aspiring cricketers, in terms of their lack of coaching, and their emergence into a culture that values flamboyance and exuberance over caution and structure are important factors that explain the ups and downs of Pakistani cricket. There is also an instability in the structure itself—in terms of leadership and the composition of the team, and in the leadership of the administration in the form of the Pakistan Cricket Board.

Having laid out the reasons for the mercurial nature of Pakistani cricket, I would like to contradict some of my previous arguments by stating that part of the unpredictable character of Pakistani cricket is, in fact, based on stereotype rather than reality. This is not to say that Pakistan is not a mercurial team, but that the stereotype of it being unpredictable strengthens what is already in existence.

The phrase 'that's cricket' or that 'cricket is a funny game' refers to its inherent unpredictability. Few games are as dependent on the vagaries of weather and the pitch, besides the randomness of missed catches, run outs and umpiring errors.

Cricket, according to Ashis Nandy, is a game that permits anarchy, plurality and randomness.

> It is a game of chance and skill which has to be played as if it is wholly a game of skill...cricket is a game which is nearly impossible to predict, control and prognosticate. There are too many variables and many of the relationships among the variables are determined by chance (2000: 25).

All countries have shown their share of inconsistency, driven by the unpredictability of the game itself. But, in the case of Pakistan, stereotypes came to define the team even when they did not apply.

Over the years, specific cricketing cultures have developed in all cricket-playing nations, partly through the way they played their cricket and partly through a view that 'what's bred in the marrow comes out in the batting'. In other words, cricket reflects a nation's cultural heritage and character: its history, its personality, its culture, its social make up, its insecurities, its politics and its religious commitment.

As a result, the West Indians were 'Calypso Cricketers'— aggressive, colourful and flamboyant. They reflected the huge talent and panache of the Caribbean people. The Australians were frank, truculent and open-hearted, like most Australians. The English were cautious, low-key and disciplined. India's image has changed along with its own global image. Once the epitome of the colonial gentleman—elegant, exotic, but genial—the team has changed along with India's rise as an economic powerhouse. From being a talented but almost timid team, the new generation is self-assured, aggressive and untainted by its colonial baggage.

Pakistan was youthful, brash and mercurial. Like the country itself, there was chaos and disorder, brilliance and exuberance. As typical of most polychronic cultures, Pakistanis may be lacking in organisation and discipline but are unmatched in natural ability. But stereotypes dominated reality and, as Hall (1997) argues, *stereotyping is often employed to construct negative representations of people and groups,* so that even when the West Indies added an uncompromising professionalism to their natural flamboyance, they were still seen as carefree calypso cricketers. Yet their punishing training and practice regimes, coupled with their natural ability, are what allowed them to dominate for decades, beginning in the 1970s. Similarly, Pakistan has had periods of stability during which they were uncharacteristically consistent: under Misbah they won 11 series and lost only five and, as mentioned earlier, Pakistan's overall win ratio would not have been possible without a degree of consistency. Yet, the mercurial tag would remain in place.

Pakistan's mercurial nature may not be as consistent as it has been made out to be, but it is a defining feature of their cricket. Attempts at trying to tame its volatile talent need to be carefully considered. The globalisation of sport and of cricket has brought standard coaching techniques and training regimes to all countries. However, cricket would be much the poorer if teams began resembling one another, losing their indigenous characteristics and becoming standardised.

This article has sought to explain where the roots of Pakistan's inconsistency lie: from its haphazard domestic structure and frequent changes within the team, to a cricketing culture that has developed to value high-risk match winners, rather than consistent performers. It is this ethos that has allowed Pakistan to produce some of the most exciting innovations in world cricket, including reverse swing and the doosra. They have also produced some of the world's most memorable cricketers. Their unpredictability produces the kind of roller-coaster ride that makes for unforgettable sport, as has been demonstrated in some of Pakistan's most remarkable victories. Cricket and sport will be much the richer if Pakistan and other teams retain their distinctive characteristics.

◆

NOTES

1. See Samiuddin (2014), Hussain (2015), and Heller and Oborne (2016).
2. Pakistan's Test Match record (percentage of wins) places them below Australia, South Africa and England, but above India, Sri Lanka, New Zealand, West Indies, Bangladesh and Zimbabwe. Their one-day record is even more impressive, with only Australia and South Africa having a better win percentage.
3. This excludes stand-in captains.

REFERENCES

Hall, Stuart. 1997. *Stereotyping as a Signifying Practice*. London: Sage Publications.

Heller, Richard. 2016. 'Tape-Ball Cricket: A League of its Own', *ESPNCricinfo*, http://www.espncricinfo.com/story/_/id/17011001/richard-heller-popularity-tape-ball-cricket-pakistan (accessed 4 June 2016).

Heller, Richard and Peter Oborne. 2016. *Green on White*. London: Simon & Schuster.

Hussain, Abid. 2015. 'Tape-Ball Tales', *The Cricket Monthly*, http://www.thecricketmonthly.com/story/929545/tape-ball-tales (accessed 5 December 2017).

Little, Charles and Chris Valiotis. 2012. 'Cricket in Pakistan', in John Nauright and Charles Parrish (eds.), *Sports Around the World: History, Culture and Practice*, vol. 1. Santa Clara, California: ABC-CLIO.

Nandy, Ashis. 2000. *A Very Popular Exile: The Tao of Cricket; An Ambiguous Journey to the City; Traditions, Tyranny and Utopias*. New Delhi: Oxford University Press.

Oborne, Peter. 2014. *Wounded Tiger: A History of Cricket in Pakistan*. London: Simon & Schuster.

Samiuddin, Osman. 2014. *The Unquiet Ones: A History of Pakistan Cricket*. NOIDA, India: HarperCollins.

◆◆

CRICKET IN BANGLADESH

HABIBUL
HAQUE
KHONDKER

INTRODUCTION

In the autumn of 2017, during the entrance examination to Dhaka University, the most prestigious educational institution in Bangladesh, students were asked several questions on Mashrafe Mortaza, the inspirational captain of the Bangladeshi Test team. It was testimony to not only Mortaza's popularity and influence on young Bangladeshis, but also to the status of cricket in the public imagination of Bangladesh. Cricket has emerged as a national sport, often uniting a nation, albeit temporarily, divided by seemingly irreconcilable, political and ideological factionalism.

In neighbouring India, cricket has become a true symbol of national unity. As Astill (2013: xi) puts it:

> No other British legacy in India, save perhaps the English language, has proved more popular or enduring than cricket. Nothing unites Indians, in all their legions and diversity, more than their love for it. No other form of entertainment—not even Bollywood or politics— is so ubiquitous in India's media, and no Indian celebrity more revered than India's best cricketers.

In Bangladesh, while the youthful majority has found cricket to be a rallying point, there are sections of the populace that are sceptical as the team's performance in Test matches has been inconsistent. Bangladeshis are not known for a high degree of patience. When the sky-high hopes of the nation are realised by a winning match, there is euphoria. This is followed by a dark spell of gloom, amounting to a near-national tragedy when the team suffers a defeat, dashing their high, and often unreasonable, expectations.

The year 2017 has been a turbulent one for Bangladeshi cricket. In their tour of New Zealand from December 2016 to January 2017, the team almost achieved a milestone in the first Test, touching 600 runs (595/8 declared). Yet the team lost to New Zealand as it collapsed in the second innings. Bangladesh conceded two Tests, three One Day Internationals (ODI) and two T20s in that series. Bangladesh, as usual, went to New Zealand with high hopes, having beaten the Kiwis in three ODIs on their home ground, in late 2013, and drawing the two-Test series, conceding the only defeat in the sole T20 match. On 31 August 2017, when Bangladesh defeated the Australian team in a Test match at Sher-e-Bangla National Cricket Stadium at Mirpur,[1] Dhaka, a new chapter unfolded in Bangladeshi cricket. This was reminiscent of Bangladesh's victory over Pakistan in 1999, which paved the way to Bangladesh's achieving Test status in 2000. The team's victory over Test-playing opposition—against Pakistan at Northampton in the 1999 World Cup—put Bangladesh on the cricketing map. The Bangladeshi team was officially recognised as a Test side on 10 November 2000 and has taken 16 years and 12 days—the least amount of time among all 10 Test-playing countries—to reach that landmark. It took half a decade for the team to secure a Test victory. The first Test win came at Chittagong, in 2005, in their 35th Test against Zimbabwe. Bangladesh's visit to South Africa in October 2017 marked a string of defeats, casting gloom and shattering morale. After suffering an inning's defeat in both Tests to South Africa, 'questions have been raised about Bangladesh's away performances in the Test circuit'.[2]

It is now an accepted theory in Bangladeshi cricketing circles and amongst cricket observers in general that the country's strength lies in short-format cricket (ODI and T20), while it remains a novice in Test cricket. For example, in April 2015, when Pakistan toured Bangladesh, Pakistan won one of two Test matches, and the other was drawn; but Bangladesh won all three ODIs and one T20. And in June the same year, Bangladesh won two of three ODIs against India, while the only Test was drawn. In July–August 2015, Bangladesh won two of three ODIs against touring South Africa, while the two Test matches were drawn. Against the visiting English team in

October 2016, Bangladesh won two of three ODIs, and the two Test matches were shared by the two teams.

In the International Cricket Council (ICC) Champions Trophy played from 1 to 18 June 2017, Bangladesh, which started off with the ambition of securing a place in the top five, ended up losing narrowly to Pakistan, and convincingly to India, in the semi-final. And, then, in August when Bangladesh beat Australia, any doubt about the quality of its players was removed. It may be unambiguously stated that Bangladeshi cricket has come of age exactly 17 years after it achieved Test status—a badge of honour for any team. On both occasions, the team was mentored by a cricket-loving prime minister. Prime Minister Sheikh Hasina not only took a personal interest in cricket, but also made sure that the team got the resources it needed. Cricket management, under her watch, saw remarkable improvement and professionalism. Former cricket stars and those knowledgeable about cricket were put at the helm of the affairs of the cricket board.

Cricket has come a long way in Bangladesh, having successfully jettisoned the stereotype built and nurtured during the Pakistani days (1947–1971) that Bengalis are not cricket material. As Bangladesh moved to secure its place in the cricketing world, it was also viewed with cynicism by commentators of certain friendly countries each time it suffered a setback.

This paper explores the social history of cricket in Bangladesh, situating cricket as an aspect of sporting culture in larger political and cultural contexts, and relating this increasingly popular sport especially to the questions of nationalism, cosmopolitanism and globalism. I have argued elsewhere that cricket is at once a global and a national game, and, thus, sheds important theoretical light on the intermingling of the phenomena of globalism and nationalism (Khondker, 2010: 152–71). More recently, Roland Robertson, a leading scholar of globalisation and glocalisation (a synthesis of the global and local), and I have argued that cricket, especially its limited over-commercialised version, is a glocal game (Khondker and Robertson, forthcoming). Thus, while the present paper provides a sociology of cricket in Bangladesh, it is underpinned by some key theoretical issues in sociology. Cricket, like all sports, represents important aspects of the culture of a society and its changing dynamics. Cricket is particularly interesting in the South Asian context because of its entanglement with colonialism that historians have pointed out time and again (Appadurai, 1996: 80–113; Guha, 1998: 155–90).

The history of cricket in Bangladesh goes back to colonial times when Bengal was a part of British India. The first cricket club was set up in Dhaka in 1867. In 1947, the territory that now constitutes Bangladesh, or East Bengal, as it was then known, became a part of Pakistan. During the period from 1947 to 1971, which many Bangladeshi scholars regard as semi-colonial rule, cricket was dominated by non-Bengalis, and the small number of Bengalis playing cricket in the major cities came from the upper strata of society. Cricket was marked by social exclusion and was dominated by West Pakistan. I grew up in a small town in south-east Bangladesh, where cricket was introduced by the remnants of the local zamindar class who were mostly Hindu. In the 1960s, as many upper-class Hindus began to leave the then East Pakistan for India, and as a new Muslim middle class began to evolve, the children of these middle-class Muslim families began to play cricket.

Cricket was brought to the Indian subcontinent by colonial rulers and remained a game of the elite during the colonial period. In independent Bangladesh, cricket not only gave Bengali-speaking players a chance to prove themselves, but was also democratised, rendering it more inclusive. A number of top players today hail from rural areas and are from non-elite backgrounds. This democratisation of cricket has also become a source of national pride and heightened a sense of national belonging. The trajectory can best be described as one from exclusive to inclusive cricket.

THE PAKISTAN PERIOD (1947–1971)

During this period, cricket generated a great deal of interest among young people in both western and eastern parts of Pakistan. While it cannot be denied that cricket was more popular in West Pakistan, it was not altogether absent in East Pakistan. In 1955, the first-ever home Test between Pakistan and India took place in Dhaka stadium. The stadium saw some memorable cricket matches, when a dynamic Pakistan took on the Australian team (captained by Richard Benaud) or the West Indian team (skippered by Gary Sobers) or the English team (led by Ken Barrington). While Dhaka stadium was the site of such great sporting events, the participation of Bengalis was more as cheering spectators rather than as players. Pakistan's team was made up of players exclusively drawn from the western province. That Bengalis were not cricketing material was a myth created by the Pakistanis and shared by their cricketing authorities. In first-class cricket, the then East Pakistani players often turned in lacklustre performances, thus reinforcing the stereotype.

In my secondary school days (1963–1967), cricket became quite popular with middle-class Muslims and Hindus, as well as Muslim boys from the lower-middle classes. The peasant class preferred to play vigorous football, especially in muddy fields. As the son of a civil servant in a small town, I was more interested in playing a whole range of games: football in the morning, cricket during the day, volleyball in the late afternoon and, sometimes, badminton in the evening. The entry of urban Muslim boys from middle and lower classes into cricket made it more lively and popular across the board. In 1969, I played for my college team that won the Jessore Board Championship, beating a number of strong rivals—among them B. L. College, Daulatpur; and Khulna and B. M. College, Barisal. I was the opener for our team. Later, I would occasionally get a place in the first-division cricket league in Khulna, the divisional headquarters. I was one of the three players from Bagerhat, a subdivision in East Pakistan, who played for one of the leading teams of Khulna, Uttoron Club. Our team had reached the final of the league. For the final, a three-day match, both sides hired leading players from Dhaka. Seven members of our team were brought from Dhaka, three from Bagerhat, and the skipper was from Khulna. We had Raquibul of the Under-19 team for Pakistan, with whom I opened. Our opponent's side, too, was studded with players from Dhaka—Latif, Daulat, Rauf Ansari, Anwar, Taher, Shafiq-ul-Haq Hira, among others.

To say that there was not much cricket in what came to be Bangladesh is not factual. However, cricket remained an exclusive game limited to the urbanites. Rural Bangladesh, with its agricultural economy and social structure, remained outside the pale of cricket. Its popularity as a national sport can also be attributed to the expansion of television coverage. Television was introduced in 1964 and its transmission was confined to the provincial capital, Dhaka. I grew up in the 1960s, listening to the running commentaries of cricket on radio. One prominent cricket commentator at that time was Omar Qureshi, whose stylish commentating created a large following among urban middle-class youth. Bengali cricket commentators from Akashbani Radio, Kolkata, were also poetic and brought Test cricket to our living rooms. Thanks to their vivid commentaries and punditry, we could literally see Gary Sobers' batting, or Lance Gibbs' spin spells, or Tiger Pataudi's brilliant and gutsy knocks, with all their nuances explained and analysed. In Bagerhat, a small provincial town, Ken Barrington and Richie Benaud became household names with middle-class, school-going lads.

Cricket thus remained an exclusionary game in East Pakistan during those days, dominated as it was by non-Bengali elites and a sprinkling of Bengali elites. The metropolitan bias in cricket was noticeable. In the small towns, cricket was patronised, to an extent, by declining numbers of local zamindars, many of whom were migrating to India. They left a legacy which was taken forward by the rising middle class in small towns. As a cricket player in a small town, I had occasion to watch a match between the Bagerhat team with the Dhaka Gymkhana team that played in the first-division cricket league in Dhaka. The Gymkhana, a club for the Ismailia community, was an arena for the upper crust of the non-Bengali business class, well known for their wealth and business acumen. The fair-skinned, slightly plump players, wearing white silk shirts and dazzling cricket gear, took on the Bagerhat team in the Prafulla Chandra College ground. Bagerhat hired a couple of players from Khulna, some 19 miles away. When the match started, the Dhaka team looked invincible. After almost five decades, I still have memories of that match as a spectator. The Dhaka team, with its stylish players and looks, went down, badly beaten by the rag-tag Bagerhat team that included Kamal, a fine off-spinner. One of the two hired players from Khulna included Manoj, a stylish batsman, who tore apart Dhaka Gymkhana's bowlers. In my youthful mind, this victory debunked a number of myths—the foreign-looking players from Dhaka were not unbeatable; and the more important lesson that dawned on me was that cricketing talents were not confined to Dhaka and could be found in small non-metropolitan towns, such as Bagerhat (e.g., Kamal) or Khulna (e.g., Manoj).

This marginalisation of Bengali players did not create any Bengali role models for young Bangladeshi players. Once in a while, a supposedly 'Bengali' player (i.e., a resident of East Pakistan) would make it to the 15-member squad of the Pakistani team. On one occasion, it was Nasimul Ghani, who debuted for Pakistan in Test cricket against the West Indies, in 1958, as a bowler. He also scored a century as night watchman against England in 1962, receiving accolades for his performance as an all-rounder. Later, Neaz Mohamed and Daula—both bowlers, and Urdu-speaking *muhajir* (migrants from India)—who played in Dhaka were included. The only Bengali-speaking player who made it to the team was Raqibul Hasan, who was included in the Test squad in 1968–1969 as twelfth man against New Zealand (Krishnan, 2000). However, the first cap that Raqibul won for Pakistan was for his inclusion in the Pakistani Under-19 XI in 1967–1968.

Raqibul was the first Bengali player to be included in the Pakistani squad against the Commonwealth XI in 1971. The match started on 26 February. On day four, 1 March 1971, the match was disrupted as General Yahya Khan, the president of Pakistan, postponed the 3 March opening of the National Assembly. Raqibul's bat carried a 'Joy Bangla' sticker, which created quite a stir in view of the revolutionary atmosphere of the time. There were rumours of a police warrant against him for his rebellious, albeit symbolic, action.

The liberation movement took off, first as a reaction to the unilateral postponement of the sitting of the National Assembly, and, second, after Bangabandhu Sheikh Mujibur Rahman's historic public address on 7 March, where he issued a call for national liberation. Following the Pakistani army's military crackdown on 25 March, Raqibul, like many others, had to flee to safety in India. As the liberation war continued, the Swadhin (Independent) Bangla Football Team was formed. Raqibul, too, proposed a Swadhin Bangla Cricket Team, which he formed. Even as the cricket season approached, Bangladesh became independent on 16 December when the Pakistani troops, under the command of Lt. Gen. Niazi, surrendered to the joint command of Indian and Bangladeshi forces headed by Maj. Gen. Aurora.

THE EMERGENCE OF BANGLADESH

In the early years, cricket received very little patronage from a cash-strapped administration, and Raqibul, like other first-class cricketers, began to feel frustrated. In late 1974, as Raqibul and about 40–50 former first-division cricket players assembled at the Jatiyo Krira Sanghstha (National Sports Association) to lead a procession to Prime Minister Bangabandhu Sheikh Mujibur Rahman's office, Sheik Kamal, the Prime Minister's son—a keen sportsman and a good cricketer as well—volunteered to act as a go-between and persuaded the prime minister to declare his support for cricket. A perception, compounded by bureaucrats, that cricket is an expensive game, a game of the rich and an economically hard-pressed government's post-war rehabilitation and reconstruction led to its neglect in the initial years. By the end of 1974, a Cricket Control Board (later renamed Bangladesh Cricket Board [BCB]) was formed, and the then Minister for Education and Sports M. Yousuf Ali was made the president of the Board, with Muzaffar Hossain Poltu as general secretary and Ashraf Chowdhury a member of the Board.

The first international team to visit Bangladesh was the MCC team in 1976, partly to survey the conditions of cricket in Bangladesh. The MCC's visit was more of a fact-finding mission. Ashraful Haque—a first-division cricketer studying in the UK, scion of an elite family—who was in London at that time accompanied the MCC team. Apparently, Haque had cultivated Robin Marlar, Cambridge Blue and cricket writer for *The Sunday Times*, who also wrote about the plight of Bangladeshi cricket in the years of economic difficulties following Independence. Marlor hoped that Bangladesh would participate in the World Cup sooner rather than later. Raqibul was selected as captain of the Bangladeshi team to play its first match against MCC, which comprised a number of county cricketers. In the first two-day match played at Rajshahi, Bangladesh North Zone performed reasonably well. Wahiduzzaman Montu opened with Raqibul Hasan.

The first international match played by Bangladesh ended in a draw. This match included skipper Raqibul's unbeaten 73. In the second two-day match in Chittagong, Bangladesh was convincingly beaten by MCC; yet, Bangladesh's lacklustre performance was compensated by Ashraful Haque's 68. In the only unofficial three-day Test under the captaincy of Shamim Kabir, Bangladesh scored 266/9, that included Yousuf Babu's 78. Bangladeshi bowlers performed competently as well, with Khandker Nazrul Quader Lintu's 4 wickets for 54 runs and Daulat's 3 for 67. Lintu, a promising leg-spinner and a brilliant student at Dhaka University, dropped out of cricket to pursue higher education overseas. The last two-day match was also drawn in which Raqibul scored 74 of Bangladesh's 203 for 9 declared. Bowler Yousuf Babu claimed 4 wickets for 37 runs.

Cricket in post-independence Bangladesh has become more inclusive and democratic. One would normally think of democratisation as a political process, involving changes in the system of government from authoritarian rule to more participatory democratic rule. Yet, there is another side—a social aspect—of democratisation that opens up space for social mobility. This is a process that allows people from the margins to take part in mainstream events. This transition from an exclusive system to more openness and inclusion is an aspect of democratisation at the level of society in which Bangladesh's cricket has thrived.

The professionalisation of cricket and other sports came in the 1990s with improvements in infrastructure in the late 1980s, especially under military ruler President H. M. Ershad, himself a keen sportsman. The present home of cricket, Mirpur Cricket Stadium, was built in his tenure and named Sher-e-Bangla Cricket Stadium. Originally designed as a football (soccer) stadium, in 2004 it was converted into a cricket stadium that hosted Scotland in an ODI in 2005, and the first Test match against the West Indies in 2007. The stadium hosted the World Cup in 2011, and the Asia Cup in 2012 and 2014.

Herself a consummate cricket fan, Sheikh Hasina's personal support and official patronage played an important role. It was during the tenure of the Awami League government under her leadership (1996–2001) that Bangladesh attained Test status. Charge of the Bangladesh Cricket Board was given to Saber Hossain Chowdhury, a respected politician who also acted as special assistant to Prime Minister Sheikh Hasina. British-educated Chowdhury is a popular public figure in his constituency, one who wins support with his fine manners, civility and organisational capability. He played an important part in professionalising cricket in Bangladesh. During this period, cricket players of the national team received handsome financial rewards, and cricket became a lucrative profession. Since the late 1990s, Bangladeshi cricket has been managed by figures who brought their corporate experience to cricket management. Gone were the days when cricketers were employed by banks or national airlines so that they could earn a livelihood.

FROM EXCLUSIVENESS TO INCLUSIVENESS

Between 2015 and 2017, of 13 Test debutants only one, Taskin Ahmed, was from Dhaka. The rest, including Mustafizur Rahman, Mehidy Hasan and Mosaddek Hossain, came from small towns. Says Nazmul Abedeen Fahim, Bangladesh Cricket Board's Manager, 'We believe we can find any talent from anywhere in Bangladesh. It is slowly becoming a pan-Bangladesh effort, which gives boys from smaller towns more opportunities.'

> Previously, a boy from a small town would have a hard time figuring out how to become a cricketer in Bangladesh. Now they have local heroes, the likes of Soumya Sarkar from Satkhira, or Imrul Kayes from Meherpur, or Mehidy Hasan from Khulna. They now know the path to becoming a professional (Isam, 2017).

This inclusiveness began with the recruitment of Mashrafe Mortaza, a small-town boy from Narail, a district in south-western Bangladesh, who made his debut in Test cricket in 2001. In 2012, when Gazi was given a chance to play first-class cricket in the city of his birth, Khulna, he proved his mettle. Gazi has had to a travel a long way from Pautakhali, a district town of Barisal, to Dhaka, to find a place in the national team (Isam, 2012). Bangladesh has seen major improvements in the expansion of the catchment area for recruiting talented players.

ENTER CORPORATE CRICKET

The Bangladesh Premier League, popularly known as BPL T20, was formed in 2011 by the BCB after a brief spell of the National Cricket League. The BPL, comprising seven teams (see Table 1), is studded with cricket superstars from round the world: Chris Gayle, Brandon McCulum and Darren Sammy are part of Rangpur Riders, whereas Afghan cricket stars Mohamad Nabi and Rashid Khan are members of Comilla Victorians. To the consternation of foreign cricket sceptics, the celebration and consumption of short-format commercial cricket has placed Bangladeshi cricket on the global map. The rise of corporate cricket is the flipside of Bangladesh's remarkable economic growth since the 1990s.

Table 1 BPL Teams

Team	City	Owner	Captain
Chittagong Vikings	Chittagong	DBL Group	Luke Ronchi (New Zealand)
Comilla Victorians	Comilla	Legends Sporting	Mohammad Nabi (Afghanistan)
Dhaka Dynamites	Dhaka	Beximco Group	Shakib Al Hasan
Khulna Titans	Khulna	Gemcon Group	Mahmudullah (Bangladesh)
Rajshahi Kings	Rajshahi	Mango Entertainment	Darren Sammy (West Indies)
Rangpur Riders	Rangpur	Bashundhara Group	Mashrafe Mortoza (Bangladesh)
Sylhet Sixers	Sylhet	SylhetSports	Nasir Hossain (Bangladesh)

The success of commercialised cricket is also the face of new economic growth in Bangladesh since the 1990s. Currently, Bangladesh enjoys an economic growth rate of seven per cent.[3] Bangladesh's export-driven capitalist development has given rise to a number of local corporations that can inject substantial financial resources into the game, attracting leading cricketing superstars from round the world.

GENDER AND BANGLADESHI CRICKET

With the advent of cricket in Bangladesh, women were to be seen in the viewers' gallery of the Dhaka stadium, rooting for their favourite stars and teams. Women are now also seen on cricket fields. The Bangladesh Women's Cricket team attained one-day status after they beat the US team by nine wickets in the Women's World Cup Qualifier in 2011. The team took part in the Asian Cricket Council (ACC) championship in 2007, which it won. It took the team seven more years to take part in the International Cricket Council (ICC)

World Women's T20 in 2014. The emergence of women's cricket is both a sign of their dedication to the game and a reflection of the overall empowerment of women in Bangladesh. In 2017, Bangladesh was ranked 47th of 144 countries worldwide in gender empowerment by the Gender Empowerment Report 2017 of the World Economic Forum.[4] There has been a noticeable improvement in the overall conditions for women, despite the existence of a patriarchal social structure.

CONCLUSION

One of the interesting paradoxes of the Bangladeshi team is that while as a team it often struggles, the team has some highly talented players, such as Shakib Al Hasan who was named the Wisden Cricketer's 'Test Player of the Year' for 2009. He was also named in the World Test XI in the ICC Awards 2009, becoming the first Bangladeshi player to receive the honour. In 2011, Tamim Iqbal was named in the Wisden, a year before Sri Lanka's Kumar Sangakkara received that honour. For Bangladesh to move forward, much work lies ahead in building a team based on a high degree of *esprit de corps*. And it is only a matter of time.

ACKNOWLEDGEMENTS

I am grateful to cricketer Raqibul Hasan, now a match-referee, for sharing his biographical narrative with me in a telephone interview. I also thank Mahbubul Haque Khondker for his useful comments.

◆

NOTES

1. The two-Test series ended in a draw as Australia beat Bangladesh in the second Test in Chittagong by seven wickets.
2. *Daily Star* (Dhaka), 10 October 2017, Star Online Report.
3. 'Bangladesh vs. Pakistan: East Overtakes West', *The Economist*, 9 September 2017: 46.
4. *The Global Gender Gap Report*. The World Economic Forum. 2017. Geneva.

REFERENCES

Appadurai, A. 1996. 'Playing with Modernity: The Decolonization of Indian Cricket', *Modernity at Large*. Minneapolis: University of Minnesota Press.

Astill, James. 2013. *The Great Tamasha: Cricket, Corruption and the Spectacular Rise of Modern India.* New York: Bloomsbury.

Guha, R. 1998. 'Cricket and Politics in Colonial India', *Past and Present.* November.

Isam, M. 2017. 'How Bangladesh is Finding and Developing its Talents', 20 July 2017.http://www.espncricinfo.com/story/_/id/20108383/mohammad-isam-how-bangladesh-develops-players

———. 2012. 'Sohag Gazi Overcomes Small-Town Doubts', 19 November 2012. http://www.estpncricinfo.com/bangladesh/content/story/592061.html

Khondker, H. and R. Robertson. 2018 (forthcoming). 'Glocalization, Consumption and Cricket: The Indian Premier League', *Journal of Consumer Culture.*

Khondker, H. 2010. 'Globalization, Cricket and National Belonging', in Chris Rumford and Stephen Wagg (eds), *Cricket and Globalization.* Newcastle Upon Tyne: Cambridge Scholars Press.

Krishnan, Sankhya. 2000. 'Meet the Only Bengali to have Played for Pakistan', 1 July. http://www.espncricinfo.com/ci/content/story/88526.html

◆◆

THE JOURNEY OF INDIAN WOMEN'S CRICKET FROM THE 1970S

SHANTHA RANGASWAMY

Whenever I reminisce about the trajectory of women's cricket in our country, I sometimes wonder if that journey actually took place, or if it is just a pleasant dream. With the passage of time, it seems as if these pioneers could well have been characters out of a novel, or perhaps a scene from a motion picture.

It is actually very difficult to recapture those golden moments. I distinctly remember walking five to six kilometres each way, every day, to practice sessions. Fortunately, the traffic those days in Bangalore was not as bad and it was not overcrowded. It is virtually impossible to walk that route now. But, then, I've jumped the gun, haven't I? It will be hard for any reader to comprehend what we went through unless it is described in detail. Generally, one does not like to go down memory lane to recollect the hardships one faced. But, at the risk of sounding like Rani of Jhansi or Joan of Arc, I relished most of those events, and am quite sure many of my compatriots would join me in stating that we enjoyed those tough moments.

I grew up in a joint family where many cousins, and their friends, would join in for a weekend feast of cricket—albeit played with tennis balls. But there were many like me who waited for a platform to display our prowess with bat and ball. I had already represented the victorious Karnataka state team in ball badminton and had captained the Karnataka state softball team too. The very first year that the Karnataka state team participated in the National Championship was under my captaincy; we were runners-up, and I was adjudged the best all-rounder in the country and was honoured with the Maharani Padmini Award.

In 1973, the Women's Cricket Association of India (WCAI) was formed in Lucknow. The first National Championship was held in April 1973, in Poona, with two-and-a-half teams participating— yes, 2.5 teams, precisely. The only teams available were from Bombay and Maharashtra, and a half-team from Uttar Pradesh. The extra Maharashtrian players filled in the blanks for Uttar Pradesh. Obviously, the first National Championship was conducted in a hurry sans publicity, thereby eliciting a poor response. The second National Championship was held a few months later in November 1973 at Varanasi with 16 teams participating, including the team from Karnataka, which I captained. We had beaten the previous runner-up Maharashtra in the initial stages, while Bengal upset Bombay, the reigning champion. Most of the players were in their early to mid-teens and Bengal had a formidable team; little wonder that Bengal emerged as the winner in that championship. Karnataka lost to them in the final. I had the small consolation that I was adjudged the best all-rounder. Bengal continued to dominate the domestic scene for years until the Indian Railways formed a team with the cream from most states. The Indian Railways team has dominated the scene ever since, with most Railways' players representing the Indian team.

There is an interesting anecdote pertaining to the second National Championship held at Varanasi. Bengal and Karnataka had beaten more fancied teams; and Bengal had to face the latter's wrath. Some players of the losing teams played havoc with the Bengal players' white cricket gear. One needs to remember that most women cricketers those days came from lower-middle-class families with modest incomes. We would wash our white dress between matches so that we could play with clean clothes in the next match. Some of the mischievous elements in the teams that lost sprinkled ink on the freshly washed white clothes that the Bengal players had hung outside. This mischief came to light the next day, and the Bengal players were naturally livid. I seem to remember that these players were almost caught, as they had left a trail of ink from the Bengal dormitory to their respective rooms! Looking back, it does sound childish, but then one has to remember that most of the players were then just 15 or 16 years old.

Dormitories were by far the best accommodation we were provided. Sometimes we had to make do by sleeping on the floors of classrooms. The current lot of players—so used to air travel and decent hotel accommodation—will shudder with fear and trepidation if they have to travel in unreserved train compartments and sleep on the floor as we did. Those days, the National Championship was a tournament that saw the participation of all state teams, but was generally played on a knock-out basis. Most teams that lost had to leave the very next day, thereby rendering the exercise of securing train reservations almost impossible. Often, our travel in the initial stages was in unreserved compartments, sitting near toilets. Since we were provided with only dormitory accommodation, we had to, per force, carry a suitcase for our clothes, a kit for our cricket gear and a hold-all for our bedding. One can well imagine our problem in trying to board a train with 18 to 20 members of the team, baggage, etc. It was even more difficult if we had to board a train in smaller cities from which trains did not originate. The inter-zonal championship for the Rani Jhansi Trophy commenced in 1974, but as the tournament was conducted on a league format, the experience of travelling by train was comparatively better as we had a little more time to book our tickets.

But, in retrospect, this was never looked upon as relevant because the passion to play overshadowed all these obstacles. A unique factor was that the pioneers realised that we needed to perform well to ensure the game's longevity. It is pertinent to mention here that during the mid-'70s, when women's cricket entered the international arena, a few other women's games also started in India. But the euphoria of these women's sports lasted for only a few years, while women's cricket went from strength to strength.

◆◆◆

In 1975, the Australian women's team toured India and the first match of the series was against South Zone at Bangalore. The match was preceded by tension between officials of the women's cricket associations of Tamil Nadu and Karnataka. The issue was a trivial one. While Karnataka wanted me to captain the team, Tamil Nadu wanted its captain Sudha Shah to lead. Eventually, I led the South Zone team. The first Test was played at Pune. During this series, it was decided that local players would lead the team. Ujwala Nikkam of Maharashtra led the Indian team in the first Test. That Test did not go well as far as I was concerned, as I made only nine runs in the first innings and did not get to bat in the second. Besides, I hardly got to bowl. The second Test was at Delhi, and with no leading player from there in the squad, Sudha Shah of Tamil Nadu was named captain. There were murmurs of dropping me for this Test. A selector from a different zone told me that I needed to deliver if I wanted to retain my place in the squad. Apparently, the selector from my own zone had planned to drop me, perhaps as a fallout of the Bangalore episode in which I had played no part.

I was told to go in at number four position in the batting order. With not much to show on the board, and with two wickets down, I entered the middle. As I left the pavilion, I loudly announced that it would be a do-or-die match for me. Fortunately, I clicked with the bat, scoring 92 in the first innings, and top-scored again in the second. But more was in store. Australia needed 118 to win. With most of the bowlers refraining from bowling (most of the players were in their mid-teens), the onus fell on me to keep pegging from one end. Diana Edulji took over at the other end, after the medium pacers had bowled a couple of overs. Those days, the last day of the Test match witnessed a minimum of 20 overs (mandatory) in the last hour. I distinctly remember the last stage. I was bowling the last over, with the opponents needing five runs to win with three wickets in hand. Fortunately for me, the well-set Australian opener Lyn Smith was at the non-striker's end, batting on 60-plus. The first ball was misfielded, conceding an extra run. But it meant the set-opener remained at the non-striker's end. I dismissed the batter—clean bowled by the next ball—and in walked their captain, Cecilia Wilson. She kept swinging her bat, but made no contact, and finally fell to the last ball of the game, again clean bowled. The match had turned on its head, with fortunes fluctuating. The result was a draw, with the Australians needing three runs to win, and we needing one wicket. It was a nail-biting finish, akin to a T20 finish, although T20 matches did not exist then. So, from being dropped, I grabbed the Eve of the Match award with 112 runs and six wickets, including the five in the second essay. I had escaped the sword of Damocles by the skin of my teeth. To top my cup of joy, I was named vice-captain for the next and final Test at Eden Gardens, Kolkata. Sreerupa Bose, the local player, was named captain.

If we had saved the second Test by grit, we almost won the third. Batting fourth, we were set a target of about 186. When I went in to bat at my customary position, our wicketkeeper and opener Fowzieh Khalili was batting. Not surprisingly, we were instructed to play for a draw, illustrating our defensive mindset. After a few overs, Fowzieh and I discussed the situation. I felt that the good batting strip gave us an advantage that ought not to be lost. Despite instructions to pull down the shutter, I persuaded Fowzieh that we ought to give it a try as there were enough batters down the line to play for a draw, if necessary. What flourished was a good third-wicket partnership, with both of us getting decent scores. But in our attempt to get quick runs, both of us got run out. I made 55 runs; Fowzi, 45. The fight continued after we left the middle, but not for long, as the fear of loss impelled the captain to instruct the players to settle for a draw. Imagine this—we were just 12 runs short of the target, with four–five wickets in hand. But, ultimately, the team achievement was a defeat-less series, despite the fact that we were two-year-old babes in the international arena.

The reason I have elaborated on the very first series—which we later learnt was an unofficial one as the Australians fielded an Under-25 team—is because the team's good performance ensured the longevity of the game. As pioneers, we were well aware that our performance mattered, as failure would have seen the premature death of the game from the public perspective. Even to this day, I maintain that our most significant achievement is that we ensured that the game continued to thrive by performing well consistently. Not the first century I scored against New Zealand the next year, nor the series win against the West Indies under my captaincy, gives me as much satisfaction as the overall performance of the team. I have said this often enough: The single most significant achievement of the pioneers is that we laid a solid foundation for cricket in India, on which edifice the game has grown exponentially.

The next year saw the New Zealand team arriving in India. Having been named captain for the entire series, it was my best series yet, with 527 runs in the five-match series, with a century to boot in the fourth Test at Pune. My strongest memory of that knock is seeing a gentleman and a young girl running on to the middle to congratulate me as I reached the century mark. The gentleman was Diana Edulji's father. The young girl was Nilima Joglekar nee Barve, who was to be part of the team later the same year when we toured New Zealand.

We notched up our first Test win when the West Indies team came to India later the same year. While I was already established as a batter, this series saw my bowling reach great heights. In an interview, West Indies Captain Louise Browne stated that I was a better bowler than a batter. I know she meant it in a positive way by highlighting my bowling ability, as by then I had established myself as a batter. On the day we won the Patna Test before a huge crowd exceeding 40,000 spectators, the whole city had erupted, celebrating our win. I remember a victory procession that took two hours from the stadium to a women's college in the neighbourhood, as people had lined up along the streets to cheer us, and finally ended with dance and song.

◆◆◆

The golden year for Indian women's cricket was 1976. Both New Zealand and the West Indies toured India, and finally we went to New Zealand for a six-week tour. The highlight of the New Zealand tour was that we played in their National Championship. The Indian team did not lose a single game on that tour. We either won, or drew our matches. The Indian team was also exposed to a new experience. Except for the Test match at Queenstown, where we stayed as a team in a hotel, we were paired off and stayed with either Indian or Kiwi families. After the initial hesitation, we got used to the pattern; I stayed mostly with Indian families. But an amusing episode is worth recounting here.

On that tour, we went directly from the airport to the homes of the families which were to host us. Fowzieh Khalili and I were mostly paired off to stay with the same family. The term 'billeted' was new to us then; it meant staying with families. As we reached our hosts' homes, we were asked if we wanted to have 'tea'. Almost all of us declined, as tea at dinner time would only have killed our appetite. Upon which, our hosts showed us to our bedrooms and wished us good night. We went to bed hungry, as we hesitated to ask for dinner until offered. Next day, when the team members assembled for practice, all of us complained to our manager about the lack of dinner. We then learnt that 'dinner' in India was 'tea' in

New Zealand! Since we had declined 'tea', our hosts presumed we had eaten on the flight. But this experience stood us in good stead when we moved to the next centre, where there was a resounding yes when we were asked by our host family if we wanted tea.

At the Test match played at Dunedin, rain affected play for four days. Fortunately, I made a century in that Test. I remember Nilima Joglekar—who was now a member of the team—ran on to the pitch to congratulate me. So, for both my centuries, Nilima had been the common factor. We later learnt that the New Zealand tour of India in early 1976 was not treated as official by the International Women's Cricket Council (IWCC)—but the Dunedin Test was. It was almost impossible to comprehend the logic because the team that played against us in Dunedin, and in most of the Tests in India, was virtually the same. The 527 runs that I made in the series when New Zealand toured India, and Diana Edulji's many wickets, went down the drain. I sometimes wonder if my name would have entered the records as the first-ever centurion if I had not scored that century in Dunedin. But it is never too late. The International Cricket Council (ICC) can still examine the issue and set right this anomaly, and declare as official those Tests played against New Zealand in India.

◆◆◆

The one disturbing factor that haunted women cricketers of that era was that many of us lost a few playing years because of poor administration. After the 1978 World Cup in India, there was no official tournament until the 1982 World Cup and the 1984 Australian tour of India. Again, from 1986 to 1991, there was no cricket played. This effectively meant 12 wasted years without playing any series—even as most of us were in our prime—and we had to endure this for want of a strong organisational set-up.

In fact, most of us collected funds under the banner of the India Club and in 1979 toured Holland, England, the West Indies and the United States. We played matches in Guyana, as well as in Trinidad & Tobago where we were treated as state guests. We also played against the men's teams, comprising largely of the immigrants in the United States. But there is more to the story than just our tour. We brought out a souvenir to raise funds. Chandra Tripathi, the then

Chairperson of the WCAI, got wind of this and visited my home in Bangalore. She suggested that if we handed over to the WCAI whatever we had collected, she would send the Indian team to the West Indies. I rejected the suggestion outright, and politely told her that it was improper and unfair to those who had toiled to collect the funds.

Still, many women cricketers are indebted to Chandra as she was responsible for Diana Edulji's job with Indian Railways, which led to many more recruitments. Chandra was the daughter-in-law of Kamalapathi Tripathi, the then Railway Minister. When Madhava Rao Scindia became the Minister for Railways, he ensured that many more women cricketers got jobs. Women's cricket in India is thus indebted to Chandra, Scindia, Diana and Sharad Pawar, among others.

The WCAI started functioning efficiently from 1991 onwards, initially when Anuradha Dutta took over the reins of administration, and from 2002 onwards with Shubhangi Kulkarni as secretary. While the 2017 performance of the Indian team in the ICC World Cup hogged the limelight, there are many who are unaware that the Indian team achieved the same result in the 2005 World Cup in South Africa when Shubhangi was at the helm.

Incidentally, the IWCC had merged with the ICC towards the end of the 20th century. In fact, the 2000 Women's World Cup at Christchurch, New Zealand, was hosted by the New Zealand Cricket Council—the men's body. It was only in India that the Board of Control for Cricket in India (BCCI) took its time to take over the administration of women's cricket. While most women's governing bodies merged with the men's boards, it was only in 2006 that the BCCI took over the women's cricket administration. This was possible mainly due to the efforts of the then President of the BCCI, Sharad Pawar. Initially, when asked by the ICC, the BCCI was not keen to govern women's cricket. Jagmohan Dalmiya, the then President of the BCCI, wrote to the ICC, authorising the WCAI to administer the game in India. But it was the advent of Pawar as president that saw a sea change in attitude. It is reliably learnt that Pawar had to virtually force his decision on the BCCI. But unlike countries where women's cricket councils merged with their male counterparts, there were many men occupying posts in the WCAI who wanted to continue to stay in power. To circumvent this, the BCCI started its own women's wing, which was the most significant development for Indian women's cricket in the 21st century. This progressive initiative by Pawar enabled women cricketers to play under the BCCI umbrella, which meant better practice and travel facilities, and access to trained coaches. Although the team reached the finals of the 2017 World Cup, which we lost narrowly, I would rank the BCCI's takeover of women's cricket as the single most significant factor for the overall improvement of the game. I state this primarily because it opened up unexpected avenues at the grass roots level that benefited many women cricketers.

◆◆◆

It has been almost five decades since women's cricket began in India—1973, to be precise. When we started playing, the initial reaction was ridicule, to begin with, followed by curiosity, and, finally, appreciation as we held our own against other countries that had begun playing a few decades before us. This process of growth—from ridicule to curiosity to appreciation to adoration—has not come about overnight. It is the result of the sweat and toil of many women cricketers over almost five decades. Now it is time to look back and rejoice as our national team has continued to do well. But in the process, let us not forget to gratefully acknowledge those pioneers who did this for no financial benefit—just passion for the game. To reiterate a comment I made in an interview some 30 years ago: Women cricketers are more passionate about the game than their male counterparts, as they have served the game with sincerity without expecting anything in return. They served the game with no financial benefits, which may be hard to believe; but like other pioneers, I have never earned a rupee from the game in my entire cricketing career that spanned two decades. Nonetheless, we have all carved a niche in the history of the game—the sheer joy of serving the game and our country was more than sufficient. I wish I could compose poetry—I would have written an ode to all my teammates, even as I am aware that they deserve much more than just that. But, it is a good place to begin.

◆

INDIAN PREMIER LEAGUE
The Great Indian Story

MIHIR BOSE

In 2009, after the second Indian Premier League (IPL) season, Shikhar Dhawan reflected on what this new tournament meant. Before the advent of the IPL, Dhawan had made his mark on Indian domestic cricket as a rising young star. He had been part of the Delhi Ranji Trophy winning team, and won the Player of the Tournament award in the U–19 World Cup in 2004. He had even won a Border–Gavaskar cricket scholarship to train at Australia's Adelaide Academy. Yet none of this matched what the IPL did for him. As he put it:

> Playing in the IPL was almost like being in an international match. Winning the Ranji Trophy or the U–19 World Cup award did not give me the kind of visibility that the quick-fire IPL knocks gave me. I have had good knocks in Ranji matches, and when you do that the selectors obviously take note. But the power of the [IPL] matches that are telecast live and watched by millions is immense. Not only the selectors, even the fans get to know you and start talking about you.

Nothing sums up what has happened better. The shortest form of cricket, with each side restricted to 20 overs, the IPL has revolutionised the fortunes of players, both Indian and overseas, and so transformed cricket that England, after more than a century of world domination, has now had to cede power to India. And this new Indian League, which will celebrate its tenth anniversary in 2018, is the ultimate expression of Indian soft power. It means that for the first time a major team sport is not controlled by the West.

INDIA'S ASTONISHING JOHANNESBURG MIRACLE

Yet this transformation is a very Indian story. The 20-over game was not only not an Indian invention, but it was shunned by Indians when the English came up with the concept, so much so that the then secretary of the Indian board initially refused to take part in the first T20 World Cup in South Africa in 2007, snorting in derision, 'Twenty20. Why not ten-ten, or five-or one?'

India reluctantly sent a side to South Africa, with its greatest star Sachin Tendulkar dropping out. Rahul Dravid, who had just captained India to their first series victory in England since 1986, also refused to go, and was happy for Mahendra Singh Dhoni to take over as captain. There, in the land where Gandhi fashioned satyagraha, Dhoni led his young team to a sensational victory, beating Pakistan in the final in a thriller. Although the IPL was already being planned, it was this victory that provided the ideal launch pad for the tournament. Back in 1983, India's victory in the then 60-over World Cup at Lord's, just as unexpected as the T20 triumph in South Africa, had triggered a revolution in Indian cricket. Before that, Indians shunned the one-day format and seemed wedded to five-day Tests. Yet they now abandoned five-day cricket for this more instant tamasha. But the effect of the 1983 victory was not instantaneous; it was some years before the one-day game took over in India. The effect of the victory in South Africa was almost overnight.

On 24 January 2008, exactly four months after Sreesanth had caught Pakistan captain Misbah-ul-Haq to give India victory, rich Indian businessmen met at the Board of Control for Cricket in India's (BCCI) headquarters in Mumbai. At the end of the bidding process, eight franchises based in Bangalore, Chennai, Delhi, Hyderabad, Jaipur, Kolkata, Mohali and Mumbai were sold for USD 723.59 million, nearly double the reserve price. Four months later, the first IPL was held—a format of the game that most Indians had not even been much aware of before the miracle of Johannesburg. Even in a country like India, where change can come quickly, this was sensational. In the decade since, Indians have so taken to this form of the game that they have in the process destroyed many myths.

One myth was that the only form of cricket that can attract crowds and television income is international cricket. For almost 60 years, all over the world, domestic cricket had been subsidised by the international game. This is in stark contrast to other team sports such as football, rugby, American football, basketball and baseball. This was even more so in India where, for all the talk of cricket being religion, the crowds only came to worship when the national team was playing. Even in my youth, Ranji Trophy matches, the premier domestic competition, struggled to attract crowds. Now crowds are so sparse that you can walk in free for a Ranji Trophy match, even one featuring Mumbai, the most successful side ever. Yet, in contrast, the IPL draws enormous crowds and, what is more, these matches are played in the heat of the Indian summer. This is another break from the past, as in April and May, traditionally, cricket in India gave way to football and hockey.

The economic power of the IPL cannot be overstated and continues to confound most experts. In 2008, broadcast rights to the IPL's first season were sold for 10 years to Sony-World Sports Group for USD 1.5 billion. This was considered remarkably good money, as in the previous year, ESPN Star offered the International Cricket Council (ICC) USD 1 billion to telecast all ICC events, including quadrennial World Cups and Champions Trophy for eight years between 2007 and 2015. That a domestic competition could fetch more revenue than international competitions was sensational enough; what has followed since is quite remarkable. In September 2017, IPL rights were sold to Star India for five years for ₹16,347 crore, which was more than the worth of all the other T20 leagues that have mushroomed in the wake of the IPL in the last decade.

THE NEW INDIAN CRICKET EMPIRE

But while these figures are impressive, the IPL story is best told by the impact it has had on the world of cricket and why India, once pariah of the cricket world, is now the place cricketers cannot keep away from. The pre-IPL world revolved round an English summer. The moment the English cricket season started in late April, cricket all over the world effectively ceased. Such was the power of the English game that cricketers from all over the world came to play in England. The impact of the English game on the world game was emphasised, following efforts made by the English authorities to revive interest in the game. In the 1960s, English cricket, keen to attract crowds back to the county game, relaxed the strict residency rules for qualifying for county cricket. Overseas cricketers flooded in and the English county game effectively became the finishing school for overseas cricketers, with great players like Vivian Richards and Imran Khan on display throughout the English summer.

India was a bit player in this English summer garden party. Unlike the West Indians and Pakistanis, not many Indians played county cricket. In the early post-war years, Indian cricketers did spent their summers in England. But, unable to play county cricket and desperate to earn when there was no cricket in India, they played in league cricket in the north of England. This meant being the only professionals in amateur club sides which played on Saturday afternoons. If they scored a 50 or took five wickets, a hat was passed round the crowd to collect money that supplemented their meagre income. The cricketers spent the rest of the week doing a bit of coaching and were put up with families in various fairly dismal Lancashire towns.

It is a reflection of the standing of Indian cricket—and how poorly rewarded Indian cricketers were—that some of its greats spent many a summer in England during the 1950s and 1960s. The list included Vijay Hazare, the man who captained India to its first-ever Test victory; Vijay Manjrekar, one of India's best batsmen; Vinoo Mankad, one of its greatest all-rounders; and Subhas Gupte, the man Gary Sobers considers the greatest leg-spinner in the history of the game.

Indeed, Mankad's story illustrates how the IPL has changed the cricket world. In 1952, Mankad's left-arm spin led to India's first-ever Test victory at Chepauk (Madras, India). India was to tour England that summer but Mankad, poorly paid, had to earn money, and with the Indian selectors refusing to guarantee him a place in the touring team, he decided to play for a League club in Lancashire. But after India's disastrous showing in the first Test at Headingley, losing four wickets for no runs—still the worst start in Test history—Indian selectors were forced to turn to Mankad. They paid off his contract; Mankad played in the second Test at Lord's where, despite another defeat, he performed so brilliantly that it is known as Mankad's Test.

Now, observe the transformation wrought by the IPL. It is 24 January 2008, and bidding is about to start at the BCCI headquarters in Mumbai's Wankhede Stadium for the franchises that will own the teams taking part in the inaugural IPL tournament.

The Ambani brothers are there; so is Bollywood starlet Priety Zinta, her then boyfriend, the businessman Ness Wadia, along with other businessmen, such as Mohit Burman and Vijay Mallya. The cars carrying the dignitaries reflect the India that has emerged since the 1991 opening up of the Indian economy. Priety Zinta and Ness Wadia have come in a black Lexus, Mohit Burman in a silver Rolls Royce, Mallya in a red Bentley with another red Mercedes in tow. Yet, what is the name of the gate they have come through? Mankad Gate, after a cricketer who could never have afforded such a car and was at times so poor that he slept on the concrete benches along Marine Drive, just across the way from the stadium.

Just as remarkable is the IPL's effect on the world's cricketers. In the 1950s, unable to attract international sides, a team of various international players—dubbed the Commonwealth Team—was organised by former Lancashire wicketkeeper, George Duckworth. In 1951 and 1972, England sent a team captained by a man who had never played Test cricket—both Nigel Howard and Tony Lewis made their Test debuts as captain in India and, as it happened, both of them in the opening Test of the series in Delhi. The result was that some of the greats of English cricket of the 1950s, such as Len Hutton, Alec Bedser, Godfrey Evans, Fred Trueman, Jim Laker and Dennis Compton, never played Test cricket in India.

This attitude of keeping Indian cricket at arm's length continued well into the 1980s. In 1979, Australia played six Tests, but this seemed to take so much out of the Australians that their next visit was in 1986. Then another 10-year wait till 1996, but only for one Test, before a three-Test series in 1998 marked the start of more regular visits. On that trip, India was so unfamiliar to the Australians that only eight of the touring party of 15 had ever played a Test in India, and Shane Warne caused something of a stir before the series began by stating that he was 'not a fan of exotic cuisine'. This prompted Qantas, the Australian national airline, to fly in 1,900 tins of baked beans and spaghetti for the team.

Yet, with the advent of the IPL, Shane Warne in 2008 coached the Rajasthan Royals to victory and learnt to speak Hindi. By then Bret Lee, the Australian fast bowler, was quite fluent in Hindi. During the 2003 World Cup, some Indian fans even complained that he had abused them in Hindi; he had even been used as brand ambassador by Indian companies. Such was Lee's appeal that businessman Kumar

Mangalam Birla exchanged text messages with him, and when Birla was guest editor of the *Economic Times*, it ran a profile of Lee on 6 April 2008, just as the first IPL was getting started.

SEEKING INDIAN CRICKETING GOLD

Ever since 2008, cricketers from round the world have flocked to India. This is hardly a surprise. Suddenly, the best in the game can make the sort of money earned by high-ranking footballers, and just for a few weeks' work. Ben Stokes, England's best all-rounder, is a classic example. Stokes was not selected for the 2017–2018 Ashes series because of an off-field incident in September 2017. He was held on suspicion of causing actual bodily harm, following a disturbance outside a Bristol nightclub. According to the police, 'A 27-year-old man suffered a fractured eye socket in the incident on Queens Road, Clifton.' Stokes was later released and after the police had completed a preliminary inquiry, a file on the incident was passed on to the Crown Prosecution Service (CPS), with the police seeking advice on how to proceed. With the CPS decision pending, Stokes was not selected for the 2017–2018 Ashes series. Many cricket experts felt his absence was one of the reasons why England lost. Yet, come the IPL, the 26-year-old was ready to play and, indeed, could not wait to come to India. Not surprisingly, with salary caps increased by 20 per cent, he could now earn an estimated USD 4 million for under eight weeks of cricket. As this article was being written, the CPS decided to charge Stokes; and England, feeling they could not do without their charismatic all-rounder, selected him for the New Zealand tour.

Such has been the effect of these riches that players like West Indian Chris Gayle have preferred the IPL to playing for their country. Gayle played in the 2017 IPL, but not for the West Indies when they toured England later that summer. For almost three decades, from the 1950s to the 1980s, the West Indies team was one of the most dominant in the world. A player not wanting to play for the West Indies was unthinkable. But with the Caribbean unable to match the earnings of a few weeks of the IPL, Gayle's preference for a form of the game in which he is much in demand, and where his batting has set records, can hardly be a surprise. Gayle is one of several West Indians who have turned their back on what was once the most-feared team in the world. So have spinner Sunil Narine and all-rounder Dwayne Bravo. As Bravo put it, 'I am not going to give up the contracts that I have around the world to come back and play in the domestic tournament. I did it already and I got burned.' Observe the contrast with Mankad—we can only speculate about what he would have done had there been an IPL in the 1950s.

ENGLAND BECOMES INDIA'S CRICKETING COLONY

But perhaps the most dramatic impact of the IPL is the effect it has had on England. When it was was launched in 2008, English cricket, unable to believe that Indians could match their expertise, scoffed at it. Such was their disdain that in order to counteract the IPL and to ensure their cricketers were not attracted to Indian money, they teamed up with Allen Stanford, an American financier and promotor of sport. The England and Wales Cricket Board (ECB) signed a controversial agreement for a multi-million-pound series of matches. Stanford flew into Lord's on board a private helicopter laden with a treasure chest supposedly filled with dollar notes, which later turned out to be fake. A few months after the IPL had been successfully launched, England flew out to Antigua to play against the Stanford Superstars for a prize pot of USD 20 million, with the 11 players on the winning side promised that each of them would walk away with USD 1 million, with a further two million going to squad players, and coaching and management staff. The ECB clearly saw this as making sure no English players would be tempted by the IPL. But within months, Stanford was charged with fraud worth USD 8 billion and is now serving a 110-year federal prison sentence, although he continues to deny any wrongdoing and has vowed to clear his name.

Since then English cricket has had to bow to the power of the IPL, so much so that despite the fact that the IPL overlaps with the English cricket season, English cricketing authorities now allow their best players to miss the first two months of the season to take part in this great Indian gold mine. Two centuries ago, the British came to India to make money and founded an empire. Now their cricketers are willing to miss a part of their cherished season to make the sort of money they could never make anywhere else.

The IPL has also developed bonds between Indians and foreigners, among other things. This is best illustrated in the case of Sarvesh Kumar, a medium pacer who got a chance to play for

Hyderabad Deccan Chargers in the IPL's first season. A cricketer from a working-class background—his father worked as a welder in a government-owned ordinance factory in Hyderabad—he had long admired Australian wicketkeeper–batsman Adam Gilchrist, so much so that when Gilchrist wore yellow he wore yellow. Gilchrist played for the Deccan Chargers and gave Sarvesh his chance. Sarvesh agonised about what he should call his Australian hero. 'Everyone called him Gilly or Gilchrist. But I was confused; how could I call such a senior player Gilly? But I found a way out by calling him Brother.' The story illustrates the impact of the IPL, providing Indian cricketers, even those like Sarvesh who never made it, a chance to mix with the best in the game but yet be Indian in their social attitudes.

IPL AS MASS ENTERTAINMENT

The IPL has had its critics, with some arguing that it is all about the money. According to Santosh Desai, CEO of Future Brands, speaking in the early years of the IPL, 'The exploitation of the game in [the] IPL is too naked. Patriotism, which has sustained the game for more than a century, is replaced by narcissism.' This ignored the fact that maharajas could hardly be called patriotic. They had had their own motives for promoting the game, which had nothing to do with the Indian nation as they did not believe in that idea.

Desai's other point is even more emphatic.

[The]IPL has little cricketing logic but sound television logic. The Indian youth want to watch big names and celebrity parties, where the camera has an obsessive focus on cleavage. They want a Bollywood awards show with a dash of instant-result cricket.

There is some merit in that argument. Rohit Gupta, President, Sony Entertainment Television, would say his company got involved because,

We are a mass-based entertainment platform...The bulk of our audience is in rural India and our appeal goes deeper than sports channels. Our pitch was that we could draw in more viewers because we can enable the marriage of cricket with entertainment.

This dictated the format of the tournament; matches had to be between three and three-and-a-half hours, as they were in the National Basketball Association (NBA) in America or the English Premier League (EPL). They had to be shown when a family could watch. And as Gupta put it:

> There had to be some action of some sort all the time. There could never be a dull moment during the entire period of the match. The matches did eventually keep the viewers hooked.

So, the fact that Harbhajan slapped Sreesanth in the first season of IPL, something that would have been considered outrageous in pre-IPL cricket, made for great viewing.

The IPL matches were also designed to attract women, many of whom had never watched cricket before. As one such newcomer put it:

> I liked the pace of the format and also the excitement. I liked the fact that the game could turn this way or the other in minutes—just like life…. Each match seems like a fast-paced movie. It would be topical and everyone in the family can watch it together.

IPL AND BOLLYWOOD

And just to emphasise how the IPL could bring families together even more than the movies, she went on to say, 'In the case of the movies every member would have different taste.' In cricket, after all, a six is a six and cannot be interpreted in multiple ways.

Of course, the IPL has also allied itself with both big business and Bollywood. Indian cricket was always allied to money. In its early years, the maharajas, keen to curry favour with the British, financed it. In the first decades after Independence, any businessman seeking to promote his company and advertise his power had a cricket team. Rival businessmen competed on the cricket field, trying to lure the best cricketers in the country to play for them; and competition to win the Times of India Cricket Shield, a cricket tournament run by a newspaper group, which helped market business, was intense. So intense that, at times, the matches out-rivalled and often proved more competitive than the Ranji Trophy, the country's premier first-class domestic tournament.

Also, Bollywood was part of Indian cricket, as demonstrated during the 1959 Test in Mumbai against Australia. With the Test drifting to a draw, actor Raj Kapoor walked into the Indian dressing room at the CCI and persuaded the Indian captain Ramchand to declare the innings closed. In 1966, this was taken further when visiting West Indian captain, Gary Sobers, widely considered the greatest all-rounder in the history of the game, immediately after a test in Mumbai announced his engagement to Bollywood star Anju Mahendru, although this did not lead to marriage. However, the IPL has taken this alliance with Bollywood to a level never before seen in cricket or, for that matter, in Indian society. Kolkata Knight Riders, the franchise cricket team of the city, is owned by Bollywood actor Shah Rukh Khan, actress Juhi Chawla and her spouse, Jay Mehta.

The IPL has brought to India the American concept of cheerleaders at sporting matches. After every four or six runs, glamourous cheerleading squads go into dance routines. It has a dual function. The idea has been to get the crowd motivated into cheering their teams at the stadium. And these, remember, are teams that did not exist before the IPL was launched. They also provide the audience watching on television, for whom cricket may be new, an additional reason to stay tuned. If the cricket does not enchant, then the dancers will. The first season of cheerleaders drew criticism as being un-Indian and a Western conspiracy. There were problems, some rather funny, others more serious. For instance, there was Janine Kallis—younger sister of former South African cricketer and present head coach of Kolkata Knight Riders, Jacques Kallis—who was a cheerleader for Chennai Super Kings, breaking into dance and cheering against her brother's team. In 2011, South African cheerleader Gabriella Pasqualotto, who worked for Mumbai Indians, blogged about 'flirtatious' and 'inappropriate' behaviour by cricketers, naming some of them, and was thrown out of the tournament.

IPL'S IMPACT ON CRICKET DEVELOPMENT

But is the IPL just razzmatazz? Has it done nothing to influence the game as played on the field? Purists may scoff, but this format has influenced the wider game and there can be no doubt about its tremendous impact. While the IPL has its Bollywood-style flashiness, cricket skill is also involved. True, this very specialised form of the game will never match the complexity of a five-day Test, or provide the drama and the game-within-game conflict that almost mirrors real life. Tests will always be seen as the high benchmark of the game. Yet, the IPL has improved cricketing skills and this can be seen in Test cricket. For Indian cricketers, this has meant a sharpening of fielding, traditionally a neglected aspect of the game, and it has also meant that Indians have learnt how to finish matches, as opposed to starting well and then fading so badly that victory turned into defeat, a common lament of Indian cricket. The IPL has given Indian cricket and its cricketers a confidence it did not have in the past. Now they do not look up to the world outside in fear. The world comes to them and they feel the equal of any cricketer in the world.

IPL PROBLEMS

Yet, in very Indian fashion, it has had its problems. Lalit Modi, the creator of the IPL, was ousted three years after he launched the tournament with the BCCI accusing him of misconduct, indiscipline and financial irregularities. In 2013, he was banned for life after a committee found him guilty of these charges. For good measure, the Enforcement Directorate (ED) launched an investigation against him for alleged financial irregularities, but Modi has not been found guilty of any. The Government of India had even revoked his passport in 2010, but the decision was overturned by the High Court in 2014. Modi, who moved to London after he was ousted, has always claimed he did nothing wrong. As he told me in 2010:

> I can very clearly tell you that I have not pocketed any money from the IPL. I created something out of nothing. I didn't do it for myself and the benefit, 100 per cent, accrues to the BCCI. The BCCI has benefited and will benefit in the next 10 years in excess of $2 billion. That was never in their projections. I'm very proud that I've been able to create something that is of tremendous value, has world recognition and has put India on the map.

The IPL has also seen the re-emergence of cricket corruption and the most dramatic changes in the running of cricket in India since the BCCI was formed in 1928. It has seen the downfall of BCCI President N. Srinivasan, once one of the most powerful men in world cricket. It started when the Justice Mukul Mudgal Committee Report looked into the betting charges against Srinivasan's son-in-law Gurunath Meiyappan and Raj Kundra. They were officials of the two IPL teams: Meiyappan of Chennai Super Kings (CSK), and Kundra of Rajasthan Royals (RR). Following this, the Supreme Court set up the Lodha Commission, which banned Meiyappan and Kundra for life from all forms of cricket, and suspended CSK and RR for two years. The Lodha commission also had a wider remit of looking into how the BCCI was run. The 189-page report, supported by 146 pages of annexures, called for major structural reform of the organisation. If implemented it would mean a reincarnation of the BCCI into a totally different organisation. What all this means is that the BCCI, which has long seen itself as a non-government organisation beyond the law, is now firmly subject to the legal system of the country. Never before has a non-government organisation had such judicial scrutiny. The end result of all this has been that the Supreme Court of India is so involved that it is, effectively, administering the game and directing how the BCCI should be run. Yet, through all this, the IPL has remained immune. It carries on making money, both for the BCCI and for cricketers, and provides the sort of entertainment that cricket fans of India have never had before.

◆

II

NATIONALISM
COMMUNALISM
RACE
CLASS
AND
GENDER

INNOCENCE AND INDIAN CRICKET

SATADRU SEN

Modern Indian sports are colonial legacies, and their early histories are inseparable from the history of race and empire. Questions of race, however, are elusive in writings on Indian sport in the decades after 1947, and when they appear, their content remains unexamined. Indeed, it is as if Indian sport became simultaneously deracialised and dehistoricised with independence, disconnected from developments outside the field. Yet Indian sports continued to be played in historical spaces, of which the most influential were national space and a reconfigured world of race. 'Successes' and 'failures' on the playing field were constructed and experienced with reference to these wider fields.

Race is, among other things, a moral construct: the presumption and ascription of conditions such as innocence, guilt, delinquency, perversion, and even, sin. It is innocence that concerns me here, and tangentially, sin. Reshaped by Victorian schoolmasters in a particular moral image, cricket reflected a transition within whiteness that rejected the corruption of Georgian society for a new purity—captured by metaphors of what was and what was not cricket—that also encapsulated ideologies of empire, Spartan masculinity and class. These ideologies allowed Englishmen to be innocent in the world just as they were on the playing field. As an imperial phenomenon, sporting innocence overflowed whiteness, allowing for the phenomenon that C. L. R. James rather admired (as 'the code'), and Fanon bemoaned (as a traumatising chasm between aspiration and identity). Indians who learned cricket learned a subjectivity that saw the sporting community as an embodiment of innocence, even as they learned that innocent natives were not quite white.

I suggest in this essay that while innocence has been a persistent ideal in cricket, it has also been unstable. It has shifted from the self-perception of a small, weak, modernising class that Salman Rushdie imagined as 'midnight's children', that was isolated from both the world and its own demographic hinterland, but that nevertheless imagined itself as engaged in the pursuit of justice, including justice for others. It has moved towards a different model of innocent isolation: the isolation of non-responsibility, in which the very existence of others (in the political sense) is an irritant to the fan, the crowd, the consumer and the ethnically identified citizen.

One pattern visible in Indian cricket since independence is a correlation between the practices of the Indian nation state and the boundaries of the sporting nation, which has served to expand the field and the crowd, to sustain them at a certain level and, ultimately, to limit them. Another is the role of the sport in the emergence of an Indian racial identity that is globally competitive, and that borrows readily from global idioms of racial competition. In both regards, cricket has been influential in producing Indianness in public spaces. Between the 1950s and the 1980s, this was both an extensive and a limited phenomenon. Large numbers of people followed and played cricket. Matches in domestic tournaments were often well attended, and Test matches routinely sold out stadiums seating up to 80,000. Live commentary on All India Radio took the game into millions of homes, and small crowds gathered over transistor radios at bus stops and tea stalls, listening to games they could not attend in person. Cricket in this form was a ritual of consuming technology, within the modest means of the middle class in a 'socialist' economy. For children, the national team provided icons with an overarching appeal: no matter where in the country one lived, one was fixated upon the same dozen or so players, although one might have 'home state' favourites. The rituals of neighbourhood cricket, played on any available patch of open space, were the same in any Indian city or town. Thus, just when foreign observers, such as Selig Harrison, became convinced that centrifugal tensions would tear India apart, cricket facilitated an Indianness that transcended regions and regionalisms. This was the innocence of the Union and the Republic.

As part of that consciousness, the nationalised subject learned to look beyond national boundaries. Cricket connected Indians to a world of sport and competition: they learned the names of

Caribbean players, the peculiarities of stadiums in Australia, and the subtleties of English 'playing conditions'. They acquired that cosmopolitan knowledge as Indian fans. In the same spirit, cricket became an instrument of Indian foreign policy in a world of justice: India was the first country to push for a boycott of apartheid South Africa, to which I will return. It was against India that South Africa played its first international cricket when apartheid ended. It was thus as part of a wider stance on decolonisation, the Cold War and Non-Alignment.

Cricket also reflected the limits of the Indian nation. There were economic limits that were also the limits of leisure. Even transistor radios and cheap seats at the stadium were not within the reach of all. People whose earnings depended on how long they worked could not take a day, let alone five days, off to watch cricket. (The other side of that coin is the likelihood that high unemployment left men with time to follow Test matches.) Moreover, in the 1950s, patronage of the sport passed from the princes (a notoriously debauched demographic) and was taken up by the government and private-sector companies that gave cricketers jobs and salaries. This provided players with the security to pursue the sport on a full-time basis, but the money was modest and nobody became rich playing cricket. This modesty, like all modesties, was a moral position: it belonged with, and to, the morality of Nehruvian socialism, with its somewhat self-righteous ethos of sacrifice and strife.

Then, there were city limits. The constituency of the game remained urban and middle class. Test cricket marked not only a line between the city and the village, but a line between cosmopolitan and provincial cities, centres and backwaters. Players who made it to the national team came overwhelmingly from the bigger cities and the middle class. So did women who became cricket fans. The women's game remained severely underdeveloped even in the cities. It is not that people in mofussil towns, villages and urban slums did not play cricket, or that girls ignored the game. Many middle-class Indian girls have played with their brothers. But whereas boys could continue to play the game in a reasonably structured way, few girls were given to understand that the game was compatible with female adulthood, which had to conform to a model of innocence that has its roots in Partha Chatterjee's well-known 'nationalist resolution'. Innocent of finance, bureaucracy and coaches, women's cricket—

and rural cricket—remained improvised, irregular and self-contained: akin to Jerry Leach's famous narrative of Trobriand cricket, in which Pacific islanders play their peculiar form of the game.

Results displayed a similar picture of limited success. In Test cricket, Indian defeats far outnumbered victories. An internationally competitive team seemed to take shape only in the 1970s and 1980s, and even then overseas wins remained rare. Exceptional players were all too exceptional, in the sense that their teammates were mediocre; they were also not exceptional enough, in the sense that the opposition was even better. The Indian pool of talent and resources was too limited. Even middle-class Indian boys lacked access to equipment, practice facilities and coaching that Australian and English players could take for granted. Players from poorer backgrounds lacked all those things, plus a few others: proper nutrition, access to schools and tournaments, time to play. Indian successes were victories against the circumstances, sustained in part by the small size of the world of international cricket, in which even mediocre teams had a place, and in which it was possible for the threadbare and the well-shod to share a stadium and a national fantasy of making do.

The two levels of Indian cricket in this period—the organised, urban-middle-class level, with its coaching, tournaments and demarcated pathways of upward mobility, and the unorganised, improvised level of subaltern cricket—were not entirely discrete. Middle-class schoolboys also played neighbourhood cricket, often alongside boys from the slums. They switched codes as they switched contexts. The stadium itself was a space where classes and codes came together in semi-segregated fashion: separated by differently priced stands, but immersed in a common crowd and a shared ritual of watching the same game. The men in the cheap seats (there would be few women here) were more given to shouted comments and crude jokes than the ladies in smart sunglasses. But they also showed a sophisticated appreciation of the subtleties of Test cricket. They knew the esoteric terminology, admired and applauded opponents, and knew what was 'not cricket'. They dressed within their means, but did not come in rags. When the proletariat went to the stadium or clustered around the radio on the street, they too switched codes, or accepted the hegemony of a notion of civilisation that basked innocently in the winter sun. Neville Cardus, that philosopher of a summery English innocence, would not have felt entirely out of place among them once he had got over the shock of so many natives.

THE WORLD OF LIBERALISATION

Like every aspect of public life in India, this stodgy edifice of sporting respectability was shaken up by the economic changes of the 1990s, generally described as liberalisation: the abandonment of the rhetoric of socialism and centralised regulation, and the unleashing of an ethos of unapologetic entrepreneurship, self-enrichment and consumerism. It brought to Indian cricket not only a flood of money, transforming the game into a major generator of revenue, it expanded the pool of players and spectators, bringing in people who were indifferent to the codes and expectations by which the previous generation had lived. In this period, Indian cricket became an undisputed global power, and confronted an existential crisis of corruption. New forms of innocence were not only required, but duly produced by the same economic engine that drove the corruption.

Indian cricket in the 1990s was marked dramatically by the intertwined phenomena of revealed sins and Sachin Tendulkar. The decade saw a series of scandals: senior players were implicated in, or at least accused of, various financial and sporting improprieties. These included tax evasion and 'match fixing'. As allegations flew and secret recordings emerged, the spectacle of corruption itself became a commodity, consumed in the new commercial media. In that hothouse of money and scandal, Tendulkar emerged as a young batting prodigy. His undeniable greatness on the field was matched by his enormous appeal to advertisers, and by his apparently impeccable propriety. Unlike older players with their suddenly acquired Rolex watches and bookie friends, the baby-faced and squeaky-voiced Tendulkar set new standards of patriotism and circumspection even when he was no longer a teenager: every move was calculated to be scandal-proof, and every word as bland and insubstantial as a public-relations statement. This was the new innocence, personified. He was everybody's child, and everyone's imagined child-self, frozen and bubble-wrapped in purity. The circumspection itself was marketed by his managers and admirers as part of his image: he was, it was often said, very protective of his privacy.

That new concept of privacy as an accessory of innocence went beyond middle-class modesty: it was inseparable from Tendulkar's astonishing earnings. (A rough estimate, in the early 2000s, would be USD five million annually, and sometimes a tax-free Ferrari crashed through the cordon of privacy.) Those earnings no longer came from a token job; they came from corporate sponsorship. Cricketers advertising products were not new in India, but the scale and scope of such activity in the 1990s was. Tendulkar thus epitomised the consolidation of a new, sophisticated relationship between cricket and acceptable wealth, legitimising the acquisitiveness and aspirations of the middle class in a time when there was, apparently, no longer a contradiction between private aggrandisement and the collective pleasures of nationhood.

In the new millennium, the Indian national team began to win with a frequency that was unprecedented, and the perpetual underdog suddenly became recognised as one of the top teams in the world. The Board of Control for Cricket in India (BCCI)—the board that runs Indian cricket—had become very rich from television revenues. It now eclipsed the Australian and English boards in terms of income, and was the pre-eminent financial power in the sport. The new wealth allowed it to invest—albeit unevenly—in the infrastructure, personnel and methods of modern professional sport: the training facilities, coaches, dieticians, and specialists in fitness and sports medicine that Indian hockey and football could seldom afford. Simultaneously, the expansion of the middle class threw up an abundance of talent.

In this euphoric moment, however, there were already signs of trouble, some overt and others that were not immediately recognised. The development of T20, a very short version of the game that is essentially cricket reduced to stunts and highlights, was seen by Indian media entrepreneurs as a money-making opportunity. With the support of retired cricketers, such as Kapil Dev, they organised a T20 League—the Indian Cricket League (ICL)—that offered attractive remuneration to regional, national and even international players. The BCCI, unwilling to tolerate the challenge to its monopoly on players and revenues, cracked down very hard on the ICL, using its financial clout in world cricket to ban participating players from all international competition. When the ICL collapsed, the BCCI promptly created its own T20 competition, the Indian Premier League (IPL), in which privately owned teams were associated with particular Indian cities. The IPL offered lucrative contracts to Indian and overseas cricketers, muscled in on the international cricket calendar, and became a television phenomenon.

It also instantly became a problem of innocence. The IPL was in many ways the perfect symptom of the Indian version of globalised capitalism, monopolistic privilege and the 'gold-rush' culture of liberalisation. It took its cues wherever it could find them, but preferred American and Indian cultural material: the floodlit cricket was accompanied by imported white cheerleaders in skimpy clothes, Bollywood music and personalities (who played a dual role as owners and mascots of the teams), and fireworks. Players were publicly 'auctioned'. The pavilion, from which players traditionally descended like gods or angels, was replaced by the 'dugout', from which troglodytes emerged. All India Radio and Doordarshan commentators, now hopelessly dull, made way for exuberant 'journalists' and ex-cricketers paid to endorse the spectacle in hyperbolic terms. Board members of BCCI themselves owned IPL teams, giving themselves the right to regulate their own profit making, and drafting bylaws that denied any conflict of interest between the private ownership of IPL teams, management of the national game and the allocation of television revenues. Politicians drew visibly close to the IPL, supporting their protégés among the managers of the game, and it remained unclear whether they were curbing or facilitating the irregularities of the cricket board. Board members who were team owners also had their protégés: N. Srinivasan, the powerful and tenacious president of the BCCI, also owned the Chennai Super Kings IPL team; M. S. Dhoni, the captain of that team, was also the captain of the Indian national team and the highest-paid cricketer in the world.

In this acid of apparent financial, sexual, aesthetic, linguistic and political corruption, the link between sport and nationhood stood to be corroded. The IPL teams were affiliated with cities, not the nation. The BCCI's attorneys increasingly took the position that the Board was not a national entity at all, but a private organisation. Given the history of Indian cricket, this amounted to a startling repudiation of the ideological and communitarian focus of the sport, and an admission of the naturalised nexus between corporations, politicians, sports bureaucrats and celebrity athletes. It was a logical culmination of the privacy that had been heralded by the Tendulkar phenomenon, but it exposed the inconsistencies of that ethos and generated sharp discomfort. The public's fascination with the moneymaking on display was tempered by a discernible revulsion at the corruption and greed, especially as the novelty of cheerleaders and Bollywood stars at cricket matches wore off. Lalit Modi, the architect of the IPL, soon found himself accused of financial impropriety and fled the country. After a series of lawsuits, new match-fixing scandals and the intervention of the Supreme Court, some conflicts of interest were mitigated and the worst offenders were weakened.

The efforts to clean up the IPL could not, however, hide the transformation in the crowd. Attendance at Test matches plummeted after the 1990s; fans made it clear that they preferred the 'entertainment package' of T20 to the arcane pleasures of the longer game. It could be said of them that they were not serious cricket fans, but being 'serious' about the adult equivalent of 'play' is a historically specific mode of respectable innocence, and it was now alien to them. The phenomenon was not exclusively Indian: it affected every cricket-playing country outside the old, white circle of England, Australia, New Zealand and a portion of South Africa. Within India, the pattern was clear: Test cricket hung on (precariously) in the older centres, and was dying in the peripheries of the nation, the city and the stadium, where economic liberalisation had transformed the relationship between consumption and respectability. These peripheries were made up not only of old cricket fans who had revised their ideas about pleasure and leisure, but also of new fans whose expectations were different to begin with. These fans were not subalterns in the economic sense; the poor were never a part of the marketplace of cricket in the IPL era. They were, however, newly moneyed and brashly confident, and showed no interest in the pedagogy of the stadium or the hegemony of those who insisted upon a 'straight bat'. They did not applaud opponents; they were not liberals. They were not invested in the nostalgia and history—the Victorian and Nehruvian modernities—that Test cricket prioritised. Short-format cricket was instant and disposable gratification: a sport akin to basketball, in that it did not call upon the fan to learn and remember legends, scoreboards and plays over periods of decades.

Nor did it call upon the Indian fan to learn about a historically shaped world of justice in which he or she might play a political role. Instead, it encouraged an entirely passive self-importance. Indian cricket was the new global centre, sucking foreign players into IPL teams and bullying other national cricket boards (to their alarm, resentment and acquiescence). When the cricket board insisted that it was 'private' and teams were identified with owners, the thrill of national victory came substantially from the awareness of Indian power in the financial and administrative world of cricket.

MONKEYS OF INNOCENCE

It is in the context of this shift in what constitutes cricketing 'knowledge' that we can understand the incidents in 2007 when Indian fans in Baroda and then Mumbai made monkey gestures at the mixed-race Australian player, Andrew Symonds. It was justifiably condemned by some Indian commentators, not to mention Australians. There is some room for debate on the specific condemnation, which was a charge of racism. As a form of spectator behaviour, monkey gestures directed at black players come from the copybook of European football, where racism is a highly developed problem, and which is now accessible on television to newly moneyed sports fans even in a provincial city like Baroda. Given that African students are routinely abused on Indian campuses and city streets, it would certainly appear that racism of the European sort has established its Indian pedigree. This is, however, misleading. Anti-black racism, like anti-Semitism, requires discursive meat: a deep consensus about what race is, what blackness is, what a Jew is like, and so on. Those discourses are so threadbare in India that it is doubtful whether a monkey gesture in Baroda means what it would in Barcelona or Liverpool.

What, then, does it mean? What might an Indian, who has opened a boutique named 'Hitler' in Ahmedabad, or picked up a copy of *Mein Kampf*, mean when he says that he agrees with Hitler, assuming he is being sincere and not merely provocative? He means that he empathises with what he perceives to be a desire for order and a stifled nationalism: the Romantic notion of a community defined not only by its humiliation but also by its failure to *be* a community united in purpose, yearning for unity, purity, revenge and fulfilment. What is peculiar about the Nazis is not the fact of mass murder, but the extent to which they imbued murder with the magic of industrial–bureaucratic efficiency. That magic is largely alien to India: it is desired in a general way by the middle class, but resisted in its particulars by nearly everybody, including the middle class. Indian admiration for Hitler is, in that sense, an 'innocent' empathy, or the misidentification of one set of frustrations with another. Likewise, the behaviour of the monkeys in Baroda and Mumbai was a kind of innocent pleasure: that of being a crowd in the winter sunshine, having a bit of fun at the expense of a total outsider who was just passing through anyway. The members of the crowd knew that they were being hurtful, but had only the vaguest idea of the historical context and political significance of the pain, and hence, of the scale of the offence.

The apparently apolitical nature of this innocence is its most sharply political quality. To illustrate this, it is useful to recall the boycott of apartheid South Africa, not only by India, but by the other racially identified worlds of cricket. Former Australian Prime Minister Bob Hawke once recalled an exchange he had in 1970 with Don Bradman. Bradman was then a cricket administrator, and Hawke a labour union leader trying to persuade the Australian cricket establishment to stop playing against South Africa. When Bradman invoked the shibboleth that the innocence of sport ought not be sullied with politics, Hawke retorted that it was the apartheid regime that had done the sullying by preventing non-white players from representing their country. Bradman was startled but persuaded, and the result was a two-decade period when South Africa became a twilight zone of cricket: missing, but present at the other end of a wormhole of race, money and gambled careers.

Hawke may have overstated his own role, and that of Australia, in the boycott of South Africa. The Basil D'Oliveira crisis (in which South Africa refused to accept the presence of the coloured, South Africa-born D'Oliveira in the English team) had already moved England closer to a boycott. The non-white Test-playing countries—India, Pakistan and the West Indies— had of course not played against South Africa at all. (It is telling that the term 'boycott' entered the lexicon of cricket journalism only when England, Australia and New Zealand ambivalently agreed to participate.) Within Australia, anti-apartheid sentiment was not unknown in 1970. The country was a part of the global half-revolution of 1968, with its student radicalism and protests against the Vietnam War, in which Australian troops fought. That rejection/loss of innocence informed the agenda and methods of the South Africa campaign. Nevertheless, there was something quixotic about Hawke's stance. Bradman's surprised innocence was by far the more typical response, and not just in Australia. In England, the D'Oliveira affair had generated more irritation than outrage: it was as if D'Oliveira had ruined a good thing, otherwise known as the purity of sport, which was also the solidarity of the white Commonwealth. Organised sport in modern societies is always a reactionary edifice, aligned with the interests and identities of those who take privilege for granted and identify it with banalities like purity and innocence. Administered from closed circles of feudal, Tory and then corporate power, cricket is more reactionary than almost any other spectator sport. It had simply not occurred to Bradman to push the comfortable envelope of whiteness, until Hawke pushed it for him. He was innocent.

The boycott of South African cricket was one of the most extraordinary instances of political boycott in recent times, laying the groundwork for the divestment campaign of the 1980s and substituting for the diplomatic isolation that Western governments refused to deploy. It was extraordinary because it was always the agenda of a minority: the English, Australian and New Zealand cricket establishments went along with it because of a peculiar convergence of pressures, some emerging in their own radicalised backyards, and some coming from outside. Those external pressures—the mobilised existence of a non-white world of cricket— were vital, and they were not fully acknowledged in their own time. Had the Anglo–Australian establishment not acknowledged a South African problem, the fiction that world cricket could be represented by an 'imperial' council made up of pink dinosaurs even in 1970 would have cracked like an egg. As it happened, it did crack, albeit gradually. Since the 1990s, there has been much grumbling in England and Australia about the rise of the 'Asian bloc', with its apparently genetic tendencies towards corruption, touchiness and disregard for tradition. But that rise began earlier, over South Africa, when one model of racially informed innocence confronted another.

There was nothing uniform, predictable or reliable about pro-boycott sentiment in the non-white Test-playing countries either.

This becomes evident as soon as we look at India and the West Indies. South Africa was not automatically relevant to Indian cricketers, fans and administrators: many would have shrugged and accepted 'normal' sporting relations, and gone to see Barry Richards, Mike Proctor and the Pollock brothers play against Pataudi, Prasanna and Gavaskar. The position taken by the Indian board reflected the apartheid regime's own misgivings about playing against non-whites, and the foreign policy initiated by Nehru, in which anti-colonialism, non-alignment and boycotting South Africa found a mutual compatibility. It was, thus, partly a state-directed idealism. Foreign policy tends to float above public opinion in large countries, and India was no exception. But in India, cricket was a largely middle-class affair, and that middle class was genuinely—if casually—hostile to racism of the sort represented by South Africa. That hostility, moreover, was integrated with the politics of the organised Left: it is difficult to imagine South Africa being allowed to play in Calcutta in the years of *Amar nam, tomar nam, Vietnam* demonstrations.

In the West Indies, the politics of the boycott had deeper soil. Through a combination of writing, activism and play in the 1950s and 1960s—the overlapping phenomena of C. L. R. James, Learie Constantine and Frank Worrell—racial self-assertion in cricket had become the basis not only of a politics of justice, but also of a sport-based nationhood found nowhere else in the world. Yet the West Indies, along with England, Australia and Sri Lanka, provided apartheid South Africa with a steady dribble of 'rebel' cricketers in the years of the boycott. These included not just those on the margins of the big time, such as Sylvester Clarke and Collis King, but those who were sought out by the South Africans precisely because they were stars: Colin Croft, Alvin Kallicharran. In South Africa, they faced predictable racism, tried to come to terms with the dubious privilege of being treated as 'honorary whites', and accepted the unreliable affection of white crowds that enjoyed this remarkable complicity of pariahs. One of the ironies of the South Africa boycott is that the same white nation that contemptuously refused to share a field with Basil D'Oliveira suddenly became eager to play against Lawrence Rowe, and would have given anything to have Viv Richards.

There is, in this reverse supply of black bodies from the New World to Africa, an unacknowledged tragedy of modern sport.

The rewards were modest compared with what professional cricketers stand to earn today. The contracted periods were limited not only by the shelf-life of athletic ability, but also by the endgame of apartheid. None of it was enough to compensate for destroyed careers and reputations. That did not concern South African plotter–poachers like Ali Bacher, or players like Proctor, whose lives were not adversely affected by their innocent games. They remained respectable even after the end of apartheid, shielded by the aura of sport itself.

For Caribbean players, however, South African cricket was a drug that left a trail of moral ambiguity and real damage. It is difficult to blame professional athletes in an economic backwater for responding to the cash available in South Africa. This is especially true of those on the margins of the phenomenally strong West Indies squad of the 1980s: they had not benefited from Kerry Packer's World Series Cricket circus, and their reward for not joining the circus had been snatched away by their own cricket board when the Packer players returned to the fold of respectability and innocence. They cannot be compared with English and Australian players who joined 'rebel tours' or signed up to play domestic cricket in South Africa; their earnings in their own country were precarious. Also, unlike the middle-class milieu of the Indian game, Caribbean cricket included the poor who had skills to sell and mouths to feed. Not going to South Africa came with the danger of sliding into squalor. Ironically, going to South Africa had the same effect.

Caribbean cricket, James pointed out many years ago, is played within a powerful class-based code of propriety, i.e., within its own code of innocence. Breaking the boycott was highly improper, and the repercussions are unsurprising. In the 1970s and 1980s, cricket was not yet played in a weirdly skewed universe in which a Third World country was both the goldmine and power-centre of the sport. It was an embattled imperial order, and the poorer, relatively vulnerable, black scabs paid the price: white players who went to South Africa were, by and large, rehabilitated far more easily into the cricket establishments of their homelands, and faced little in the way of earnest opprobrium. Kim Hughes, Graham Gooch and the inappropriately named Geoff Boycott were embedded within populations that generally saw the boycott of South Africa as political correctness: an artificial agenda promoted by uppity natives who did not understand the innocence of sport, especially cricket, with its mythology of village greens, spotless whites and permanent hegemony. Unlike the West Indians, they were fundamentally innocent.

The innocence of Indians with their monkey gestures and luxury cars is not identical to that of Englishmen and Australians playing in South Africa and returning cheerfully to civilisation. But it is a movement in the same general direction, marked by the assumption (in the Indian case, assertion) of centrality in the world, floating above the evidence of sin, and unruffled by guilt, i.e., the concerns of the margins, which are no longer worth learning or embracing. It is the innocence of having arrived. The monkeys in Baroda were, after all, 'aping' not Symonds, but the metropolitan crowd in Madrid and Sydney.

◆

CRICKET IN ABSTEMIOUS TIMES

SANKARAN
KRISHNA

INTRODUCTION

Things matter. They signify class distinctions, they are important when it comes to fashioning selves, we often fetishise them, and it is frequently the case that the possession of certain goods lends an aura or patina of desirability to some, while their lack leaves others feeling like lesser beings. In this brief essay, I reminisce on the relationship between people and things in India, as refracted through the lens of cricket during the two decades or so following the death of our first Prime Minister, '*Chacha*' Nehru.

To be a middle-class Indian in the 1960s and 1970s was to harbour an insatiable lust for foreign goods in an overall milieu of scarcity. On school and college campuses across the nation's metros, one's social status hinged on access to Levi's jeans or Simon and Garfunkel cassette tapes (not to mention fluency in English and familiarity with the pop culture of the West). Our leadership's ascetic commitment to self-reliance through import-substituting industrialisation was all too often translated into shoddy homegrown goods made by coddled monopolists protected from competition. The term 'export quality' was frequently used to denote that rarity: a desirable or well-made local product—Alphonso mangoes or Bajaj scooters, for instance—and it not so subtly implied that we Indians were not as deserving of high quality as those who lived abroad.

Foreign goods were imbued with class, scarcity and a whiff of the illicit. Terms like 'smuggler' and 'smuggling', and leering references to 'import–export' businesses, were ubiquitous in the vocabulary of the time. The Emergency (1975–1977) era was marked by a special focus on the nexus between smuggling and the degeneration of the body politic. The dreaded Maintenance of Internal Security Act (MISA) targeted those in the business of illegally purveying foreign goods to Indians. A blockbuster film like *Deewar* (starring our angry young man Amitabh Bachchan, and an inadvertently apt title for our protectionist economy) was a fictionalised biography of the smuggler Haji Mastaan who rose from penury to wealth in Bombay's docks. The moral economy of the film pivoted on vigilantism: Bachchan may have portrayed a scofflaw with ill-gotten gains, but he was not very different from, and indeed preferable to, the corrupt milieu that surrounded him. Shashi Kapoor, who played Bachchan's police officer brother, might have had the best line of dialogue in the film ('*mere paas maa hai*'; I have Mother with me), but we all knew *maa's* heart lay with Bachchan and not Kapoor.

Cities had sanctioned spaces where, for a hefty premium, you could buy foreign goods on the black market (although their authenticity could never be guaranteed): Madras' Burma Bazaar had its counterparts in all the major cities. Our attitudes towards these foreign goods were riven with contradictions. We were patriotically proud that both Coca Cola and IBM were forced to leave India when they refused to adequately indigenise their operations. You could even say, as Kesavan (2016) insightfully suggests, that we were proud of our austerity and commitment to self-reliance, and of our refusal to take the easy way out and simply import desired goods, as nearly all our neighbours had done. Yet, in a schizophrenic vein, we cast our envious eyes at the easy availability of stereo systems and blue jeans in societies less beholden to ascetic ideas of self-reliance. Friends or relatives returning to India on visits from the West or the Middle East were expected, like Santa Claus, to shower us with gifts which we would proudly display, enjoying a momentary fillip to our status, as it were. We were a bit like the guest at a dinner party who had rather sanctimoniously denied himself a second helping of dessert when he really would not have minded one at all.

OF MIDDLE-CLASS MISERLINESS ON MAIDANS

As an aspiring schoolboy cricketer of limited abilities and questionable courage, I encountered the results of our economic policies in the quality of the gear with which we had to play. I still wince at the memory of batting in gloves with 'padding'—emaciated strips of green, spiky rubber supposed to protect my fingers from the hard cricket ball. Worse still, there were only about three or four pairs of such batting gloves in the kitbag that served the entire team. So, it was all too common to have to bat in gloves still reeking with the sweat of previous batsmen. There were never enough pads to go around either, so it was common for right-handed batsmen to play with protection only around their left-leg (as it was the one that faced the bowler), and vice versa for left-handed batsmen.

Improvisation was an indispensable feature of sporting life in such abstemious times. The leather strap-and-buckle supposed to keep your pad snug around your legs was of such shoddy quality that it disintegrated quite rapidly. Never mind—wrapping a handkerchief and knotting it tightly across held the pads in place, at least momentarily. A frequent sight on maidans all across India was that of batsmen out in the middle exchanging bats every time they changed ends: only one was good enough to play with, the other just a useful prop. Brand new cricket balls were expensive and used only for proper matches. For the most part we made do with highly durable cork balls or worn-out tennis balls. Given the rough and patchy terrain, even in some of our better cricket grounds, a new cricket ball rapidly lost its shine, and with that, any swing or movement. It is hardly surprising that as a nation we produced legions of high-quality spinners but few worthwhile fast bowlers. (The discerning reader will immediately point out that similar conditions across the border never impeded Pakistan from churning out one brilliant fast bowler after another over the years. All I can say is that, as on many other fronts, our dear neighbour defies rational explanation.)

Improvisation also extended to the multiple forms of cricket we played. If you did not have stumps, a piece of charcoal and a wall sufficed to create them—with the added bonus that you now did not need a wicketkeeper either. If there was just a bat and ball and there was no wall anywhere in sight, we switched to 'French' cricket, with the batter's legs (below his knees) serving as the stumps. Runs were scored by hitting the ball away and circling the bat around your midriff, with each circle counting as a run, until the ball was recovered. (Interestingly, the batsman was the only one who knew for sure how many runs he had made: the trick was to report a number that walked a fine line between permissible inflation and one that elicited accusations of cheating.) If you could only play on one side of a narrow street, you had to direct every shot away from the houses and especially the windows. Given the large number of players wanting to bat, you were out if: (i) you were caught even on the first bounce; (ii) your shot hit a window pane; (iii) the ball struck you below the knees; (iv) your score reached 25; and in a variety of other ways.

Cricketing 'whites' rather quickly became 'light browns' or 'jaundice yellows', given our dust and sweat. Photographs of cricket played in places like England or Australia or New Zealand showed a brilliant contrast between the gleaming white or cream-coloured flannels of cricketers and the resplendent green of the grass. In India, we seemed to operate with a palette of about 50 shades of brown. In any case, the same white shirt that served as the school uniform during the week often doubled as a cricketing shirt on weekends, adding to its tired appearance. When our national cricket team toured the West Indies to face their fearsome pace attack in the mid-1970s, we could fully relate to reports of brave Mohinder Amarnath washing his bloodied cricket shirt in his hotel room every evening after the day's play.

Quality cricket bats were both expensive and a rarity. Initials like GM (for Gunn and Moore) or SS (for Stuart Surridge) or the grooved, red logo of Gray Nicolls emblazoned across the bats of famous cricketers filled us with envy as we stared at the photographs. Their meaty middles and gleaming blades were quite a contrast to the anemic bats with which we played. On many of our willows, the famed sweet spot either did not exist or was possibly no more than the size of a one-rupee coin. One of the unintended consequences of such bats was that they rapidly separated players with that uncanny ability to time their shots perfectly from the rest of us. The same bat that felt like an unresponsive hunk of wood to me leapt to life in their hands, as the ball pinged sweetly off the middle and went scudding to the boundary. I have often thought that the incredible sense of timing of some of India's batsmen from that era—Gundappa Viswanath readily comes to mind—had much to do with learning their cricket with such substandard bats.

Magazines like *Sportsweek*, with its stellar cast of columnists from all over the world, were hugely popular. The British Council library became a regular part of my Saturday routine, and the *Cricketer* magazine was much sought after by various readers. A big part of the thrill of reading these foreign cricket magazines was, of course, the glossy, coloured photographs of a quality we rarely got to see in India. The pictures of sleek cricket shoes with sharp spikes were a world removed from the clunky leather boots with worn-out metal studs that were common on cricket grounds in India. It was as if the contrast between aerodynamic Western automobiles and our stodgy old Ambassador car was being re-enacted, only now in the domain of cricket equipment.

The back pages of the *Cricketer* were full of advertisements for cricketing gear. Batting gloves with nice, plump, sausage-like padding encasing each finger; pads that seemed to be made of light, foamy plastic rather than heavy canvas; bats with scooped middles that looked like sleek scimitars—and with prices listed in British pound sterling that translated into an exorbitant number of Indian rupees—enraptured us. Just as was the case with the back covers of Archie comic books from the United States, chock-full of pictures of dune buggies or inflatable swimming pools or other such incomprehensible pleasures; all this enticing merchandise gave us a glimpse into a very different world.

WHEN A WORD WAS WORTH A THOUSAND PICTURES

Our era of deprivation was most acute when it came to media technologies of sports coverage. Long after television had penetrated living rooms in much of the world, India remained a glorious exception. Until the early 1980s, coverage was limited to our major metros and monopolised by the stodgy 'babus' of the Ministry of Information and Broadcasting. Programmes began around 6:00 pm and shut shop by about 10:00 pm with the news, the last assiduously watched by stern *patres familias*, and for which pin-drop silence was demanded. With the exception of *Chitrahaar* (Hindi film-song clips), much of it was dreary fare, exemplified by re-runs of *I love Lucy* (a slapstick comedy that had been originally broadcast in the United States in the mid-1950s), or programmes about the relative merits of different types of fertiliser (a dubious topic, given that audiences were primarily in a handful of big cities at the time).

Well into the 1970s, then, the Indian cricket fan had to make do with radio commentary, especially when we toured abroad. In its own way, though, radio enhanced the experience of following cricket, rather than detracting from it. For my generation, India's greatest cricketing moments—or its more frequent plunges into the abyss of defeat—are inseparable from the voices of various commentators. With radio, unlike television, you had to work hard: triangulating the words you heard with grainy newsprint photographs of cricketers and remembered images of different cricket grounds in various countries to produce a rich movie of the match in your mind's eye. We were not an audience of passive recipients; being a cricket fan was an active work of imagination.

For example, Sunil Gavaskar's admirable display of grit and technique during the Old Trafford test of 1974—when he scored a century in the biting cold, with the ball swinging all over the place—is indelibly associated with John Arlott's Hampshire burr over the British Broadcasting Corporation (BBC). The voices of commentators in faraway lands waxed and waned through the ether to reach my transistor radio in Madras. One had to constantly keep twiddling the dial, changing the position of the receiver, and engaging in all sorts of acrobatics to stop the temperamental short-wave transmission from fading away. (In retrospect, I suppose it did develop one's fine motor skills, besides virtues like patience.) Without realising it, we also learned to distinguish the 'propah' accents and Queen's English of some of the BBC commentators from the nasal twang of the Australians or the lilting cadence of their Caribbean counterparts. Omar Kureishi of Pakistan oozed class, and the long and incredibly musical names of cricketers from Ceylon (as it was then called) seemed to be virtually sung by their commentators. Tracking the coverage also educated us about time zones and world geography in ways that our school textbooks never could have.

On many occasions, All India Radio would send its own two-member crew for overseas tours, with one of them doing the ball-by-ball in English, and the other in Hindi. The former spot was often the preserve of a certain Suresh Saraiya, one of the real characters in the annals of cricket commentary. Saraiya may well have been the man Mark Tully (1991) had in mind when he titled his memoirs *No Full Stops in India*. With his pronounced Gujarati accent, Saraiya spoke a variety of English I have not heard before or since—it was completely bereft of punctuation. He paused when he needed to catch his breath, but otherwise the words poured out of him in a torrent of free association, unburdened by any concern for grammar or syntax or pronunciation. I do have to thank Saraiya, though: he unwittingly ended up greatly improving my Hindi, and especially my command over numbers in that language. I disliked his commentary so intensely that I preferred listening to the elegant and understated Ravi Chaturvedi, who was often his partner on overseas tours. Chaturvedi was a master of the pause, letting silence give you an opportunity to imagine the tableau unfolding in distant lands, rather than drown them in verbosity. (Incidentally, Saraiya's cricket commentary found a sort of counterpart in Raju Bharatan's cricket writing for the *Illustrated Weekly of India.* Bharatan was deeply knowledgeable about the game, and was also an excellent reviewer of Hindi films and music. Unfortunately, he exemplified the cliché about puns being the lowest form of wit; he could never resist one, and they were invariably groan-inducing.)

During test matches, life ground to a halt and everything revolved around cricket. By day, the commentary monopolised our attention; evenings were for post-mortems of events; and early mornings spent reading newspaper reports of the previous day's happenings, and poring over the handful of black-and-white action photographs. If the match was excitingly poised, everyone crowded around the radios, with the latest scores exchanged between strangers on the street and in buses. The guys in school who owned a pocket transistor saw a sudden surge in their popularity and, despite the surveillance of teachers, somehow, the latest score always got around the classroom, through notes and whispers.

Cricket commentary was a major distraction from studies and we often felt guilty at the hours wasted when we should have been hitting the books or preparing for major milestones, such as board exams. I remember a good friend in college once coming to my hostel room late one night with a most unusual request. He had in his hand a bunch of Eveready batteries that he wanted to leave with me. I was not to return them to him until the end of the semester, even if he were to beg me on his knees. He said he had been unable to resist tuning into the cricket commentary and ended up wasting all his time. If he did not get his act together soon he was likely to flunk the upcoming exams, so would I please help him? I have now forgotten if the ruse worked and how he did on his exams—but he did come by to collect his batteries, once the exams were over.

Today, cricket is watched on TV and via the Internet all across the world, all around the year. One could literally see Dhoni's eyes light up as he prepared to launch that sixer that won India the World Cup at the Wankhede stadium in 2011. While the excitement in the stadium and the rest of the nation was transmitted in real time all across the world and made for a simultaneity that was wonderful, there was nothing left to the imagination: it was all there, laid out in front of you in high definition and with slow-motion replays— quite a contrast to the last time we won that Cup, back at Lords, in 1983. On that occasion, at a most critical period in the final match, Doordarshan's live television coverage, predictably, went AWOL. Everyone went frantically back to transistors and short-wave radios to keep abreast of what was happening. Kapil Dev's athletic over-the-shoulder-catch to dismiss Viv Richards—the turning point of that match—was not seen by most of us, but heard. It would be a while before we could see what had transpired during that hiatus in television coverage.

The absence of television coverage also enhanced the importance of the written word. The prose of cricket writers such as Neville Cardus, Ray Robinson, E. W. Swanton, or our own K. N. Prabhu, instilled in many of us a love for the written word that has lasted to this day. Their penchant for understatement was a useful corrective to the vivid prose of American authors, such as James Hadley Chase or Sidney Sheldon, whose novels were quite popular among schoolboys. Over the years, some of us went on to discover the writings of C. L. R. James and to more fully understand the political, racial and colonial worlds beyond the boundary of the cricket field.

CONCLUSION

I seem to have traversed a strange trajectory over the course of this essay. In trying to depict the austerity (one could even say genteel poverty) of Indian middle-class life in the afterglow of Nehru, I have instead found myself returning repeatedly to all of the ways in which those times were rendered creative and even enchanted because of those very same deficits. One major reason for that is, of course, almost everyone in that middle-class milieu shared in the austerity and lust for quality goods—home-made or foreign. The pain, or even cognisance, of deprivation is heightened when some of us feel singled out for it and others seem exempt. That was not the case back then. And, honestly, it really is no fun to have better things than all your friends; you'd much rather have exactly what they have.

But another, more important, reason is that while middle-class India may have been relatively deprived in comparison with suburban United States or post-war Britain, the truth is that we sensed we were a somewhat privileged oasis in a desert of poverty and destitution, especially in the big cities. You could not help being aware, even as a schoolboy, that a brand new cricket bat or ball was a luxury when many around you could not be sure of their next meal, or lived in a slum at the edge of your housing colony. You could never shake off that sense of being rather fortunate, and, indeed, that a descent into the abyss that surrounded your little enclave could never be definitively ruled out in your own future either.

The abstemiousness was justified—more intuitively than consciously, I suspect—by a sense that the national journey was still in its early years and certain forms of trivial enjoyment could be deferred until we became a more inclusive and egalitarian society. Without romanticising those earlier times, or confusing my own nostalgia for a younger self with something more than just that, I do have a disquiet about the untrammelled enthusiasm for, and easy availability of, things in contemporary India. I fear it has come at a price: a greater ability to keep the less fortunate out of our sights and minds as we enjoy the nation.

◆

REFERENCES

Kesavan, Mukul. 2016. 'Before the Change: When Austerity, Simplicity Ruled Everyday Middle-class Life', *Hindustan Times*, 24 July.

Tully, Mark. 1991. *No Full Stops in India*. New Delhi: Penguin.

◆◆

SPORTS, RADIO AND MEMORY
Looking Back at the 1970s

AVIJIT GHOSH

Memory has a split personality. It can hitch you on a rocket to euphoria. Or, put you in a deep blue mood. But last month, while watching the 1975 World Cup hockey final between India and Pakistan, I realised that memory is also a manipulator. It makes you remember things the way you want it to, and not necessarily the way it actually was. For memory isn't exactly a replay of the past. It is a carefully edited copy of a film that we view through the prism of nostalgia.

My memory of the game that India won 2–1 to become the world champion for the first, and only, time was further modified by the fact that I had heard its running commentary on the radio, and not seen it on live television or at a stadium. Watching the full match on YouTube last month, I realised that memory and imagination had combined to construct a game that was only partly played in the grassy Kuala Lumpur stadium. The rest I had invented on my own.

I was a Class VII student then. In my mind's archive, I had always pictured Ashok Kumar dodging past the Pakistan defence and scoring the match-winner. The truth is, as the video shows, it came off a goalmouth melee. Watching the final, I also realised how much hockey has changed beyond recognition, a fall-out of the introduction of artificial grass in the 1976 Montreal Olympics, which altered the game's DNA and marked the beginning of Indian hockey's rapid decline.

In recent years, snatches of milestone moments have also made their way to the video broadcasting site: India's 1980 Moscow Olympics triumph; athlete Milkha Singh's 1960 so-near-yet-so-far

Rome Olympics run; even the incomparable Dhyan Chand and company, toying with Germany before a home crowd at the 1936 Berlin Olympics. But a full recording of a major international contest involving India is rare. Our finest feats in international sports, during the 1970s or in earlier decades, can only be replayed through the mind's eye, even though the possibility of a recording lying in a fusty, foreign archive always exists. But watching grabs of old, grainy film can be deceptive. Like an anonymous WhatsApp video, they might not tell the full or the real story.

In any case, to anyone who grew up in the 1970s or earlier in middle-class India, watching international sport wasn't really an option. Television had arrived in India in the 1950s, but its reach was restricted to the country's cosmopolitan elite. For everyone else, TV was little more than a photograph in a book.

Nobody really missed TV, though. It simply didn't exist as an accessory of desire. For millions of enthusiasts, the engagement with international sports was about sound, not sight. The radio and the portable transistor radio, usually just referred to as the transistor, were the primary windows to the world of domestic and international sports.

Hardcore cricket fans even listened to the commentary of Ranji Trophy or Duleep Trophy games. Sometime in the early 1970s, I remember tuning in for the final of the now-forgotten Rohinton Baria Trophy, the all-India inter-university contest considered the best platform to showcase young talent. If memory serves me right, Mohinder Amarnath scored an unbeaten 171 to anchor Delhi University to title when the championship was held in Patna. Incredibly, he had already played a Test match in 1969.

Radio gave wings to every imagination. Clutching the intimate transistor set, one could create one's own version of Gundappa Viswanath's perfect square cut or body-feint past any defender like Chuni Goswami. Unlike today, when the brain's memory card gets overloaded with a surfeit of images and even international matches have the shelf-life of a burger, in those days every vital moment of a game was remembered and reproduced at a college canteen, a school bus stop, a government office or a village square. In other words, the world of sport was also the playing field of the raconteur. Constant retelling allowed sporting moments to acquire new forms and evolve with each narration.

The world of sound created its own stars in every walk of life. Back in the 1950s and 1960s, I am told, my father used to tune in to the radio every Independence Day to listen to Melville de Mellow—a voice so warm that it seemed to be shaking hands with you. Like many others, my father's admiration for De Mellow began after listening to him speak non-stop during Mahatma Gandhi's funeral in 1948. And it endured for decades.

My father was often reminded by my grandmother to tune in to All India Radio at 4 am for the rousing recitation of 'Chandipaatth' by Birendra Krishna Bhadra on the day of Mahalaya. Bhadra was a cultural institution in Bengal. When he was replaced by the iconic Tollywood star Uttam Kumar for a year, the move was deemed sacrilegious. He was eventually restored.

One of my elder cousins adored Ajoy Basu, who pioneered radio commentary on sports in Bengali. There was a certain charm about Basu who was blessed with the gift of recreating moods like a classical singer, which, I was told later, also endeared him to a legion of women listeners.

KANGAROOS CALLING

I entered the world of live commentary in the winter of 1969 when Bill Lawry's Kangaroos came calling. We then owned a neat Phillips two-band radio, with a green cat's eye. Like a half-willing lover who needed foreplay to be aroused, it would slowly warm up to the world of sound. But I was too young to be granted access to it. We also had a three-band Murphy transistor, which was actually owned by a cousin who lived with us. One of my first memories of excitement in sport is of him shouting aloud that some rookie Viswanath was out for a duck.

I only have fleeting memories of that Test series between India and Australia. I was gradually getting acquainted with the finer facets of the game. But I do recall a few dinner conversations between my cousin and my father. I remember my father telling him that we had found a batsman of class in Viswanath, who had scored a cultured century in the second knock after the horror show in the first. Viswanath was then only 20. For once, my cousin seemed to agree with him.

Both, especially my cousin, were more excited than usual during the Delhi Test because two Bengalis—middle-order southpaw Ambar Roy and paceman Subrata Guha—were part of the playing unit. India famously won that match by seven wickets at Feroze Shah Kotla. Barring a special delivery by Guha that sent Lawry's stump cartwheeling, the Bengal boys contributed little to the win.

Both were given another chance in the Calcutta Test, the presence of two home-bred boys further fuelling the feverish excitement created by any Test match. Only a handful of Bengalis had played Test cricket. Among the most notable were opener Pankaj Roy (43 Tests, five centuries and a world-record opening partnership of 413 with Vinoo Mankad against New Zealand that lasted over 50 years) and wicket-keeper Probir Sen, who once famously stumped Don Bradman during a four-day game against South Australia and effected five dismissals in India's historic first Test win against England in 1951–1952.

Those were memories of another day. But there was a link to the past and present. Ambar was the nephew of Pankaj Roy. And there was a firm belief—certainly in my family—that he was as good as his uncle, if not better. All such hopes were dashed by the time the Test ended. India lost the match by 10 wickets. Ambar scored 19 and 18. He never played a Test again. Guha went wicket-less. He, too, never played a Test again.

The barren years for Bengal, characterised by a total lack of presence in the Test-playing XI, created a victim narrative, at least in my home. In the years that followed, I grew up listening to tales of the great injustices meted out to Bengali cricketers—such as opener Gopal Bose, who was part of the ill-fated 1974 England tour but never got to play a Test—particularly from my *jamaibabu* (brother-in-law). Bose did turn out for an ODI, but in the cricket-conservative 1970s few cared about the shorter format. And it stayed much the same way till the summer of 1983. Speedster Barun Burman's name would also crop up during such conversations.

The absence of a Bengali in the national cricket team during those growing-up years shaped my sensibility in a different way. As someone who grew up in different towns of Bihar, I chose my idols without the baggage of regional prejudice. For me, and indeed for most of my Bihari friends, a topic like 'who's better, Gavaskar or Viswanath' made little sense. We loved both unconditionally. It was the same for the spin quartet: Bedi, Chandrasekhar, Prasanna and Venkataraghavan. That is not to say we didn't have our favourites;

mine was always Gavaskar. The point is, our fondness wasn't shaped by parochialism.

By the time Tony Lewis' team was visiting India in the winter of 1972–1973, I was a certified sports addict. Those days I only played what could be roughly described as mohalla cricket, with bits of football and hockey thrown in. I participated in intensely contested matches with neighbouring localities. Sometimes they ended in brawls. I remember that cricket was mostly played with cork and tennis balls; that footballs had two components: a bladder which was inflated using a pump, and a leather cover into which it was stuffed; and that hockey sticks were shaped out of behaya plants (pipe canes).

TIGER'S TALE

Around this time, I was also gifted my first book on sports—*Tiger's Tale: The Story of the Nawab of Pataudi*, the autobiography of Mansur Ali Khan Pataudi—by another cousin who worked as an electronics engineer in Jamshedpur. If I remember correctly, it was priced at ₹3. Some of its vocabulary sailed like harmless bouncers over my head, but I loved re-reading the portions I understood. I lost the book when we were shifting to another town since my father, who worked for the state intelligence bureau, had a transferable job. The loss caused a lingering regret. Moreso, since I could never find another copy in bookstores again. Many years later, while working for *The Telegraph*, I met Pataudi for an interview. After it was over, I spoke to him about the book and wondered why it was never printed again. I have no idea, he said. When he passed away in 2011, I offered to write his obituary in *The Times of India*. I searched for the book again but it was futile. Even now I keep enquiring about it in bookstores and trawl the internet hoping to find a copy. I will keep looking till I find it. It is a slice of my childhood.

Another lasting ache from those pre-teen days was missing the 1973 World Cup hockey semi-final between India and Pakistan, because the game's timing clashed with my tuition schedule. India won 1–0; forward B. P. Govinda scoring the goal. Missing out rankled for weeks, especially since India lost the final to the Netherlands.

Listening to cricket commentary, whenever available, was my number one priority, taking precedence over even *Binaca Geetmala*, the weekly countdown show on Bombay cinema chartbusters, broadcast over Radio Ceylon. Hockey or football games were over in less than two hours. But cricket commentary was daylong and stretched to nearly a full week. Tests were fought over six days because, as old-timers will recall, there used to be a rest day in between the five playing days.

During the Christmas holiday of 1972, I was sent to spend a fortnight at my maternal grandmother's sprawling home in Khamarbere village in West Bengal's Bankura district. My *chhoto mama* (mother's younger brother) lived there, often shuttling between Bankura town, famous for its terracotta horses and where his family lived, and the village which was his workstation.

The Jyoti Basu era was yet to begin in Bengal and the Communist slogan, 'Land to the Tillers', was yet to be put into practice. My *mamas* (maternal uncles) still owned acres of land and were prosperous farmers. The ponds—and there were quite a few—were key rural assets. Catching fish in the morning, to be later served as lunch or dinner, was a daily ritual carried out by the household staff. Lush with bamboo groves, *kamranga* (star fruit), *jaam* (blackberry) and other fecund trees, even a small temple in the capacious compound where an emaciated priest would offer prayers, morning and evening— the surroundings reminded one of the film *Pather Panchali*.

Ours was among a handful of homes blessed with electricity. The supply was erratic and the wattage sickly. It was impossible to read a book even in the light of a 60-watt bulb at night. When I reached Khamarbere with my mother, I discovered to my horror that the radio set wasn't working.

In 1971, Ajit Wadekar's team had wrenched out two improbable triumphs against the West Indies (1–0) and England (1–0), and there was all-round excitement about the series with Lewis' Marylebone Cricket Club (MCC) team. Lewis' men had carved out an unexpected win in the first Test at Kotla in Delhi. And like millions of Indians, I couldn't wait for the start of the second Test at Calcutta.

Missing out on the running commentary was non-negotiable. The problem was that there was only one transistor in the entire village. It belonged to an eccentric gentleman, rather aptly nicknamed Khepa (a crank). It was serendipity that Khepa agreed to my chhoto mama's request to lend his transistor for a week, but on one condition: we would use our own battery.

To this day, I can still picture myself sitting in the courtyard under the winter sun, listening to the radio, guava in hand. And I can still hear snatches of the Bengali commentary of that game. When Farokh Engineer got out after scoring 75, the highest individual score on either side in the match, the commentator just kept repeating, 'Out. Out. Out. Out. Out. Out. Out.' That was part of his style and not because words had failed him. When India won the low-scoring thriller by 28 runs, the commentators combined to transmit the rapturous mood at Eden Gardens to rest of the country. I walked on air.

SWITCHING CHANNELS

In the spring of 1974, we shifted from Ranchi to Arrah. The distance between the two towns—the first located in south Bihar and the other in central Bihar—was less than 300 km, but I soon realised that they could have been on two different worlds.

Ranchi—or the Heavy Engineering Corporation colony, to be precise, where we lived, about 15 km from the cheerful town—was a mini India of sorts, as any other public sector colony. It was orderly, respectable and modern. It was an India that was slowly and wilfully coasting towards the next century.

Arrah was a counter narrative. The headquarters of Bhojpur district had one foot firmly planted in the 19th century. Caste was omnipresent; it was the glue that forged a bond between two strangers, as also the reason to kill a fellow man. In the district's interiors, Naxalites had found firm footing. The radical Reds often left their imprint on the town's walls: the standard *Comrade Mao Ko Laal Salaam* (Red Salute to Comrade Mao), and the menacing *Mudi Katwan Se Hoshiyar* (Beware the head chopper).

In school, I learnt to negotiate these two worlds of contrast. Ranchi had a bunch of pedigreed English-medium public schools. Arrah had none. In Ranchi, it was easy to get hold of a copy of *Sportsweek*. In Arrah, you could try the A. H. Wheeler stall at the railway station. Sometimes you could get very lucky. To buy any readable stuff on sports in English, you took the local train to Patna, about 50 km away. I don't think that either Rohan Kanhai (*Blasting for Runs*) or Sunil Gavaskar (*Sunny Days*) would believe that someone travelled that distance to buy their autobiographies as I did, tagging along with my father during the summer holidays.

I watched my first Ranji game, played between Bihar and Bengal in Patna's packed Moin-ul-Haq stadium. I don't remember the year, but I do recall that both teams had a number of Test discards and a couple of unlucky ones who had missed out on an international career for reasons other than talent.

Bihar had Ramesh Saxena, a gifted stroke-player and a murderer of spin bowling, who earned high praise from Erapalli Prasanna in his autobiography, *One More Over*. Wicket-keeper batsman Daljit Singh, who later earned national recognition as the curator of the pacer-pleasing Mohali wicket, was another player to watch out for. Bengal had the polished opener Gopal Bose, Ambar Roy, Subrata Guha, Barun Burman, and left-arm spinner Dilip Doshi, who was years away from making his Test debut.

The game ended in a draw, but towards the end Saxena delighted the crowd with an audacious assault on the strong Bengal attack. This was my first taste of batting as fireworks. To this day, I believe it was only cynical regional politics that chronically plagued the Board of Control for Cricket in India's (BCCI) selection, which kept Saxena out of Team India. That too at a time when its middle order was as fragile as a *khakhra* (wafer-thin Gujarati savoury).

I wasn't there to watch it, but another Patna game left indelible memories on the psyche of thousands. It was the Indian women's cricket team, wrenching out a dramatic five-wicket win over the West Indies. The sight of a young Diana Edulji, dancing down the pitch to smote boundaries, jolted many preconceived notions about what women can do in a region where patriarchy ruled. Some of my school friends who watched that match developed a grudging admiration for women's cricket thereafter. The Indian team's bus took more than two hours to reach the hotel, because both sides of the road were lined with cheering crowds. They must have felt like stars that evening.

During my early days in Arrah, I spent a lot of my time at the Ramna Maidan where the local football league was played. Most football fans will tell you that they got interested in the game by either accompanying their father or an elder brother or an uncle to the stadium. It is like the baton in a relay race which is passed on from one generation to the other. That's how a deep and durable association with a particular club is formed.

In my case, that wasn't true. My father had a tough job on his hands: tracking the rise and spread of left-wing extremism in

Bhojpur and Rohtas districts. And that left him with little time for the family.

But my interest in sport, I realise now, was part of my DNA. My father was an athlete of reasonable merit in his youth. He also kept goal for Gardanibagh Athletic Club in Patna, and refereed a charity football match between Mohun Bagan and Tripura XI. And he always read *The Statesman's* sports pages carefully.

The league, which I watched almost on a daily basis, had a bunch of institutional teams such as the electricity board, municipal department and banks. They were pretty decent outfits, because each of them had recruited talented local players on sports quota. I also remember a club that went by the name Hero FC, which had a flamboyant goalkeeper. The team I backed, it goes without saying, was the local police unit. Objects in the rear view mirror appear closer than they are, and fonder too. But I do think that watching the Arrah Football League was time well spent.

Being an officer with the intelligence bureau, my father had to read all the newspapers which carried local news. Besides the venerable *The Statesman*, we also used to get copies of *The Indian Nation* and its Hindi counterpart, *Aryavrat*, as well as *The Searchlight* and its Hindi sister publication, *Pradeep*. They are all long gone, but even today they remain an invaluable source of information for researchers. These newspapers gave prominence to local news and even occasionally published the standings of the Patna Football League. Imagining myself to be a loyal fan, following a family tradition, I would faithfully follow the fortunes of Gardanibagh Club. I would always tell the score to my father, especially if his ex-club had won. He always smiled.

A WEEKLY ADDICTION

We would also subscribe to *The Illustrated Weekly of India*, then edited by the irreverent Khushwant Singh, and eagerly wait for the sports and music articles by Raju Bharatan. But my distinct memories of good sports journalism are from *Dharamyug*, a sister publication of the *Weekly*, for the Bennett and Coleman group. *Dharamyug* brought out two special issues—the first was after India won the hockey World Cup. The second was a tribute to the women's cricket team: Shantha Rangaswamy, Diana Edulji, Fowzieh Khalili, Srirupa Bose, Sharmila Chakravarty—they were all there.

Around these years I also started a scrapbook of India's finest moments in sports. I would go around homes asking aunties and uncles if they could lend me the previous day's newspaper, clip a sports photograph, and return the paper. Some would refuse on the excuse that the *raddiwala* (recycler) wouldn't buy clipped newspapers. Others would be gracious. Even today I have a couple of those scrapbooks.

I have a copy of the match report published in *The Indian Nation,* when India famously chased down 404 at Queen's Park Oval, Port of Spain, Trinidad, a defeat that forced West Indian captain Clive Lloyd to dump spinners and start his hunt for fearsome fast men.

And I still possess one-half of the match analysis filed by Ajit Wadekar for *The Illustrated Weekly of India* after the Bishan Singh Bedi-led side swept past Glen Turner's New Zealand, in 1976–1977, in Bombay. I also became an amateur cricket statistician, diligently keeping scores of the Indian team in every Test series.

Amidst all this, I played the sport too. At school, I developed the reputation of a dour opener who found it extremely difficult to score runs, but was hard to dismiss. It doesn't sound much, but growing up at a place where slow batting condemned you to the rank of sissies, it required plenty of self-belief to stick to your strengths. In time, after shepherding my team to a couple of wins in inter-class games with scores such as 22 not out in an overall score of 92, I gained social acceptance. But what made me an object of envy was my knowledge of cricket statistics.

I was one of the few who would even follow an Australia–Pakistan match via newspapers.

By Class VIII, I had also acquired my own three-band transistor that I treated with a fondness generally reserved for pets. Like seasons, one Test series after another came and went. So did players and captains, even sports commentators: Suresh Saraiya, Ravi Chaturvedi, Anant Setalvad, Joga Rao, Murali Manohar Manjul, Jasdev Singh, Akash Lal, Sunil Doshi. I could recognise each one's voice.

Then, slowly, the business of growing up caught up with me. My world changed. So did I.

Now, sometimes, I try to listen to the running commentary on radio. It is not the same thing, though. One feels like stoking the embers of a fire that's long gone. I give up too soon. Sometimes, I also turn to YouTube for succour. Recently, I saw snatches of the 1972–1973 Test series, uploaded perhaps by some incurable nostalgia-addict like me.

And, sometimes, in more pensive moments, I just ponder over the old scrapbooks and try to relive the past. As social scientist Susan Visvanathan wrote—memory is a gift; to remember is to return.

◆

WHEN POLITICS RAN RIOT AT EDEN GARDENS

SOUVIK
NAHA

alcutta's cricket spectators tend to believe they are the best; the world sees them as volatile and fiercely partisan. The city's reputation was tarnished in 1996, when a section of spectators interrupted the World Cup semi-final, unable to tolerate India's impending defeat to Sri Lanka. The incident so vitiated their image that many considered the Test match against Pakistan in 1999, which was also the first match of the inaugural Asian Test Championship, both a high-risk undertaking and a shot at redemption. The political hostility between India and Pakistan since 1947 has had a profound impact on their cricket contests, which has become an exemplar of communal polarisation and a test of patriotism in the subcontinent (Bandyopadhyay, 2008).

The belligerent atmosphere that comes to mind when thinking of India–Pakistan matches almost belies the fact that it was the Board of Control for Cricket in India (BCCI) that moved the motion of Test status to Pakistan in a Marylebone Cricket Club (MCC) meeting in 1952. Pakistan's first-ever cricket series was against India in the same year. The cricketers were provided high security and asked to stay alert to trouble. During the tour, when the train carrying Pakistani cricketers stopped in Surat, a city with an 87 per cent Hindu population, knocks on the windows alarmed everyone in the team. As one of the cricketers opened a window in response, he saw a crowd thronging the platform that had waited for several hours to garland the players. The adulation was reversed a few days later as some Hindu Mahasabha cadres welcomed the touring party to Nagpur with anti-Pakistan slogans (Mahmood and Sohail, 2003). The politically motivated behaviour of cricket followers was manifest most visibly during the India–West Indies One Day International (ODI) match in Srinagar, Kashmir, in 1983. Thousands of spectators waved the Pakistani flag in the gallery, cheered the fall of Indian wickets, and shouted anti-India slogans throughout the match.[1] The crowd became so hostile that Sunil Gavaskar, the Indian captain, wanted to abandon play and forfeit the match. Later, in his autobiography, he wrote of having felt that the match could well have taken place outside India (Gavaskar, 1984).

Cricketers, too, were drawn into the surrogate war of establishing national supremacy. Several incidents affirm the percolation of political propaganda among cricketers. Fazal Mahmood made an impassioned speech at a dinner during the Calcutta Test match in 1954 in support of British India's partition, notwithstanding the misery it had brought to millions (Mahmood and Sohail, 2003). Aftab Gul refused to sign a charity bat, which was to be auctioned to raise funds for the cholera-affected people of Bangladesh in 1971.[2] Most of the India–Pakistan Test matches were drawn as cricketers, allegedly, were unwilling to risk losing and hence resorted to defensive play. During the 1979–1980 series, Pakistani cricketer Majid Khan controversially commented that Indian Muslims would sacrifice their lives during a war between the two countries but in cricket they would always support Pakistan.[3] During the 1987 World Cup, a heated argument between two young Muslim boys in Gwalior, 11-year-old Qadir and 13-year-old Nasir, ended in a mishap. As Qadir had predicted India's win in the tournament, and Nasir Pakistan's, the boys started to fight to settle the score, resulting in Nasir's death and Qadir's arrest by the police.[4] The increasing tension and violence among spectators prompted the two cricket boards to use neutral venues in the 1990s. The Test series in 1999 marked the return of Indo–Pakistan cricket to India after 13 years, and coincided with the undertaking of several confidence-building measures between the countries in February 1999.

RIGHT, LEFT AND THE TEST MATCH

However, Right-wing extremist group Shiv Sena's threat to disrupt matches cast a shadow over the series before it began. Sena demonstrators vandalised the BCCI's office and had the Test match shifted out of Mumbai. They dug up the pitch and threatened to unleash snakes in New Delhi. Pakistan's captain Wasim Akram, dismayed by such intimidation, said, 'We are going there to better the relations between the two countries, and I hope the Indian government will not allow a handful of people to deprive cricket lovers of some action and tension-packed cricket' (R. Bhattacharya, 2005: 12). The CPI(M) government in West Bengal found in the fiasco a political opportunity to upstage other states, and offered to host the entire Test series in Calcutta should the rest of the country prove to be too volatile.

The Shiv Sena warned the West Bengal government against a possible backlash.[5] They appeared to have sent a letter, posted in Calcutta. It could have been a hoax as the party had no organisation in the city, and caused little alarm. A reader from Nadia district sent a poem to the newspaper *Aajkal*,[6] the first stanza of which read: *Diyechhile onek badha/dal niye tumi Thakre/sesh kalete bujhle kemon/ porle hoye eka re* (You and your goons/Spared not a single trick/But in the end, Thackeray/It's you who is cornered). Anti-Shiv Sena posters were plastered round Eden Gardens. *Aajkal* presented this action as a statement of the city's secular outlook.[7] *Ganashakti*, the state government's mouthpiece, was understandably appreciative of the CPI(M) for having stood up to the Shiv Sena's threat. Its editorial spoke of admiration throughout the cricket world for the Left Front Chief Minister's eagerness to organise the Test series. It asked the people to cooperate with the state to dispel the myth of the playing field as a site of proxy war.[8] Test matches in Chennai and New Delhi were not shown on Doordarshan, but MP Gurudas Dasgupta arranged for the live telecast of the Calcutta match through a separate stream for the state at the BCCI's expense.[9] Other newspapers were not so congratulatory of the government; instead, spectators were asked to monitor their own behaviour.

The excitement generated by the match was evident in the presence of a record-breaking 465,000 spectators over five days, negating predictions—the weekday schedule, the state board examinations, the high price of tickets and the attraction of television viewing (Steen, 2014). The police arrested 53 people on various charges on the first day. The Calcutta Improvement Trust's lawyer requested the Calcutta High Court's Green Bench to postpone the hearing on pollution at the Rabindra Sarobar area, as the cricket was too distracting for him to plead his case.[10] A patient, admitted to hospital for a heart attack, released himself on a personal bond to watch the second day's play. He suffered another attack and was taken back to the hospital.[11] In the midst of this madness, on the fourth day, with the game evenly balanced, Sachin Tendulkar collided with Shoaib Akhtar while attempting an easy third run. Tendulkar might have made his ground before the collision, but television replays showed him outside the crease when the ball hit the stumps. As an unhappy Tendulkar left the ground, the public thought of his dismissal as unfair, and rained bottles on the ground in protest. Tendulkar came out to pacify the crowd. It took 67 minutes for the match to resume. Nobody was hurt and the crowd did not threaten to further disrupt the match.

The day's play closed with India in a precarious position. Any hopes of an Indian victory was pinned on local boy Sourav Ganguly who was unbeaten at the end of the day's play. Ganguly fell cheaply, followed by the rest, leaving India on the brink of defeat within half-an-hour's play on the final day. A gesture from Yousuf Youhana reportedly provoked the disappointed spectators, who now started to burn newspapers in the gallery and hurl stones, fruit and plastic bottles on to the field.[12] Some people tried to stop others from throwing bottles in vain. As the police sprang into action, spectators at Block B of Eden Gardens taunted them, calling them traitors. Block C responded with a volley of fruit, which the police blocked with shields. The public set fire to Blocks J, K and L. It took the police three hours to eject 65,000 people. One spectator claimed that the police chased them even as they were dispersing peacefully. Some fell into drains near the Raj Bhavan, some slipped on the road trying to evade mounted police, and some regrouped near the Mayo Road–Red Road crossing and stoned the police.[13] Only around 200 people were left to witness Pakistan's 46-run victory.

The sport diplomacy exercise ended as a huge embarrassment for India. Among the 250 persons arrested, 49 came under civil prosecution. Home Minister Buddhadeb Bhattacharjee denied the charge of police atrocity, maintaining that people were evacuated without the use of force or panic. He added that a similar incident in Chennai or Mumbai would have turned worse. The Calcutta police were better prepared than their counterparts from other states to maintain security and order.[14] The tension between Jagmohan Dalmiya, President of the Cricket Association of Bengal (CAB), and the police did not reach the boiling point of the 1996 World Cup semi-final, as the former did not blame the police eventually. The *Bartaman* newspaper implicated Dalmia as well as the sponsors and betting syndicates for plotting the riot. Sujoy Chakraborty, Additional Superintendent of Police, denied every accusation against the police, and admired the courage and diligence shown by the constabulary in controlling the crisis. *The Telegraph* reported that the CAB's medical room treated 17 people, a record since the unit started functioning in the 1980s; but its sister publication, *Anandabazar Patrika*, put the number at 33 and also asserted that people were treated like cattle. *Ganashakti* credited the Social Welfare Service for admirably treating 34, administering first aid to a further 50, and sending two to be admitted to PG hospital. The Home Secretary was asked to probe the crowd's behaviour and submit a report to the state government within three months.[15]

BATTLE FOR THE NATION

Historians have drawn attention to the role played by the media in intensifying Indo–Pakistan rivalry by drawing 'battlelines', highlighting the history of military conflict and strained diplomatic relations between the countries. This martial imagery polarised Hindus and Muslims in both India and Pakistan even further, at times provoking clashes. The organisation of the bilateral series resonated more with diplomatic initiatives than any positive measure towards achieving peace. Hence, the proclaimed unity remained a pipe dream; the cloak of harmony often slipped to reveal the underbelly of political motives and national sentiments (Dasgupta, 2005). The media's connivance in provoking the public during Indo–Pakistan cricket matches was accentuated during the riots on the fourth and fifth days of the Calcutta Test match in 1999. A part of the local media was apprehensive of communal tension boiling over to the cricket field. *The Statesman*[16] summed up the popular mood before the match: 'A cricket match is a cricket match. But a cricket match against Pakistan is *the* cricket match.' A correspondent to the daily wrote,[17] displaying a misguided understanding of cultural citizenship:

> [The spectators] are 'sane' in their self-professed intent but fret, fume and are not averse to frothing at the mouth in the event they notice someone waving an 'enemy flag'... [They] won't much stand for any revelry indulged in by the supporters of the Pakistan cricket

team. Of course, as [an] excuse for their ire, they will say these supporters are Indian citizens….Can't someone love a country of his choice, however vague the inherency factor may seem, and yet remain faithful to the nation he is a citizen of? In fact, had there been an aberration or two in the behaviour of these people, it is due chiefly to the fear psychosis they are forced to live in.

The state government's assurance about the non-communal nature of the Calcutta crowd proved to be unfounded as spectators at Block B were heard shouting 'Pakistan hai hai' on the second day. When some people objected, they were told that it was a protest against Wasim Akram bouncing Harbhajan Singh and nothing communal was intended.[18] Aajkal[19] reported that the city's Muslims seemed to be unhappy that spectators did not vigorously applaud good performances by Pakistani cricketers, hinting that Indian Muslims favoured Pakistan. As an implication without explanation as to why Indian Muslims empathised with Pakistani cricketers, the news supported the long-standing allegation against the supposedly anti-national behaviour of Muslims in cricketing matters. Soumya Bhattacharya in The Telegraph[20] wrote of the hypocrisy of spectators in Block C waving a placard that read, Indi-Pak pyar to hona hi tha, when the camera zoomed in, but as soon it panned away shouted, Pakistan murdabad. He pointed out that the general standard of spectatorship had declined, writing, 'Only one stereotype is missing in that steamy cauldron, among the screaming, flag-waving, foot-stamping multitude: Calcutta's characteristic cricket-lover, that well-informed, well-read person...' A college student in Block D boasted that the people of Calcutta were not weak, unlike their counterparts in Chennai who had applauded Pakistan's victory. The spectators had come to celebrate India, and Pakistan would not be allowed to win at any cost. Following Tendulkar's run out, screams were heard that the Pakistanis were cheaters. An angry father taught his four-year-old son to extract the maximum noise from two empty bottles by banging them together. Rahul Bhattacharya (2005: 128) later reminisced about the clamour around him: 'Butchers, cheats, Pakistan murdabad!' 'F…g Muslims, go back to [your]own country.' 'Cheats! Bastards! Hai hai! Go back!'

The headline of the Anandabazar Patrika[21] on the fourth day was Chap Thele Swargajayer Bhar Aj Sachineri (It is Sachin's Task to Conquer Paradise), fuelling expectations which were cruelly crushed. It continued its quest of reclaiming Bengal's lost supremacy on the morning of the fifth day, titling its main match report, *Banglar Hate Aj Bharater Bhagya* (Bengal Holds the Key to India's Success), which announced that it was time for Ganguly to prove that he was a hero.[22] One of its journalists lambasted Azharuddin for raising his bat to acknowledge the applauding Pakistan players on reaching 6,000 Test runs. There was no reason for the captain's gesture, according to this line of reasoning, since the opposition was not playing cricket but had launched a battle. Pankaj Roy wrote that Akram's professionalism vandalised cricket's tradition, and a number of former cricketers said that Tendulkar was obstructed and wrongfully given out. It was reported that Gavaskar urged Pakistan's coach Javed Miandad to revoke the appeal, arguing that such a gesture would be remembered as a landmark in the peace process of the subcontinent.[23]

Soumya Bhattacharya (2006) later criticised *The Telegraph*, which he wrote for during the match, for its inflammatory match report entitled, 'Akram Loses India, May Win Test'. He saw supporters coming to the stadium on the fifth day, brandishing the morning newspapers and angrily discussing the injustice done to Tendulkar. *The Telegraph* wrote that Akram could have offered Pakistan Prime Minister Nawaz Sharif the heart of all of India had he made the gesture of calling Tendulkar back, but instead tried to win the match.[24] Its editorial stated that even though the batsman was technically out, Akram violated the spirit of cricket by appealing, which was symptomatic of the declining moral standards of players and spectators. Next day, it published the comments of British journalist Peter Deeley in response to the daily's perturbing reports, countering that he was mistaken about the newspaper's intention. The journalist concerned had not blamed Akram for crowd trouble, but had merely reflected public mood without making any judgement. Akram apparently said after the match, 'It is all because of you people and your reports. You have held them [the crowd] responsible for the wrongdoings but I will never blame them' (S. Bhattacharya, 2006: 132). *Ganashakti*[25] downplayed the fourth day's incident, considering the outburst quite regular, given India's precarious position in the match. It admitted to the city's disgrace, but declared that the behaviour of spectators had improved so much that the match was merely suspended, not abandoned, as in 1967 and 1996. However, the fifth day's incident so changed the position of every newspaper that no clear editorial policy could be discerned from the contents.

The main report in *The Telegraph*,[26] under the headline 'At Eden, Cricket Hangs its Head in Shame', minced no words. It condemned spectators, noting that they were no different from the Jamaat-e-Islami fundamentalists who had hurled stones at Indian Prime Minister Atal Bihari Vajpeyi's motorcade the same day, during his visit to Lahore Fort for peace talks. Both groups were people with no sense of history, engaged in the common effort of subverting history. The cricket field was now a site where jingoism had official sanction for a parade. Rupak Saha reported that the CAB ought not to organise any match for the next three years.[27] The editor of *Ganashakti* was more critical of spectators, having written that cricket was now ruled by commerce, and that spectators of this changed cricket were false fans.[28] No longer envisioning the people of Calcutta as an anti-communal brigade who had foiled the Shiv Sena's plan, he accused a section of the spectators of instigating communal hatred and raising hate posters in the galleries. The newspaper defended the police against allegations of brutalising spectators, arguing that a group of young people taunted the police into beating them, and later incriminated the government by showing their wounds to the media. Nevertheless, it remarked that most of the spectators were victims of communal propaganda that had flung cricket, religious identity and the Kashmir situation into crisis. It claimed that the incident was not spontaneous, but rather was orchestrated by political opposition to discredit the state government. Not so supportive of the government's role, *The Statesman* reported:[29]

> Jyoti Basu's and Buddhadeb Bhattacharjee's interpretation of Calcutta—a culturally sophisticated island nurtured on Marxist values—is a fantasy; no other Indian city erupts so easily at the tiniest non-excuse; nowhere else is civic freedom held in such contempt. But it has taken the ultimate bourgeois pastime—Test cricket—for the point to be rammed home....Calcutta cannot comprehend that there's more to lose in cricket than merely a match...[The behaviour of spectators] indicate[s] a pattern of

lumpenism, which is activated whenever the home team slips at a crucial stage of the game. Since Mr. Dalmiya cannot ensure the Indian players always come up trumps, and since the apology placards some Calcuttans displayed after the India–Sri Lanka match have been proved to be a mere PR stunt, for the sake of cricket, and for the sake of this country's reputation, the city that reaches for plastic bottles every time Sachin or Sourav is dismissed, must be considered beyond the pale.

The Trinamool Congress organised a protest march, demanding Buddhadeb Bhattacharjee's resignation, which ended in the arrest of 59 members, including 32 women.[30] Basu remarked that such incidents of violence were common in sport, especially when ruffians had access to the stadium as ticket holders. His efforts at self-exoneration failed to influence his political rivals. The BJP General Secretary Rahul Sinha demanded an investigation; Trinamool leader Mamata Banerjee demanded an apology from the state, insinuating that Basu had masterminded the disturbances to hinder the peace process. The Youth Congress President Paresh Pal asked for a refund of the fifth day's ticket.[31] The demonstrations fell well short of their target. The sports press stopped its criticism all too suddenly and focused on the next Test match. Dalmiya used his clout to save Eden Gardens from being blacklisted by the International Cricket Council (ICC). While the blemish of communalism did not entirely fade, it never returned with the same vengeance during the Indo–Pakistan matches played later in the city.

CONCLUSION

The riot was caused by a combination of antagonism towards Pakistan and resentment at coming up second best. Indo–Pakistan matches have, in this way, generated an idea of nationalist loyalty that needs to be explicit and compliant to a certain political discourse of nationhood. This discourse asserts that one's legitimacy as a citizen depends on one's adherence to a national symbol, i.e., cricket. Such an articulation of legitimation, arguably, helps a group to take a majoritarian position and dominate the nonconformists. Journalists have inaccurately compared this test of nationalism that is often asked of Muslims to the infamous Tebbit Test in Britain, which was about asking resident South Asian-origin people to prove their right to be British citizens by supporting English cricket teams against India and Pakistan. The two contexts are fundamentally different, as the British test was about ethnic South Asians growing out of their traditional group loyalty, and the Indian test has been about Indians being asked to support their country, irrespective of their religion. Indians who question this arrangement open themselves to allegations of harbouring anti-national sentiment. They are seen by the majority to be inimical to the establishment of a unitary nationalism. Their actions symbolise simultaneously the shortcomings of a nation that fails to inculcate a sense of national belonging in its citizens, and the problem of alienation of a community from Indian society, prompted by a mutual unease between religions. The shared mistrust between India and Pakistan seemed to have been removed on the occasion of the 'Friendship' cricket tour in 2003–2004, but later events have resulted in suspension of all bilateral sporting contact.

◆

NOTES

1. *Jugantar.* 18 October 1983.
2. *The Times of India.* 20 June 1971.
3. *Amrita Bazar Patrika.* 3 February 1980.
4. *The Statesman.* 20 October 1987.
5. *Aajkal.* 12 February 1999.
6. *Ibid.* 14 February 1999.
7. *Ibid.* 15 February 1999.
8. *Ganashakti.* 15 February 1999.
9. *Anandabazar Patrika.* 16 February 1999.
10. *Bartaman.* 18 February 1999.
11. *Ibid.* 19 February 1999.
12. *Anandabazar Patrika.* 21 February 1999.
13. *The Telegraph.* 21 February 1999.
14. *Ganashakti.* 21 February 1999.
15. *The Times of India.* 24 February 1999.
16. *The Statesman.* 15 February 1999: 16.
17. *Ibid.* 17 February 1999: 1.
18. *Aajkal.* 18 February 1999.

19. *Ibid.* 19 February 1999.
20. *The Telegraph.* 20 February 1999: 10.
21. *Anandabazar Patrika.* 19 February 1999: 1.
22. *Ibid.* 20 February 1999: 1.
23. *Ibid.* 20 February 1999.
24. *The Telegraph.* 20 February 1999.
25. *Ganashakti.* 20 February 1999.
26. *The Telegraph.* 21 February 1999: 1.
27. *Anandabazar Patrika.* 23 February 1999.
28. *Ganashakti.* 21 February 1999.
29. *The Statesman.* 21 February 1999: 8.
30. *Anandabazar Patrika.* 22 February 1999.
31. *Bartaman.* 24 February 1999.

REFERENCES

Bandyopadhyay, Kausik. 2008. 'Feel Good, Goodwill and India's Friendship Tour of Pakistan, 2004: Cricket, Politics and Diplomacy in Twenty-First-Century India', *International Journal of the History of Sport,* 25 (12): 1654–70.

Bhattacharya, Rahul. 2005. *Pundits from Pakistan: On Tour with India, 2003–04.* New Delhi: Picador.

Bhattacharya, Soumya. 2006. *You Must Like Cricket? Memoirs of an Indian Cricket Fan.* London: Yellow Jersey Press.

Dasgupta, Jishnu. 2005. 'Manufacturing Unison: Muslims, Hindus and Indians during the India–Pakistan Match', in Boria Majumdar and J. A. Mangan (eds.), *Sport in South Asian Society: Past and Present.* London: Routledge: 239–48.

Gavaskar, Sunil. 1984. *Runs 'n Ruins.* Calcutta: Rupa.

Mahmood, Fazal and Asif Sohail. 2003. *From Dawn to Dusk: Autobiography of a Pakistan Cricket Legend.* Karachi: Oxford University Press.

Steen, Rob. 2014. *Floodlights and Touchlines: A History of Spectator Sport.* London: Bloomsbury.

◆◆

'INDIANS MAKE US ANGRY!'
Australian Perceptions of Touring Indian Cricket Teams, 1947–2017[1]

IAN SIMPSON

T he group of Indian cricketers that arrived in Australia in October 1947 was the first sporting team to represent the newly independent nation overseas and, as such, was invested with important political overtones. Selected in the context of Partition, the team represented Indian hopes that a new national identity might be created, based on political unity and religious harmony. As the Bombay journalist Homi J. H. Taleyarkhan commented in his preview of the tour:

> On India's sports fields we still find Hindus, Muslims, Sikhs, Scheduled Classes, Christians, all brushing shoulders, playing in the happiest spirit of amity, knowing no distinction of class or creed…They are all SPORTSMEN OF INDIA [sic], playing for ONE INDIA [sic]—for the glory of one nation (1947: 159).

But Australian cricket officialdom, and the Australian media, both of which to this point had treated Indian cricket with indifference, made no acknowledgement that the tour carried any kind of postcolonial significance.

THE FIRST TOUR, 1947–1948: 'YOUR FELLOWS PLAY THE CRICKET WE LIKE'

The Indians arrived with modest ambitions, the leading batsman V. S. Hazare confessing their intention was to play, learn and enjoy. The team's results suggested this reticence was perhaps justified: there were individual flashes of brilliance, such as Hazare's two centuries in the fourth Test at Adelaide, but, ultimately, the tourists could not match the depth of an opposition that was essentially the core of Bradman's 1948 'Invincibles' Ashes team. By the fifth Test in Melbourne, the Indians were 'disappointing and spiritless' and could offer little resistance. The series was lost 4–0.

Nevertheless, the Indians had quickly established a reputation for playing entertaining, adventurous and attacking cricket in a style which Australian crowds liked to think was uniquely Australian, in contrast to the relentless, 'win-at-all-cost' approach that had begun to characterise the Australian team under Bradman's leadership. The former Indian batsman K. S. Duleepsinhji, who had played for England against the Australians in the 1930s and was now covering the tour as a journalist for English and Australian newspapers, reflected the warmth of local feeling when he related how he had been constantly approached by Australian cricket followers telling him, 'Your fellows play the cricket we like. They are sportsmen, and we hope they win the first Test' (1947).

At the same time, Australians were fascinated by the mysterious otherness of the Indian cricketers. The Sikh batsman, 'the picturesque, turbaned Rai Singh', became an instant celebrity when the Brisbane *Courier–Mail* featured him in a front-page photograph, padding up before net practice, with extensive discussion of his religion, his cultural practices and, most of all, his turban. Yet the alluring, Oriental mystique Australian commentators were constructing around Indian cricketers, the 'collection of dreams, images and vocabularies', in Edward Said's phrase, contained an essential dualism in the suspicion that the visitors were physically frail and vulnerable, particularly when confronting the Australian pace bowlers (1978: 73). But there was, as yet, no questioning of the Indians' courage or resolve.

THE 1960s AND 1970s: 'FAIR-DINKUM CRICKET'
However, cricket provided only a tenuous link between the two countries for some time. Australian teams visited India in 1956 and in 1959–1960, but if anything, the Australian cricketers' experiences there only consolidated what the journalist Mike Coward has termed a 'rat and riot mentality' where the players viewed India as a place of unhealthy food, cramped and unhygienic accommodation and political volatility (1990: 4–5). The Australian Cricket Board did not invite another Indian tour until the 1967–1968 season,

when the tourists were outclassed 4–0, though winning praise once again for their entertaining and attacking approach. India had beaten both the West Indies and England in 1971, its first series victories recorded overseas, marking a 'psychological inauguration of a new boldness in Indian cricket', in Arjun Appadurai's view (1995: 40). Consequently, Bishen Bedi's side came to Australia in the 1977–1978 season not to compete, but to win against an Australian team left in turmoil by the defection of its first-choice players to World Series Cricket, and were considered unlucky to lose the series 2–3.

Nevertheless, despite India's growing competitiveness, the Australian press continued to frame Indian cricketers as Oriental types. Journalist Malcolm McGregor later recalled how the Indians' exotic aura had fascinated him:

> As a kid in an Australian country town, I was riveted by that [1967–1968] series....From my juvenile perspective, the Indians were exotic, mysterious creatures straight from the novels of W. E. Johns—their team led by the Nawab of Pataudi Jnr. [sic] no less. Had they turned up to play on bejewelled elephants, I would not have blinked (2012: 12).

During the 1977–1978 tour, Australian journalists employed a particular vocabulary drawn from the trope of Oriental wizardry to explain the dominance of India's quartet of spin bowlers—Bedi, Prasanna, Venkataraghavan and Chandrasekhar. Consequently, Australian batsmen were frequently said to be 'mesmerised' by the Indian slow bowlers, or 'held in a trance', or even 'throttled by the Indian rope-trick'. No Indian player better personified Australian ideas of Oriental mystique than the 1967–1968 captain, Mansur Ali Khan, the Nawab of Pataudi, with his dashing image, his aristocratic background and his boyhood nickname, 'Tiger'. But Pataudi appeared a complex character to the Australian public because he was also seen to embody traditional Victorian sporting qualities: selflessness, dedication, physical endurance and, above all, the courage he displayed in his furious assaults on Australian fast bowling, despite being restricted by a hamstring injury. The picture of Pataudi painted by a Melbourne *Age* reporter was of how 'the twain of Eastern dexterity and Western determination have been married in this one player...I ask myself what other player in the world could have overcome his dual physical disability with a combination of occidental gutsy know-how and Oriental dexterity' (Tyson: 1968). The 1977–1978 Tests were also celebrated for restoring traditional cricketing values. At the close of the final Test, the two captains, Bedi and Simpson, were photographed with their arms around each other's shoulders. In Simpson's words, 'This is the best thing that has happened for fair-dinkum cricket.'

THE 1980s AND 1990s: 'INDIANS BRING OUT THE AGGRESSIVENESS IN US'

If the 1977–1978 season was the summer of good sportsmanship and camaraderie between the two sides, the tours of 1981 and 1985–1986 provided a taste of the coming winter. Displays of churlishness, animosity and aggression marked each contest as India seriously challenged Australian ascendency, drawing both series. In an interview following the final day of the first Test at Adelaide in December 1985, Allan Border, the Australian captain, attempted to explain the tensions that had grown between the two cricketing nations:

> I think the Indians bring out the aggressiveness in us....There is just something about playing against them which tends to make you a little more aggressive. I don't know what it is, but it is there (Coward: 1985).

The Australians were irritated by what they regarded as the constant and over-zealous appealing by the Indians (but also, quite paradoxically, by their passive natures. One Australian player described the Indians as 'unnerving' because 'you don't know what they are thinking about you'). The tourists, for their part, were indignant over a series of controversial decisions made against them by the local umpires, culminating in the Indian captain Sunil Gavaskar threatening that India would forfeit the Melbourne Test in protest.

While increased acrimony on the field clearly coincided with India's emergence as a serious rival in Test cricket, Border's views signalled how the Indian–Australian consensus about the nature and purpose of Test cricket, and any assumptions about the shared cricketing values of the British Empire, were dissolving as each nation developed differing views of its place in the global cricketing hierarchy and even, it might be suggested, differing views of national identity. In India's case, Anandam Kavoori has suggested, the players had experienced 'a moment of postcolonial delinking' and a growing sense of self-determination and confidence following their unexpected victory in the 1983 World Cup. This new attitude was personified by the figure of the technically flawless, relentlessly competitive batsman Sunil Gavaskar who, Kavoori argues, had revisited 'the tools of the masters' and replaced the discourse of mimicry with one of mastery (2009: 153–54). For Australians, sensitivities about India's rise as a cricketing power were not eased by the recognition that the home side's own fortunes had floundered since the World Series split in 1977. Between the 1977–1978 series and 1985, Australia had lost 35 Test matches, won only 22, and drawn 23. 'We're the worst in the world,' lamented the *Daily Telegraph's* Jim Woodward in 1985, and in his view, the coming series against the Indians would decide the title of world cricket's wooden spooners.

Two related trends in Australian cricket commentary emerged during the 1980s. First, and coinciding with India's success, Australian cricket writers began constructing, with grudging respect, a new model of the modern Indian cricketer; a hard-edged competitor who was confident, assertive, physical and intent on doing whatever was necessary to win. The prototype of this new Indian cricketer was Gavaskar, but Australian critics later identified the same characteristics in Ravi Shastri, then in Sourav Ganguly and Harbhajan Singh (and currently in Virat Kohli, its apotheosis). Second, sections of the Australian media, which had long since given themselves a responsibility for subverting the confidence and morale of visiting sporting teams, began to raise questions about the Indians' character, moral strength and courage. This charge had echoes of Mrinalini Sinha's analysis of British Raj contempt for 'the effeminate Bengali', updated and transported to the Antipodes. However, regular displays of determined resistance by touring Indian cricketers made these accusations difficult to sustain. Sandip Patil, hit in the head by a bouncer in the first 1981 Test at Sydney and taken to hospital, re-emerged near the close of India's second innings, batting in one of the new helmets, and then scored 174 at Adelaide in an 'innings of rare character'. By tour's end, Patil 'had built up a name for courage and heroic stroke play and an ability to play his natural game against all the odds' (McFarlaine, 1981: 82–84). In Melbourne, both Shivlal Yadav and Dilip Doshi bowled throughout the match with broken bones in their feet. Phil Wilkins, originally critical of India's lack of gumption, declared after these revelations, 'Don't ever describe the Indian cricketers as cowards to me again' (1981). Nevertheless, and despite all the evidence to the contrary, Australian journalists were reluctant to lay aside their criticism that Indian cricketers lacked courage and revived the accusation during later tours. The punning headline to a *Sydney Morning Herald* report on India's batting collapse at Sydney in January 2000, 'No tikka', had such longevity that it was revived several times to describe similar collapses during later tours.

Australian journalists were also persistent in describing Indian cricketers as figures of Oriental mystery; India's spinners continued to be cast as 'conjurors and sleight of hand men', for example. Commentators were also intrigued by the importance of religion in the daily lives of the Indians. Krishnamachari Srikkanth, the opening batsmen, quickly became something of a phenomenon for his whirlwind batting, but the local press also celebrated him as personifying the confounding enigma that was India. When Richard Sleeman arrived for an interview with Srikkanth in Sydney's Boulevard Hotel, he found Srikkanth had converted his room into a Hindu shrine. For Sleeman, the scene encapsulated 'the great incongruity of India, where centuries-old faith and ritual flourished in a rapidly-emerging nation' (1986).

As other touring teams were beginning to find during the 1990s, the Indians were confronted not only by a resurgent Australian team, but also by what appeared to be an increasingly unwelcoming cricketing scene. The Indians' longstanding sense of injustice was amplified by contentious umpiring decisions that continued to favour the opponents; local umpires delivered finger-wagging lectures to the visitors during play; pitches once famous for their slow, turning nature transformed into hard, bouncing greentops; and Indian players found guilty of dissent on the field were fined, while Australians were exonerated for similar breaches. Peter Roebuck sensed the antagonism directed towards Indian teams was an expression of the current intensification of Australian jingoism and paranoia:

> A monster called nationalism is loose among us and is causing dreadful trouble, for visitors sense it and react to it....Having imagined cricket to be a game of meadows and manners, these Indians are learning the lessons of the street....They are learning fast, taking the best from their opponents, yet maintaining their own identity (1992).

Roebuck's concerns raised two questions for future Indian tours: whether or not expressions of Australian cricketing nationalism could be contained before degenerating into even more extreme forms; and whether Indian cricketers might eventually come to the view that, in order to defeat the Australians, they would need not only to play like Australians, but to behave like them as well.

INTO THE 21ST CENTURY

During the 2003–2004 Indian tour of Australia, Steve Waugh, the Australian captain, argued that the contest between the two nations had become 'the biggest in world cricket'. Television ratings for the 2011–2012 Indian tour provided substance for Waugh's belief, as India surpassed the Ashes as the biggest attraction for local audiences. There were many reasons why India now mattered in Australian eyes. First, India had undoubtedly become a serious challenger to Australia's status as the world's premier cricket team. Moreover, India now matched its economic dominance of the game with increasing political clout through its control of the International Cricket Council (ICC), and Australian cricket authorities were not merely obliged to conform to cricket's new order, but appear grateful. 'This summer has been a breakthrough season for the future of Australian cricket,' enthused Stephen Dabkowski in the *Age*. 'The competitive, lively Test series against India has finally plugged Australia into the financial powerhouse of world cricket' (2004). Australian cricketers took advantage of their high profile in the Indian Premier League from 2008 to develop business interests and write columns in Indian newspapers. There was even a physical Indian presence at Australian cricket grounds as companies, including Hero Honda and Royal Stag, bought signage rights and

Indian expatriates and groups of tourists formed the 'Swami Army' to sing and cheer in support of the visiting team.

But despite these developments, a series of heated incidents highlighted how relations between Indian and Australian cricket remained fractious, culminating in the confrontation between Andrew Symonds and Harbhajan Singh during the Sydney Test in 2007, which saw the Indian bowler reported for racial abuse, and then suspended by the match referee for three matches. The Indian team management appealed to the ICC and threatened to abandon the tour, prompting the ICC to appoint John Hansen, a New Zealand High Court justice, to oversee the appeal. Hansen downgraded the charge to a less serious 'abusive language' and fined Harbhajan 50 per cent of his match fee, observing in conclusion that it was Symonds who should accept responsibility for provoking the incident. The principal architect behind the Indians' harder, more confrontational brand of cricket was Sourav Ganguly, captain from 2000 to 2005. Caricatured at first by the Australian media as a wealthy, almost effete Bengali aristocrat, Ganguly won begrudging respect (and the ultimate Australian accolade of exhibiting 'mental toughness'), particularly for his fighting century at Brisbane in 2003 despite being hit several times by the Australian fast bowlers. Ganguly's players seemed assured, even 'cocky', personified by the belligerent opening batsman, Virender Sehwag, who insisted the Indians were prepared to return the Australians' sledging in kind: 'The Australians are famous at sledging and if they start it, we will not be quiet. Why should we take it lying down?' (Dorries, 2008). When India fought back to win the 2003 Adelaide Test after the Australians had scored over 500 in their first innings, the Adelaide *Advertiser's* reporter proclaimed India had redefined itself as a Test nation and left the Australian side 'battered physically and psychologically' by playing 'Australian-style cricket'. In Robert Craddock's view, 'Once the softest of away teams, the Indians have become road warriors against the game's top side' (2004).

Ganguly might well have won local respect for being 'the first captain to think like an Australian', but he also became the subject of a campaign of 'villain production' conducted by sections of the local media. Richard Hinds suggested the reason Ganguly, and before him the Sri Lankan captain Arjuna Ranatunga, so infuriated the Australians was because their assertiveness and defiance exposed an insecurity in the national sporting psyche that should have been overcome long ago. On the field, there was a predictable resurgence of sledging by the Australians. But the local cricket culture as a whole now appeared tainted by racial slurs. Several journalists reported instances of Indian spectators and journalists being called 'coolie', 'curry muncher' and 'Muslims', and having bones and full bottles of water pelted at them. An Indian executive, who had been living in Australia for 15 years, said he feared for his safety as he left the Adelaide ground. At Melbourne, members of the Swami Army were taunted with cries of 'go home', 'you came here on a refugee boat', and even 'you created Osama bin Laden and Saddam Hussein'. A reporter for the *Age* witnessed a nearby spectator screaming 'F— off, ya black c—s, ya shouldn't even be in the f—ing country!' at the Indian batsmen. Peter Roebuck, always an acerbic analyst of Australian cricket culture, insisted it was time for Australia to 'confront its ugly side', while Gideon Haigh lamented how the scenes demonstrated how 'patriotism mutates quite easily into nationalism and into xenophobia'.

The unwelcome combination of the race issue and growing crowd restiveness continued to mark later Indian tours. Before the Perth Test in January 2012, the Indian captain M. S. Dhoni requested additional security at the ground following reports of crowd abuse of Virat Kohli, while fielding at Sydney, and of Ishant Sharma, during a social function in Perth. When Kohli assumed the leadership of India following M. S. Dhoni's retirement from Test cricket during the 2014–2015 tour, he was widely characterised in the Australian media as the most confrontational captain to lead a touring side (was Douglas Jardine, the architect of Bodyline, so easily forgotten?). So thoroughly did Kohli's players emulate the Australians in their intensive match preparation, their aggressive tactics and their boisterous behaviour on the field, that for Greg Baum it seemed, borrowing from football idiom, as if the two teams had swapped jerseys—'India are the Australian-style belligerents in this series' (2014). When the former captain Steve Waugh tweeted that 'Kohli plays like an Australian', many took the comment as extending Kohli the highest mark of respect. In a sense, these views represented the ultimate in Australian cricket's myopia and self-regard: the only cricketers capable of overcoming Australians, so it seemed, were Australians themselves, or in the case of the modern

Indian cricketer, their clones. The Adelaide journalist Graham Cornes, however, attributed the blame for the continuing animosity between the two sides largely to the Australians. Their belligerence was undeniably underscored by racism, Cornes argued, but also by a growing awareness that their inherent sense of superiority was being challenged by an increasingly assertive and self-assured Indian team. The Australians were 'flat-track bullies' who could not accept their intended victims were standing up for themselves (2015).

SOME REFLECTIONS

Throughout the post-war period of White Australia, Australians had refused to acknowledge Asian peoples as their equals; yet their initial response to touring Indian cricketers was to welcome them with an essentially benevolent, imperial view as individual sportsmen, illustrating perhaps the lingering influence of British Empire ideology in Australian society. After the Indians were seen to demonstrate an adventurous approach to the game and the personal qualities of resilience and fortitude, values which Australians liked to claim were uniquely theirs, they became widely popular. Nevertheless, Australians found it difficult to divorce these perceptions from Orientalist assumptions about difference and inferiority; as we have seen, Australian commentators persisted in framing Indian cricketers as racial types. Thus, the colourful exotic (Rai Singh), the Oriental prince (Pataudi), the conjurors and wizards (Bedi and his spin bowling colleagues).

But Australians struggled to define or understand the modern Indian cricketers who emerged during the latter decades of the century with their win-at-all-costs mentality. In India, there has been much discussion about the causes and nature of this transformation. In Ashis Nandy's view, this process was simply a result of Indian cricket becoming a 'consumable sport' that reflected globalised values, with an emphasis on managerialism, professionalism, competitiveness, profit and results defined by statistics (1989: 86–87, 92–93). Changes within Indian culture and society also contributed, as the Indian media provided increased exposure of the game through widespread use of vernacular languages in commentary and analysis, and marginalised groups responded to the financial rewards that cricket was increasingly able to offer. Associated with these trends was the emergence of what Boria Majumdar identifies as 'an aggressive hyper jingoistic sentiment', where success for the Indian cricket team came to represent success for the nation as a whole (2011: 200–201). Insofar as cricket can be construed as a synecdoche of contemporary consciousness, as Nandy maintains, then Indian cricket is a representation of India's modernity (or at least one version of it) with all that might involve—globalised, commercialised, mercenary, assertive, competitive, successful.

Much of this analysis might, of course, be applied equally to Australian cricket. As Gideon Haigh has reminded us, cricket has always served as an avenue for expressing national identity and achievement. Yet outside a select few, local commentators have found it difficult to adjust to the transformation in the Indians' approach to the modern game, nor, indeed, to the fact that post-imperial India has been undergoing a continuing 'reassertion of identity', in Shashi Tharoor's words (2017: 190). This is hardly surprising given that studies of India, once flourishing in Australian universities, have languished for some time and in Australian schools are practically non-existent.

The modern manifestation of Indian cricket rubbed uneasily against an Australian counterpart that from its resurgence in the late 1980s increasingly reflected the rise of another strident and bellicose variety of nationalism, drawing for its symbolism from a particular interpretation of Australian history that emphasised heroic sacrifice and military achievement. The extent to which Australian cricket had cast itself as a nationalist symbol, expressed in martial terms, was exemplified when Steve Waugh and his 2001 Ashes touring team were photographed in the trenches on the Gallipoli battlefield, slouch hats and all, in a promotion devised by the Australian Cricket Board in cooperation with General Peter Cosgrove, the prominent Australian military commander and current Governor-General. Indian–Australian Test cricket in the 21st century had become a contested arena in which each team asserted the right to represent its own version of a pugnacious national identity and, consequently, conflict was unsurprising; indeed, conflict came to be welcomed on both sides as an essential ingredient. When the question of race figured in radical conceptions of national identity, as it had historically in the case of Australia and continued to do, then the temperature of the contest was bound to be even more heated.

Australian perceptions of touring Indian cricketers have shifted from 'exotic, mysterious creatures', to 'road warriors', to players who appear at least as combative and disputatious as the Australians themselves. Yet Australian cricket commentators have never been completely cured of their fascination for the language of Orientalism. Here is Malcolm Knox, describing the innings of 66 played by V. V. S. Laxman at Sydney in January 2012:

> Laxman, who is my favourite batsman in world cricket, dominated the partnership with his twirls and clips. He is so compelling because after 130-odd Tests it's still impossible to work out how he gets so much energy into the very last instant of his shots. He practised hard in the nets this week, and I spent some time watching him without being any the wiser. He can be out of position, flat-footed, beaten in flight, and the next moment the ball is whistling towards the boundary because of some conjuring of his wrists that was faster than the observer's eye. His timing is so good that no matter how lightly he brushes the ball, it always runs faster than the chasing fieldsman. He played some lovely strokes yesterday, but one leg-side flick, off James Pattinson, left the bowler scowling and muttering as if he'd been cheated. He swore he'd seen the ball hit the stumps, but apparently it was going wide of mid-on for four.

The secret to the batsman's artistry is incapable of rational explanation: the 'conjuring', the wristiness, the powerful flicks, the timing, the way the honest bowler is left bewildered; it all could as easily have been written about Ranjitsinhji when he batted in Sydney, over a hundred years before.

◆

NOTE

1. The headline to an article by Mike Coward, published in the *Sydney Morning Herald*, 18 December 1985, in which Allan Border, the Australian captain, described his team's reaction to what they perceived as Indian cricketers' on-field aggression.

REFERENCES

Appadurai, Arjun. 1995. 'Playing with Modernity: The Decolonisation of Indian Cricket', in Carol A. Breckenridge (ed.), *Consuming Modernity: Public Culture in a South Asian World*. Minneapolis and London: University of Minnesota Press.

Baum, Greg. 2014. 'It's more like home but Indians can't get a foothold', *Sydney Morning Herald*, 26 December.

Cornes, Graham. 2015. 'Have-a-chat Virat shows he won't back off', *Advertiser*, Adelaide, 2 January.

Coward, Mike. 1990. *Cricket Beyond the Bazaar*. Sydney: Allen and Unwin.

————. 1985. 'Indians make us angry: Border', *Sydney Morning Herald*, 18 December.

Craddock, Robert. 2004. 'Road warriors stunned champions', *Advertiser*, Adelaide, 3 January.

Dabkowski, Stephen. 2004. 'Indian cricket fever spins plenty of dollars for Australia', *Age*, Melbourne, 3 January.

Dorries, Ben. 2008. 'India's sledge pledge', *Courier–Mail,* Brisbane, 14 January.

Duleepsinhji, K. S. 1947. 'Hope you fellows win Test', *Courier–Mail*, Brisbane, 27 November.

Kavoori, Anandam. 2009. 'Playing with Postcoloniality: Four Moments in Indian Cricket', in Anandam Kavoori (ed.), *The Logics of Globalisation: Studies in International Communication*. Lanham, Maryland, USA: Lexington Books.

Knox, Malcolm. 2012. 'Clarke's Test heroics will stand test of time', *Sydney Morning Herald*, 27–28 January.

Majumdar, Boria. 2011. 'A New Dimension? India, Australia and the Cultural Politics of Sport', in Brian Stoddart and Auriol Weigold (eds.), *India and Australia: Bridging Different Worlds*. New Delhi: Readworthy.

McFarlaine, Peter. 1981. *Cricket in Australia: Season 1981–82*. Melbourne: Garry Sparke and Associates.

McGregor, Malcolm. 2012. *An Indian Summer of Cricket: Reflections on Australia's Summer Game*. Geelong: Barrallier Books.

Nandy, Ashis. 1989. *The Tao of Cricket: On Games of Destiny and the Destiny of Games*. New Delhi: Penguin.

Roebuck, Peter. 1992. 'It's time to eat our humble pie...but with a Vindaloo filling', *Sydney Morning Herald*, 7 January.

Said, Edward. 1978. *Orientalism*. London: Penguin.

Sleeman, Richard. 1986. 'The man with thunder in his bat gets that ton at last!' *Daily Mirror,* Sydney, 3 January.

Taleyarkhan, Homi H. J. 1947. *Cricket: United India in Australia*. Bombay: Thacker and Co.

Tharoor, Shashi. 2017. *Inglorious Empire: What the British did to India*. Melbourne and London: Scribe.

Tyson, Frank. 1968. 'No other man in the world', *Age*, Melbourne, 4 January.

Wilkins, Phil. 1981. 'Au revoir (until next summer)', *Cricketer*, April.

❖❖

INDIA'S SPORTING FRONTIER
Race, Integration and Discontent in the North-east

DUNCAN
MCDUIE-RA

INTRODUCTION

N orth-east India is increasingly being viewed as an incubator for national sporting talent. The success of athletes from the North-east, representing India at the global level, such as Mangte Chungneijang Mary Kom (Mary Kom), and of teams in national competitions, such as Aizawl FC, narrate a region teeming with potential sports stars, national heroes, product endorsers and potential customers. Sporting success is seen as a way to bring the recalcitrant frontier further into the national fold. At the same time, sporting infrastructure in the region continues to grow, responding to and fuelling local aspirations for sporting careers in metropolitan India and beyond. Exploring sport in the North-east highlights conversations about the frontier and its place in India that are different from, though often entangled in, conversations focused on security, identity and migration. As Carrington writes, 'Sport engenders national conversations about race, discrimination, opportunity and identity that would otherwise not take place, and as such, understanding the sports–race–society nexus is of increasing importance to sociologists and other social scientists' (2013: 380). With this in mind, this article explores the sports–race–society nexus in the North-east to explore themes of belonging, integration and discontent.

In doing so, I make three arguments. First, sport has become a mechanism for the integration of the frontier into the national imaginary. According to this narrative, it is through sporting success that North-east communities can demonstrate their place in contemporary India, erasing the politics of separatism, violence and state brutality. Second, for many people in the North-east, sport is a livelihood opportunity and a form of upward mobility. Third, while sporting success offers the opportunity for acceptance in mainstream India, sporting success compounds rather than challenges racial stereotypes for North-east communities. For those who cannot run, punch or kick a ball, the experience of India remains complex and has altered little with the rise of sporting heroes from the region.

These arguments are developed through four sections. The first introduces the notion of the 'sporting frontier', which suggests the North-east is viewed as a sporting incubator for the nation. The second section explores the ways sport is viewed at the national level as a pathway to integration and, simultaneously, as a way of erasing histories of rebellion with the prospect of sporting redemption. The third section examines the relationship between sport and aspiration for communities in the North-east, and discusses these in relation to livelihoods and mobility. The fourth and final section considers the limitations of this view of the North-east, and the complex politics it masks.

As with virtually any writing on the North-east, it is important to make a series of disclaimers at the outset. By discussing the North-east, I am not implying that the region is homogenous or that the intersections of sport, race and politics are identical in all parts of the region, and for all communities. However, I am concerned with the ways sport both constructs and reproduces notions of a largely homogenous frontier, exemplified by racial distinction from 'mainland' India: a racial distinction that is imputed with assumptions about physicality, athleticism and potential. In exploring these assumptions, I am not subscribing to them. Further, this brief article is neither a history of sport in the North-east, nor an account of various sporting pioneers, or early encounters between communities on the frontier, or colonial and/or other counterparts in sporting competition. Indeed, individual sportspersons, teams and achievements are less important to this article than what Creak, writing in the context of the Lao People's Democratic Republic, identifies as 'links between the human body, ideas and practices of physical culture, and the constitution of social, cultural, and political power…' (2015: 16). Therefore, I am interested in the present sporting moment, gravid with the history of colonisation, rebellion and state-making, and what this can tell us about contemporary India.

THE SPORTING FRONTIER

The North-east is represented in various ways within India and beyond: violent and unruly, anti-national, remote, backward and exotic. These representations merge people and place, culture and landscape, politics and history, and rest upon a distinction between the frontier and the rest of 'mainland' India. These have been discussed at length by multiple authors, as have responses by communities from the North-east, not just in academic writing but also in the media, literature, art and popular culture. The North-east is being reconfigured in contemporary India, following a decade plus of intensified encounter between communities from the North-east and communities in mainland India through accelerated migration, changing labour markets in metropolitan India, and economic niches carved out for and by North-east communities, along with an easing (not cessation) of violence in the region, more aggressive economic and security policies captured in the Look East/Act East rhetoric, and attendant policies. The far has become near for both communities in mainland India and communities in the North-east. Sport is entangled in this recalibration.

Sporting success has drawn attention to the region as an incubator of sporting talent with potential *national* benefits. On the one hand, sport enables individuals and teams, though, arguably, not entire communities, to challenge the lingering stereotypes earlier discussed. Running, jumping, kicking, punching is a way to put one's community, territory, state 'on the map' at the national and even global level. On the other hand, sport affirms many of the stereotypes about the region and its people. Race and gender intersect in portrayals of North-east athletes who run up and down hills, eat plenty of meat, have limited restrictions on female mobility, and, often implicitly, are driven by a desperate desire to leave the region to the allegedly safer confines of metropolitan India. According to this portrayal, armed conflict and militarisation produce bodies that are fit and fearless, and these are unleashed on the rest of the Indian population to startling levels of success, especially in sports that involve violence and/or speed: boxing, weightlifting, martial arts, football. The North-east is often imagined as a resource frontier, historically and contemporaneously. This is usually taken to mean natural resources—coal, uranium, oil, rivers, crops—although it also applies to human resources, ranging from hospitality workers to entertainers to sportspeople.

In arguing that sport is entangled in the recalibration of the region, I am not suggesting that communities in the North-east only recently started playing sport, recently started travelling out of the region to participate in sporting activities, or recently started to see sport as a pathway to an alternative future. Rather, I argue that as the North-east comes to be represented in multiple ways, and with renewed complexity, sport is far more present in ways of imagining the region. This owes a great deal to the sporting success of individuals and teams from the region, but it also indicates an overall shift, a recalibration of the region in the national imaginary—a recalibration that has many parts and, as I have argued elsewhere, does not always direct attention and resources to the issues facing communities in the region (2015a: 114–15). Before discussing the significance of sport at the local level, I will focus on the most visible manifestation of the sporting frontier: the push for integration.

INTEGRATION

Attempts to better integrate the North-east and its communities into the Indian national whole have had an erratic and varied history. Arguably, the last half-decade has seen a more aggressive and overt push for integration from the centre, epitomised by Prime Minister Modi's visits to various North-east states in the months leading up to, and following, the 2014 election; the very public memorials for murdered Arunachal Pradesh student Nido Tania in Delhi; the felicitation of model North-easterners, such as Mary Kom; the formation of the Bezbaruah Committee in 2014 to address racial discrimination and violence; and the flawed 'Eye am Indian' campaign that sought to promote inclusion by encouraging the adoption of overtly racist mimicry of the epicantic fold.[1] There have also been adjacent market-led initiatives that produce and reflect integration initiatives, including the consideration of the North-east as an untapped market for Indian capital, and the consequent proliferation of its symbols and objects throughout the region.

Integration is a two-way conversation. As debates on race and racial discrimination have become more common in India, communities in the North-east have been more vocal about being accepted and being treated as Indian citizens. This is often presented

Wishing Manipuri athletes luck in the 2012 Olympics. Imphal. Photo: D. McDuie-Ra, 2012.

simply as recognition; recognising (ethnic and racial) difference will produce an acceptance of citizenship. Far less attention is given to the ways by which individuals and communities resist integration in everyday acts and the complexities of citizenship for many communities in the North-east. Rather, the issue has become one of identifying the best paths to integration, not on whether integration is desired in the first place. Sport is integral to the ways integration is conducted and imagined.

There are many different carriers of integration through sport between the North-east and mainland India. Mary Kom is an obvious focus. Following her 2012 Olympic success, Mary Kom can be considered 'as a singular figure, representing not only her own ethnic group, but an entire region of diverse ethnic communities long considered (and self-identifying) as outside the boundaries of the Indian nation' (McDuie-Ra, 2015b: 305). In my previous work on her cultural significance, I compared her image and its deployment with that of Irom Sharmila, another prominent woman from Manipur who, at the time, had been on a hunger strike against the Armed Forces Special Powers Act 1958 (AFSPA). Sharmila's 'wasting body, protesting the violence of the Indian state, contrasts with Mary's fit and active body, furthering the glory of the same India. One evokes India's shame, the other Indian pride' (ibid.: 319). Aside from the politics around her deployment as an 'ideal North-easterner', especially during the so-called 2012 exodus,[2] and the erasure of her ethnicity in the casting of Priyanka Chopra to play her on screen, Mary Kom represents both the pathway to national success that other athletes from the North-east should emulate, and the existence of a sporting frontier that requires attention and incubation. Kom's success cleanses the frontier of violence, of anti-India sentiment, and hints at the possibility of harmony. Critically, harmony is imagined nationally. There is little sense in the integration narratives that sporting success may heal local violence and tensions between, say, tribal and non-tribal communities in Manipur (or even between tribal communities). Sporting success animates ideals of integration between specific territorial units: India and its frontier.

Football is another crucial carrier of integration, though its contours are different; it is a more situated encounter. The success of teams and players representing sub-national territorial units in national competitions does not only draw attention to the athletes, but to the polities they represent. In other words, it helps put patches of the North-east on the map, as it were. Aizawl FC's victory in the 2017 I-League was a remarkable achievement, but one also layered with geopolitical significance. The club has only been professional since 2012, and only in the first division of the I-League since 2015, but has a history dating to 1984. The majority of its players are from Mizoram and surrounding territories and the club has a distinctive grass-roots identity, in contrast to, say, the much more superficial (and arguably cynical) North-east United FC in the Indian Superleague. Aizawl FC's victory came just over 30 years after the Mizo Accord was signed between the Mizo National Front and the Government of India, officially ending two decades of armed struggle punctuated by remarkable instances of state violence against its own citizens, including bombing and 'grouping' of villages. It is interesting to note that in the same year, NEROCA (a club developed from the socio-cultural organisation known as the North Eastern Re-Organising Cultural Association), an Imphal-based team with over 50 years of history, won the second division title and will join the 2018 first division.

Football, in general, is an interesting arena for recalibrating the territorial heartlands of India. Aizawl FC, NEROCA and Shillong Lajong make up a third of the I-League teams for 2017–2018, and all three clubs have deep local roots, mirroring the success of Goan and other south Indian clubs. Players from the North-east play throughout India and beyond; some, such as Jeje Lalpekhlua, receive international recognition and opportunities. Yet, it is the success of football teams from the North-east in flagship national competitions that counters the stereotype of a backward and undeveloped region while, simultaneously, reinforcing the notion of a sporting frontier: an incubator of rare talent. Aizawl, Mizoram and the North-east are 'on the map' for talent shown kicking a ball, but little else.

A third, though less visible, carrier of integration through sport can be read in attempts to expand sports popular in mainland India to the North-east. This reverses the flows discussed in the previous two examples. The case of cricket in Nagaland is perhaps most illustrative. Its epicentre is the new day–night cricket stadium at Sovima in Dimapur. The entrance features an interpretation of a Naga village gate, made from concrete and bamboo, with a buffalo motif. The site features six massive towers that soar into the sky, with 60 or so spotlights on each. Stadium seating stands on the northern edge of the ground overlook the slightly misshapen field. At the southern end of the ground is the adjacent Nagaland Cricket Academy, housed in a three-storey glass and concrete box, with a cement reference to a *morung* entrance attached to the front. A plaque informs that the complex was opened in 2012 by the President of the Board of Control for Cricket in India (BCCI), who at the time was also the Union Minister for Agriculture, in the presence of the (then) Chief Minister of Nagaland Neiphiu Rio, also President of the Nagaland Cricket Association. The entire complex is remarkable in a city desperately short of sporting facilities, where the existing stadium in Oriental Colony is more useful for learning to drive than exercise, and where cricket is far less popular than football, basketball and just about any other sport imaginable.

In 2016, Rio appealed to the BCCI to pay more attention to Nagaland. He stated: 'Cricket binds the country, it is like a religion. It integrates the country and we should be made part of it' (Samyal, 2016). With the national body eager to promote the game on the frontier, there are opportunities to access funds and enrol Nagaland in national and international cricket circuits. But the stadium also symbolises the desire to be accepted as part of India. Located on the edge of the so-called Beverley Hills of Nagaland, the stadium is

Nagaland Cricket Stadium gate. Sovima (Dimapur). Photo: D. McDuie-Ra, 2017.

nestled among the mansions of the political elite, many of whom have made their fortunes through appropriating state funds—elites likely buoyed by the idea of teams from India coming to play cricket in their backyard. Yet, the stadium is also on the road to Camp Hebron, the ceasefire camp on the outskirts of the city. Former insurgents and their families, who have fought against the Indian state, have to pass by this structure—and its fawning gesture to Indian sporting and political cultures—on their way to and from Dimapur. Perhaps the most ironic moment comes for BCCI officials visiting the stadium and returning to the city, as they pass through a gate several kilometres closer to the city that reads 'Kuknalim', the rallying cry of the Naga movement.

OPPORTUNITY

In the North-east, sport is tied to aspirations, to the idea of 'making it' locally and, perhaps, nationally. Making it is not simply about mobility; it is about finding a way to make a life, to have an identity as a 'somebody' and as a valued member of a community. While this is true in many contexts, in parts of the North-east badly affected by violence and militarisation with limited livelihood opportunities and the growing normalisation of migration as one of the few ways to make a living, sport can be a way to stay rooted. It is also a way to stay out of trouble or to emerge from it, especially in communities affected by substance abuse and trauma.

Take, for instance, a Saturday morning at Khuman Lampak Sports Complex in Imphal. At first glance, the now 17-year-old complex appears a shabby mix of construction debris, makeshift shelters and dilapidated sections of buildings. Yet the complex is a hive of activity, especially on early weekend mornings. Children and young adults from Manipur's different communities can be seen jogging, stretching and training for various sports. Almost all wear the ubiquitous training tracksuit with MANIPUR emblazoned on the back in various shades. Billboards in the complex feature famous Manipuri athletes: hockey players, footballers, boxers, weightlifters and archers. Inside, athletes from all over the state come to train, many housed in nearby dormitories. Manipur sporting teams comprise members of all the state's ethnic groups: significant, given the fissures and violence that have shaped inter-ethnic relations since the 1990s. Residents of Imphal also come to the complex for organised competitions, and to exercise. Parents and social organisations encourage sports to try to keep young people 'off the streets' and away from underground groups and out of the path of the Indian armed forces. Former athletes work as coaches and run training academies that recruit children and youth to train for state teams. Manipur has a severe narcotics problem owing to unemployment, post-traumatic stress and narcotics trafficking through the state. Sport is used extensively in rehabilitation from narcotics addiction by scores of rehabilitation clinics in Imphal. Furthermore, an interest in sport by children and teenagers is taken as a way of avoiding narcotics addiction through distraction, goal setting and exposure to positive role models. It does not always work, but it is integral to ways of mentoring and parenting young people.

Sport is also a legitimate pathway to employment in a region with limited options. This includes successful athletes being able to make a living outside the state and as returnee athletes, working as coaches and trainers, and, more importantly, sport provides the opportunity for recruitment into the state police and other government posts. This is not restricted to famous athletes, and sport has become a pathway to all kinds of jobs and is encouraged as a way to make things happen in a context where conventional pathways can be blocked. This is especially attractive for members of poorer families unable to send their children outside Manipur for education.

Similar scenes are repeated in sports grounds, indoor stadiums and improvised pitches all over the region. There are two further points to make here about sport in the North-east itself. First, the focus on those who 'make it' at the national or global levels overlooks the smaller scale mobility enabled through sports: the opportunity to spend a few months or a few years in a state capital or

Improvising a football pitch for 3-a-side tournament. Imphal. Photo: D. McDuie-Ra, 2012.

DUNCAN MCDUIE-RA : INDIA'S SPORTING FRONTIER

district headquarters; the opportunity to take trips to tournaments in towns and cities in mainland India; and the opportunity to have schooling, training or tuition paid. Second, the notion of the sporting frontier draws attention to the potential contributions of athletes from the North-east to sports that have an infrastructure and a support base in mainland India. However, there are other sports that enjoy widespread popularity at the frontier, but which do not show up at the national level. These include conventional sports and so-called action sports that do not require organisation such as BMX (bicycle motocross), skateboarding, breakdancing (B-Boying) and parkour—all of which can be witnessed in the suburbs and peripheries of the urban North-east, often by groups of young women and men who learn techniques through videos on the Internet and then put them into practice, even making their own videos that are posted and shared. Action sports, especially skateboarding, are tied to cultures of delinquency and rebellion— even as they have become more accepted as mainstream sports. Here, the appeal is not mobility but identity; ways of being that have virtually no connection to mainland India but, rather, to the urban environments of the United States, Australia and north Asia.

A RACIAL NICHE?

To close this paper, I will explore whether being good at sport changes anything for communities in the North-east, especially for individuals who cannot run, punch, jump or kick. On the one hand, it does. Success in sport draws focus to parts of the region that are unknown or ignored in the rest of India and even on the frontier itself. Sport is a mechanism for redemption for communities cast as backward, disloyal and anti-India. It is a pathway to, and sometimes evidence of, integration and inclusion of communities from outside the Indian national and territorial imaginary. For many people in the North-east, sporting success is a way of putting their homelands and communities on the map, of acceptance, of generating good news, of portraying them as willing participants in national life. Yet, it is a very particular type of inclusion. North-eastern athletes fit a racial niche. Their success is evidence of difference: diet, climate and gender relations, mixed with conditions of desperation. Sport compounds, rather than challenges, stereotypes about the region and the women and men who call it home. Race drives these stereotypes, and physicality remains fundamental to the livelihood opportunities available to many men, and especially women, from the region: entertainment, hospitality and service industries that relate to their appearance alongside sport that emphasises fierce, martial bodies. It is also a particular form of territorial recognition. Sporting success helps to enrol the frontier into a more cohesive idea of Indian Territory, into the inviolable idea of sovereign India.

On the other hand, sporting success has changed little for those living their everyday lives in the North-east. The conditions that make sport so attractive are rarely mentioned in accounts of the sporting frontier, except perhaps to highlight against-the-odds stories of triumph. This raises a further question as to whether sporting success erases the (varied) politics of the North-east, which is difficult to answer definitively. However, the most pressing issues facing communities in the North-east—land, natural resource extraction and profiteering, territorial control—particularly with regard to in-migration, autonomy, extortion, corruption, human rights abuse, post-conflict social reconstruction and reconciliation, are distant from celebrations of sporting success. This is where the North-east departs somewhat from other contexts where ethnic minority communities and recalcitrant territories are enrolled into national consciousness through sport. There has not been, for example, any overt protest at the national or global level by an athlete from the North-east over AFSPA. There are many possible explanations for this, including the relative disunity amongst communities in the North-east, the perilous position of North-eastern athletes in national and global arenas; there is just too much to lose, the reality that many of the best athletes from the region spend a great deal of their lives outside it, and that statements uttered may not always be heard. In his account of the victorious Manipur women's football team in the 11th Women's National Football Championship in 2003, Mills suggests a banner held by a member of the team, reading 'Manipur rules, We're #1', is perhaps a statement of resistance to India and an assertion of ethno-nationalist identity (2006: 73), although without further evidence it is difficult to tell from that single banner.

Perhaps the issue is the arena, the space, or the scale where politics is sought and read. At the local level, sporting competitions *are* spaces for political statements. Sport has been part of reconciliation between different tribes and factions after divisive episodes of violence. In Nagaland, football has been a tactic in reconciliation in various ways, including the 2008 match between Naga civil society groups and members of different armed factions held in Chiang Mai, Thailand, where talks were taking place, and later the same year in Kohima. A further case in point is the annual 5th Dr. T. Ao Memorial Football Tournament in Aizawl in February 2014. Coming just weeks after Nido Tania's murder in Delhi, the tournament features the senior men's football teams from the North-east states and is a major pan-North-east event. Ministers, officials and guests from all over the region attend, along with the players themselves, and groups of travelling supporters. The field in Aizawl is made from artificial turf, can be lit up at night, and sits close to the top of a hill *inside* the Assam Rifles headquarters in the centre of the city. Despite being held within an army base, the tournament has a festive atmosphere.

The stadium is built on three sides of the field and a steep wall bounds the fourth side, where the hillside has been cut away to level the ground for the field. All seats in the stadium have a view of this wall as they watch the action on the field. On the wall, and under the floodlights, was an enormous portrait of Nido Tania with 'Justice

Practice before kick-off at the Dr. T. Ao Memorial Championship. Aizawl. Photo: D. McDuie-Ra, 2014.

for Nido Tania' written underneath. At the flagship tournament for North-eastern sports, Nido's murder provided a source of solidarity: shared outrage, shared marginality, shared mourning. The banner depicted Nido as 'one of us', the 'us' being North-easterners and the 'them' being the perpetrators and the justice system that faltered. It is also significant that the Arunachal Pradesh team, the team from Nido's home state, was not at the tournament. Nido was depicted as someone from the hills, the frontier, the North-east, not simply someone from Arunachal Pradesh, or the Nishi tribe. Sport can be a venue for politics, but much of this takes place away from the national gaze.

Sporting success has put the North-east 'on the map'. The notion of the sporting frontier and the success of athletes and individuals has put the North-east in the limelight. It has encouraged the connection between sport and integration in mainland India, and on the frontier as well. Locally, it has opened up the possibility of greater mobility and livelihood opportunities. For those who do not excel at running, ball-sports, boxing, weightlifting or martial arts, and for those those who try but fall short, or those who begin a career and burnout, life back on the frontier is hardly changed by their success. There may be improved facilities, new coaches, greater expectations, and new inklings of possibility for lives changed through sport, but there is still AFPSA, military occupation, limited livelihood options, landscapes ruined by extraction, and memories of trauma and brutality. Members of North-east communities still feel racial discrimination, disproportionate levels of sexual harassment and the burden of crushing stereotypes—both at home and in metropolitan India. To celebrate the benefits of sporting success without attention to everything unchanged is to make only partial use of the sports–race–society nexus in understanding contemporary India, its frontier and the recalibration of the two.

◆

NOTES

1. See McDuie-Ra (2015a: 82–103) for a more detailed account of the various integration initiatives mentioned here.

2. The exodus refers to the return of North-east migrants to the frontier from various Indian cities in August 2012, following incidents of racially targeted

violence, allegedly in retaliation for violence against Bengali-speaking Muslims in Assam. For details, see McDuie-Ra (2015a: 43–52).

REFERENCES

Carrington, Ben. 2013. 'The Critical Sociology of Race and Sport: The First Fifty Years', *Annual Review of Sociology*, 39 (1): 379–98.

Creak, Simon. 2015. *Embodied Nation: Sport, Masculinity, and the Making of Modern Laos*. Honolulu: University of Hawai'i Press.

Mills, James H. 2006. '"Manipur Rules Here": Gender, Politics, and Sport in an Asian Border Zone', *Journal of Sport and Social Issues*, 30 (1): 62–78.

McDuie-Ra, Duncan. 2015a. *Debating Race in Contemporary India*. New York/ Basingstoke: Palgrave MacMillan.

———. 2015b. '"Is India Racist?": Murder, Migration and Mary Kom', *South Asia: Journal of South Asian Studies*, 38 (2): 304–19.

Samyal, Sanjjeev. 2016. 'Major Hurdles in Bid to bring North-east into National Cricket Mainstream', *Hindustan Times*, 17 May.

◆◆

REINFORCING DIFFERENCE
The History of Women's Involvement in Physical Activity in India

PAYOSHNI
MITRA

O n 1 August 1911, the *Manchester Guardian* reported:

> There is one person in Calcutta to whom the remarkable win of
> a Bengali football team over a crack British regiment will bring a
> lively satisfaction. This is Miss Tagore (Mrs. Dutta). It is mainly
> due to Miss Tagore that the Bengalis have taken to European
> sports at all. She alone was responsible for the great athletic
> movement among the gentle youth of Bengal, which in its
> exaggerated form took the character of the 'Bengali Volunteers'
> of whom so much was heard during the partition agitation. Miss
> Tagore belongs to the great progressive house of Tagore, the first
> family in Bengal seriously to embrace the Brahma Samaj schism
> of Hinduism. She had been carefully educated and it was from
> reading the works of Rudyard Kipling that she conceived the
> idea of introducing her countrymen to an active participation in
> field sports. She organised a gymnasium for the boys of her own
> family, and then other families instituted similar centres, until
> it became quite common in Bengal to see native youths playing
> cricket or football.[1]

This report was published after Mohun Bagan, one of the oldest and
most famous football clubs in India, scripted its famous victory in the
IFA (Indian Football Association) Shield, beating the East Yorkshire
Regiment, an English team, on 29 July 1911. A sport like football,
which was not yet of great sociopolitical significance in Indian
life, had, for the first time, given colonised Indians much-needed

psychological assurance. It was a remarkable victory for Indians and especially for the Bengali, who was stereotyped as a man of 'sedentary' pursuits and 'delicate' limbs. But what did a certain Miss Tagore have to do with it? Who was this Miss Tagore who started the great athletic movement in late 19th and early 20th century Bengal?

The Miss Tagore referred to in the report was certainly Miss Sarala Devi Ghoshal, who later became Sarala Devi Chaudhurani after marriage to Rambhuj Dutta Chaudhuri. The London correspondent of the *Manchester Guardian*—who, according to Sarala Devi, was one Mr. Radcliffe, former editor of *The Statesman*, Calcutta—mistook her for 'Miss Tagore' as she was related to the eminent Tagore family through her mother, the poet Rabindranath's elder sister, Swarnakumari. At a time when the lives of women in India were still restricted to the *antahpur* (indoors), the English press thought the happiest person on that victorious day was Sarala Devi, a Bengali woman. And, indeed, they may well have been right. Sarala Devi had long worked hard to erase the stigma of physical frailty from the public image of ordinary Bengali youth. She dedicated her initial life, especially her life before marriage, to cultivating a culture of physical fitness and strength among Bengali youth, something that, according to the *Manchester Guardian,* was the equivalent of an athletic movement in Bengal.

Sarala Devi initiated the *Birashtami Utsab* (1902) and the *Pratapaditya Utsab* (1903) in order to reinvent the heroic quality of the Bengali man and defy the British-made stereotype of a vulnerable Bengali male. Her writings in the journal *Bharati*, including 'Byayamcharcha' (physical exercise) and 'Bilati Ghushi Bonam Deshi Kil' (a Native Cuff versus a British Punch), were all intended to inspire the 'frail' Bengali to acquire strength through physical training. Sarala Devi engaged herself in building *akharas* (gymnasia) and supporting boys' associations in order to fulfil the duties of an ideal woman, the resurgent mother of colonised sons. During the Swadeshi movement and later, luminaries like Vivekananda and others emphasised the Hindu concept of glorious motherhood. Some scholars argue that Sarala Devi's project too carried forward the idea of the glorious Indian mother.

◆◆◆

Before marriage, when she had devoted most of her time to inspiring the Bengali male to be physically active and challenge the British-made stereotype of Bengalis, she had written vividly on Indian and Bengali women. But her most important work with women started after she was married. Throughout her life, Sarala Devi appears to have had an unflinching faith in the power of women. To quote Bharati Ray:

> For Sarala, woman-power was real. In an article entitled 'Ramanir Karya' (The Duties of Women), published in the journal *Suprabhat*, edited by Kumudini Mitra, she argued that women were the driving force in society, men merely the machine.[2]

Yet, despite her great confidence in the womenfolk, Sarala Devi never feels the need for women to be physically strong. There is a strange denial of the female body, as if it is incapable of demonstrating extraordinary physical strength. The one reference to the necessity of physical exercise for women is an account of her introduction of dance to middle-class households:

> Today in every house, in every school, at every meeting, girls dancing is a common sight. In those days, even taking a couple of rhythmic steps on stage was frowned upon. Once, with a lot of trepidation, I taught some young girls a bare semblance of rhythmic movements while Rabindranath's lyric: 'Come dear friends, let us dance together holding hands and singing songs', was being presented.[3]

After marriage, she dedicated herself to advancing the lives of women in India and especially in the Punjab, but her focus was on educating them. She paid scant importance to physical education for women.

Even though her actions had defied the conventions of her time, she was very much aware of her limits. Still, it is interesting to observe a woman leader like her who wrote endlessly, embraced politics, emphasised strength and physical resistance, encouraged the culture of the body, and inspired thousands of young men in Bengal to take up physical exercise and sport seriously. Sarala Devi's emphasis on the need for the younger generation to build a strong body is to be seen in very few nationalist leaders of the time. Swami Vivekananda recognised the importance of physical strength and endurance, but his main emphasis was on spirituality. Vivekananda's ideal woman was also the 'mother'. In a lecture delivered in California,[4] he expressed his disapproval of Western/ American women's lives and beliefs, and spoke highly of the concept of glorious motherhood in Indian Hindu society. There was a typical denial of the body, and bodily needs and activities, when it came to Indian women. While he emphasised spiritual masculinity, he also recognised the need for men to build strong bodies as he repeatedly pointed out the importance of *Karmayoga*.[5] But, besides the few references to the hard work that Indian rural women have to engage in as part of their household duties, he never paid attention to physical strength, or the need for it, in women. It seemed as if every ounce of an Indian woman's energy was to be directed towards 'mothering' her child.

◆◆◆

Many pamphlets and books from the late 19th and early 20th centuries reveal how women's education and extra-curricular activities were designed to create a good Indian woman— housekeeper and mother. The *Encyclopedia of Indian Physical Culture*,[6] written as late as 1950, was subtitled 'A comprehensive survey of [the] Physical Education in India profusely illustrating various activities of physical culture, games, exercises, etc., as handed over to us from our forefathers and practiced in India'.

Like most other similar books of the time, it discusses physical education for men and boys. However, unlike most of them, a separate chapter is dedicated to girls and women. In 'Games Peculiar to Girls and Ladies', written by Laxmibai Mujumdar, games and exercises demonstrated through pictures, and detailed descriptions are notably similar. None of them requires free and uncontrolled movement. In 'cat and mouse', an elderly woman as the middle player controls the movement of the other two younger players. One game is called 'cradle', unquestionably reminding us of the concepts of motherhood and mothering that are traditionally considered central to a woman's life. Another game suggests running to the corners of a pillared courtyard, thus trying to work within regulated space. Yet another game—'lock and key'—suggests moments of 'no movement', of restriction or stasis, controlled externally. The entire chapter points to a very important fact of Indian girls' and women's lives, and their access to physical activity and games. Interestingly, most of these games restrict one's movements: either by drawing a line, the over-stepping of which indicates that the game is lost; or by touch, so that if one is touched by the 'thief', who is chosen by a process of elimination, one loses the game too. Therefore, all these games in a way try to teach the girls a lesson—the ideal of controlled action.

This is not a rarity, as such practices may be seen time and again in our history. The role of women was restricted mostly to housekeeping and mothering, and whenever they had to exert themselves, it was for the sake of the family or the nation. Innumerable examples abound of women doing physically demanding household work, such as pounding corn in a mortar, fetching water from afar, churning buttermilk, washing heavy clothes, or cleaning utensils. But the concept of physically exerting oneself for the sake of physical activity or enjoyment is mostly absent among women in Indian tradition. Even individuals and their projects, which were designed to re-establish the culture of physical activity, fitness and strength—projects that appeared to be more or less liberal—tried to conform to the norm by directing women's programmes towards building better housekeepers and mothers.

In 1905, Sarala Devi outlined a scheme for an ideal girls' school in India. In it she revealed her unlikely approval of this notion of housekeeping as central to a girl's development. Not only did she think that women needed the support of a man's physical strength and intelligence, she also believed that women were naturally backward and helpless (Goshal, 1901: 4).

> Of course it is not possible to do away altogether with the weakness and helplessness of women. But it is the duty of every sensible member of human society to try and effect as much improvement in this direction as lies in his power (ibid.: 5).

It was probably with this duty in mind that she wrote *A Scheme for an Indian Girls' School*. While the preliminary educational curriculum would be more or less similar to that of any boys' school, she believed that a girls' school ought to teach its students arts that would be of daily use to them 'in their future domestic life'. The list included quilt-stitching, carving stone-moulds for domestic purposes, *alipaná* (sacred motifs/paintings), lessons in singing, cooking, nursing the sick, an English education—especially the art of conversing in English—Hindi, Urdu and Sanskrit in higher classes, *bratas* (taking of vows), the celebration of national festivals, housekeeping, taking charge of a younger girl in school by a senior girl, among others. It also included certain games. To quote:

> They will also be taught any suitable games for girls that may be extant amongst the Marhattas, the Guzrathis or any other Indian race—especially such as tend to promote the grace of the figure by due exercise of all the limbs (ibid.: 15–16).

◆◆◆

The scheme that Sarala Devi framed, therefore, did not offer anything unconventional. This emphasis on mental faculties, and the disregard for physical strength and exercise, could be seen in most Indian schools, especially in Bengal. If the history of physical education in the schools of Bengal is revisited, it may be observed that for more than a century the problems have been more or less the same. Certainly, there was a resurgence of physical education during the nationalist movement, but it gradually died out with time after India's independence. Physical education had always received lower preference, as the focus of school education had at all times been about the nurture of mental faculties. Although some physical education accounts of 1911–1912 reported gradual improvements in facilities for girls in European schools, reports of Indian schools in the years to follow highlight the need for playgrounds and other facilities and equipment, the absence of trained instructors, and a lack of genuine interest in fitting physical education into the curriculum. In a speech at the 27th meeting of the Social Study Society of Calcutta on 20 February 1918, Manindra Chandra Sinha said:

> Next, let us take the need of physical development. Anyone who has had a cursory view of things will tell you that our schools are

overcrowded and very often are located in unhealthy surroundings
and ill-ventilated rooms. With all these disadvantages, the boys are
forced to wade through books after books till their brains are filled
with undigested items of knowledge of little value to themselves,
and of less use to those who come in contact with them.

Before they are forty, which by the best savants is considered the
prime of life, they slip into the sixth age, so picturesquely described
by the Bard as, 'shifting into the lean and slippered pantaloon
with spectacles on nose and pouch on side'. Before the Bengali is fifty-
five he is already 'sans teeth, sans eyes, sans taste, sans everything'.[7]

Sinha also tried to emphasise the necessity and importance of the
Boy Scouts movement among Indians. This brings us to another
very important movement in the history of women's involvement in
physical activity and sport in India: the Girl Guides movement.

◆◆◆

The first Girl Guides Company was set up in 1911 by Dr. Cullen
in Jabalpur, Madhya Pradesh, two years after the Scout movement
came to India. As in the case of Boy Scouts, only English and Anglo-
Indian girls were admitted in the initial years. In the next two years,
the Girl Guides movement reached Calcutta and started expanding
in and around the city. There were as many as 14 such groups in
Calcutta and Howrah by 1914. The first Indian Guide company
got under way in 1916 in Pune. In 1920, Abala Bose became the
first-ever Indian woman to be appointed Guide Commissioner.
Janet Aldis, while recalling her experiences in India in the early 20th
century, wrote *A Girl Guide Captain in India*. In a chapter entitled 'We
go to Madras', she writes:

> We are packed pretty tightly in our carriages, and as we creep down
> the mountains we collect companies. At one station we were joined
> by half a dozen Indian Girl Guides and their Captain, from the
> Zenana Orphanage. It must be a great adventure for them; but they
> do not give any outward sign of the excitement that must be stirring
> inside. They sit as demure as mice, enveloped in their pretty *saris* of
> blue and white (1924: 198).

This description, however demeaning and patronising, also indicates the attitude of Girl Guides in India, which conformed to the ideal of Indian womanhood. The book ends with a quote from Sir Robert Baden-Powell's *Indian Memoirs* (1915):

> Also the Girl Guides have now made a great start in India, a promise to exercise a most valuable influence in the education of girls in that country. The principles in which they are trained are very much the same as those which guides the education of the Boy Scouts, but the details are those which apply to womanhood, in the shape of nursing and house-keeping, and the many details connected therewith (ibid.: 252).

This emphasis on nursing and housekeeping in the case of girls is found throughout our history. For example, while a Boy Scout's oath framed him as one whose priority is God and the King and the people,[8] the focus of the Bluebird's oath—a junior branch of the Girl Guides—was on the people at home, along with God and the King–Emperor.[9] *The Bluebird Book* is the story of a young girl, Nillawa, who learns through her adventures with the Bluebird how to 'sweep and cook and look after our baby' and be happy by being 'the most useful housewife'.[10] In spite of being a movement that upheld the need for physical activity, the Guide movement too tried to create perfect housekeepers and housewives. Consequently, these movements and initiatives created and perpetuated a woman-specific philosophy of sport and physical education that recommended moderation and control as vital to women's physical activity. In short, it was a deeply gendered enterprise that reinforced the inscription of gender roles in every walk of life. Movements such as the Girl Guides failed to forge a new identity for girls in early or mid-20th century India, and certainly did not liberate them from their gendered destinies.

◆

NOTES

1. See *Manchester Guardian*, 'Athletics in India', 1 August 1911.
2. See Ray (2002: 58). Bharati Ray supports her argument by quoting from 'Ramanir Karya', *Suprabhat*, Chaitra 1316 BS, 1907 AD.
3. *Ibid.* See Chaudhurani (2003), and Bhattacharya and Sen (2003: 155) for the translation.

4. See Swami Vivekananda (1982: 685–91). This is from his lecture on 18 January 1900 on the Indian woman at Shakespeare Clubhouse, Pasadena, California.

5. *Karmayoga* means the discipline of action and it is based on the teachings of the *Bhagavad Gita*, a sacred Sanskrit scriptural text of Hinduism.

6. See Mujumdar (1950: 6). 'During the last fifteen years we have been able to publish the Physical Culture Encyclopedia in Marathi in ten volumes.' He adds, 'The aim of the present publication is to make available to the English-knowing public the whole of the science of Indian physical culture.'

7. Speech delivered by Sinha (1918).

8. Rules of The Boys Scouts Association, India (Calcutta: Indian Headquarters, July 1921) cites 'the promise of the Boy Scout' as 'to do my duty to God and the King', 'to help other people at all times', 'to obey the Scout Law'.

9. See *The Bluebird Book: The Civil Guide Association of India. A Handbook for the Junior Branch of the Civil Guide Movement in India* (1932).

10. *Ibid.* p. 3.

REFERENCES

Aldis, Janet. 1924. *A Girl Guide Captain in India*. London: Office of *The Girl's Own Paper* and *The Woman's Magazine*.

Baden-Powell, Sir Robert. 1915. *Indian Memoirs*. Delhi: Gyan Books.

Chaudhurani, Sarala Devi. 2003. 'My Life Changes Track', Chapter 14 of her autobiography, *Jibaner Jharapata*, in Malini Bhattacharya and Abhijit Sen (eds.), *Talking of Power: Early Writings of Bengali Women from the Mid-Nineteenth Century to the Beginning of the Twentieth Century*. Trans. by Bhattacharya. Kolkata: Stree.

Goshal, Sarala Devi. 1901. *A Scheme for an Indian Girls' School*. Revised and reprinted from the *Journal of Mahabodhi Society*, July and September. Calcutta: Manomohan Press.

Mujumdar, D. C. (ed.) 1950. *Encyclopaedia of Indian Physical Culture*. Baroda: Good Companions.

Ray, Bharati. 2003. *Early Feminists of Colonial India*. Delhi: Oxford University Press.

Sinha, Kumar Manindra Chandra. 1918. *Bulletin of the Social Study Society of Calcutta*, vol. 27. Calcutta: The Central Press.

Vivekanada, Swami. 1900. *Vivekananda Rachanasamagra*. Kolkata: Nabapatra, 1391 BS, 1982 AD.

◆◆

FOCUS
SPORT

Pal Pillai · Ali Bharmal · www.focussports.in

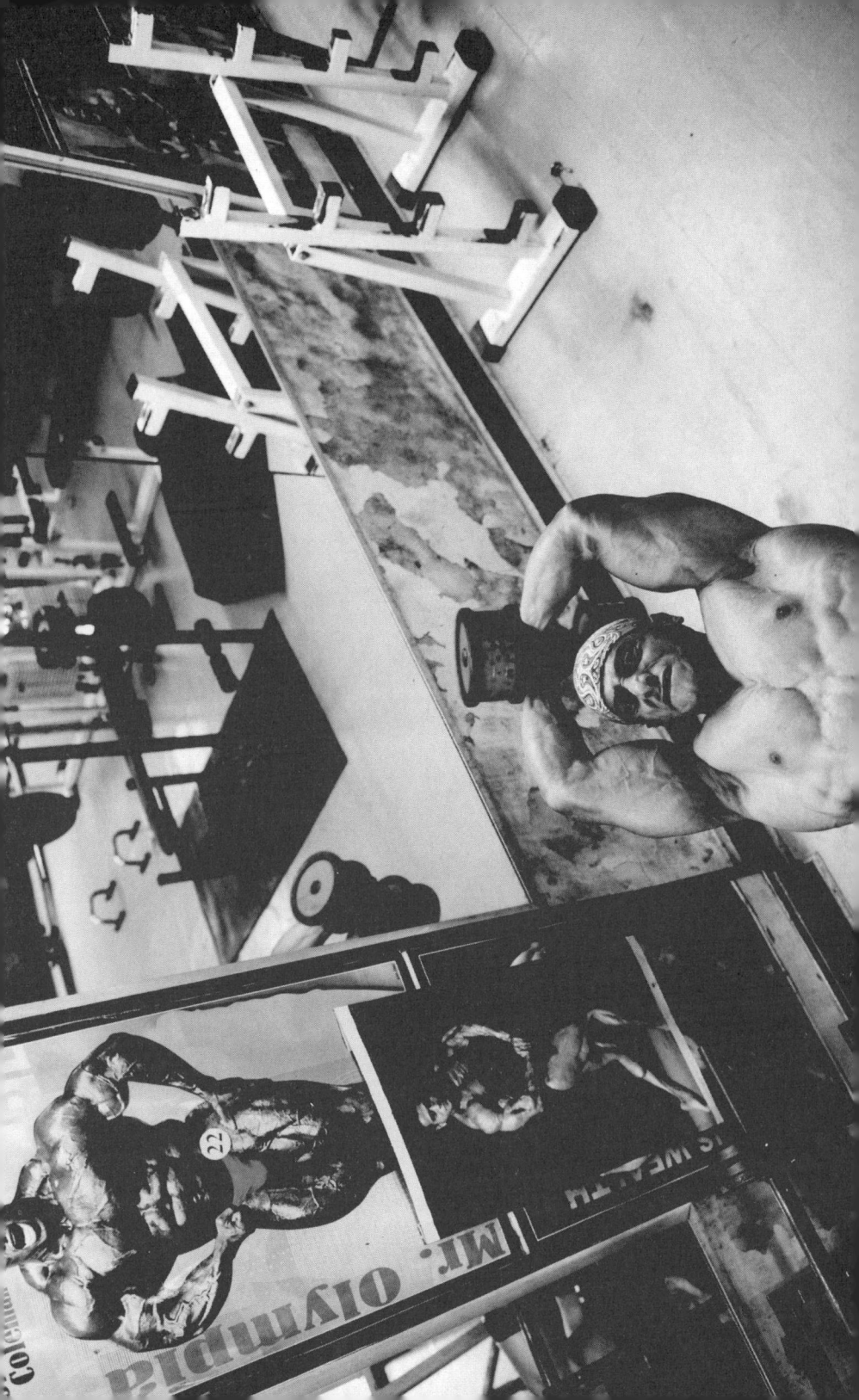

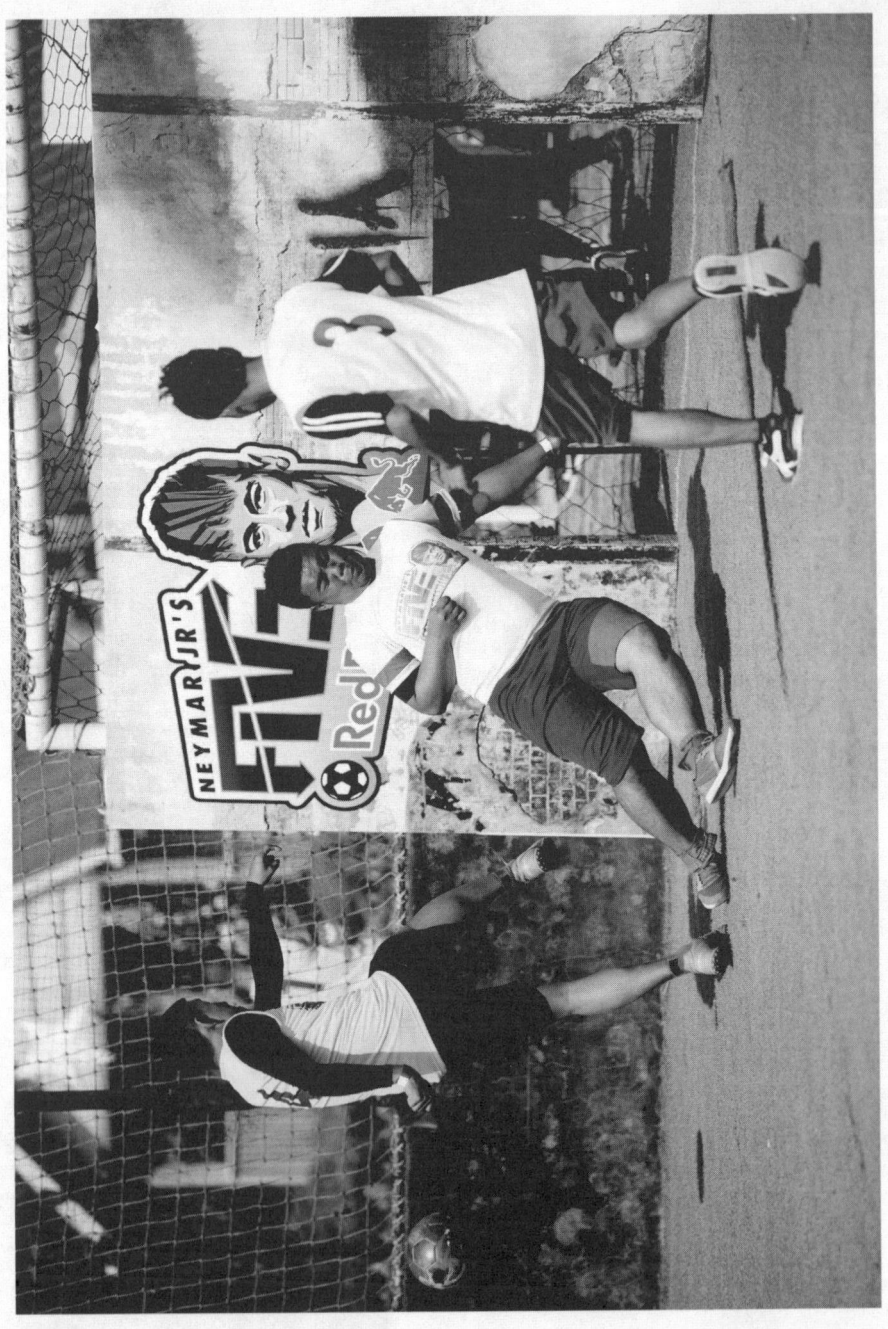

III

BEYOND CRICKET

THE DECLINE OF HOCKEY IN PAKISTAN

SHAHARYAR
M. KHAN

From the heady days of the 1950s, 1960s and early 1970s, when Pakistan epitomised the attacking style of subcontinental hockey, winning Olympic golds in Rome and Mexico, several World and Asian titles and frequently defeating India in bilateral matches, hockey in Pakistan has declined to the extent that Pakistan finds it difficult to qualify for the Olympics and the World Cup. We are regularly handed the wooden spoon in international championships, such as the Azlan Shah Cup, and find it challenging to match European and Australasian teams. The reason for this sharp decline is linked to a series of factors that included crucial rule changes that disadvantaged Asian teams, technological developments and the rise of cricket as Pakistan's favoured sport.

EARLY OLYMPIC SETBACK

The 1948 Olympics were the first in which Pakistan participated. The team selected relied heavily on pre-Partition reputations such as A. I. S. Dara who won an Olympic gold medal in 1936. Ahsan Mohammad Khan and Major Shakoor from Bhopal accompanied the squad as part of the management team. Other pre-Partition stars, such as Feroze Khan, were past their prime by 1948, and the brilliant winger S. M. Jaffer had drowned in a swimming accident. Pakistan won all its league matches but lost in the semi-finals, while India went on to win another gold medal to add to its previous victories in all the Olympics it had competed in to date: 1928, 1932 and 1936. I was in London in 1948 and, like other Pakistan supporters, was disappointed that we had failed to win a medal in our national game.

The rebuilding process was started at home with young players such as Latif-ur-Rehman (the Blackflash), Abdul Hamid, Munir Dar, Habib-ur-Rahman (the dribble wizard) and Anwar Ahmad Khan (my school teammate from hockey-mad Bhopal) taking the lead. At the 1952 Helsinki Olympics, European teams such as England, Germany and Holland, and Australia were beginning to match India in their hockey playing prowess. Pakistan did not make the finals, having lost to Holland in what was a single elimination tournament. The tide finally turned at the 1956 Melbourne Olympics where Pakistan topped their group, defeated Great Britain in the semi-finals, and were narrowly beaten by India (1–0) in the final. Anwar Ahmad Khan (centre-half), Hamidi (inside-right) and Munir Dar (full-back), regarded as stars of the future, were now matching India in skill and ability.

OLYMPIC GLORY

But it was at the Rome Olympics in 1960 that Pakistan won its first gold medal. Pakistan had stormed through the group stages, defeating Australia 3–0, and Poland and Japan 8–0 and 10–0, respectively. There were quarter- and semi-final victories against Germany and Spain before Pakistan overturned the result from four years earlier, defeating India 1–0 in the final.

The victory saw the national team elevated to super stardom and Naseer Bunda, the goal scorer in the final, became a household hero. I remember vividly on the day of the hockey final I was playing a cricket match against St. Edwards Martyrs in Oxford. I excused myself with my captain for the duration of the final. Dressed in whites, I went to the nearest house on the ground's perimetre with a TV antenna, and when the lady of the house met me at the door, I politely requested if I could watch the match on her television set. She kindly agreed, and I nearly tore up her cushion while waiting for the final whistle after Bunda had scored his famous goal. At the time I was Third Secretary at the Pakistan High Commission and when the victorious team stopped over in London, the High Commission gave them a warm welcome with musical soirees and sightseeing visits. I made lifelong friends with manager Dara, Brigadier Hamid, Brigadier Atif, Munir Dar and other stars in the team who appreciated the warm and earthy welcome we gave them in London.

GOLDEN ERA: 1970–1995

After Rome, Pakistan's successes followed in the Olympics in Mexico (1968) and Los Angeles (1984), in the World Cup (1971, 1978, 1982) and in the Asian Games. However, Pakistan's golden era began in the mid-70s with the World Cup and Hockey Champions Trophies (HCT). Pakistan regularly defeated India in bilateral series, even on India's home turf. This golden period was manned by an impregnable defence by the Dar brothers—Manzoor and Munnawwar—with two outstanding centre-halves, Anwar and Akhtar Rasool. The goal scoring was in the hands of fleet-footed Islahuddin, Samiullah (nicknamed the 'flying horse' for his devastating speed) and Hassan Sardar, aided by the superb penalty corner drag-flicker, Sohail Abbas. The strategic incursions were left to the two inside-lefts—Mohammed Shahbaz and Shahbaz Ahmad—as also Hanif Khan's precision passes at inside-left.

I remember well when posted to Foreign Office Headquarters in Islamabad in the mid-1960s and 1970s, I would regularly attend international and national hockey events. In those days, hockey was keenly supported by the public, and crowds of 20–30,000 would gather at international matches against Holland, Kenya and India. At the time, Pakistan was an outstanding team with a bevy of stars. We won most of these matches with our stars becoming household names in Pakistan, lifting the morale of the nation, especially when we defeated India. Those were heady days when hockey flourished in schools, clubs and departments.

But by the beginning of the 1990s, AstroTurf and the introduction of new laws had begun to undermine the primacy of the subcontinental style of hockey.

I recall raising a team of amateurs in Islamabad called the Potohar Panthers with retired internationals Naseer Bunda and Qamar Ali Khan; my Cambridge captain, centre-forward Colin Carruthers, posted to the British High Commission; and some Australian diplomats. Legendary cricketer Majid Khan would also play right-half for the Panthers. We usually played local club teams from Rawalpindi and I noticed the high standard of hockey in clubs at the time. Occasionally, we played against local army units, who were far too good for the journeymen Panthers, but I could see the depth of talent in Pakistan from these mid-level fixtures.

DECLINE

Then, by the late 1970s, a wave of cricket fever swept across Pakistan when television, radio and the media began to overshadow public interest in hockey. Gradually, cricket replaced hockey as the chosen sport of the people across the country, capturing the fervent attention of young and old, rich and poor. The interest in cricket increased exponentially—while hockey declined in the public eye—with Imran Khan, Zaheer Abbas and Majid Khan emerging as stars, replacing the likes of Hassan Sardar, Islahuddin and Akhter Rasool. This decline continued so that cricket, rather than hockey, was seen as the national sport, with the consequent magnetic pull of youth towards cricket. Gone were the days when one noticed young men in shorts, cycling out to their clubs, hockey sticks in hand. By the time Pakistan won the cricket World Cup in 1992, it was apparent that interest in hockey was declining in favour of cricket.

At around the same time, there began the European and Australasian countries' attempt to break the stranglehold of Asian teams. European and Australasian governing bodies took advantage of the Indo–Pakistan rivalry to push through a series of laws and rules that changed the entire strategy and flow of hockey.

First, it became mandatory to play matches on AstroTurf and not on natural grass where South Asians played hockey. The argument put forth by the Europeans was that they wanted to make hockey a faster, more spectator-friendly sport on the smooth surfaces provided by AstroTurf. They also drastically changed the laws so that, for instance, there were no 'offsides'. Attackers could place their forwards next to the defending goal-keepers from where they deflected hard hits into the goal. Long passes were encouraged, as were through passes to 'offside' attackers. Stick-work and body dodges, the hallmark of Pakistani and Indian teams, evaporated in favour of seeking penalty corners and scoring goals from them. Field goals from artistic free-flowing forwards such as Dhyan Chand, Balbir Singh, Naseer Bunda or Hamidi became rare, and the percentage of goals through penalty corners increased. The end result was that the artistry and beauty of the game was sacrificed at the altar of hard-hitting long passes that prevailed in soccer, and the deep stationing of forwards due to the 'no offside' rule.

These rules and synthetic surfaces required a player to be supremely fit, rather than one who relied on stick-work and deft body dodges to defeat a defender. A European journalist once likened playing modern hockey on AstroTurf to playing in a swamp, as the ground requires constant watering to keep the surface smooth. Tactics and fitness levels also changed to suit AstroTurf. Converting penalty corners became the primary source of goals, and artistry was sacrificed for speed and fitness. The great Anwar Ahmad Khan told me that in his time it was considered insulting to make a back-pass. Now possession requires that you constantly pass back—a la football.

Besides the controversial no offside rule (even football has an offside rule), the laws have been changed to downgrade the importance of deft approach work by forwards towards the goal. There is no obstruction penalty for placing a player's body between a defender and an attacker. Also, there is no penalty for 'back sticks', nor for the former offence of turning. All these changes reduce the importance of stick-work and body dodges in favour of speed and stamina.

This drastic change of by-laws and strategy requires vast investments in grounds with AstroTurf. They also require constant maintenance with hoses and sprinklers. For finance-starved Pakistan, importing AstroTurf has not been a priority, while European and Australian countries find it relatively easy to purchase and maintain these artificial surfaces. For instance, Pakistan has, at best, six or seven functioning AstroTurf grounds. When I visited the Netherlands I was informed that in one Rotterdam club alone there were eight! An Amsterdam club had six, where schoolchildren, women's clubs and universities could practise. The result is that this basic training and tactics of modern hockey are learned from a young age—a luxury that is completely denied to Pakistani youth, who learn their hockey on grass or *bujree* (gravel) surfaces. The Pakistani youngster still aims to achieve distinction through sheer dedication to the game, but it is a hugely uphill task. More prosperous India is doing a better job of overcoming the economic gap, but these days it also generally returns from the Olympics without a medal, which are now typically shared between Australia and the European countries with their abundant resources.

The answer to reversing this trend is for India and Pakistan to join forces and revert to playing hockey on different surfaces. Just as in tennis, we should play our hockey tournaments on natural grass. Tennis is played on a grass surface in Wimbledon, a clay court in Paris, and hard courts in the United States of America and Australia—to which players have to adjust their tactics. Why not have tournaments on grass in Delhi, Calcutta, Karachi and Lahore? Unless drastic changes are made, Pakistan and India will continue to lose out.

◆

A STORY OF TWO DIFFERENT WORLDS
Indian Hockey's Glory Run and the Unending Struggle

SUNDEEP
MISRA

t is akin to going to the moon—and then unable to create the formulae to fire the rockets once again. That is probably how we could describe India's climb down from eight Olympic golds to no medal at all since the 1980 Moscow Olympics—38 years from the time an Indian hockey team stood on the Olympic podium, let alone the colour of the metal. In fact, if every hockey fan was brutally honest with himself, the last pure Olympic gold that we minted was in Tokyo 1964, when Charanjit Singh's team beat Pakistan in the final. It has been 54 years since Tokyo. Moscow 1980 was slightly devalued as every team worth its salt stayed away because of the American boycott. India beat Spain 4–3 in the final to clinch the gold.

In the 1960s and 1970s, fans were known to say 'hockey is in India's air'. But with growing pollution in the form of bad practices and an ancient coaching system weighed down by the arrogance of illiterate hockey presidents, India is now trying to turn the wheel while others have reinvented several times over the engine that drives world hockey. The rulers of the 'hockey world' are now being ruled. Can they reclaim what was once their crown, their turf, and yet again rule over the hockey grounds of which they were once the true zamindars?

The rot set in around the 1960s—1960, to be exact. When Milkha Singh broke the world record in the 400m but could not pick up a medal as he had finished fourth, it was up to the hockey team to somehow nullify the disappointment on the track. On the hockey pitch, then played on turf, India was the Boss. However, it turned out differently. There was confidence in the Indian ranks. After all,

India had been unbeaten since 1928, except for the intervening war when the Olympics were not held. In those times, India never travelled unless it was to the Olympics where they played practice games before going into competition and winning the gold. While it is true that competition was tough, other teams did not have too much knowledge of India's game. We were an unknown entity; so when confronted with the silky wrists and skills of the Indians, it was always a lost cause for the Europeans. So if India had the ball, taking it away was by implication a mistake made by India.

When the team left for Europe, there were no signs that this tour would be ill-fated. Led by the brilliant veteran left-back Leslie Claudius, playing his fourth Olympics, it had the necessary ingredients that go into making a gold-medal winning unit. In goal was Shankar Laxman, and the forward line boasted names like Udham Singh Kullar, Charanjit Singh, R. S. Bhola and Mohinder Lal. In the half line were Govind Sawant, Joginder Singh and Jaswant Singh, while the full back was the tall and extremely talented Prithipal Singh.

India qualified for the quarter-finals after winning three league games and then came up against Australia. It was only an extra-time goal by Bhola that ensured a semi-final spot. Many years ago, in an interview, Bhola would say, 'I remember distinctly that the Australians were stopping us before we passed the ball. They were using crowding tactics. We, as a team, were used to space and the dribble, but unable to do that left us confused.' In other words, the other teams were gaining knowledge. India was reluctant to see the signs, or simply arrogant. The match against Great Britain was close, and a 16th-minute goal from Udham Singh saw India into the final. It was momentous—the first India vs. Pakistan Olympic hockey final. The final turned out to be a classic as Pakistan went ahead in the 11th minute through a goal by inside-left Naseer Bunda. India attacked furiously but could not break the rival defence, and Pakistan eventually emerged victorious. Pakistan was the King of Hockey. India, heads hung low, stood with the silver. It would be the first Indian team to lose to Pakistan in an Olympic final, or in any final, for that matter. But at that time, instead of an analysis of how we relinquished our hold on the gold, Pakistan's win was termed as a flash in the pan by the Indian Hockey Federation (IHF). Nobody was looking inwards; there were no post-mortems. To be honest, there was probably no one with an insight into the changing world of hockey to understand its problems. Worse, consumed by the defeat against Pakistan, no one noticed that Europe and Australia were meanwhile taking a different route. But the team knew they were beaten by a good side that played good offensive and brilliant defensive hockey. Hockey tours between countries were very few then. Flying was expensive, and European weather too fickle to go on long tours and encounter rain-filled days while playing matches on slippery-slick grounds. But before heading to Tokyo for the 1964 Olympic Games, the Indian team decided to tour New Zealand.

TOKYO 1964: THE LAST OF THE GREAT TEAMS

It was a dreary afternoon in Masterton, New Zealand. It had been raining continuously in Wairaarapa Province. As the Indians got off the bus and stepped onto the ground, alarm bells were ringing. The Indian captain Charanjit Singh called a team meeting and made it very clear that no player would take risks on a ground as soggy and wet as the one on which they were about to play a match with the provincial team. Looking at Prithipal and Gurbux Singh, Charanjit said, 'I don't want any injuries before we reach Tokyo. No heavy tackles, just try and clear the ball.' He also made it very clear to the forwards that they would need to hold onto the ball and make scoring opportunities.

The Indians had a good tour of New Zealand, winning all their games, and were now ready for Malaysia before flying to Tokyo. Rains greeted them in Malaysia where, after landing in Kuala Lumpur, they drove to the town of Ipoh to play a few practice games.

After resting for a day, the Indians arrived in Tokyo. The city was full of banners and Olympic preparations. They rested for a day at the Olympic Village. The hockey team had been travelling and playing now for almost a fortnight. Back in the Village, Charanjit called a meeting with coach Dharam Singh, with manager Inder Mohan Mahajan in attendance. India's first match was with Belgium and the team wanted to start off with a win. The pitch was a concern as it had been raining heavily for the last three days. However, Charanjit pointed out that the Indians had played on slippery surfaces in New Zealand and Malaysia before coming to Tokyo, and that was an advantage.

The Indians did not plan according to strategy. All tactics were in tandem with the players in their respective positions. Most coaches had not seen the teams in their pool before they came to the Olympics. But Dharam had seen Belgium at a practice game and he now passed on the wisdom to the players. 'Get the goals,' was always his mantra.

The pitch was beautiful when India lined up for its campaign opener. Flat, green, it was made for skills which the Indians had in plenty. After the first 10 minutes, it was apparent that Harbinder Singh was still unfit after his long lay-off from an injury. Bandu Patil seemed almost pedestrian, not going into empty spaces. Haripal Kaushik, one of the seniors in the team, was the only threat, playing old-school hockey, darting in and out of the Belgian defence. The first short corner came India's way midway in the first half. Prithipal's hard stinging shot entered the net, but the Australian umpire pulled up the shot for undercutting. Belgian goalkeeper Jean-Marie Buisset played a brilliant first half to keep the Indians away and maintain a goal-less scoreline.

Fortune turned India's way in the 63rd minute. Harbinder finally got through the Belgian defence, but his shot was saved by the goalkeeper at the expense of a short corner. India's fifth short corner was taken by Prithipal, who ensured the ball did not rise. It was low, all along the carpet, and hit with enough power to beat Buisset in the Belgian goal. India had the lead. Prithipal had started the Tokyo Olympic campaign with a brilliant strike. A few minutes later, Haripal held the ball long enough to draw out the defenders and slot it into a corner for the second goal. It was a messy game. But importantly, it was 2–0 in India's favour. Meanwhile, neighbour Pakistan struggled to a 1–0 victory over Japan. If Dharam Singh was worried about a scoreline, it was Australia's thumping 7–0 win over Britain.

Back in the Village, both captain and coach were worried about penalty corners, which were being disallowed. Haripal was critical of the umpiring. 'They won't allow so many goals from penalty corners,' he said. 'They won't let us score often.' Rules had been tweaked a bit. Undercutting was allowed, only if it did not constitute dangerous play. Now, who would finally take a call on 'dangerous play'? It was the umpire who would whistle, disallowing a goal. Or, as Haripal insinuated, India would not be allowed to score goals from short corners, simply because they had the world's best convertor in Prithipal.

As is apparent, rules were being changed to favour the Europeans even then. But India, stuck on a high horse that skills could alone manage the sport for them, still refused to fight for high positions in the IHF. In other words, India had no say in the international body.

Even in his room, Prithipal started practising the short corner. He would bring in the stick and touch the ball on the full. He knew he was not always undercutting the ball. But he wanted to hit it low and strong, like the opening goal against Belgium.

If the match against Belgium was average, the game against Germany was abysmal. Nothing worked. The forward line was disjointed, while the mid-field of Charanjit and Jagjit played into the hands of the Germans. Germany led. Without Prithipal the team would never have scored, and the defence would have been easily pierced. Harbinder and Mohinder's absence was probably playing on the Indians' mind—their mindset was defensive. After the break, Germany had a few chances again and twice their forwards missed after picking up rebounds off Laxman's pads. In the 53rd minute, India had a short corner. Prithipal took his time, and kept the shot low and wide of the goalkeeper to find the equaliser for India. But the hopes of India raising its game came to nothing. In reality, the quality of play deteriorated and the long whistle came as a relief. India walked off, knowing they were lucky in holding the Germans. They had given up a point, but were alive with a 1–1 draw.

India was lucky to have a rest day before taking on Spain and that could have been crucial as far as injuries went. When the team arrived at the ground, the drizzle started. The Indians hated playing in the rain. On the other hand, the Spanish seemed more energetic, eager for the match. Charanjit stepped gingerly on the ground and almost slipped. The mood was set. Psychologically, the Indians were already on the back foot.

Both teams tried to take the upper hand in the first half. After a goal-less first half, the Indians entered the ground after a pep talk from Dharam. In the second half, Spain shocked India by taking the lead. Eduardo Dualde converted a short corner, which Laxman could not even see. The play got rougher and when Prithipal undercut a shot, which hit a Spanish defender, the crowd began hooting at the Indians. In the very next minute, in a one-to-one situation, Prithipal barged into Spanish winger Amat who fell on the ground. The match was stopped for a minute and the umpires spoke to both captains. Late in the second half, Joginder was obstructed and the Japanese umpire gave a short corner to India. Prithipal's shot beat the goalkeeper but Jose Colomer, the defender on the line, held the ball and India was awarded a stroke. Mohinder converted, and India had equalised. It was a match which India would want to forget. Bad tactics, rough play, frayed tempers was all India had to show for their performance. After the match, the *Hindustan Times* reported that 'India indulged in dangerous play'. Willie, a former German centre-half, was quoted as saying, 'India taught the world how to play hockey. But here we see India playing the man instead of the ball. Nobody will have any respect for India.'

Against Canada, India played with their old confidence. They moved the ball around and with two goals from Harbinder and Prithipal, won 3–0. Pakistan had already qualified for the semi-final from the other pool while in Pool B India led with 10 points, followed by the Netherlands and Spain with nine each. Anything was possible in India's pool. India could be eliminated while the Netherlands and Spain could reach the semi-final.

There was tension in the air when the team bus arrived for the crucial match against the Netherlands. Spain had beaten Belgium 3–0, which meant an Indian defeat against the Dutch would eliminate the last Olympic silver medallist. But first they had to beat the Netherlands. India controlled the game in the first 10 minutes, winning a long and a short corner. Prithipal hit a perfect shot, which was blocked by the Dutch goalkeeper, but there was no forward to pick up the rebound. A minute later, in the 10th minute, Prithipal had another opportunity at a short corner. It was beautifully taken, the shot low and powerful enough to beat the goalkeeper. India was ahead 1–0.

The equaliser came in the 45th minute when India saved a short corner, which resulted in a long corner. Amazingly, India reacted too slowly as Dutch forward Franciscus Fiolet beat Laxman with a powerful hit.

The Dutch had a short corner in the 55th minute. There was a melee in front of the Indian goal with too many Indian and Dutch sticks all jumbled together. Suddenly, out of the blue, the Dutch inside-left Francis van't Hooft picked up the ball and shot it past Indian goalkeeper Laxman. The Dutch fans in the stands started celebrating. Even the Dutch players threw their sticks up in the air. The Indians seemed deflated, defeated, not believing what had happened. Suddenly, the whistle sounded, but not for goal. British umpire Kendrick Eaves had disallowed the goal, saying it was off-side. There was still life left in the match.

In the 60th minute, India played with 10 men as Mohinder was ordered out for dangerous play against van't Hooft. But India still attacked. Harbinder was in a wonderful scoring position when he was blocked. India had a short corner. Prithipal's shot was powerful, but it bounced off the goalkeeper's pads. V. J. Peter darted in from nowhere to shoot the ball into goal. With a few minutes left, India hung on to their 2–1 lead, and won the match and a semi-final spot.

The semi-final line-up was now Pakistan vs. Spain and India vs. Australia.

The sky was clear on 21 October 1964. The ground was dry. Only the corners were slightly wet. Anyone taking long corners had to watch out while hitting the ball. But the shock came in the 11th minute of the match when the Australians scored. Patrick Nilan found himself in the Indian circle after getting a pass from Eric Pearce to shoot past Laxman. The forwards started mounting pressure. Harbinder had a great opportunity. But even after all the hard work and drawing the goalkeeper out, he could not put the ball into an empty goal. Five corners came and went. Harbinder was once more in a one-to-one situation with the goalkeeper, but could only feebly push the ball onto the pads.

Finally, in the 22nd minute, the equaliser came India's way when Prithipal's shot beat the out-stretched goalkeeper and defender on the line. India took the lead a minute later when Harbinder's scoop was wrongly stopped by the goalkeeper, leading to a stroke by the umpire. Mohinder converted strongly. Two minutes later, Prithipal scored his second goal of the match by converting another short corner. India now led 3–1 at the break.

The Australians did try hard but were unable to break the Indian defence. For the first time in the tournament it seemed the Indian defence was unbeatable. In the other semi-final, Pakistan beat Spain 3–0 to enter the final.

It was now India vs. Pakistan in the Olympic final.

The weather had not improved on Friday morning. It had rained all Thursday. Tokyo was dripping wet. Still, fans made a beeline for the stadium. Training was almost impossible.

In the first five minutes it was apparent that both teams were not giving much away. Pakistan, with their wings, probed in the third minute, racing into the Indian circle. But the push on the wet ground was slow. India built its attacks slowly. Pakistan was better in the mid-field. At the break, both teams were goal-less.

With dark clouds hovering, light was a problem. The organisers switched on the floodlights—it was only 3 pm. India made the move in the 41st minute when Darshan Singh raced down the flank on the left, beating three defenders. His shot was saved by the Pakistani goalkeeper, Hamid, but at the expense of a short corner. As Prithipal came up, the crowd went silent. There was huge pressure on the Pakistani defence. Prithipal took his time, and let loose a lightning shot that beat Hamid and struck a Pakistani defender on the foot. As the Indians raised their hands appealing for a stroke, umpire Guust Lathouwers also pointed to the spot. Mohinder came up and flicked the ball into the left-top corner of the net. Celebrations broke out in the stands as the Indian fans started doing the bhangra.

In the next 10 minutes, Pakistan attacked relentlessly—but India held out.

The International Hockey Federation Secretary-General, Rene Frank, spoke to the media after the medal ceremony:

> I have never seen a match played with so much of tension and emotion. India deserved its victory. On the day, it was the better side. Pakistan lost its cool and thus the match. There is no doubt that India is the World Champion since 1928, except for losing in the final in 1960. You have the best talent in the world.

DESPITE TALENT, CONSISTENCY BECOMES AN ISSUE

India did have the best talent in the world; Rene Frank was not wrong about that. It was managing that talent, selected from across the country, which was the problem. India's 1964 gold glossed over the issues, which were glaring: defensive structures, diminishing strike power and an over-reliance on players like Prithipal, which would continue in the years to come. Even though India won the Asian Games gold in 1966, they were being overtaken by the Europeans who were working on the skills and understanding required to stop the multiple Olympic champions. By the time India decided its line-up for the Mexico Olympics, the team was hit by selection and captainship woes. The lack of a professional set-up ensured chaos and, for the first time in Olympic history, an Indian team with two captains arrived to defend its Olympic gold. Stuck between Prithipal and Gurbux Singh, and the stupidity shown by IHF President Ashwini Kumar, India was a disjointed side. After losing to New Zealand in the opening match and playing close games throughout the competition, Australia beat India 2–1 in the semi-finals. For the first time, an Olympic final would be played without India. And, also, for the first time, an Olympic final would have Australia in it. In later years, Australia would go on to play four more finals, winning its first Olympic gold in 2004. India would play one more final in 1980, winning gold.

By 1972, the situation had transformed so dramatically that, for the first time in Olympic history, both Pakistan and India would not win the gold. It would be Germany—then West Germany—that beat Pakistan 1–0 in Munich. Pakistan had beaten India 2–0 in the semi-final. The shift was now clear. Holland, West Germany, Australia, Spain, Great Britain and New Zealand were making big strides in breaking the hegemony of India and Pakistan.

Even talent-wise, India was losing players while Pakistan, in the late 1970s and then in the 1980s, brought out some tremendous ones. In 1975, India strung together a team led by Ajit Pal Singh, which won the first-ever World Cup, beating Pakistan 2–1 in Kuala Lumpur. The 1984 Los Angeles Olympics boasted an Indian team which, in the opinion of the Australian great Ric Charlesworth, was 'one of the best teams to have not won an Olympic medal'. But India's fifth-place finish was the start of a story that spoke of under performance rather than lifting levels to play out of their skins.

With the 1983 World Cup win in cricket, many changes took place across the sporting landscape of India. As money poured into cricket, which later led to the Indian Premier League, other sports, including hockey, suffered. Infrastructure is always the first casualty. Indian hockey, already struggling on AstroTurf, could not compete with the Europeans as the laying of artificial pitches was expensive.

While Holland, slightly smaller than the Indian state of Haryana, had 500 plus turfs, India had less than 10! Two entire generations of players played school and junior hockey on grass. Some even saw AstroTurf for the first time when they attended a national camp—it was like growing up malnourished.

In the middle and intervening years, some big defeats left India reeling. The Asian Games final defeat to Pakistan by 1–7 in New Delhi left the sport struggling, devastated, like a critically ill patient stuck in the ICU for a few years, until the junior programme started working again and the flow of players began. Pakistan, on the other hand, discovered players like Shahbaz Ahmed, Wasim Feroz, Mansoor Ahmed and Tahir Zaman, among others, and entered two consecutive World Cup finals in 1990 and 1994. They won in 1994, beating Holland in the final in Sydney. We would do well to remember that India and Pakistan had finished 12th and 11th, respectively, in the 1986 World Cup in London. Pakistan had climbed back.

The election of K. P. S. Gill, Punjab's super-cop, as President of the IHF, brought a wave of optimism. It was during Gill's tenure that India reached the Junior World Cup final in 1997 in Milton Keynes, and then won the World Cup in 2001 in Hobart, Tasmania. But on other fronts, it slipped. It failed to reach any podium finishes in the Olympics or the World Cups. By the 2008 Beijing Olympics, India had failed to qualify for the first time in its illustrious Olympic history.

Gill was sacked. In came Narinder Batra, already on the Board with Gill.

Ambitions soon changed drastically for Indian hockey. Foreign coaches of the calibre of Terry Walsh and Roelant Oltmans were brought in. Nevertheless, sackings were fast too. Walsh won India the 2014 Asian Games gold—but was sacked. Oltmans was sent packing after a Hockey World League (HWL) semi-finals campaign was derailed after losses to Canada and Malaysia. But the hunt for a semi-final spot in the World Cup and the Olympics continued.

Of late, the situation appears positive. In Graham Reid, India has a coach with proven pedigree. Reid was assistant to the great Ric Charlesworth when Australia won the 2014 World Cup. Of course, detractors would say when Reid took charge of the Australian 2016

Rio Olympic team, it crashed out in the quarterfinals; for the first time in 28 years, an Australian team didn't medal.

Reid has delivered so far taking charge after the 2018 World Cup where India lost in the quarterfinals. The improvement in the team is visible and the bench, which looked somewhat lean now sees a healthy number of more than 40 players knocking on the senior selection team door. 'We have started well in the Pro League and hopefully do well at Tokyo 2020,' said Reid, after India beat Australia in the shoot-out in the second home game of the 2020 Pro League at Bhubaneswar.

The gap between the top six teams in the world has been considerably reduced. India are now 4th in the latest FIH rankings. With many foreign coaches plying their trade across nations, skills, tactics and ideas have levelled the playing field substantially. But it is consistency that counts, and that is why the Netherlands, Australia, Germany and Belgium, especially Belgium—in the last three to four years—that has shown the necessary verve; Belgium won the 2016 Olympic silver, the 2018 World Cup and the 2019 European Championships. India needs consistency. At the 2017 Hockey World League finals, it held Australia to a draw, and then lost to England, which was a step back.

But, as in 1964, when one of the better teams was assembled in Indian hockey, it is the selection of the team that will count for Reid in Tokyo. India badly needs a podium finish at the 2020 Games. Knowing that the last time when Tokyo held the Olympic Games the Indian team won gold could be an inspiring moment for the present team. It has been 40 years since India won an Olympic gold. And as for a true, full-blooded—not devalued—Olympic competition, it has been more than half a century: 56 years, to be exact from 1964. Pedigree, form, skill, coaching, talent—everything seems to be coming together in what many believe could be the return of the old days. There is confidence, too, and momentum. Perhaps, after all these years, there could be salvation in Tokyo 2020.

◆

THE FUTURE OF INDIAN FOOTBALL

NOVY
KAPADIA

I n the two years since I wrote my article there have been drastic changes in Indian football, especially in the organisation of domestic tournaments.

The India Super League (ISL) has replaced the I League as the top-tier competition in the country as per a proposal presented by the Asian Football Confederation (AFC) after a meeting in Kuala Lumpur in October 2019. This was attended by the All India Football Federation (AIFF) officials and I-League and ISL club owners. The agenda was domestic structural reforms in India.

As per the road map, the ISL champion would also be entitled to a play-off place in the AFC Champions League, and I-League champions would participate in the secondary competition, the AFC Cup.

The key demand of I-League clubs to start the promotion-relegation system in the ISL has been shelved till 2024–25. The demand for inclusion of I-League teams with immediate effect was ignored. In the 2020–21 season, two I-League clubs will be inducted in ISL, "subject to criteria being fulfilled". These two spots may go to the popular teams, East Bengal and Mohun Bagan, as these legacy clubs have a much bigger fan following than any of the 10 ISL franchises. Also, in the 2022–23 season, the winner of the I-League could be promoted to ISL with no participation fee (range of ₹12–15 crores per annum), but will not get a share of the central revenue.

A kind of apartheid system prevails in Indian football with the I-League clubs, which regularly nurture and develop young talent, feeling neglected and unwanted. Some of the consequences are disastrous. About 30 clubs have closed down in 2011–19 and over 25 all-India tournaments have also shut shop in the last two decades. The players are also affected by this uncertainty and neglect. In a nutshell, young players, clubs and domestic tournaments have become victims of this prolonged dispute between the ISL and I-League clubs.

Meanwhile, the senior national team has also stagnated. In 2019, India played 13 matches, winning just two (both against Thailand), drawing four and losing seven. India's chances of progressing to the third round of the 2022 World Cup qualifiers are remote. In Group E of the qualifiers India is on three points from five matches, in fourth position and a point behind Afghanistan. Croatian Igor Stimac (played in the 1998 World Cup, where his country finished third) took over as national coach in May 2019, but improvement has been marginal. Approach play is better, but results have been unflattering. India struggled to draw against lowly ranked Bangladesh in Kolkata and against Afghanistan.

In the 2017–18 season, the youngsters from India's U-17 World Cup squad were drafted into the Indian Arrows team that played the I-League. Many have now been roped in by ISL franchises, but sadly most of them have either struggled to settle at their club or earn regular playing opportunities. Many of them have just stagnated or faded away. Goalkeeper Dheeraj Singh Moirangthem, who received his first call-up to the national team in November 2019 as a reserve and skipper, and central midfielder Amarjit Singh Kiyam, who made his debut against Curacao at the King's Cup Thailand in June 2019, are the only two from the U-17 squad who are in the reckoning for the senior national team.

As there is no relegation or promotion in the ISL, the basic structure is flawed. The young Indian players in the ISL teams do not know how to grind out a result and do not know how to take responsibility when playing for the country as foreigners are the main players in the franchises. Many of the Indian players at the 2019 World Cup qualifiers had limited match experience as they are mainly reserves for their franchises. Coach Stimac has rightly lamented that he is struggling to find a goalscorer, as except for Sunil Chettri none of the Indian forwards are regular starters in their ISL franchises.

◆◆◆

India shattered the record for the largest attendance at the Under–17 World Cup, with 13,47,143 spectators attending the event. This was the greatest legacy for Indian football, as it showed that the country is not just obsessed with cricket, but there are passionate fans for other sports also. Gianni Infantino, President of FIFA, who attended the final along with other FIFA executive members, was suitably impressed and said that in India the future is football.

Another positive legacy is the construction of six world-class all-seater stadia, including the Yuba Bharati Krirangan (Salt Lake stadium) in Kolkata where the matches were held. These stadia can be used to change the outlook on Indian football. Leading European clubs—Real Madrid, Barcelona, Chelsea, Manchester United and Arsenal—can now play in any one of the six cities in their pre-season summer tours. These clubs generally play in Japan, China, Malaysia and Singapore, but can now include India. This could lead to long-term TV and merchandising deals.

Thus, hosting the U–17 World Cup is India's second tryst with destiny (after qualifying for the 1950 World Cup in Brazil, but not sending a team to participate), and an opportunity that should not be wasted. India is the fifth Asian country after China, Japan, South Korea and the UAE to host the U–17 World Cup. The other nations built on the momentum of having hosted a global football event and have all made the senior World Cup finals at least once. Can India emulate them?

For nearly one week, from 6 to 12 October 2017, the U–17 Indian football team got extensive media coverage. Players became household names and received adulation from fans and ample media exposure. Spectators at the Jawaharlal Nehru Stadium, Delhi, chanted the names of their heroes: goalkeeper Dheeraj Moirangthem; Anwar Ali; Boris Thangjam; Jitendra Singh; Komal Thatal, with his fancy hair style; and the six-foot-tall goal scorer, Jeakson Thounaojam. A product of the Minerva Football Academy, Punjab, Jeakson headed in a corner kick against Colombia, a match India lost 1–2.

The humble backgrounds of the players were highlighted; their hobbies; their football heroes (Cristiano Ronaldo was the most popular, with seven of the Indian squad listing him as their icon); and the clubs they supported (Real Madrid was the team of choice, with 12 saying they backed the current European and La Liga champions, and only four supported Barcelona) were all written about.

The Indian team played gallantly in the Group A matches against superior opposition, lost 0–3 to the United States, 1–2 to Colombia and 0–4 to Ghana. Creditably, they were not overawed and made a positive impression. The spirited displays by the team aroused optimism for the future, which is yet another positive legacy. Several of the U–17 team were selected for the Asian U–19 qualifiers in Saudi Arabia in November 2017. Again, India was eliminated in the group league stage, losing 0–5 to Saudi Arabia, drawing 0–0 with Yemen, but beating Turkmenistan 3–0.

So, October–November 2017 saw a positive outlook on Indian football and there is optimism for the future. Dheeraj Moirangthem, according to Baichung Bhutia, was the find of the tournament. His shot-stopping ability, positioning and awareness has been appreciated by many experts who watched the U–17 World Cup. His sterling performances under the bar kept the margins of defeat respectable in the three Group A matches. Moirangthem became immensely popular and more celebrated than Gurpreet Singh Sandhu, the goalkeeper of the senior Indian team.

Most of the players in this age group are from humble backgrounds and have fire in their bellies, as success can lead to a professional career and upward social mobility. Midfielder Abhijit Sarkar's father pulls a rickshaw in Chinsurah, Bengal; tall defender Anwar Ali's father grazes cattle in Punjab; tenacious Jitendra Singh's father is a watchman in new Alipore, Kolkata; Sanjeev Stalin's mother sells clothes on a Bangalore footpath; the skipper's parents sell fish in Imphal; and midfielder Jeakson Thounaojam has an ailing father and is dependent on his mother, who sells vegetables in the market. Ninthoi, another midfielder from Manipur, lost his father in the summer of 2017 and lives in a two-room, tin-roofed shack. Only goalkeeper Dheeraj Singh and midfielder Suresh Singh, and the two recruits from overseas—Sunny Dhaliwal (Canada) and Namit Deshpande (USA)—are from middle-class families.

But what is the future of these players? The AIFF offered the entire squad contracts for two years, with a monthly salary of ₹50,000. The team would be kept together and, with some additions from India's U–19 squad, would participate in the 11th I–League which kicked off in the last week of November 2017.

The AIFF announced that Luis Norton would continue as coach. This caused some heartburn as AIFF's technical committee was not consulted. Chairman Shyam Thapa said he had no idea how this decision was taken. Continuing with Luis Norton seemed sensible, but wisely the AIFF appointed Indians as assistant coaches. Floyd Pinto, who has been associated with the Indian U–19 team for some years, is the assistant coach. Former international Yusaf Ansari is the goalkeeper's coach. Ansari's role is to make the goalkeeper alert and aware that moves can be started from the back. Pinto helps to transmit Nortion's ideas to the players by speaking in Hindi if necessary. Norton returned to Portugal during the Christmas week of 2017 for a family wedding and Pinto coached the team in an I–League match against Shillong Lajong on 26 December 2017. Playing effectively, Indian Arrows convincingly won 3–0. Ansari and Pinto have also been effective in coping with adolescent anxieties.

The U–17 World Cup showed that even at the teenage level, the gap between leading European and South American countries and India is still large. Also, the team sheets revealed that, even as adolescents, the players had contracts with professional clubs and played in their youth teams in competitive leagues. For instance, runner-up Spain had five players from Real Madrid and four from Barcelona. Champion England had four from Chelsea and three from Manchester City in their playing eleven. It is obvious that in these countries the clubs are doing developmental work. In India, with almost the entire squad being from the AIFF Academy, it is primarily the AIFF that developed players, not the clubs. This was a wake-up call for people involved with football in India. Clubs in India must get more proactive in youth development activities.

Administrators are realising that Indian children are being exposed to football training much later than in other nations. Creditably, steps are being taken to rectify this. The AIFF has started the U–13, U–15 and U–18 leagues in the country. All ISL franchises and I–League clubs are being persuaded to invest seriously in youth development programmes. Hopefully, attitudes will change as, until recently, everybody spoke about catching them young but no concrete steps were taken. Youth teams have to be trained properly and not just assembled hastily. In a U–15 league fixture in Kolkata,

Mohun Bagan beat ATK 13–0. The score line suggests that the latter was one such hastily assembled squad.

To date, Mizoram is the only state that seriously implements grass roots developmental programmes. They have an U–18 league to support the Mizoram Premier League. The Mizoram Football Association (MFA) intends to start both U–15 and U–12 leagues in all districts in 2018. However, the most revolutionary step they have taken is in the Champhai district on the Indo-Myanmar border. The MFA has joined hands with 8one Foundation, a private organisation, to start the Young Legends league in three age groups: U–8, U–10 and U–12 (Bhargab, 2017).This concept was initiated by Richard Hood, Head of Player Development, AIFF, and matches will be played for nearly eight months. It is to be seen if such concrete steps are emulated in other parts of India.

The AIFF claims to have given recognition to over 100 football academies all over the country in the last two or three years. Hopefully, they will function seriously and give a new direction to football in the country. Shaji Prabhakaran, former FIFA South Asian Regional Football Development officer, said that 'We need to focus constantly on youth development. Clubs must take an active role in identifying and developing talent. As long as that doesn't happen it will be very difficult to bridge the gap' (Dias, 2017).

Famous foreign clubs have started academies in India. Arsenal, in collaboration with Tata Tea, organises annual inter-school tournaments in different metropolitan cities to scout for talent. They started this project in 2007. The chosen players are taken to Arsenal's academy for specialised coaching. Following Arsenal's example, many renowned foreign clubs—Barcelona, Liverpool, Everton, Crystal Palace, Bayern Munich, Sporting Lisbon, Celtic—have made attempts to upgrade football in India by starting academies or training schools, or selecting players for training in their academies.

These clubs also have other hidden motives. The popularity of English and European football is increasing rapidly with live telecasts of the English Premier League (EPL) and UEFA (Union of European Football Associations) Champions League matches, beamed in by satellite TV. So, supporting English clubs such as Manchester United, Chelsea, Manchester City, Liverpool and Arsenal reflects the growing importance of contemporary India's globalising elite. Urban cosmopolitan youth have the desire and spending power to purchase the merchandise of leading foreign clubs and join their global fan base.

It is this thriving middle class which the foreign clubs are targeting as potential customers and fans. Consequently, many renowned foreign clubs hope that helping Indian football will lead to an increased sale of their merchandise. However, the expertise of foreign clubs may benefit the growth of Indian football, even if they have ulterior motives for getting involved. But serious efforts to develop Indian football have to be taken by the AIFF and existing clubs. Hopefully, the FIFA U–17 World Cup in October 2017 was a wake-up call to implement schemes that can be built upon for the future.

THE ISL AND THE PARADOX OF INDIAN FOOTBALL

The President of the Asian Football Confederation (AFC) Sheikh Salman came to Kolkata in October 2017 to attend the FIFA Council. He hinted that in the 2018–2019 season there would be just one national league in India, which ought to include teams from both the ISL and the I–League. However, there is no clarity as yet on how this merger will take place. The AIFF, in the meantime, has shelved the decision about the merger, declaring that from November 2017 to April 2018, both the ISL and I–League would run simultaneously (Chakraborty, 2017).

There is a change in the image of the ISL in its fourth season. It has expanded from eight to 10 teams and will be of four months' duration, rather than the previous 10 weeks. It is now no more a glamorous showcase event but a traditional league. With a longer season, and thereby increased costs, many teams have opted not to sign a marquee player for this season. So, due to the increased number of teams, the longer duration of the league and the decrease in the number of foreigners, the fourth ISL in the 2017–2018 season is very crucial. As compared to previous seasons, there are few famous names among foreign players. Thus, it is to be seen if attendance and media profiles come close to the levels of the previous years (Duerden, 2017).

By adding new teams and extending the duration of the fourth ISL to four months (from 17 November 2017 to 17 March 2018), the AIFF was signifying that this is going to be Indian football's premier league in the future. In June 2017, two new clubs joined the ISL: Bengaluru FC, twice winner of the I–League and runner-up of the 2016 AFC Cup; and the newly formed Jamshedpur FC, sponsored by the Tatas. The scenario has changed. For the first three seasons, the ISL ran as a private tournament without any affiliation. But their biggest triumph in 2017 is that they earned recognition from both the AFC and FIFA. The ISL champions will now feature in the AFC Cup qualifying play-off. The rules of recruitment have also been changed: the 10 ISL franchises can now only field five foreigners in their playing eleven and recruit a maximum of eight foreigners.

Why has the ISL been successful since its inception in 2014? This fledgling competition has developed a glamorous brand image and has extensive TV viewership due to high-profile owners, big name signings and famous coaches. Hero ISL received a tremendous response across its third edition (2016), with a total viewership of 216 million as compared to about 207 million in 2015.

The convergence of the media, celebrities and business has been responsible for the success of the ISL so far. Essentially, the league is supported by broadcaster Star Sports, which telecasts the matches on several of its channels. The ISL franchisees, who provide the glamour quotient, are miscellaneous film celebrities, such as Abhishek Bachchan and John Abraham, and cricketers such as Sachin Tendulkar and M. S. Dhoni. Besides, the league is backed by Reliance Industries, which has committed to significant investments in the game and is a key source of initial funding. Compared to the officially sanctioned I–League, the administration of the ISL is more commercially driven.

A major reason for the ISL's popularity over the last three seasons is the big name and marquee signings, which has elevated football's status in the country. This is due to the financial clout of the owners. It has also helped captivate audiences and contributed to the development of local players. Season one featured the likes of Alessandro Del Piero, Luís Garcia, Joan Capdevilla, David Trezeguet and David James; season two had Nicolas Anelka, Florent Malouda, Adrian Mutu, Elano Blumer, Roberto Carlos and Simão; and the third edition consisted of renowned players such as Malouda, Diego Forlán, Lúcio, Hélder Postiga, and Northern Ireland veteran, Aaron Hughes. Legends such as Zico (FC Goa), Marco Materazzi (Chennaiyan FC), Gianluca Zambrotta (Delhi Dynamos),

Steve Coppell (Kerala Blasters) and David Platt (FC Pune City) have become coaches of the various franchise teams in these three seasons, which has helped raise the profile of Indian football.

There were fewer big name signings in the fourth ISL. The most renowned player to join was the Bulgarian international and former Manchester United striker Dimitar Berbatov who, along with team-mate Wes Brown, played for Kerala Blasters. The Kolkata-based franchise was renamed ATK after the club's part-owners Atletico Madrid sold their share of 25 per cent in the summer of 2017. The ATK signed former Republic of Ireland striker Robbie Keane, and ex-Bolton Wanderer's goalkeeper, Jussi Jasskelainen.

There were still some high-profile coaches. The Dutchman Rene Meulensteen, who worked under Alex Ferguson at Old Trafford, was coaching Kerala Blasters. The ATK had roped in another Manchester United legend, Teddy Sheringham. It is the 51-year-old Sheringham's first managerial job and was assisted by Ashley Westwood, who was in charge of Bengaluru FC when they won the I–League in 2014 and 2016. There were two other English coaches in the ISL in its season. Former Aston Villa boss John Gregory was in charge of Chennaiyin FC, and Steve Coppell was with Jamshedpur FC. There was a strong Spanish connection too. Alberto Roca, who has coached Barcelona's B team, was in charge of Bengaluru FC. The 40-year-old Sergio Lobero, former coach of Spanish second division Las Palmas, coached FC Goa. Another Spanish coach was 61-year-old Miguel Angel of Delhi Dynamos. He has been at the helm of many Spanish clubs, such as Racing Santander and Real Valladolid. The 41-year-old Portuguese Joao Carlos Pires de Deus was North East United's fourth coach in four seasons. He has managed lower division Spanish and Portuguese clubs. Mumbai City FC's Costa Rican coach Alexandre Guimarães was the only head coach among the ISL franchises to return from last season. Roca was with Bengaluru FC when they were in the I–League last season. Serbian Ranko Popovic took over from Antonio Habas at FC Pune City.

There were nine Europeans among the 10 coaches in the ISL. Guimarães (Mumbai City FC) is from Central America. He was happy that the ISL is of a longer duration and feels that every coach would benefit from the extended season. He said, 'A longer league means every manager will have more time to impart their ideas to their team and know players better' (Alvarez, 2017).

For football to gain momentum in India, the ISL–I–League conundrum has to be sorted out soon. The biggest stumbling block is the inclusion of the legacy clubs East Bengal and Mohun Bagan, the country's two biggest football brands. Both the Kolkata clubs collected the bid documents from the ISL in 2017, but did not submit them. The major bone of contention is the franchise fee of ₹15 crore, which they refused to pay, and requested special favours from the ISL organisers. Their plea was that they were not corporate entities and deserved special consideration, especially in view of their legacy and contribution to Indian football. Both the clubs also do not want to play their home matches in Siliguri (East Bengal) and Durgapur (Mohun Bagan). This rule exists because the Kolkata franchise ATK has territorial rights for five years. This means no other franchise/club can operate from the city. This rule can be easily amended as, in all developed football nations, several professional clubs thrive together in one city. In London, Arsenal, Tottenham Hotspur, Chelsea and West Ham United coexist, as do Manchester City and Manchester United in Manchester, AC Milan and Inter Milan in Milan, and Real Madrid and Atletico Madrid in Madrid.

While clubs like Mohun Bagan and East Bengal have a rich history and a huge fan base, they also have to modernise their administration and learn how to cope with market forces. They could learn a lot from the use of social media and slick marketing of the ISL franchises.

The ISL has also resulted in considerably higher payments for Indian players. At the ISL player's draft, held in Mumbai in July 2017, the 10 franchise clubs spent ₹37.33 crore on 134 players. Including the money spent on retained players, the total expenditure was ₹48.85 crore. This is a massive increase on the ₹24 crore spent by the eight ISL franchises in the first-ever players draft in 2014. The big money spenders were new entrants Bengaluru FC, with ₹6.01 crore on 17 players, and Kerala Blasters, with ₹5.93 crore for 16 players.

For the first time, seven Indian players were paid over ₹1 crore. The five who were retained for this price are Sunil Chhetri (₹1.5 crore; Bengaluru FC), Jeje Lalpekhlua (₹1.4 crore; Chenniayin FC), Sandesh Jhingan (₹1.2 crore; Kerala Blasters), Amrinder Singh (₹1.2 crore; Mumbai City FC) and C. K. Vineeth (₹1 crore; Kerala

Blasters). The two players in the draft with a base price over ₹1 crore were Eugeneson Lyngdoh (₹1.1 crore; ATK) and Anas Edathodika (₹1.1 crore; Jamshedpur FC). These figures suggest a financial boom in Indian football.

There is also a windfall for developmental players featuring in the ISL teams. The 27 U–21 players in the 10 franchises are all set to earn a combined salary of ₹6 crore, as they have been offered multi-year contracts. The highest paid is international winger Udanta Singh of Bengaluru FC, at ₹1.95 crore for three years. Chennaiyin FC has also invested in youth. Its highest paid developmental player is left-back Jerry Lalrinzuala, who has a contract of ₹1.20 crore for the next three years. Midfielders Germanpreet Singh and Anirudh Thapa, in the same team, have also signed three-year contracts worth ₹67 lakh and ₹47 lakh, respectively.

Delhi Dynamos have given three-year contracts to four U–21 players. The highest paid is the Assamese midfielder Vinit Rai at ₹52 lakh. Defender Sajid Dhot and goalkeeper Sukhdev Shivaji Patel will earn ₹47 lakh each, and a roving forward from Mizoram, Lallianzuala Chhangte, will get ₹33 lakh. Jamshedpur FC has recruited Jerry Mawihmingthanga, another player from Mizoram, at ₹15 lakh a year. Kerala Blasters has signed local boy Prasanath Karuthadathkuni for ₹60 lakh. Consequently, established internationals and young players have benefited by the ISL draft (Shilarze, 2017).

Players have opted for ISL clubs as they have a more professional structure, better coaching and support staff. Accordingly, money in Indian football has increased, thanks to the deep pockets of the ISL owners, but only the top players are getting richer. Indian football does not yet have an economic structure, whereby younger players, and even those who do not make it to the top, earn a living wage.

The paradox is that those who have not made the cut at the player's draft are now looking at an uncertain future. Mohun Bagan and East Bengal may offer reasonable contracts in hiring players for the I–League. However, it is uncertain how much the other clubs will pay.

This uncertainty is particularly acute in Goa. Salgaocar Football Club (winner of the National Football League in 1999 and I–League in 2010 and 2011) and Dempo Sports Club (five-time winner of the NFL/I–League) are not competing at the national level any more. They will only play in the Goa professional league and local tournaments.

At a time when Indian football needs more established clubs to grow and prosper, Salgaocar Football Club, Dempo Sports Club and Sporting Clube de Goa withdrew from the I–League as they believed that the AIFF's policies were flawed, putting the future of budding players at stake. This is best exemplified by the fate of the talented striker, Milagres Gonsalves. He played in the first ISL final for Kerala Blasters. He is no longer wanted, has given up football in disgust and migrated to England, where he works for a courier company. Similarly, many Goan players are looking for alternative employment.

Till a few years ago, football was a thriving industry in Goa, rivalled only by mining and tourism. When Dempo won the fifth I–League in 2012, its budget was about ₹12 crore. Goan players had lucrative contracts, and international midfielders Climax Lawrence and Clifford Miranda, defenders Samir Naik and Mahesh Gawli, had annual contracts worth ₹1 crore.

As Churchill Brothers and Sporting Clube de Goa, the other Goan clubs, also offered good money, the employment prospects for local players were good. In the ninth NFL in 2005, there was a record number of six clubs from Goa: Salgaocar, Dempo, Churchill Brothers, Sporting Clube de Goa, Vasco and Fransa FC. Vasco has financial problems and is unable to field a competitive side, Fransa has folded up, and Churchill Brothers is the only representative from Goa in the I–League. The ISL has FC Goa.

When six Goan clubs were active in the NFL/I–League, about 125–150 footballers from one of India's smallest states were employed. The scenario has now changed. FC Goa has roped in six players from Goa: Brandon Fernandez, Seriton Fernandez, Pratesh Shirodkar, Jovel Martins, Anthony D'Souza and Bruno Colaco. Midfielder Lenny Rodrigues and Joyner Laurenco are with Bengaluru FC. Delhi Dynamos have taken goalkeeper Albino Gomes, winger Romeo Fernandez and defender Rowilson Rodriguez. The ATK has taken defender Augustin Fernandez, and FC Pune City has invested in Adil Khan. Chennaiyan FC has bought leftback Fulganco Cardoza and winger Francis Fernandez. So the top Goan players have got contracts in the ISL, but for the younger players in the state, the future is uncertain. Churchill Brothers may recruit six to seven players from Goa in the I–League. But the unemployment crisis for players in Goa will still exist. It is a big setback for the development of football in the state.

The same predicament exists in other states too. This game cannot thrive by lucrative payment to about 100 players only. After all, from quantity emerges quality. Youngsters will not opt for football as a career if the future remains precarious.

Football in Kerala suffered a setback as institutional teams such as Kerala Police, Titanium and State Bank of Travancore (SBT) disbanded for lack of domestic tournaments in which to participate. These teams employed many players from Kerala, and some like I. M. Vijayan, Jo Paul Ancheri, Sharaf Ali, the late V. P. Sathyan and C. V. Pappachan became internationals and were very popular.

In the closing years of the 20th century, FC Kochi became the first professional club to start in Kerala. As a matter of policy they also employed local players. Unfortunately, FC Kochi closed down within six years because of financial problems. Next came Viva Kerala—they too did not last long. Prayag United also lasted a couple of seasons in the I–League, but then shut shop due to insufficient funds.

Kerala Blasters football club in the ISL is very popular and does hire some local talent. However, there are insufficient clubs in Kerala to nurture emerging talent. Some players, such as striker Justin Joby, have been signed by East Bengal and other I–League or ISL clubs. Nonetheless, the decline of club football in Kerala has led to a paucity of talented players emerging from the state.

The ISL claims to have designed a long-term grass roots programme targeted at children aged 6–14 which will help in popularising the game all over the country. Its ambition is to ensure that about five million children will actively play organised football by 2018. This is a laudable project, but if so many children are going to be playing the game then more clubs, grounds and facilities will be required in several Indian cities. To achieve this aim, the ISL will have to work in tandem with AIFF and the existing clubs in Indian football, especially those in the I–League, first and second divisions. For its long-term grass roots programme to succeed, the ISL has to work with the existing domestic club structure in India. Franchises can create city-based teams for a competitive league, but to improve

Indian football across the country a harmonious relationship with local football federations and clubs is required. They must not feel threatened by the ISL and fear that their existence is at stake (Kapadia, 2017).

Relaying the main playing surface at all the stadia and providing top locker room and floodlight facilities are important initiatives undertaken by the ISL. But just the refurbishment of football infrastructure and stadia in which the ISL matches are played is not enough. The success or failure of ISL's grass roots initiatives can only be assessed after a minimum of, say, seven or eight years. In the short run, its primary objective is to cultivate an interest among children. The ISL rules also demand that each team spends ₹2 crore for the development of the game at the grass roots level and builds an academy within five years of formation in their respective states. However, this laudable idea is not being taken seriously. Some franchises are finding short cuts. For instance, FC Pune City has just taken over the existing academy of the now defunct I–League team, Pune FC. Delhi Dynamo's academy is based on talented players spotted by the Subroto Mukherjee Cup officials in their annual tournament for schools.

The investors and partners of the ISL franchises must be prepared to play a long game, as the league is still far from turning profitable. Ticket sales are small, clubs do not own their stadia, and foreign players and coaches remain expensive routes to success and credibility. Initial estimates that investors could reap a return on their investment within the competition's first five years are just ludicrously optimistic.

◆

REFERENCES

Alvarez, Rohan. 2017. 'Many Takers for Longer ISL', *The Times of India*, 11 November: 31.

Bhargab, Samrah. 2017. 'Champhai takes Baby Steps in Indian Football', *Hindustan Times*, 10 November: 24.

Chakraborty, Shamik. 2017. 'Kolkata Infrastructure is from the Past Century', *The Indian Express*, 9 November: 24.

Dias, Shayne. 2017. 'After High of U–17 World Cup, Time to Focus on Future', *Hindustan Times*, 6 November: 18.

Duerden, John. 2017. 'ISL Grows as Merger gets Closer', *World Soccer Magazine*, October: 70–71.

Kapadia, Novy. 2017. *Barefoot to Boots: The Many Lives of Indian Football*. New Delhi: Penguin Books.

Shilarze, Saharoy. 2017. 'Big Money for New Kids on the Block as ISL Franchises Invest Heavily on U–21 Players', *The Times of India*, 10 November: 29.

◆◆

FOOTBALL IN POST-INDEPENDENCE BANGLADESH

KAUSIK
BANDYOPADHYAY

The history of Bangladesh since Independence has often been described as a story of political turmoil, social tension and economic underdevelopment. Yet the sphere in which the nation has always shown a sense of purpose and vitality has been *culture*. An inner sense of *Bengali* nationality was visible in the diverse domains of culture during Pakistani rule—language and literature, to music and sport—demonstrated distinctively in efforts ranging from the Language Movement in East Bengal to the formation, in 1971, of the Bangla Football Team in West Bengal (Bandyopadhyay, 2012: 87–97). The role of a mass-based civil society was so predominant and crucial to shaping the national culture of Bangladesh from the days of the Language Movement that political–social–economic instability could not impede the growth of an everyday sports culture.[1] The media, especially since the 1980s, both printed and visual, played a stimulating role in generating interest among the masses in games and sports as integral parts of the nation's popular culture.

When Bangladesh emerged as a politically independent nation in 1971, football as a 'played, watched and read game' was undoubtedly the most popular spectator sport, albeit without any worthwhile impact on the international stage, and continued to remain so until the mid-1990s. While the mass passion for football ensured the game's growing popularity in Bangladeshi society in the first two decades following Independence, the internal dynamics of its organisation and culture became intertwined with the emerging political culture and social processes. While football was integrally related to everyday life in Bangladeshi society until the early 1990s—international football still enjoys great following in the country—the domestic game witnessed a steady decline in the last two decades or so, owing to a variety of factors such as poor management, infrastructural debilities, administrative lapses, anomalous finance, and the lack of vision and leadership. This essay is an attempt to comment briefly on this evolution of football culture in Bangladesh since 1971.

◆◆◆

When Bangladesh attained independence, football was the most popular sport in the country with nearly 95 per cent of its sporting activities focused on this game and more than 2,000 football clubs operating across the country (Rashid, 1988b: 78). Smarting under economic devastation, the masses of the war-torn nation, particularly the youth, became more concerned with resolving the immediate issues of economic survival. Even then, football soon began to draw attention as well as currency. However, the challenges before the newly formed Bangladesh Football Federation (BFF, 1972) as well as the clubs were manifold, ranging from the lack of resources and infrastructure to declining interest in playing the game (ibid.: 79). The BFF could not ensure a uniform and stable set of rules in running the most important and popular event of its annual calendar—the Metropolis League—leading to confusion and anomalies almost every year (Islam, 1993: 49). In such a context, ever since the 1970s, match-fixing was also a feature of Bangladeshi football (Rashid, 1988a: 57–60). Clubs could not demonstrate their earlier commitment to the development of the game by rearing young talent at their own initiative; neither could they any longer rely upon a steady flow of talent from suburban areas or villages. This created a paradox in football in independent Bangladesh: the increasing popularity of the game ran in striking contrast to a declining interest in actual participation in the game.

There was another unique hazard faced by football in the early years following Independence. Regular players of different clubs used to play for local teams at local tournaments in lieu of handsome cash emoluments, despite the risk of injury and public wrath, which could endanger their careers. This system of hiring club footballers for local tournaments was known as *khyap* (play on hire) or *khep* (Said, 1993: 70–72). While there developed a paucity of sports grounds in post-Independence Bangladesh, barring a few clubs that had their own grounds, most of the League clubs had to hire the university grounds for practise and training. Apart from the usual competition and tussle among the clubs for access to available grounds, there was the additional problem of paying local thugs for the use of those fields (Kabir, 1993: 77). The lower-division clubs, on the other hand, unable to afford the expense of hiring such practice grounds, competed with each other for access to the outer stadium grounds of the Bangabandhu Stadium at Motijheel (ibid.: 78). Along with this change in the landscape of Bangladeshi football, the everyday culture that grew around the Bangabandhu Stadium, centred on football since the 1950s, seemed to undergo a decline in the 1990s. The *adda*s, which were the order of the day in earlier decades, no longer remained fashionable in the 1990s. Football's decline and cricket's fast-growing popularity, along with the shifting of club premises from the stadium area, were considered to be major factors behind this trend (Mahmud, 2005b: 137–39).

In May 1972, soon after Independence, Calcutta's Mohun Bagan Club came to play an exhibition match in Dhaka. Although the new nation was yet to recover from the scars of the recent war of independence, a select Bangladesh XI put up a spirited show against the visitors and surprised everyone by beating their more renowned opponents by a solitary goal scored by Salahuddin.[2] The performance instilled an enormous amount of confidence in millions of football lovers across the country and widely increased the popularity of the game. In the same year, a Dhaka XI participated in the Bordoloi Trophy held in Guwahati (in Assam, India), and was runner-up in the tournament (Mahmud, 1993a: 196; Mahmud, 1999: 82). 'Although the boys from Dhaka ended up as runners-up,' it was noted, 'they displayed a brand of football that matched the expectations of the game's large following' (Mahmud, 1999: 82). Bangladesh got its first true international exposure at the 19th Merdeka Football Tournament, held in Malaysia, in 1973. It was Bangladesh's youth team, under the supervision of its German coach, Warner Beckelhopt, which brought home the country's first international victory on 10 October 1978, when it defeated Yemen, 1–0, in the 20th Asian Youth Football Championship (Mahmud, 1999: 83; Mahmood, n.d.) The senior national team recorded its first victory at the international level in the qualifying round of the Asian Cup, in 1979, when it beat Afghanistan, 3–2.

However, the national team could never really match Asian standards, save on very few occasions. One such occasion was the victory of the Bangladesh Red team in the 6th President's Gold Cup in 1989, in which teams from South Korea, India, China, Thailand and Iran also participated (Mahmud, 1993b: 196; Mahmud, 1999: 83; Mahmood, n.d.). Similarly, Bangladesh's wins in the Four-Nation Meet in Myanmar, in 1995, in the 1999 and 2010 South Asian Federation (SAF) Games tournament, and at the South Asian Football Federation (SAFF) Championship in 2003 were hailed in contemporary media (Mahmood, n.d.). Meanwhile, Bangladesh organised the Bangabandhu Cup to celebrate the silver jubilee of Independence, which was considered to be 'truly a milestone in footballing history' (Mahmud, 1999: 83). In the 1982 Asian Games, Bangladesh got its first victory by defeating Malaysia, 2–1 (Mahmood, n.d.). The nation first appeared at the qualifying stage of the World Cup in 1985, while its only attempt at an Olympic qualifier was in 1991 (ibid.). However, it did not perform well on either occasion.

While the national team mostly suffered appalling defeats at the international level, individual clubs and players made Bangladeshis proud in the same period. Both Dhaka Mohammedan Sporting Club and Abahani Krira Chakra—the leading clubs of the country—performed well in foreign tournaments,[3] particularly in India, while some of their players such as Aslam, Najib, Munna, Kaiser and Sabbir became popular in the Calcutta League. However, it was Salahuddin who became the first-ever Bangladeshi professional footballer on foreign soil when he played for the Caroline Football Club of Hong Kong.

◆◆◆

Despite this occasional success, Bangladesh has never been able to show consistency in the development of the game, either at the domestic or at the international level. Azam Mahmood (n.d.) identified three key shortcomings responsible for Bangladesh's 'continuous naïve performance' at the turn of the century:

Firstly, we are poor travellers and fare badly on foreign soil; secondly, due to poor stamina and tactics, most of the goals were conceded in the last minutes of the match, turning many stunning results into negative; thirdly, the sharp peak-valley in the level of performance.

Post-Independence, three of Bangladesh's traditional and well-known clubs—Wari, Victoria Sporting Club and Azad Sporting Club—lost their sheen by the 1980s. The most dominant feature as well as the attraction of domestic football in Bangladesh in the decades following Independence was the arch rivalry between Dhaka Mohammedan and Abahani, who 'are unquestionably the forerunners to quench the peoples' lust for football since independence, thereby taking the popularity of the game to newer heights' (Mahmud, 1999: 83). The passion and excitement this derby match used to generate in Bangladesh in the 1970s and 1980s invites comparison with the arch rivalry between Mohun Bagan and East Bengal in India. Besides the usual scenes of excitement and emotional outbursts, the encounters between the two teams continue to generate rampant indiscipline, hooliganism and spectator violence, leading to the damage of public and government property. Many fans even fell victim to recurrent spectator clashes and hooligan violence over the years. Faruq (in 1978), Jahangir (in 1979), Anwar (in 1986) and Shahid (in 1990)—to mention a few—remained martyrs of club rivalry in domestic football (Tito, 1993: 118–20). The players, the referees, the spectators and the club officials—all had their share of responsibility in making the Mohammedan–Abahani conflict very violent, particularly in the 1980s (Rashid, 1988c: 72–77). However, the obsession with this arch rivalry has dwindled in the new century with the deteriorating standard of football, the rise of new clubs, and the concomitant decline in spectator attendance (Baki, 2008: 19).

The institution of the President's Gold Cup in the early 1980s was deemed to be an important step towards the development of football in Bangladesh, particularly by giving international exposure to its footballers and spectators. The Cup, which cost five lakh takas, was donated jointly by the Department of Sports and Culture, the Government of Bangladesh and the National Sports Control Board at the instance of President Ziaur Rahman. While the tournament was organised with the avowed objective of bringing national teams or representative teams of similar standard from foreign countries to give adequate exposure to the Bangladeshi side, participating teams fell far short of such expectations. From the very beginning, the tournament was marked by an utter lack of vision and planning, and the marked failure of the organising committee to make arrangements with due priority (Rashid, 1988d: 87). For many, the organisation of the tournament was nothing more than a political instrument to heighten the image of the government and draw international attention to its achievement. Disillusioned with the President's Gold Cup, many believed that the huge expense of the tournament would have been better utilised in making available basic provisions to poorer clubs and arranging for long-term training for young talent from across the country (ibid.: 91). Therefore, the Cup, which could have made a worthwhile contribution to the growth of the sports movement in the country, failed to fulfil expectations.

Political turbulence and natural calamity—two recurrent features of Bangladeshi life since its independence—sometimes severely affected sporting activities. In 1990, for example, the Dhaka Football League, the most popular annual sporting event of the country, could not take place due to political agitations. After the fall of Ershad's dictatorial regime, for the first time a sports personality, Sadek Hosain Khoka, became the sports minister in 1991. This was considered to be a much-needed development for the advancement of sport in the country.[4] However, he soon became chairman of the National Sports Council, too. It is said that with Khoka's accession to power, 'corruption in sports started and the downfall of the sports arena has begun'.[5] It was also in 1991 that coastal areas of the country were devastated by a tornado. The BFF organised a few exhibition matches with Dhaka's big teams in order to raise funds for victims hit by the natural disaster. More importantly, three Calcutta giants—East Bengal, Mohun Bagan and Mohammedan Sporting—came to Dhaka to play in a fund-raising tournament, which showcased the game's role as an instrument of philanthropy.[6]

Despite rising mass attraction to football, the game remained amateurish for a long time. Neither the BFF nor the clubs made any viable long-term effort to professionalise the game. Although the standard of the game had begun to decline from the late 1980s, the players used to receive huge sums of money, thereby creating a peculiar blend of amateurism and professionalism. For example, Salahuddin, one of the best footballers of post-Independence Bangladesh, was paid around 10,000 takas for a season in 1973, which was increased to about three lakh takas by the mid-1980s. In striking contrast, Monem Munna of Abahani Krira Chakra was offered 30 lakh takas in 1991 for a transfer.[7] However, with the onset of satellite television in the 1990s, people all over the country were witness to the global standard of the game through live telecasts of the World Cup, and the European and Latin American Leagues, and could clearly understand the huge difference in standards between the global and Bangladeshi game. This certainly played a role in decreasing the popularity of the domestic game.

Along with the peculiar semi-professional set-up of football, the dichotomy between club and nation also became a critical factor in the development of the game. The players, attracted by the incentives of playing for clubs, began to ignore their duty towards and performance for the national team. This was but natural in a set-up where playing for the country did not ensure them any material benefit, besides incurring the risk of injuries which could hamper their professional career for the clubs that paid them handsomely (Mahmud, 1993a: 25).

♦♦♦

For many, the gradual decline in the status of football in the 1990s was a result of the appalling failure of the BFF to adapt to changing priorities of the global game and the peculiar semi-professional character of football administration in the country. For others, poor club administration was to blame for the dismal state of football. Without caring about the standards of the game, the three top clubs of the country—Dhaka Mohammedan, Abahani and Brothers Union—squandered money for short-term success. Financial anomalies apart, the decline in spectator attendance became alarming in the course of the last decade of the 20th century (Sohag, 1993: 124–25). The national team, too, put up dismal shows on the Asian circuit, ranging from the South Asian Federation Games to the Olympics qualifiers.[8] In the late 1980s and early 1990s, although footballers from Dhaka used to play for Kolkata's big clubs,[9] the trend completely changed with time. The continued dependence of the top League clubs on foreign players[10] for success and fanfare resulted in a sharp decline in the quality of native footballers, which became a source of worry and lamentation for football lovers. The BFF, however, seemed to turn a blind eye to this reversal of fortune. Rather, the Leagues in Dhaka and in the districts became irregular around this time, with a consequent decrease in the number of matches, leading to a decline in public interest in the game.

Peter Velappan, the Asian Football Confederation secretary, once said, 'Bangladesh has the resources necessary for the development of football. Measures have to be taken under proper planning to get to the goal' (Mahmud, 1999: 83). While Bangladesh has produced a galaxy of quality footballers since the 1950s,[11] it could not field a team with the ability to perform consistently at the international level. Foreign coaches were employed periodically, but success was limited to winning the SAFF championship or the South Asian Federation Games gold medal. While many foreign footballers raised the standard of local football in the 1980s and 1990s, this trend seems to have been reversed in the past decade or so with a number of substandard African recruits playing for the top clubs (Mamoon, 2011a: 38–40). Hence, the nation's success in football has always lagged far behind its vast popularity. The reasons behind this anomaly, as already discussed, need to be addressed immediately. As Dulal Mahmud suggested in 1999:

> Socio-economic condition may be one of the main reasons. But, perhaps even more important is the non-enforcement of a comprehensive long-term plan of action with a true spirit of professionalism. Immediate steps should include making football a regular event in educational institutions from the grass roots to the university level (1999: 83).

The start of the professional league in 2007—the first in South Asia—was an important move, albeit much delayed, in the direction of synchronising the structure of Bangladeshi football with the changing global dimension (Manik, 2007; Joy, 2007). It was initiated as part of the Asian Football Confederation's (AFC) Vision Asia programme. The selection of Kazi Salahuddin as the president of BFF, along with the installation of a new government in 2008, also raised hopes about serious changes to be effected in the structure of Bangladeshi football. Despite Salahuddin's best efforts, which mobilised both media and sponsors for the cause of football in the midst of cricket's enormous popularity, factionalism and politics still remain major hurdles to Bangladesh's rise to a worthy footballing nation on the international map.[12] With the growing popularity of cricket in the last decade, the future of domestic football in the country has become more uncertain.

◆◆◆

Despite this continuing stagnation in domestic football, international football has always remained hugely popular in Bangladesh. Bangladeshis had traditionally been attracted to Brazilian football and its greatest star, Pele. The artistic style of Brazilian football and its consistent performance in World Cups between 1958 and 1970, along with Pele's skill, turned the Bengalis of East Pakistan into ardent fans. However, independent Bangladesh's tryst with World Cup soccer began in 1974 when the final match was telecast on Bangladesh Television (BTV), making a great impression on the few who watched it. However, the masses learnt of the Cup details only through radio and newspapers, as television in those days was a rarity. The victory of Argentina on home ground in the next World Cup, in 1978, with live telecast of some of the matches of the tournament on BTV, made a great impact on the nature of football following in Bangladesh.[13] Fans came to be divided into two blocs— Brazilian and Argentine—while their rivalry ranged from exuberance to violence.[14] Instinctively, perhaps, Latin American football has always been a fad with Bangladesh. However, the course of football fandom in the country was completely transformed with live telecast of all the matches of the 1986 World Cup that gave birth to one of the greatest footballers of the 20th century, Diego Maradona, who won the championship for Argentina (Mahmud, 2005a: 111–12). It is said that Maradona, with his creative genius and artistic display, created such a stir in Bangladesh that a whole generation became die-hard Argentine fans (Manik, 2006: 9; Mamoon, 2011b: 13), with that tradition still continuing due to the present Argentine sensation, Lionel Messi. Ever since 1986, Bangladesh appears to have become an Argentine soccer colony during the World Cup.[15] Every four years, this is borne out by the enthusiasm of the Bangladeshi masses when Argentina plays in the World Cup, albeit without success thus far. In the new century, the kind of public enthusiasm witnessed during Argentina's matches in the World Cup draws comparison only with the enthusiasm of the masses for their national cricket team.

This mass attraction towards the global game could therefore be discerned in the everyday life of the nation, and ranges from journalistic efforts that cover and reflect this football fever, to the peoples' intense affiliation and loyalty towards World Cup teams. Thus, the football fever that engulfs the entire nation for those four weeks once in four years not only shows the Bangladeshis' obsession with the game, but also throws light on football's immense influence on their everyday life. The everyday forms of football culture have been visible in nearly every walk of life and are well represented through various forms of popular media in the wake of the World Cup. These everyday experiences of football during the World Cup clearly point to the sport's importance in the realms of society, religion and culture, and beyond the spaces of leisure, entertainment or commerce.[16] For a nation which never came close to playing in the World Cup, and which hardly expects to achieve that in the near future, World Cup-fever remains an opiate for the masses dejected with the performance of their national team over the years, as well as an escape from the drudgeries of daily life.[17] However, despite this enthusiasm, a lamentation that continues to torment more than 160 million Bangladeshis is: When will Bangladesh or, rather, will Bangladesh, ever, play in the World Cup? The question, given the current state of football affairs in the country, remains unanswered.[18]

ACKNOWLEDGEMENT

This article contains some of the facts and arguments offered in my earlier writings on sports in Bangladesh, particularly *Bangladesh Playing: Sport, Culture, Nation* (2012).

◆

NOTES

1. For a broad discussion on the evolution of sports culture in pre-Independence Bangladesh, see Bandyopadhyay (2012: chapters 1 & 2).

2. *Dainik Ittefaq*, 14 May 1972. Also see Mahmud (1999: 82).

3.   It was Abahani that become a champion on foreign soil for the first time when they won the Nagji Trophy in India in 1990. See *Khelar Bhuban*, 1 June 1991, p. 8. Abahani and Mohammedan started representing Bangladesh at the Asian Club Cup and Cup Winners Cup from 1985 and 1987, respectively. See Mahmood (n.d.).

4.   *Khelar Bhuban*, 1 June 1991, 1: 5–7.

5.   'Evil Force Controls Sports', *Khelar Bhuban*, 8 May 2007: 14.

6.   Abahani emerged champions in the tournament. See *Khelar Bhuban*, 20 June 1991: 6–10.

7.   Munna, however, refused the offer to play for his beloved club, Abahani. See Mahmud (1993a: 24).

8.   The only notable performance of the national team was the victory of Bangladesh in a four-nation tournament held in Myanmar in 1995.

9.   Monem Munna, who played for Kolkata's East Bengal Club, became the cynosure of all eyes in Bengal. He earned the greatest renown as a Bangladeshi soccer star playing in India.

10. Foreign footballers began to play in Bangladesh from 1974, when Dhaka Mohammedan employed C. Prasad and Prabhakar Mishra from Calcutta's Mohammedan Sporting Club. Since then a host of players from different countries of Asia, Africa and Latin America have played for bigger clubs of Dhaka. In 1989, the BFF prohibited the import of foreign players, thereby preventing them from playing in the Dhaka League. In the last two-and-a-half decades, however, foreign footballers, particularly from Africa, have proved to be substandard, thereby adding poorer quality to Bangladeshi football's overall standard. For a useful discussion on this, see Mamoon (2011b: 38–40).

11. For a detailed discussion on the most renowned footballers of Bangladesh over the years, see Saber (1990) and Mahmud (2006).

12. See interview with Ajoy Barua, 29 March 2007. Veteran sports journalist Ajoy Barua of *Dainik Sambad* narrated how ever since the 1990s, politicking and corruption became the order of the day in soccer administration in Bangladesh.

13. See Subhro (2007). Utpal Subhro, one of contemporary Bangladesh's best sports journalists, has recounted his childhood memory of the impact of Argentina's World Cup victory in 1978 on the people of Bangladesh.

14. See Mohsin (2006: 54–55). Mostafa Mamoon (2011b: 62), who compares the enmity between the two fan groups to Awami League–BNP political conflict, has mentioned that a Brazil–Argentina final might result in a civil war in Bangladesh.

15. See Majumdar (2002) for a similar construction in the case of India.

16. See Bandyopadhyay (2012: 132–36) for a brief discussion on this.

17. See Iqramuzzaman (2006: 29) for some interesting insights on this.

18. See Mahmud (2005c: 123–24) for wishful thinking along these lines.

REFERENCES

Baki, Mohammad Suman. 2008. '*Abahani–Mohammedan Match Jeno "Smriti Tumi Bedona"*' (Abahani–Mohammedan Match is like a 'Pitiable Memory Now'), *Kriralok*, 1 December.

Bandyopadhyay, Kausik. 2012. *Bangladesh Playing: Sport, Culture, Nation*. Dhaka: Subarna.

Iqramuzzaman. 2006. *'Amader Biswacup Football'* (Our World Cup Football), *Krirajagat*, 1 July.

Islam, Kazi Shamsul. 1993. *'Sobinoy Nibedan'* (Modest Appeal), in Iqramuzzaman, Naqib Ahmed Nadvi and Dulal Mahmud (eds.), *Khelar Kotha Kothar Khela* (Talk of Sports, Sport of Talk). Dhaka: Bangladesh Krira Lekhak Samiti.

Joy, Arif Khan. 2007. *'B-League: System er Marpanch Naki Velki?'* (B-League: System Tricks or Hoax?), *Krirajagat*, 10 February.

Kabir, Mohammad Iqbal. 1993. *'Khelar Mather Somosya'* (Problems of Sports Ground), in Iqramuzzaman, Naqib Ahmed Nadvi and Dulal Mahmud (eds.), *Khelar Kotha Kothar Khela* (Talk of Sports, Sport of Talk). Dhaka: Bangladesh Krira Lekhak Samiti.

Mahmood, Azam. n.d. 'Football in Bangladesh.' *Banglabandhu Cup Silver Jubilee of Independence Football Tournament: Official Souvenir*. Dhaka: Bangladesh Football Federation.

Mahmud, Dulal. 1993a. *'Bittaban Footballar, Bittahin Football'* (Rich Footballers, Poor Football), in Iqramuzzaman, Naqib Ahmed Nadvi and Dulal Mahmud (eds.), *Khelar Kotha Kothar Khela* (Talk of Sports, Sport of Talk). Dhaka: Bangladesh Krira Lekhak Samiti.

———. 1993b. *'Kriranganer Dui Dashak'* (Two Decades in the Arena of Sports), in Iqramuzzaman, Naqib Ahmed Nadvi and Dulal Mahmud (eds.), *Khelar Kotha Kothar Khela* (Talk of Sports, Sport of Talk). Dhaka: Bangladesh Krira Lekhak Samiti.

———. 1999. 'Football in Bangladesh.' *2nd Bangabandhu Cup International Tournament: 1999 Souvenir*. Dhaka: Bangladesh Football Federation.

———. 2005a. *'Barir Pashe Biswacup Football'* (World Cup Football Besides Home), *Dainik Jugantar*, 31 May 2002, in Dulal Mahmud, *Stadium Er Sei Addata Aaj Aar Nei* (Adda at the Stadium No Longer Exists). Dhaka: Akhhorbritta.

———. 2005b. *'Stadium Er Sei Addata Aaj Aar Nei'* (Adda at the Stadium No Longer Exists), *Krirajagat*, 1 March 1999, in Dulal Mahmud, *Stadium Er Sei Addata Aaj Aar Nei*, (Adda at the Stadium No Longer Exists). Dhaka: Akhhorbritta.

———. 2005c. *'Sei Din Ti Kobe Asbe?'* ('When Will that Day Come?'), *Krirajagat*, 16 June 2002, in Dulal Mahmud, *Stadium Er Sei Addata Aaj Aar Nei* (Adda at the Stadium No Longer Exists). Dhaka: Akhhorbritta.

———. 2006. *Amader Footballer-ra* (Our Footballers). Dhaka: Parijat.

Majumdar, Boria. 2002. 'Kolkata Colonised: Soccer in a Subcontinental Brazilian Colony', *Soccer & Society*, 3 (2): 70–86.

Mamoon, Mostafa. 2011a. *'African Chakkar'* (African Puzzle), in Mostafa Mamoon, *Touchline Theke Biswacupe* (From Touchline to World Cup). Dhaka: Somoy.

———. 2011b. *Touchline Theke Biswacupe* (From Touchline to World Cup). Dhaka: Somoy.

Manik, Shafikul Islam. 2006. *'Ebarer Biswacup Ekti Sera Sundar Biswacup Hobe'* (This World Cup Would be one of the Best and Wonderful Cups), *Kriralok*, 15 (5).

———. 2007. 'Peshadar Football League: Suchonar Anubhuti Khub Anander' (Professional Football League: The Feeling of a Start is Joyous), Krirajagat, 10 February: 17–18.

Mohsin, Simon. 2006. 'Abaro Bangabhanga' (Bengal Partition Again!), Saptahik 2000, 23 June: 54–5.

Rashid, M. A. 1988a. 'Biyallish Goler Imarat' (The Building of 42 Goals). Khela O Kheloar (Sports and Sportsman). Dhaka: Jatiya Grantha Kendra.

———. 1988b. 'Swadhinata-uttar Football' (Post-Independence Football). Khela O Kheloar (Sports and Sportsman). Dhaka: Jatiya Grantha Kendra.

———. 1988c. 'Mohammedan Bonam Abahani' (Mohammedan versus Abahani). Khela O Kheloar (Sports and Sportsman). Dhaka: Jatiya Grantha Kendra.

———. 1988d. 'Bhinna Chokhe Sonar Kap-e' (A Different Perspective into the Gold Cup). Khela o Kheloar (Sports and Sportsman). Dhaka: Jatiya Grantha Kendra.

Saber, Moinul Ahsan. 1990. Bangladesher Football Taraka (Football Stars of Bangladesh). Dhaka: Yuba Unnayan Adhidaptar.

Said, Abdus. 1993. 'Khyap' (Play on Hire), in Iqramuzzaman, Naqib Ahmed Nadvi and Dulal Mahmud (eds.), Khelar Kotha Kothar Khela (Talk of Sports, Sport of Talk). Dhaka: Bangladesh Krira Lekhak Samiti.

Sohag, Rejaur Rahman. 1993 'Bangladesher Football Krantilagne' (Bangladeshi Football at Crossroads), in Iqramuzzaman, Naqib Ahmed Nadvi and Dulal Mahmud (eds.), Khelar Kotha Kothar Khela (Talk of Sports, Sport of Talk). Dhaka: Bangladesh Krira Lekhak Samiti.

Subhro, Utpal. 2007. Biswa Jokhon Footballmoy (When the World is Football-fad). Dhaka: Anannya.

Tito, Farhad. 1993. 'Football Jadi Jiboner Sapakhhe' (If Football is in Favour of Life), in Iqramuzzaman, Naqib Ahmed Nadvi and Dulal Mahmud (eds.), Khelar Kotha Kothar Khela (Talk of Sports, Sport of Talk). Dhaka: Bangladesh Krira Lekhak Samiti.

❖❖

INDIA'S SHUTTLE STORY
Breaking Through Barriers to Take Flight

ABHIJEET
KULKARNI

I n an informal chat a few months after taking over as India's chief national coach in 2006, Pullela Gopichand spoke of his desire to ensure that the country does not have to wait for another two decades to bring home the All England crown. He had bagged the prestigious title in 2001, exactly 21 years after the legendary Prakash Padukone had his hands around the men's singles trophy in 1980 and the tournament was always looked at as the bench mark for success in Indian badminton.

Eighteen years later, India's wait for another All England title continues but the country's shuttlers have achieved so much success in tournaments as prestigious as the one played in Birmingham, England, that the absence of this particular crown simply seems like an aberration. In terms of sheer numbers, this is a golden period for Indian badminton. Since 2009, India has a world champion in PV Sindhu, three silver and five bronze medals in the World Championships. Indian shuttlers have won 20 Superseries titles, an Olympic silver and a bronze, five Commonwealth gold medals and a plethora of other international titles.

As things stand now, India has equal number if not more men's singles players in the top-50 world ranking than badminton powerhouses like China, Korea or Malaysia in a sport that is widely believed to have its origins in the military barracks in Pune.

The game of badminton is said to have originated in the Ammunition Factory in Poona, where British soldiers started playing it in 1860, and was soon exported to England and thereafter to the world. The Badminton Association of India (BAI) was ultimately established in 1934 to govern the sport in the country, and started its national championship in the same year.

Despite India being the home of the shuttle sport, the country was never one of the powerhouses of world badminton like some of its Asian counterparts, who happened to pick up the sport much later. That does not mean that Indians were merely completing the numbers in international competitions. While Anglo-Indians dominated the domestic scene in the initial years as expected, Prakash Nath and Devinder Mohan had taken over the mantle by the 1940s and could have become the country's first real international stars. In fact, Nath holds the record of becoming the first Indian to reach the final of the All England Championship, then considered the premier tournament in the world, in 1947. Then just 23, Nath had accounted for the top seed in the very first round and advanced to the final after Mohan and he decided to decide the winner of their quarter-final encounter through a 'toss' to avoid overexerting themselves. Although Nath was considered the favourite in the summit clash against Sweden's Conny Jepsen, the news of rioting in his hometown Lahore meant that the Indian star was not in a fit state to play the match and lost rather easily. The family had to migrate to New Delhi soon after and Nath vowed not to play badminton till he restored the family business. He went on to become an entrepreneur and built an electronic machine tools business, while India lost a star badminton player.

Mohan, and later Trilok Nath Seth, continued to register a few good wins in the Thomas Cup and invitational meets, but it was Nandu Natekar who ultimately earned the tag of the first Indian to win a tournament abroad by bagging the men's singles title in the 1956 Selangor International tournament in Kuala Lumpur. It was probably a golden era in Indian badminton, in terms of the standard of invitational tournaments that were held in Mumbai and in North India, with some of the world's best players seen regularly in action. Old timers still describe how the invitational tournaments would attract hundreds of fans to the Cricket Club of India or Bombay Gymkhana to watch the likes of Natekar, Seth take on former world number one Erland Kops, Eddie Choong and Finn Kobbero. While these Indian stars dominated the domestic scene for almost a decade, with the likes of Meena Shah winning the women's singles national title seven consecutive times from 1959 to 1965, and Natekar, Seth and the versatile Suresh Goel bagging 13 of 14 men's singles titles from 1952 to 1965. It was also a period when foreign players were allowed to participate in the senior nationals and Kops even bagged a triple crown in 1959, humbling all the Indian star players.

Despite talent and skill levels matching the best in the world, Indians were normally done in by their lack of fitness, and it is often said that had Natekar worked on that aspect of his game, he could have won many more international titles. Dinesh Khanna was probably an exception to that rule. The Retrieving Machine— nicknamed for his style of keeping the shuttle in play for as long as possible—used to wear his opponents down and has the distinction of being the country's only Asian champion, when he bagged the title in the second edition in Lucknow. In fact, India also bagged the junior boy's singles title in the same event, with Gautam Thakkar carving his name on the trophy. Khanna went on to reach the semi-finals of the 1966 All England Championship and could have won many more titles had he not tried to balance his badminton career and civil engineering degree course to ensure an alternate career for himself.

It finally took the legendary Prakash Padukone to underline the importance of fitness and professionalism, and lay the foundation of India's rise in world badminton. The shuttler from Karnataka (where ball badminton was more popular than the shuttle version during his formative days) announced his arrival on the domestic scene at the age of 17 by becoming the first player to win the junior and senior national title in the same edition. Padukone's contribution to Indian badminton goes beyond his All England title in 1980—a first by any Indian—or his unofficial world number one status in 1980 and 1981. India's most decorated badminton player before the emergence of Saina Nehwal, Padukone changed the way Indians played the sport by emphasising fitness and professionalism to achieve international success. Players like Uday Pawar, U. Vimal Kumar, and even the doubles specialists, vouch for Padukone's training discipline and how it rubbed off onto the entire squad during national camps and tournaments.

But more than that, it was Padukone's success across the globe that made players believe in themselves. Padukone was an integral part of the Indian squad that won the team bronze in the 1974 Asian Games in Tehran, and then went on to become the first

Indian to win a Commonwealth Games gold in 1978. It was also his first major title on the international circuit and kick-started a golden period for him as he went on to win the Danish Open, Swedish Open, and, ultimately, the All England Championship in 1980. People lined up on both sides of the streets in Mumbai and Bangalore to welcome the country's first badminton superstar who showed the world what a person—with minimum facilities, but great abilities and discipline— could do.

Padukone's achievements also meant that the sport got an added impetus, with more and more children taking up the game. But the BAI was guilty of not capitalising on it. The Association was then run by the late Fazil Ahmed as his personal fiefdom, and stories of favouritism and ill treatment of players during the period reached such a level that 17 years later Padukone himself led a revolt against one of the longest serving sports administrators.

But between those years, India managed to produce a maverick like Syed Modi who halted Padukone's Nationals winning streak at nine, won the 1982 Commonwealth Games gold and could have become an international star had he not been killed outside Lucknow's K. D. Singh Babu stadium at the age of 26. Besides Modi, who also won the 1982 Asian Games men's singles bronze and led the team to bronze in Padukone's absence, India also bagged bronze medals in the men's doubles and mixed doubles events. That showing remains the best performance of the Indian contingent in the continental Games.

Padukone, however, was not really happy with the Indian contingent's sporadic success, and so the 1983 World Championship bronze medallist started the country's first top-class badminton academy in Bangalore, in 1994, where the cream of Indian badminton was provided free coaching and other training facilities. It was a revolutionary step at the time when most players were at the mercy of the national federation to host coaching camps under foreign coaches for quality practice with equipment of international standards.

Within two years, India had its first-ever world junior championship silver medallist when Aparna Popat reached the finals in Denmark. While Indian badminton was beginning to look up, thanks to improved performances at the international level, the players were feeling short-changed by the BAI, and Padukone ultimately raised the flag of revolt by forming the breakaway Indian Badminton Confederation (IBC). While many came forward to take credit for the change of guard in Indian badminton, with Fazil Ahmed stepping down after over two decades at the helm, it was Padukone's stature and his gentlemanly image that ensured that the sport took a step in the right direction.

Never a confrontationist, Padukone soon accepted the compromise formula offered by the then BAI President, V. K. Verma. Padukone took over as Executive President, and in his four-year term put together a robust coaching structure, started ranking tournaments with substantial prize money to the top performers, and build a strong junior programme through his own academy. But after the four-year stint he abandoned all that, as abruptly as he had started the revolt, to concentrate solely on coaching. A few years later, Padukone confessed to me that those four years had taught him he was not suited to administrative jobs. He insisted that India needed to invest in professionals to run the administration, if the country dreamed of becoming a world superpower one day. Although he never again bothered with the administrative set up, the academy produced numerous internationals, including Olympian Anup Sridhar, Nikhil Kanetkar and German Open champion Aravind Bhat, and also played a significant role in the success of Gopichand, who overcame a career-threatening knee injury to follow in his mentor's footsteps by winning the All England title in 2001.

But history will remember the 44 year old from Hyderabad as the man who ultimately took Indian badminton out of its inertia, and helped players and even fans realise India's real potential, and the possibilities that could be achieved by proper planning and sheer determination. Even as a player, Gopichand was probably the first to understand the changing dynamics of the sport where rigorous and planned physical training was an important tool for success, and had left the Padukone Academy in the late 1990s to work with Gangula Prasad at the Sports Authority of India centre in Bengaluru, as he felt that the latter could help him with the overall fitness regime.

The Dronacharya Awardee made it the backbone of his coaching structure when he started his own academy a couple of years after his All England triumph, and built the country's first-ever, state-of-the-art residential academy that would convert talent and potential into champion product. But it was not that easy. Gopichand had to mortgage his house and run from pillar to post to raise the required funds to build the academy before entrepreneur Nimmagadda Prasad came forward to support his cause. While that took care of the academy plans, the chief national coach had to fight many more battles before he managed to control the situation and implement his vision.

Having taken over the job from Vimal Kumar, Gopichand insisted that no player would be allowed to participate in international tournaments without being fully prepared and even blocked the entries of some of the senior players. That led to a revolt from the likes of 2011 World Championship bronze medallist Jwala Gutta, Chetan Anand, and many senior players who felt that Gopichand's diktat could not only hurt their world rankings, but also affect their chances of qualifying for the 2008 Beijing Olympics. At one stage it became such a huge media circus that players were constantly ranting about BAI and Gopichand trying to stiffle their freedom. He finally gave in and decided to concentrate on what he had under control—the performance of Saina Nehwal and other juniors—and was vindicated when the former became the first player to reach an Olympic quarter-final in Beijing.

Nehwal, in fact, was just 10 points away from a semi-final berth while leading 11–3 against Maria Yulianti of Indonesia in the decider before nerves got the better of her. She was just 18 then and playing in only her second major event. But she soon made amends by becoming the first world junior champion later that year in Pune. But that performance was enough for Gopichand to finally stamp his authority on the coaching system as he went about carefully putting in place a system that not only got the best out of Nehwal, but also produced a succession line in both men's and women's singles. It also helped that India was hosting the 2010 Commonwealth Games and the government was keen to provide all the support needed. Gopichand, therefore, brought back the culture of long-term national camps, with the elite group training at the Hyderabad centre for over 200 days a year, with physiotherapists and trainers working round the clock with the players. The immediate benefit of the policy saw India winning the team silver, apart from two individual golds in the women's singles and doubles, and a men's singles bronze, to help the hosts touch the 100-medal mark for the first time in the Games. But, more importantly, it provided the launch pad for Indian badminton to overcome traditional hurdles, including the lack of opportunities, proper coaching and funds, and stake its claim among the world elite.

According to the data released by the Sports Ministry earlier this year, grants worth ₹13.8 crore were given to the BAI for training and exposure tours in 2015–2016, as compared to ₹2.71 crore in 2005–2006, and the amount has only been increasing. Moreover, the top stars also get additional support from the Target Olympic Podium Scheme, while SAI has teamed up with the Gopichand Academy and BAI to support 50 upcoming badminton players with their training and tournament exposure. And Gopichand is the first to acknowledge the contribution of SAI and the Sports Ministry in the success of Indian badminton: 'It would not have been possible without the support of SAI. Badminton is an expensive sport and the support we have received for training and tournaments has been phenomenal so far.'

While SAI took care of the funding, Gopichand and his support staff went about instilling the discipline and the hunger for success among the players. During the initial stages he would stand near the breakfast table with a weighing scale to ensure that the youngsters were following diet charts given to them, and even pushing some of the players to turn non-vegetarian after it was clear that they were finding it difficult to physically cope with the rigours of the international circuit. Also, the coaching staff began instilling the winning mentality among youngsters, as they began speaking about winning tournaments rather than just protecting their rankings.

Nehwal best summed up that attitude as a 15 year old when answering a question about her chances of beating seniors during one of the national ranking meets. She shot back, 'They don't train enough. I will beat them.' If Gopichand was the master planer, Nehwal was the perfect pupil who was willing to push herself to the limit and was willing to follow every instruction to the T. In the 2006 Commonwealth Games, Nehwal was not really expected to play in the team event as Popat was still the main star. But the nine-time national champion had to pull out due to injury at the last minute, forcing national coach Vimal Kumar to blood Nehwal earlier than expected. Since she was never really expected to play, Gopichand had given her a strenuous fitness programme to follow. But once she was asked to play, everyone expected her to just concentrate on the match. However, to everyone's surprise, Nehwal continued to follow the programme, while giving her 100 per cent during the matches. 'Saina's single-minded dedication and ability to work hard made her a champion. She was the first to achieve what no one else had achieved before in Indian badminton and that inspired many others to believe that even they can achieve higher goals,' says Vimal Kumar, who worked with Nehwal for two years and also helped her become the world's number one shuttler in 2015.

Even before she turned 20, Nehwal had become an inspiration for fellow players who had once competed against her, as she became a catalyst for the exponential success story of Indian badminton. People began flocking to the stadium once again to watch Nehwal play, and the BAI's and Gopichand's smart strategy to host the World Championship in 2009, and at least two or three international tournaments, in the country inspired more and more youngsters to take up the sport. By first hosting the Grand Prix gold event and then upgrading it to a Superseries allowed the Indian players to test their mettle against some of the best players in the world, even as they began podium hunting in slightly lower-level tournaments.

Nehwal's Olympic bronze in London 2012 changed all that as it only elevated the aspiration levels of the likes of P. V. Sindhu, Kidambi Srikanth, and others. They were no longer satisfied with success in lower-level competitions and that showed in the way they trained and prepared for major tournaments. The players were now prepared to forgo ranking points and skip tournaments if they felt they were underprepared. Sindhu, who was just coming up during the period, was willing to concentrate on selective tournaments. Two back-to-back World Championship bronze medals in 2013 and 2014, besides a couple of Grand Prix gold titles, were a good return for the teenager.

Three years ago, neither Sindhu nor Srikanth—who went on to win his first Superseries title by beating the legendary Lin Dan in the 2014 China Open—had Nehwal's physical and emotional maturity that would allow for consistency on the international stage. But they had been part of national camps for quite some years and were supremely fit, enough to beat any opponent on a given day.

This has been true of almost all elite Indian players, as they are considered one of the most difficult opponents on the international circuit. 'We never lacked the skills. What we lacked was the fitness to last long matches,' Gopichand explains the transformation. So when Gopichand and Sindhu began preparing for the 2016 Rio Olympics, the former worked on his ward's self-belief and brought in a completely new dimension of discipline—by confiscating her mobile phone and making her focus on the job at hand. All those efforts did bear fruit when Sindhu became the first Indian woman shuttler to win an Olympic silver.

But the rise of many potential champions started becoming a problem since Gopichand alone was not able to give enough time to all the players. India experimented with a few foreign coaches, including the experienced Atik Jauhari. His Indonesian compatriot, Mulyo Handoyo, has been guiding Indian players for the past one year. 'Along with Mulyo, coaches like Amrish Shinde and Siddharth Jain started spending a long time at national camps. This allowed me to concentrate on the overall planning, while day-to-day systems were handled by them,' Gopichand said. The new system worked wonderfully well as Indian men singles players won five of 12 Superseries in 2017, with Srikanth winning four. In November, India had five players in the world top-20 men's singles ranking and also sent the largest contingent to the World Championship in Glasgow in August, winning two medals for the first time ever.

It, however, doesn't mean that there are no problems in the set-up that need immediate attention.

While the singles stars have been making a mark, India has still been struggling in the combined events. One can list the achievements of Jwala Gutta and V Diju breaking into the world top-10 in mixed doubles and Gutta and Ashwini Ponnappa bagging the 2011 World Championship bronze for a country that had nothing to show since the two bronze medals in men's doubles and mixed doubles in the 1982 Asian Games.

It's not to say that India has completely overlooked the doubles program but a lot needs to be done to identify talent early and then nurture them at the national camps. Most Indian doubles players have started playing in the combined events only because they were not good enough for singles. Thankfully, the added exposure to international tournaments from the junior circuit is helping players change that perception and a few juniors have already decided to shift their focus to doubles.

The young combination of Satwiksairaj and Chirag Shetty is one such success story. The two lanky players were combined together by former doubles coach Tan Kim Her of Malaysia in 2015 and they have gone from strength to strength. Having reached the quarter-finals of two Superseries events in 2017, they bagged Commonwealth Games silver in 2018 and then went on to become the first Indian pair to win a BWF Super 500 title in Thailand. They are currently ranked in the world top-10.

It was felt that coach Tan's abrupt departure in 2018 could hurt India's doubles program as a new coach may take time to gel with the players. But Indonesians Flandy Limpele and Namrih Suroto have managed to help Chirag and Satwik improve their overall fitness and speed. This has not only allowed the two to play with better freedom but also saw them beating almost all the top players in the world in 2019.

However, Chirag and Satwik's success cannot mask the fact that there is a long way to go for Indian doubles players to start matching the performance of their singles counterparts and help the team win medals in major team events.

But thanks to the adulation the top stars have been getting over the years, the hunger for success has definitely been ignited with the likes of Lakshya Sen, Ashmita Chaliha, Malvika Bansod in singles and Dhruv Kapila, Krishna Prasad, MR Arjun and Shlok Ramchandran beginning to make a mark on the international stage.

There may be many areas of improvement and Badminton Association of India needs to plan the progression better. But one cannot deny the fact that Indian badminton has taken flight after years of false dawns and a third successive Olympic medal in Tokyo 2020 would be an icing on the cake.

◆◆

A WELL-KEPT SECRET
The History of Rugby in Sri Lanka

SHANAKA
AMARASINGHE

I t was a Monday, the first day of rugby practice at New Malden. The King's College (KCL) 1st XV were a formidable bunch, and chilly October winds, semi-darkness and icy temperatures were not something a tropical postgraduate student was used to. On seeing the new, conspicuously brown, face among the lads, the coach asked me where I was from. 'Sri Lanka', I said proudly, as the team guffawed. 'This isn't cricket practice, mate,' said one senior to me condescendingly, as we broke for our first drill. I wanted to tell him about the rich history and culture of rugby in Sri Lanka, but decided quickly that picking up the captain and sitting him on his backside during our first tackling grid was a more effective method of communication. The communication was made, and I found myself starting for KCL 1st XV in two days' time. We do a lot more than play cricket. Mate.

Before the world became more cosmopolitan, any South Asian with a good command of English could almost guarantee being asked where he had learned to speak it. Similarly, I was asked, in amazement, where I had learned to play rugby. The accurate answer is that 150 years of colonialism is good for picking up both English and rugby, but the polite answer is 'in school'. Secondary school has become, and will remain for some time, the cradle of rugby in Sri Lanka—a cradle that rocked for longer than many would give credit.

THE COLONIAL INTRODUCTION

The origins of the game of rugby football are mythical. The best-known story is that of William Webb Ellis picking up a football and running with it. In Sri Lanka, though, its origins are hardly mythical but practical. With the advent of the British in 1796, Sri Lanka was passed on as a colonial subjugate by the Dutch. If there had been no such transition, Sri Lanka may well have boasted a rich tradition of hockey, football or cycling. Instead, we have some excellent, albeit redundant, canals, cricket and rugby—which were the favoured pastimes of British invaders. It took some time, as can be expected, for Sri Lanka to become a model colony. Both the Portuguese (1505) and the Dutch (1647) had been interested in trade. They were not entirely interested in conquering the whole country and confined themselves to the coastal areas, which they fortified and controlled. The British were more ambitious and, provoked by the odd native rebellion, made their way to the central hills where the Kandyan kingdom was situated, and ousted the reigning monarch. By 1815, the country was fully occupied and Ceylon began to take shape as a tea colony, with the upcountry hills being perfect for the crop—and the climate perfectly suited to rugby. With infrastructure like roads and railroads being prioritised, along with the setting up of Christian schools and knitting the social fabric together, it was not until 1879 that rugby was introduced to Ceylon, as it was then known.

The first club was inaugurated in June 1879, originally as the Colombo Football Club, later becoming the Colombo Hockey and Football Club (CH&FC), and is also referred to as the Gymkhana Club. It was across the road from Race Course, which has now become an international rugby stadium, reverting in the last decade to the glamour of its former horse-racing days.

TEA AND TACKLING

The plantation sector, which produced the world-famous Ceylon tea, was an inorganic one. Vast swathes of the central hills were deforested and cultivated, forming estates that mainly belonged to the commercial companies of the time. With the British being the sole purveyors of industry, all commercial activity was carried out by them, with natives 'making up the numbers', whether it be in the office or on the cricket pitch. Cricket found its way to Sri Lanka earlier than rugby, and the first recorded match dates back to 1832, nearly half a century prior to rugby. The South Asian physique possibly dictated this choice. Also, quite possibly, the heat. However, with the arrival of expatriates in increasing numbers to manage plantations and other businesses, and with a significant number of them being from Scotland and Ireland—with less cricketing tradition than the English, per se—rugby became the favoured game in that region. And by the time a critical mass of Europeans was domiciled to play against each other, there was no looking back.

Colombo was—as still is—the hub of all activity, and the first Club, it stands to reason, was birthed in Cinnamon Gardens, one of the more exclusive areas of Colombo, as referenced in Shyam Selvadurai's book (1998) by the same name. The Ceylonese Rugby and Football Club borders Maitland Crescent and Maitland Place, both named after Ceylon's second Governor Sir Thomas Maitland, in subtle homage to rugby's colonial origins. After the Club was formed in 1879, others soon followed, with Up Country clubs hot on Colombo's heels. The plantation sector proved to be the production line of rugby players in Ceylon, and the existing cricket clubs in Dimbulla and Dickoya soon doubled as rugby clubs. The first match between these two ancient clubs took place at the incredibly picturesque Darawella Grounds. Nestled in the valley between Horton Plains and Adam's Peak—Sri Lanka's most famous mountain—the ground has to be seen to be believed. The view is breathtaking and, by all accounts, the life of the 'planter' equally salubrious. The return leg of the first match in 1880 between Dimbulla and Dickoya was played at the equally stunning Radella Cricket Ground, which to date remains one of the few cricket grounds located at an altitude of above 4,000 ft.

The presence of these incredible grounds, in what was previously forest, shows British dedication to their sporting pastimes. Most grounds in the hills and the original Gymkhana Club in Colombo all double up as cricket and rugby grounds. With the departure of British expatriates, the rugby tradition in these parts of the island has declined. Land Reform, which came into force in the 1970s under the republican government, affected the ownership of estates. Slowly, over the next few decades, the tea industry for which Sri Lanka had become world famous lost its revenue-generating potential. The demography of plantation owners and staffers changed, and with it the sporting culture, which was so central to the expatriate way of life, faded away. Intervening insurrections and unrest in the area also contributed significantly to the downturn of the plantation industry. With several planters of running estates becoming victims of the insurgency of the late 1980s, it ceased to become the sought-after profession of the rugby-playing elite. Radella and Darawella are now rarely used in big competitions.

RUGBY IN EDUCATION

Just over a decade after the game began to be played by the clubs, it was introduced to schools by L. E. Blaze, the first principal of Kingswood College. This Methodist school in Kandy proudly wears the mantle of the first school to play rugby in Sri Lanka and has, fittingly, produced some of its best players. Kandy was the birthplace of school rugby, with Colombo schools taking to it later in the day—probably due to the higher temperatures on the coast, which were better for cricket, a traditionally 'summer' game. Trinity College, an Anglican missionary school across town from Kingswood, also took up the game, and the two Colleges played each other in the maiden school encounter in 1906, with the match ending in a 6–all draw. Ever since that encounter, rugby spread in the school system among the institutions run largely by various church denominations, and governed predominantly by British expatriates and clergymen. The Portuguese had brought Catholicism; the Dutch, Protestantism; the British dovetailed Anglican and Methodist teachings; while Catholic colleges were also instituted in Colombo, Kandy, Jaffna and other large towns. These schools were pioneers of both cricket and rugby ever since the mid-19th century, while many of them still have strong sporting traditions that state schools, begun post-independence in 1948, have since caught up to.

The most famous rugby match in Sri Lanka became, and has remained, the Bradby Shield encounter between Trinity College and Royal College. Royal College, previously known as the Royal Academy, and Trinity, began to play each other regularly in 1920. Subsequently, the Bradby Shield, donated by the then Trinity Principal E. L. Bradby, was played for in 1945. The encounter consists of home and away games, with the winner adjudged on aggregate. The encounter has graduated to becoming the most anticipated fixture on every rugby enthusiast's calendar and usually sees a mad scramble for tickets, with approximately 20,000 people in attendance and millions more watching an island-wide live coverage. Dean Richards—former Harlequin, and England and British Lions number eight—is a regular visitor at the game; Bob

Dwyer—World Cup-winning Wallaby coach—has been a guest speaker at the pre-match old boys' dinner; and a few years ago, Jonathan Kaplan—the world's number one referee—adjudicated the second leg of the Bradby. Such is its allure—and that too for a high school game of rugby.

THE ALL BLACKS PRECIPITATE FORMALITY

Another interesting characteristic of Sri Lankan rugby fans is the number of All Black (New Zealand National Rugby Union team) rugby fans in the country. With the national team not competing on the world's highest stage, the dominant team in the world has been adopted by many Sri Lankans, with the Sri Lankan flag featuring prominently on the sidelines during the 2015 World Cup final. The link between the two countries goes back over a century, however, with the All Black's game in Sri Lanka in 1907 creating the furore that led to the Ceylonese Rugby & Football Union being formed the following year.

The All Blacks were on their way to tour the British Isles, and the Ceylonese authorities guaranteed them a fee of USD 50 to play a match in Colombo. The game, played in September 1907 at the Havelock Race Course, was Sri Lanka's first rugby 'international'. The All Blacks, captained by Hercules Wright, swept aside the All Ceylon team, captained by A. F. West, 33–6. The Ceylon Sports Annual said:

> The All Blacks were infinitely superior—the acme of combination— different parts performing their functions almost with [the] regularity of a well-oiled machine. Nothing like such an exhibition of Rugby had ever been witnessed in the island.

No doubt it was a breathtaking affair to see the best players in the world dazzle in Colombo. While cable TV and the Internet have now made that almost a weekly sight in all parts of the world, the opportunity to witness a great team would have been a massive boon to the rugby public. The All Ceylon team was made up purely of expatriates, with eight members coming from the CH&FC Club.

Despite the obvious feather in Ceylon's cap, the All Blacks game caused some consternation at the Rugby Football Union (RFU), which, at the time, was to rugby what the Vatican is to

Catholicism. Rugby being a strictly amateur game, the RFU was upset that the All Ceylon team had paid a guarantee fee to the All Blacks in exchange for the game. As censure, they banned their home unions from playing any rugby in Ceylon. The only way to overcome this was to form the CR&FU and pledge allegiance, as it were, to the Crown. This process was unanimously completed in 1908, with all the clubs coming together to form the CR&FU. It is not clear whether the ban by the RFU was consequently lifted, but based on the fact that the British Lions toured half a century later, it would have been lifted at some point.

The newly formed CR&FU hosted its first international team at the 2nd Leicester Regiment stationed in Madras for a three-match series in 1910. Local broadsheets described the rugby as the best seen on the island since the All Blacks. The visitors won their matches comfortably at the Havelock Race Course.

THE CLUBS TAKE OVER

The following year, the most prestigious domestic competition in current Sri Lankan rugby was founded when Lady Elizabeth Clifford, wife of Acting Governor Sir Hugh Clifford, requested that a match be played between an All Ceylon team and a United Services team. The match was scheduled to be played on her birthday, but was, for some reason that escapes chroniclers, postponed for a week. United Services beat All Ceylon comfortably to win the first Lady Clifford Cup, as it was originally called. However, very soon after, in 1914, the army was transferred out of Ceylon because of World War I, decimating the selection for the United Services team.

In 1915, the Havelock Sports Club was founded to rival CH&FC's dominance in Colombo. Seven years later, the Ceylonese Rugby and Football Club (CR&FC) was founded by Colonel E. H. Joseph. The Club was a milestone in Sri Lanka's rugby journey, as it was exclusively made up of 'Ceylonese', i.e., Sri Lankan players. The All Ceylon team had hitherto been made up of exclusively European players, and the CR&FC took the first structured steps to challenge the status quo. They were accepted into the CRFU fold in 1926. With the advent of the Colombo clubs (CH&FC, Havelock and CR&FC), the rivalry with the Up Country clubs (Kandy, Kelani Valley, Uva, Dimbulla, Dickoya) increased, and matches became competitive and bruising. The competitiveness was good for Sri Lankan rugby on the whole, as it then undertook its first foreign tour in 1926 to play in the All India Rugby Tournament held in Madras. In 1928, Sri Lanka tied for the championship and eventually won it outright in 1929 by beating Madras, 11–8. They won their second title in 1932.

In 1930, almost 23 years after the All Blacks first toured the island, the British Lions made a stop in Colombo en route to their tour of Australasia. They beat All Ceylon comfortably by 45–0. It was the second-most high-profile team to play in Sri Lanka after the original, and controversial, All Blacks game in 1907. The Lions toured again in 1950, en route to the Southern Hemisphere.

By 1938, segregation in the rugby fraternity seemed to define the political tensions of the time. Ten years prior to independence in 1948, the make-up of representative teams from Sri Lanka was reflective of the social structure. The two teams—one exclusively white, and the other of Sri Lankan players—entered the All India Tournament. It is not clear whether the distinction was based purely on racial lines, or whether the expatriate team was coincidentally more able. However, the Western Australian team, which toured in the same year, played Up Country and Low Country (which were mixed teams), the Ceylonese team, and the All Ceylon team that was the only one to beat the Australians.

INDEPENDENCE AND RUGBY

After the experience of these foreign tours, Sri Lanka, in 1949—significantly, the year after independence from the British—hosted its first international tournament by organising, at short notice, the All India Tournament in Colombo. Sri Lanka stepped in due to difficulties faced by the original host, the Bombay Gymkhana Club, and ensured its supporters of rugby fare not seen since before the war. A local newspaper reported:

> A week hence, the CRFU will be staging the biggest Rugger tournament ever to be held in Ceylon. Never has there been such general interest centered in a Rugger match in Ceylon since the British RF team played in Colombo on their way home from New Zealand, a long while ago, as in today's final on the Race Course.

Given that the last foreign tour took place 11 years earlier, and with the misery of the war and the subsequent negotiations on

Independence, it was time for Sri Lanka to get back into the game it loved. All Ceylon narrowly beat Calcutta 5–3 in the final, with the Royal Colombo Golf Club hosting the post-match festivities. Prime Minister D. S. Senanayake was featured on the front page of the local dailies, watching the game. It was reportedly the first time that rugby had been as prominently displayed in front-page headlines. The All Ceylon team was captained by Lyn Simpson and, by all accounts, the tournament was well received.

The Clifford Cup, which was first played for in 1911, was resumed in 1950. This was also the year the British Lions toured Sri Lanka for the second time. Since its second coming, the Clifford Cup has remained the centrepiece of the domestic rugby season. While the league title has become competitive in more recent years, it is the Clifford Cup with which glamour is associated. It still holds pride of place, just as the Football Association Challenge Cup (FA Cup) in English football does to the traditionalists. In 1956 and 1957, a combined team of Dimbulla and Dickoya (fondly known as the Dim–Diks), captained by the famed Malcolm Wright, made its way into the Clifford Cup final before being beaten by the Sri Lankan-only CR&FC team, underlining the rapid rise of local rugby players.

Sri Lanka also hosted an Australian Colts side, a New Zealand Colts side and a combined Oxbridge side in the 1950s. Rugby continued to grow post-independence, with Up Country and Low Country rivalry being added to by the competition between the Colombo clubs. Added to this mix was the might of the tri-forces, as the Lankan Army, Navy and Air Force all took up the game and to this date compete in the top division. In this rapidly developing environment, the power shift from expatriate to local on the rugby pitch was also reflected by the gradual departure of swathes of English-speaking residents, predicated by Prime Minister S. W. R. D. Bandaranaike's 'Sinhala only' policy of 1956. Overnight, the policy changed the medium of instruction in schools and administration to Sinhala. Unwittingly, this alienated both Tamil- and English-speaking minorities. Most schools that took up rugby under the stewardship of Christian priests or European principals taught in English and replicated the British public school system. Suddenly, a mere eight years after Independence, many hitherto educated segments of society found that very same education inaccessible.

Many of the 'Burghers'—Sri Lankans of Eurasian descent—migrated, largely to Australia. British expatriates who had continued to do business in Sri Lanka returned 'home', as it were.

The fervour for rugby did not die down, though. And although Sri Lanka lost the kind of expats who currently keep Hong Kong in the top tier of Asian rugby, it continued to play high-quality rugby. Ironically, two of the country's highest achieving sportsmen came from these suddenly marginalised communities. Sri Lanka's only medal at the Olympics thus far had been Duncan White's silver in 1948. White was born to British ancestry and was matched on the Asian stage by his relay teammate Summa Navaratnam, whose exploits on the track earned him the nickname 'Fastest Man in Asia'. Born in Jaffna, Navaratnam's Tamil parents sent him to Royal College (previously the Royal Academy) to be schooled in the British public-school tradition. While excelling on the track, he also played rugby for Royal, CR&FC and Sri Lanka, winning the Clifford Cup as captain in 1954 and 1955. He also captained the Sri Lankan team to the All India tournament in 1955. The lightning winger with the ready smile was President of the Sri Lankan Rugby Football Union (SLRFU) when it hosted its largest tournament, the 1974 4th Asian Rugby Championship (Asiad).

THE ASIAD COMES TO COLOMBO

The SLRFU was tasked with organising the biggest sporting event that had been staged in Sri Lanka to date. Barring some crowd trouble in the Sri Lanka vs. Malaysia match, which the home team won 12–6, the tournament went off well. Japan had spent a couple of weeks in Sri Lanka to acclimatise and had run up 303 points against local opposition in its three warm-up games. The torrential downpour on the day of the final between Sri Lanka and Japan restricted the Japanese to a 44–6 victory, which gave Sri Lanka bragging rights as the second-best team in Asia. South Korea would no doubt contest this, given that the format of the tournament did not give it a passage to the final before meeting Japan, although the Japan vs. Korea game was the most riveting match of the tournament. After the conclusion of the tournament, Japanese rugby chief Shigeru Konno offered an all-expenses-paid trip to a Sri Lankan coach to visit Japan. It is not reported whether this generous offer was accepted.

Despite success at the tournament, the Asiad exposed the gulf between Sri Lanka and the Asian powerhouses. Shorn of expatriate players, the home team struggled physically. Given that both Hong Kong and Japan, currently the top two teams in Asia, rely heavily on expatriate players, one wonders whether the 1956 'Sinhala only' policy has had a lasting effect on rugby. However, a golden generation of players attempted to do what no Sri Lankan team had done before and win international honours. They did so in 1984 when they won the Bowl Championship at the prestigious Hong Kong Sevens, beating Thailand 16–10. It remains Sri Lanka's most famous victory on a global stage. Ten years later, Sri Lanka also hosted its first-ever Sevens tournament at the Sugathadasa Stadium, with several invitational teams participating under the watchful eye of Technical Director Jeff Matheson of New Zealand.

MODERNITY

School rugby continued to grow in this period with the advent of television coverage and active promotion by various SLRFU administrations, taking the game beyond the traditional public school domain. The Bradby became, and remained, the most anticipated encounter in the yearly calendar. Blaze, who introduced rugby to schools in the last century, has a trophy played in his honour between pioneers Kingswood and their Methodist rival, Wesley College. Trinity College play S. Thomas' College in the annual Canon R. S. De Saram trophy to honour the Colombo school's longest-serving warden. The colonial roots of the game are, therefore, still very much evident. However, it has in the last decade and more become a game of the masses.

Many who play cricket realise that unless you make the Sri Lankan team, there is little money to be made at the domestic level. However, the growth of rugby and its mercantile patronage means that aspiring players have some means of livelihood in the domestic circuit. Together with highly paid coaching and training jobs after retirement, rugby has fashioned itself to become a way of life. It is from this schoolboy cradle that Sri Lankan rugby is nourished. The game has spread rapidly in the last decade, with former President Mahinda Rajapaksha's sons at the forefront of the game's popularity. All three sons—Namal, Yoshitha and Rohitha—played for S. Thomas' College, captaining the College and their respective club teams. The two elder brothers captained Sri Lanka and their profile garnered vast column inches for the sport, especially in the Sinhala media which gave up its preoccupation with cricket. Their involvement brought the game a patronage that has outlived Rajapaksha's presidency. The demography following the game slowly widened, and rugby provided an avenue for social and financial success to those who may not have previously had those opportunities. Namal's captaincy of S. Thomas' in 2005 coincided with his father's election the year before. Former First Lady Shiranthi Rajapaksha—whose nephew also captained S. Thomas' eight years earlier—was a genuine rugby fan, and a fixture at the games. This raised the stakes for players, spectators and the media alike; and their collective enthusiasm, coupled with the penetration of social media and Internet streaming of games, has resulted in a mammoth school competition being battled out every year.

SPECTATOR GROWTH AND DIVERSIFICATION

It is not unusual to see crowds of 5,000 turning up to games on a Saturday afternoon, across four or five games played on the same day. The spectator count is probably higher than it is for some Super Rugby games. The top division schools spend between 10 and 40 million Sri Lankan rupees on their rugby budget for a year, which includes supplements, trainers, equipment and, occasionally, foreign coaches. New Zealand Sevens superstar Lote Raikabula is currently coaching Trinity College in Kandy, while former British and Irish Lion Eric Miller preceded him. High-profile players have also played in the Carlton Sevens in Sri Lanka, an international Sevens tournament, which was the brainchild of Namal Rajapaksha, and superceded the existing Sevens tournament organised by the SLRFU. Malakai Fekitoa and the Commonwealth gold-winning South African team all played in that tournament, which even saw former Tongan captain Willie Lose joining the commentary panel. Stirling Mortlock was also on the island some years ago to discuss the possibility of a tie-up with the Melbourne Rebels, given that Melbourne has the largest contingent of Sri Lankans living outside the island.

Ben Gollings, scorer of record points in the Sevens, was a part of the rugby coaching set-up when he took Sri Lanka to a consistent third place in the Asian Sevens behind Japan and Hong Kong. Since his departure, Sri Lanka is struggling to maintain its position in the top five amidst renewed interest from South Korea,

China and expatriate-heavy Malaysia and Philippines. Srinath Sooriyabandara was a household name on the Sevens circuit, and currently Dhanushka Ranjan has made a name for himself with some devastating running ability, putting Sri Lankan players on the Asian map. While the school game has its many benefactors, the SLRFU is reliant on corporate sponsorships that are not big enough to sustain rugby's heavy machinery while balancing the interests of the clubs that govern the SLRFU Council, and that do not want to lose their best players to the national cause.

However, rugby has risen to new heights in Sri Lanka. With the national cricket team disappointing consistently, more and more attention is being paid to rugby. More children are playing from a younger age, with over 120,000 players registered, making Sri Lanka the second-largest rugby-playing country in Asia behind Japan.

Although it has been 110 years since Sri Lanka played the All Blacks, steady progress with an increased amount of corporate funding may see Sri Lanka take them on again in a not too distant World Cup. For the moment, Japan and Hong Kong are the main targets. Even if those rivals are not hauled back, the game of rugby has achieved great things in the Sri Lankan social milieu. From being an exclusively European sport, it has evolved over time to become even more of a grass roots sport in some parts of the country than cricket. The interest in the school game is unparalleled, and it is only a matter of time before the craze spreads countrywide. Close rivalries, political patronage and the Old School Tie have combined to make rugby semi-professional. It has gone from being the remit of safari-shirt sporting planters, to a genuine career path for those who may not have had any growth opportunities earlier. Even though the game was traditionally dominated by the previously mentioned schools of Christian origin, the rise of Isipatana College as a rugby powerhouse—despite not possessing a ground of its own—characterises the depth of spirit the game has inculcated since it was taken up. The school's rise to prominence mirrors the growth of the game since it was democratised.

It may even be argued that Sri Lanka is one of the pioneering truly Asian sides which is reliant on solely home-grown talent and a resource of only 22 million people. The journey of Sri Lankan rugby has consistently mirrored its socio-political journey from colonisation to being the world's favoured tea manufacturer, to the growing pains of independence and republicanism, and finally its arrival in the social-media-driven sportainment culture. While cricket may historically be the apex sport, given its international success, rugby dominates the hearts and minds of more and more Sri Lankans on a weekly basis. It is a journey, many chapters of which remain to be penned. Sri Lanka's current ranking of 43 in World Rugby does not do justice to its rich history and tradition. Hopefully, it can build on this tradition, rather than regress from it.

◆

REFERENCE

Selvadurai, Shyam. 1998. *Cinnamon Gardens*. India: Penguin.

◆◆

IV
ANCIENT PURSUITS AND MODERNITY

THE GREAT GAMA AND HIS LEGACY

RUDRANEIL
SENGUPTA

Who can claim to be India's first sporting superstar? There is a definitive answer to this question: The wrestler Ghulam Mohammad, better known as Gama Pehlwan, who went to England in 1910, just another poor subject of the British Raj, and came back as Rustom-e-Zamana—the champion of the world—striking a telling blow for India at the very heart of empire.

It is a story beloved to wrestlers, and there is hardly a *pehlwan* who cannot recite a brief history of Gama, whose life has acquired the timelessness of a myth, a narrative as embedded in Indian wrestling lore as the exploits of Hanuman, the patron god of *kushti*.

The truth is, Gama was a star even before he left for his fateful trip to England. From Peshawar to Patna, from Junagadh to Jabalpur, in Calcutta or Dhaka or Srinagar or Madras—there was no place where Gama did not draw magnificent crowds.

Gama was born Ghulam Mohammad in 1878 or 1880 to a family of wrestlers of Kashmiri heritage. Gama's father Aziz Baksh, a court wrestler in the princely state of Datia, began taking his son to the *akhara* (wrestling school/wrestling pit) when he was just five. Gama lost his father when he was eight, but his training continued under his grandfather, and then his uncle.

That Gama's devotion to wrestling was of a rare variety was made apparent when he was just 10 years old, in a competition organised by the raja of Jodhpur, where wrestlers from around India came to test who could do the most *baithaks* (squats). Over 400 wrestlers competed, and after several hours of non-stop squats, only 15 were left. Gama was one of them. The rest were all well-known wrestlers. The raja had seen enough—he stopped the competition and declared Gama the winner. Gama later said in an interview that he could not remember how many squats he had done, but it was probably several thousand, and that he was bedridden for a week after that. By the age of 15, Gama had been formally appointed court wrestler in Datia.

Between 1904 and 1909, Gama's fame started to spread as he won a series of courtly tournaments across India. He won at the court of Rewa, at Orchha, in Gwalior and Bhopal, Tikamgarh and Indore, Baroda and Amritsar, and at Datia. Gama could not be beaten.

It was during one of these matches that a young Bengali wrestler by the name of Gobar Goho and his businessman brother-in-law Sarat Mitra hatched a plan to finance a team of wrestlers, led by Gama, to go to London and issue an open challenge. This was a time when the colonial construct of the 'weak' Indian, inferior in every way to his white overlords—but most glaringly in physical strength and courage—had a firm grip over the Indian imagination. Goho and Mitra wanted to shatter this belief, and Gama was to be their warrior.

In April 1910, the troupe of wrestlers arrived in England: Gama, his brother Imam Baksh, and cousins Ahmed Baksh and Gamu—all from the same akhara—accompanied by a cook. They lived and trained at the Oak Hotel in Surbiton, at Kingston-upon-Thames.

In its 14 May 1910 issue, *Health & Strength,* a London magazine, announced 'The Invasion of the Indian Wrestlers'. The wrestlers were to fight in the 'catch-as-catch-can' style—the precursor of freestyle wrestling, very similar to kushti—as opposed to the Greco–Roman style, which was more popular in Europe and involved standing wrestling with no leg holds, a style unknown to the Indians.

The magazine carried this challenge:

The sensation of the Wrestling World
Exclusive Engagement of India's Catch-as-catch-can Champions.
Genuine Challengers of the Universe.
All Comers. Any Nationality. No One Barred.

◆◆◆

Wrestling in India is old. 'Wrestling is as old as India, it came out of India's soil,' wrestlers unfailingly said when asked about how old they thought the tradition of kushti was.

A combat sport that resembles wrestling has been around since at least the fourth century BCE in India, though textual and archaeological evidence for wrestling as we know it—a man-to-man contest without punching, kicking or other strikes to the body, enclosed within a philosophy of non-violence, chivalry and fairness—begins to pile up only from the first century CE, acquiring real momentum in the medieval period of Indian history. By this time, kushti in India had absorbed influences from an astonishing variety of sources: the *mallayudh* (literally, 'wrestling-combat') described in the Mahabharata and Ramayana, mixed with the wrestling traditions of the Islamic world that spread across Central Asia from Iran to Mongolia.

A brief look at the origins of some of kushti's most well-known terms immediately reveals these influences: 'pehlwan' comes from *pahlavan*—champion—used across the Islamic world to describe a great wrestler, and thought to be derived from the Pahlava or Parthian tribe in Iran and its Arcaside dynasty, dating back to 250 BCE. Until very recently, the winner of the most prestigious traditional kushti tournament was given the title 'Rustom-e-Hind', from the wrestler–hero Rustom of the Islamic epic, *Shahnama*.

The origin of the word kushti is even older: it is derived from the Persian *kushti-gir*—belt-grabber—which in turn is derived from *koshti*, the sacred girdle wrapped around the Zoroastrian initiate. A simple, clerical entry from the *Ain-i-Akbari* shines a light on the astonishing reach of wrestling during the Mughal period. The entry lists the best wrestlers at Akbar's court, men who were paid hefty salaries and other privileges for their services to the sport.

> There are many Persian and Turani Pahluwans at court, as also stone-throwers, athletes of Hindustan, clever Mals from Gujrat, and many other kinds of fighting men. Their pay varies from 70 to 450 d.
>
> Every day two well-matched men fight with each other. Many presents are made to them on such occasions.
>
> The following belong to the best wrestlers of the age—Mirza Khan of Gilan; Muhammad Quli of Tabriz to whom His Majesty has given

the name Sher Hamlah, or lion attacker; Cadiq of Bukhara; Ali
of Tabriz; Murad of Turkistan; Muhammad Ali of Turan; Fulad of
Tabriz; Mirza Kuhnahsuwar of Tabriz; Shah Quli of Kurdistan; Hilal
of Abyssinia; Sadhu Dayal; Ali; Sri Ram; Kanhya; Mangol; Ganesh;
Anba; Nanka; Balbhadra; Bajrnath (Blochmann, 1873: 253).

Each name here is a door, a leap through time and space. Here
are athletes from across Central Asia: from the kingdom of Turan,
bordering Persia, inextricably linked to the *Shahnama*; from the
Persian city of Tabriz, one of the grandest cities along the Silk
Route of the time; from Abyssinia, the great cultural and trading
link between Europe, Africa and Asia; and from the ancient city of
Bukhara, also on the Silk Route. They lived, trained and wrestled
with the Jyesthimallas (the 'clever Mals') of Gujarat, a Brahmin sub-
caste whose very identity was founded on wrestling; Vaishnavites
like Kanhya (another name for Krishna) and Balbhadra (another
name for Balaram); Shaivites like Bajrnath; and warrior–ascetics like
Sadhu Dayal.

Centuries later, as the British took over India and introduced
other sports (like cricket), wrestling kept its place as the pre-
eminent sport of the people. Captain Godfrey Charles Mundy (1832:
279–85), aide-de-camp to the commander-in-chief of the
British forces in India in 1825, described a *dangal*—as wrestling
tournaments are known in northern India—in glowing terms:

> The Commander-in-chief having expressed a wish to witness
> the athletic and gladiatorial performances of the seapoys of the
> 39th infantry, sixteen of the most skilled in these sciences were
> drawn from the ranks, and in the cool of the evening repaired to Mr.
> Stockwell's garden.

A soft spot of earth was selected for the fight, and the English were
provided chairs under the shade of trees.

Mundy was fascinated by the display put on by the wrestlers.

> On meeting, they placed their heads firmly together, like butting
> rams, seized each other's wrist with one hand, whilst the other was
> twined round the back of the adversary's neck. In Indian wrestling,
> a fair fall consists in being thrown flat on the back, a consummation
> which, owing to the extreme agility and suppleness of the wrestlers,

is seldom accomplished. A front or side fall is not accounted disgraceful; on the contrary, it is common for the spent combatant to throw himself flat upon his face to gain breath; in which position, with outspread arms and legs, he defies the utmost attempts of his adversary to turn him, like a turtle, upon his back.

Mundy was most taken by a young boy of 22, who defeated six opponents in a row, four of whom were heavier than him. Mundy does not provide us with a name for this champion, but we do know that he had a

> Remarkably handsome and classical countenance, with a figure of perfect symmetry....And as he sprang into the circus looking sternly and confidently round for his first antagonist, I would not have wished for a better representation of a youthful Roman athlete.

◆◆◆

If Mundy were alive now, he would be astonished as to how little has changed at the village dangal, almost 200 years since he wrote *Pen & Pencil Sketches*.

On a mellow February morning, with winter on the ebb and the harvest festivals just round the corner, Satbir pehlwan, a young wrestler from Rohtak in Haryana, is making his debut on the dangal circuit. He has money on his mind. His itinerary is loosely defined, but the biggest dangals of the season are marked out: one in Haryana this week, Delhi in three weeks' time, a big fight near Chandigarh just four days after Delhi, then to Rajasthan, and finally, when the heat has settled and winter well forgotten, a major tournament in Uttar Pradesh. In between the big ones, there are numerous small village dangals to choose from; but those decisions will be taken on the fly. If all goes as planned, Satbir would have covered around 3,500 km by the end of the season. The pehlwan will be on the road, sleeping when he can and where he can. He will make his home in cars, buses, trains and railway stations. He will expect the villages where he goes to fight to provide food. Good food, the food of the pehlwans, with plenty of ghee, milk and thick rotis. The pehlwan will do all the things that his guru, Mehr Singh, had done more than 30 years before.

Satbir's guru had graduated, briefly, from a village wrestler to a national-level athlete in the 1980s. Mehr Singh comes from a long line of wrestlers: his father had worked the village circuit with considerable success. Before that, his grandfather and great-grandfather and perhaps even further back, though Mehr Singh cannot reach that far into the past with any certainty. The travelling wrestler is an ancient figure in India, he says, a tradition thousands of years old. He is just one of the uncountable many who have walked across the vast plains, looking for fame and money through the art of wrestling.

'The difference between me and my grandfather is that he could walk to Pakistan—even Afghanistan—if he wanted to. There were no borders in his time,' Mehr Singh says. 'I was bounded by India's borders....And the difference between me and Satbir...,' Mehr Singh stops, thinks about it, smiles, 'is that he doesn't really have to walk anywhere.'

As Satbir's car pulls up at the village near Rohtak where he will fight his first professional dangal, the wrestling has already begun. Next to where Satbir parks his car, wrestlers are using a water-tanker to shower down after their muddy bouts. A wrestler holds the attached pipe above his head and lets the water gush over him. He is wearing a red *langot* (a single piece of cloth wound around the groin, like a jockstrap). As the dust washes off his skin, the beautiful, trained muscles of his arms, shoulders and chest, and the long slabs of muscle in his thighs, glisten in the sun.

A few feet away, in a large clearing between the last line of houses and the rolling wheat fields of the village, wrestlers are kicking up dust as they scuffle. Four fights are on simultaneously, watched by a widening circle of men six to seven rings deep, the last of those concentric circles formed by cars and tractors. Most of the cars belong to the wrestlers, and there is a constant bustle as they step in and out of them to change, eat, drink, fight or sleep. People have gathered on the roofs of the bigger cars. The tractors have been parked expressly for the purpose of giving people in the last circle a raised viewing platform. Beyond this, carts selling sugarcane juice, sweet lime juice, chickpeas, peanuts, iced lollies and *golgappas* (Indian savoury snack) are doing brisk business.

A man yells incessantly into a loudspeaker, announcing the names of wrestlers, the villages they come from, their gurus and akharas, and commenting on the skills and techniques on display.

He lets forth fawning harangues on VIP guests—local politicians, bureaucrats and businessmen—who, it is announced, are great philanthropists donating money not just for the dangal, but also for a new temple in the village. He shifts seamlessly to a harsh, reproving tone for the unruly crowd, who are engaged in a constant and low-key battle of pushing and shoving, which turns intermittently into proper scuffling. The action on the field is equally riotous. Fights spill out of the arena and are taken up by partisan supporters. Villagers wielding long sticks swish around with unhinged menace to keep spectators away from the wrestling area. Flying dust makes the fights impossible to follow.

Satbir pehlwan waits patiently. He takes his time fixing his red langot, before his brother, who is driving him around, massages him with oil. As his fight approaches, he begins to limber up next to his car. He jack-knifes into push-ups. He does a few rapid squats. He jerks his thick neck muscles left and right to warm them up. Finally, his name is announced. It is the last fight of the day, a heavyweight bout, and a local giant will take on Satbir.

The two fighters, now only in their langots, stand in the centre of the arena. As tradition demands, they smear handfuls of earth on each other before they begin their bout.

The crowd is now quiet, attentive. Even the food carts have stopped business. The two heavyweights crash into each other. For the first few minutes, they push and pull to gauge each other's strength. Satbir's opponent drops down to get hold of his legs, but Satbir is quicker, and sidesteps the challenge. Now he has had the chance to move behind his opponent and lock arms around his waist. The local boy drops to his hands and knees, trying to shake Satbir off. The outsider heaves and twists, straining all his muscles to try and torque his rival onto his back. He fails. The referee separates them. Now it is Satbir who shoots for the legs, and gets them. His opponent goes down in a heap, but manages to rotate mid-air so that he lands on his chest and elbows. According to dangal rules, if the back of both shoulders of a fighter touches the ground, he loses. There are no points here, no handouts for technical nuances or superiority. Pin your opponent down, 'show him the sky'—that is the only way to win a bout. Realising that he is out of his depth, the local boy starts backpedalling to avoid Satbir's advances. More than once, he pedals straight out of the wrestling circle. The crowd gets aggressive, curses fly through the air. Better to be thrown and defeated than this shameful retreat!

Satbir gets more and more frustrated with his opponent's clumsy evasions. Covered in earth, and eyes glazed over in aggression, he is unrecognisable. Every time his opponent runs outside the bounds of the wrestling pit, he fumes and remonstrates with the referee. Why was he not being disqualified, Satbir wants to know. Why continue this farce? Finally, Satbir gives up the ghost of rules and regulations, chases his opponent into the crowd, and takes him down in a horrible mess of limbs and dust. Brawls break out immediately, spectators rush into the wrestling arena, stick-wielding peacekeepers enter the fray with war cries, the commentator screams at fever pitch and, somewhere in that dust-blind limbo, others try to separate the wrestlers and guide them outside the melee. Satbir's brother looks on with a droll smile. The pehlwan is brought to his car and they make a quick exit. The fight was, after all, with a local boy, and there is no telling who in the crowd might pull out a knife or a gun for revenge.

'Who did he think he was, Gama Pehlwan, taking you on?' Satbir's brother tells him, and they laugh as the car careens through dust paths towards the highway.

◆◆◆

If Satbir's opponent ran away from him in the wrestling arena, the Great Gama, a century ago, could not even find someone to step into the ring with him. He spent restless days in London. No one had responded to his challenge. The nationalist quest looked doomed before it could take off.

The reason was simple. While kushti continued to be the king of sports in India, in Europe it had already started to lose its value as a real sport, and had transformed into music-hall entertainment, at least in the big cities: showy, scripted matches between giant muscular men, full of 'flying holds' and dramatic reversals—what we see now on TV as World Wrestling Entertainment (WWE).

Gama and his men waited. April turned to May, May to June, June to July.

The London magazine *Health & Strength* made the reasons explicit: Gama had many offers of 'lucrative employment', the magazine said in an article, if only he would be willing to 'go down'—fight a pre-scripted bout, throw a match—'He simply doesn't understand what that means.'

Finally, Gama's challenge was accepted by an American show-wrestler called Doc Roller. On the afternoon of 8 August 1910, Gama and Doc Roller met at the baroque Alhambra Theatre, which loomed over Leicester Square. The massive hall was 'packed to the point of suffocation'. *Western Daily Press Bristol* had this to say:

> The large and Cosmopolitan crowd at the Alhambra, this afternoon, to witness the contest between Gama, 'Lion of The Punjaub', and the American, Dr. Roller, was sufficient testimony to the fascination of wrestling, for both men were newcomers to London.[1]

Hundreds were turned away at the door. Roller, at 6'1½", weighed in at 234 pounds; Gama, a half-inch below 5'8", at 200 pounds.

Gama came out to fight in his langot. 'Gama boasted nothing but a pair of red tights not worth the name of bathing drawers.' Roller wore long, dark blue trunks. Gama did a few rapid squat-jumps, 'bounding in the air like a ball', before the bell for the bout rang.

The first fall was quick, and brutal. *The Sportsman* reported:

> Gama sprang in for a leg hold at once, and Roller, very slow, was pulled to his knees….The Yank was soon up, only to be in a body grip, and, backing to the ropes put across in front of the footlights, fell over, his head coming heavily in contact with the bare boards.[2]

Shaken by the impact, and off balance, Roller had to be brought back to the centre of the mat by the referee. Here the attacks continued; Gama immediately got a waisthold, forcing a helpless Roller down on the mat with a heavy thud. First fall: one minute, 40 seconds. A 10-minute interval was taken.

'Gama opened the second bout with a smack on the neck, and then ducking quickly got a leg hold, which Roller broke.'[3] After his experience in the first round, Roller was cautious and defensive, looking to get out of Gama's way. But it did not help.

The Sportsman reported:

> The end came in 9 min 9 sec, when, after worrying his man with a vicious arm hold, Gama locked the American's legs and won with a press down from the front. ... It may interest Mr. Kipling to know that the gallery greeted the dusky victor as 'Gunga Din'.[4]

This match opened the door for what would be billed as the 'world championship', against a Polish wrestler by the name of Stanislaus Zbyszko, who had won the Greco–Roman world championship in Paris in 1906, and had since established himself as one of the foremost strongmen and show-wrestlers in Europe. When his match with Gama was arranged, Zbyszko knew full well that this was not going to be a scripted bout, but a real test of wrestling, and he trained accordingly, spending hours at a gym as well as swimming, wrestling, boxing and hill-walking every day. *John Bull*, a popular tabloid owned and run by the well-known raconteur, rabble-rouser, member of Parliament and soon-to-be-convicted fraudster Horatio William Bottomley, sponsored the Zbyszko–Gama fight. It was fixed at 250 pounds a side, and an honorary trophy—the John Bull Belt.

On the afternoon of 10 September 1910, a 12,000-strong crowd descended on The Stadium, Shepherd's Bush, London. Gama was on the attack from the very beginning. Within a minute, he had Zbyszko down on the mat. Bewildered by this frenzied opening, Zbyszko immediately went down to a defensive position—all fours on the mat, and sliding down on to his stomach at the slightest sign of danger that he would be turned on his back. With Zbyszko clinging to the mat, Gama tried hold after hold to get him to turn. A quarter of an hour later, the two men were still stuck in the same position. At the half-hour mark, Zbyszko felt confident enough to get on his feet. A flurry of attacks followed, described in some reports as a 'rugby scrimmage', and he went back to his defensive position, and the whole futile scene played out again on loop. This carried on for two hours, and the crowd got increasingly agitated.

After two hours and 35 minutes of this, the match was stopped due to fading light. The crowd, upset at the Polish wrestler's defensive tactics, surged forward riotously, and Zbyszko had to be escorted under the protection of the police. The *Western Daily Press Bristol* reported:

Gama, who appeared to be fully a stone the lighter man, did most of the attacking, and, in fact, during the whole of the time the contest took place Zbyszko only gained his feet on three occasions.[5]

A rematch was announced for the following Saturday to decide the winner.

'Fiasco at the Stadium', ran the headline in *Sporting Life*.

A more miserable, more disappointing match than this, the first professional out-of-door match of any consequence that has taken place in London of recent years, has fortunately seldom if ever taken place....It was disgraceful, a mockery of wrestling; and by it the game, which, it had been hoped, had received a healthy stimulus and recommendation to the public interest, has received one more bad shock.[6]

When the date for rematch came around, Gama and his entourage reached The Stadium. Zbyszko's name was called out several times, but he had already left England. Gama was declared the winner, and Bottomley, editor of *John Bull,* presented him with the John Bull Belt, saying he was glad to find that a *British subject* had won.

Where was the strike against colonial arrogance at the heart of the empire? This fight was not the flag of indigenous physical culture, flying against the imperial idea of Indian weakness, nor the bold and brave statement against racism, against the propaganda that Indians were inferior to their British overlords.

Instead, Gama and his men were at best good wrestlers and 'British subjects' who had done the empire proud by beating those arrogant wrestlers from the continent. At worst, they were a circus act in a city full of wonderful and exotic curiosities from all over the world.

If there was an anti-imperialist undercurrent to Gama's stay in London, it was quickly subdued. The editor of *Health & Strength* wrote just before the Gama–Zbyszko fight:

I actually received letters from readers in India pointing out that if they [the Indian wrestlers] kept on winning, their victories would give a dangerous fillip to the seditions amongst our dusky subjects that menace the integrity of our Indian Empire. But that is another story, upon which I do not propose to enter.[7]

Gama's time in England had come to an end. In the winter of 1910, the troupe made its way back home, going as quietly as it had come.

◆◆◆

In India, though, the story had acquired a different momentum. Gama was hailed as a hero, and his fame spread ever wider. He was feted as the world champion of wrestling, a title that Gama believed he had earned. Among many nationalists and physical culture enthusiasts, he became the symbol of India's suppressed strength—a glorious, wholly indigenous icon of masculinity.

The maharaja of Patiala gave him land and showered him with gifts. He was invited to the 25th session of the Indian National Congress at Allahabad in December 1910, where an Indian wrestling championship was held along with the United Provinces' exhibition. About 10,000 people gathered to see Gama, reported the *Aberdeen Daily Journal*, and 'so far, Gama, the famous Indian wrestler, has not been defeated'.[8]

Where can Gama and his legacy be found?

In Datia, the princely state in which the pehlwan grew up, there is nothing to remember him by. His akhara is long gone. In Patiala, where he was based during his glory days after that fateful trip to London, nothing is left except a *hasli*—a doughnut-shaped stone worn around the neck while doing squats—that supposedly belonged to him. The hasli lies in a dark corner in a dark 'museum', a forgotten room with a completely arbitrary collection of sporting memorabilia, at the National Institute of Sports (NIS), which is housed in the maharaja of Patiala's palace. During Partition, Gama and his family moved to Lahore. On 22 May 1960, the Great Gama died a broken, poor and forgotten man in a hospital in the city.

His legacy, though, lives on in the hearts and minds of wrestlers in India, old and young, Olympic or dangal champion, in phrases and in conversations.

'A great man,' says Yogeshwar Dutt, who won the bronze at the 2012 London Games. 'In wrestling, who is a bigger hero than Gama Pehlwan?'

◆

NOTES

1. *Western Daily Press Bristol*, 8 August 1910.
2. *The Sportsman*, quoted in Noble (2002).
3. *Ibid*.
4. *Ibid*.
5. *Western Daily Press Bristol*, 10 September 1910.
6. *Sporting Life*, quoted in Noble (2002).
7. *Health & Strength*, quoted in Noble (2002).
8. *Aberdeen Daily Journal*, 31 December 1910.

REFERENCES

Abu-al-Fazl 'Allami. *Ain-i-Akbari*. Trans. H. Blochmann and H. S. Jarrett [1873]. Calcutta: Asiatic Society of Bengal.

Mundy, Godfrey Charles. 1832. *Pen and Pencil Sketches: The Journal of a Tour in India*. Vol. II. London: John Murray.

Noble, Graham. 2002. 'The Lion of the Punjab: Gama in England 1910', *The Journal of Alternative Perspectives on Martial Arts and Sciences*, vols. I–IV. http://ejmas.com/jalt/jaltframe.htm.

❖❖

WRESTLING WITH THE HISTORY OF YOGA AS SPORT IN MODERN INDIA

JOSEPH S.
ALTER

T he argument put forward in this essay is that however 'absurd' modern yoga may appear to be, it is nevertheless characterised by a kind of 'transcendent' continuity, albeit continuity that emerges from social and cultural history rather than the prospect of holistic well-being, much less enlightenment. Underlying what appears to be radical discontinuity, gross appropriation, and both cynical and sincere claims made about what yoga means—as well as outright confusion, contradiction and misunderstanding concerning these claims—is a theory of embodied self-development that has much greater continuity than might appear to be the case, but only because the practice of yoga reflects a materialist struggle with the desire for idealistic transcendence. An understanding of the relationship between self-development and physiology provides a critical perspective on a history of cultural continuity in the practice of yoga as a struggle. This serves as a counterpoint or analytical antidote to what might be called yoga's postmodern, politicised disarticulation. The case of yoga as sport is used to illustrate this point.

INTRODUCTION

While becoming a global phenomenon with numerous local articulations, yoga has recently been politicised in ways that foreground questions of the proprietary control of tradition, intellectual property rights, the cultural politics of authenticity and nationalism more broadly (Alter, 2004, 2011). Although yoga has always been politicised, if for no other reason than because power in various forms is central to practice (White, 1996, 2003), one of the most interesting and contentious issues in the context of yoga's modernity is the sheer diversity of forms and tremendous variation in the institutionalisation of practice (Jain, 2015; Singleton and Byrne, 2008). Yoga seems to be endlessly adaptable and amenable to divergent interpretations, albeit within a history of philosophy that provides a degree of intellectual coherence and embodied spiritual gravitas, at least up to a point (Mallinson and Singleton, 2017; White, 2014). In broad terms, the practice of yoga in the 20th century has become medicalised with reference to different therapeutic systems, including biomedicine, Ayurveda and nature cure, each in significantly different ways (Alter, 2004); it has been incorporated into the logic of religious modernity and certainly into the spiritual rhetoric of many so-called 'godmen' (Strauss, 2005); it has been incorporated into health reform activism all over the world (Alter, 2007a); it has been institutionalised as a form of physical education (Alter, 2007b); and, as a competitive sport, it has come to be practised as gymnastics and bodybuilding (Alter, 2011; Yesudian and Haich, 1949, 1953). Above all else, yoga has been commercialised and professionalised in ways that are closely linked to the economics of capitalism, neo-liberalism, the politics of nationalism, and the changing environment of public health during the past 150 years (Jain, 2015; Singleton, 2010).

Examining the diverse ways in which yoga is practised by different people with very different agendas and interests, one might conclude that there is no way to find any degree of cultural coherence in the practice of yoga, and that it is best to simply conclude that political and economic interests define how and why the term 'yoga' is used in any given context. While justified, taking this somewhat reductive analytical route essentially makes the meaning of something called 'yoga' irrelevant to an understanding of its practice in any given context, be it something called 'goat yoga' in New Hampshire,[1] yoga for the enhancement of orgasmic pleasure in New York,[2] yoga for the rehabilitation of incarcerated criminals,[3] yoga as a means by which to embody an alternative, 'Hindu' modernity in Haridwar,[4] Hot Yoga in Los Angeles,[5] yoga for the treatment of asthma in New Delhi,[6] or, perhaps, most especially—albeit for an enlightened purpose-not-very-well-defined—yoga with Beagle puppies in Arlington, Virginia.[7]

In other words, it is both easy and accurate to conclude that yoga has become precisely what some say it is designed to transcend:

an epitome of the very illusion that perceptual, material reality is a domain of coherent, meaningful experience. In many ways, modern yoga can be said to ironically essentialise and concretise the philosophical principle of maya.

Much of my recent work on the cultural history of yoga in the 20th century has engaged with: (i) the problem of drawing this deconstructionist conclusion; (ii) the problem of claiming that yoga is one thing *but* not another; or (iii) the problem of radical relativism: that yoga can mean anything to anyone under specific and particular cultural circumstances. Earlier research on the practice of *pehlwani*—which, as we will see, involves an adapted form of yogic 'postural practice' within the competitive framework of wrestling in India—focused on the cultural construction of masculinity as an embodied ideology of power set within a very specific context of meaning. In other words, from a radically relativist perspective, pehlwani can be interpreted as a form of yoga (Alter, 2013).

My goal here is somewhat, if not completely, different from that which might be reached by means of these various approaches to the study of embodied meaning. This essay represents a return to a broader, theoretical consideration of the relationship between physiological experience on the one hand, and the cultural construction of ideas about the nature of that experience on the other. My argument is that, regardless of how divergent the various constructions of yoga in context can be, what makes them possible is not simply the political economy of cultural pastiche as a feature of postmodernity, or even just politics as such—as in magnanimous proclamations made at the United Nations, concerning International Yoga Day.[8]

What makes it possible for yoga to be so many different things is the inherent phenomenological disarticulation of human experience in the world from the possibility of transcendence as an embodied ideal. As a *social* phenomenon, yoga does not reflect the cultural meaning assigned to it in any specific context. However, the social history of yoga—as medicine, as sex therapy, as philosophy, as multi-species communion, or as competitive sport—can be made sense of by focusing on the way in which the practice of yoga, in any and all forms, reflects a struggle against the inherently alienating disarticulation of body and mind, not only where body and mind are disarticulated one from the other, as a function of enlightened reason in the context of European modernity, but *especially* and *precisely* in those instances where there seems to be a complete, holistic synthesis or historically structured postcolonial re-synthesis, of physiological realism and philosophical idealism. In other words, I will argue, very deep alienation, such as is manifest in the fetishisation of transcendence, produces a logic of struggle that can help to explain how and why yoga can be a sport that idealises in practice precisely that which, in the metaphysical philosophy of soteriological yoga, is understood to be the ontological problem of existence.

By focusing on the alienating disarticulation of body and mind in the social history of yoga, and how this helps us understand yoga as religion, yoga as medicine, yoga as political performance, and especially yoga as sport, the point of departure is simply to recognise that, from the standpoint of being animals in a *socially* animated world, our human bodies define a level of experiential reality that strains against the logic of idealism. Idealism is, of essence, a cognitive function of the perceptual attribution of meaning to things, including an abstract thing called transcendence, apart from semiotic relations that constitute a necessarily social logic that is essential to the production of knowledge about things. From a sociological standpoint that is rooted in the reality of sensory experience, to be human is to live subjunctively in a space defined by the struggle between consciousness and the transcendence of consciousness. Yoga in all its various forms—sublime, serious, sportive, surreal, sensuous, silly and spurious—inhabits this space.

WRESTLING AS YOGA

For anyone familiar with the sport of wrestling in India, called *kushti pehlwani*, it might seem rather absurd to claim that pehlwans and yogis have anything in common. Where wrestlers are thick, solid, physically muscular and grounded in the reality of this world, intent on achieving success by grappling with competitors (R. Sen, 2015; Sengupta, 2016), adept practitioners of metaphysical yoga are lithe, flexible and metaphysically inclined, intently focused inward, at least to the single point of mental concentration, rather than outward. Through stages of progressive isolation, the yogi is thought to have achieved an embodied state of perfect transcendental union. Rather than grappling with dualism in its various illusive manifestations, the yogi is said to embody a state of being—the immortal 'enstasy' of samadhi—which transcends the structure of the problem of perceptual reality.

There are seemingly obvious and overwhelming differences between wrestling and yoga. Most practitioners would tend to see and emphasise these differences, which are more than just superficial. And yet there is also deep—albeit complex—continuity; continuity in terms of the relationship between gross and subtle physiology in general and the embodied dynamics of sex, power and self-control in particular. While similarity along these lines reflects a certain logic of 'cultural' continuity in terms of how the body is conceptualised and experienced in South Asia, there is also a degree of overlap involving wrestling and yoga with respect to mythology on the one hand, and social and political history on the other (Alter, 2013). In other words, yoga and wrestling converge in practice at several levels of reality, manifest most clearly—and obviously—in the embodied practice of wrestlers who do yoga and yogis who wrestle.

Space does not permit more than brief reference to mythology, but it is noteworthy that the Ramayana and Mahabharata epics contain numerous references that suggest a degree of congruity between 'meditation and the martial arts', so to speak (Purandare, 1992; Rajagopalan, 1962). Lord Hanuman's strength is, in many ways, directly correlated with his singular unwavering devotion to Lord Ram, and the extent of his devotion can be conceptualised as a form of theistic yogic union. Beyond this, Lord Krishna is recognised as an iconic wrestler who defeats Kansa in an epic wrestling match, just as he figures very prominently in the Gita as Arjun's charioteer—the war chariot itself being a principal metaphor for control of the mind and the senses in the articulation of yogic practice. Although the Gita is by no means a discourse on postural *Hatha Yoga*, it most certainly represents philosophical principles that are specifically yogic. The point here is that mythology often involves the logical possibility that physical power and the martial arts reflect strength that is at once 'natural' and concrete as well as supernatural, mystical and ineffable (Diamond, 2013).

Research on ascetic warriors in the pre-modern period of South Asian history indicates a significant and interesting degree of overlap between the embodiment of various forms of power

(Pinch, 2006). In broad terms, the institutionalisation of asceticism within the framework of *akharas* (institutionalised ascetic sects) facilitated the politicisation and militarisation of sectarian ascetic orders in the 16th, 17th and 18th centuries. Based on a metaphysics of soteriology that is decidedly other-worldly, 'super-natural' physical power claimed by those who subscribed to various ascetic modes of yogic self-discipline was used as a means by which to control resources, and secure political and economic advantage in the 'real' world. This makes sense in terms of research on popular conceptions of yogic power during the Mughal and British periods, showing how people were ambivalent about the claims to power made by yogis (White, 2009). They were generally viewed, with cynical scepticism tinged with fear, as sinister practitioners of black magic intent on duping the credulous and building alliances with powerful patrons by means of a politics of deception. As comparable cases from around the world suggest—ranging from Alexander and the Oracle at Delphi, to Rasputin and the Russian Czar—the convergence of power, prophecy and contrived profundity by means of mysticism and magic is an integral feature of realpolitik. To the extent that warrior ascetics practised wrestling to embody a unique form of power within the matrices of imperial power, it would have involved a synthesis of the martial arts and the dark arts.

In the context of a history of ideas about the relationship between yoga and the martial arts, including a history of the body in South Asia which suggests that physical strength is closely linked to forms of ritual practice that synthesise purity and power (Whitaker, 2011), we can more easily understand the logic underlying Shanti Prakash Atreya's claim that pehlwani is, simply, an extension of the practice of yoga into the arena of wrestling as a way of life, and that a yogic theory of physiology—based directly on *samkhya* philosophy—provides a practical framework for athletic training. Not only does Atreya's reasoning make sense in terms of the larger mythology and socio-history of yoga, asceticism and the martial arts, it helps to explain the otherwise somewhat curious— and counter-intuitive—fact that a number of the leading figures in the development of modern yoga, including Shri Yogendra Krishnamacharya, Sri Aurobindo and Swami Sivananda, all engaged in various forms of athleticism and/or martial arts (Alter, 2011, 2013). Even though he had a rather ambivalent attitude concerning the virtue of postural practice, it is important to remember that Vivekananda famously advocated a form of modern 'muscular Hinduism' that combined athleticism with the biomorality of yogic asceticism (A. P. Sen, 2003).

In any case, as a champion wrestler and prolific writer on the subject of pehlwani, Shanti Prakash Atreya—whose father B. L. Atreya taught philosophy at Banaras Hindu University—developed an argument which can be summarised as follows, drawing both on interviews that were conducted with him by me in 1988 as well as several articles published by one of his students (Kesriya, 1992, 1993, 1996). The development of skill and strength as a wrestler is dependent on the physical development of shakti in a way that synthesises the power of the subtle body with the strength and stamina of the gross body (Atreya, 1965, 1987). *Pran* and *ojas* within the samkhyan rubric of *sukshmavyayam* transubstantiate into air and semen within the operational parameters of pehlwani athleticism, although it is important to keep in mind that semen is a subtle substance that manifests itself in terms of gross physiology as the radiant essence of a body of one colour, *ek rang ka sharir* (Alter, 1993). In other words, semen is a substance that is uniquely gross and subtle in the same form (Alter, 1994). In conjunction with this, Atreya argues that the body of the wrestler manifests a distinctive, highly energised, dynamic balance of the *triguna* strands—*sattva*, *rajas* and *tamas*—albeit a 'balance' that involves a maximisation of pure *sattvic* radiance to counterbalance tendencies toward exaggerated *rajasic* violence on the one hand, and sensually exaggerated *tamasic* immorality on the other. To effect a preponderance of controlled sattvic radiance, Atreya develops a theory of physical training based on a vegetarian diet and *pranayama* exercises, while engaged in vigorous exercises and sparring routines. Consumed as part of an exercise regimen designed to generate shakti, a pure sattvic diet, including ghee and milk and almonds, is transubstantiated into semen (Atreya, 1987).

Although Atreya does not go into detail on the subject, his understanding of the relationship between shakti and semen is worked out in terms that clearly demonstrate samkhyan principles, as yoga can be understood as the embodiment of an alchemical process of transmutation involving the *mahabhuta* elements (White, 1996). More generally, his logic abides with many of the structural principles outlined by Geoffrey Samuel and Jay Johnson (2013) in their discussion of the subtle body in the context of South Asian religions. In essence, what alchemical yoga is said to do, in terms of the language of transcendence, is produce immortality. Once the condensed essence of life in the body merges with transcendent cosmic energy, the flow of material substances in and out of the mortal body ceases, such that change and the karmic entailments of change—of which reproduction is the most obvious form—is no longer the defining characteristic of life and sensory experience. In pehlwani, absolute celibacy is analogous to 'enstatic' samadhi following the ecstasy of kundalini enlightenment, an experience often described in terms that reflect the subtle logic of internalised ejaculation.

We may conclude, therefore, that whereas wrestling in sportive practice seems to have nothing in common with *asana* and pranayama, in terms of subtle physiology, yoga and wrestling can be made to become virtually identical, at least up to that point of translation across domains of embodied experience when it further becomes clear that both simply involve hyper-exaggerated fetishisation, as fetishisation—in this mode especially—is animated by profoundly alienated human consciousness manifest in the deep desire to achieve what is impossible—to overcome mortality.

YOGA AS SPORT

Which brings us to a consideration of yoga as sport and the question of how to make sense of this particular manifestation of subtle, transcendental consciousness in the form of gross competitiveness and hyper-exaggerated, heroic individualism.

It will come as no surprise to those familiar with the medicalised history of asana and pranayama in Indian modernity to learn that yoga has been conceptualised not just as physical fitness, but as an athletic sport and a form of bodybuilding from as early as the 1930s (Alter, 2011). In fact, yogic bodybuilding probably dates to the time when Eugene Sandow travelled throughout British India in 1904, promoting his brand of moral muscular masculinity (Waller, 2011). As exemplified by the likes of Apa Pant and Krishnamacharya, as well as a large contingent of admirers in Calcutta, asana, pranayama and *surya namaskar* came to provide the means by which to embody a form of alternative masculinity that was distinctively Indian but also definitively modern in a mode suggested by muscular Christianity in the context of late colonialism (Alter, 2000).

As exemplified most clearly by Shri Yogendra and Swami Kuvalayananda, asana and pranayama were not only easily and effectively adapted for both therapy and physical education. These discursive frameworks facilitated the transformation of mysticism and magic into medicine, making it possible for yoga in postural form to become relevant to the concerns of the urban middle class in colonial India. While growing up in a small town in the Bombay Presidency, Yogendra had been a wrestler, and Kuvalayananda came of age training in the martial arts at Jummadada Vyayam Mandir under the tutelage of Professor Rajratan Manikrao, an advocate for muscular Indian nationalism. Although primarily focused on the medicalisation of postural practice within a rubric of modern scientific research, both Yogendra and Kuvalayananda developed asana and pranayama routines designed for integration into school programmes. The goal here was to implement a programme of physical education based on the moral, ethical and philosophical idealism of 'classical' yoga philosophy. This was done to establish an indigenous alternative to the YMCA. It is interesting to note that, in many ways, the logical correlation between athleticism and self-development was more obviously—and 'coherently'—articulated in the metaphysical philosophy of yoga than in the somewhat contrived logic of muscular Christianity, which places emphasis on ethics derived from the competitive sociality of sport rather than from the embodied practice of gymnastics and exercise (Alter, 2007a).

Be that as it may, it is possible to understand the 'contorted' logic of postural yoga's development as a sport by examining the case of Hanuman Vyayam Prasark Mandal (HVPM), a nationalist gymnasium established in 1914 by the Vaidya brothers. The HVPM was founded on the model of Rajratan Manikrao's facility in Baroda, but grew rapidly with a focus on athletics and sport rather than revolutionary martial arts. Once HVPM was institutionalised as a professional organisation, in 1918, the Vaidya brothers focused their energy on systematically modernising traditional Indian sports. Throughout the late 1920s and early 1930s they organised competitions, classified and sub-classified postures, systematised asana routines, sought to formalise the techniques for executing these routines, and established the rules by which to judge proficiency and expertise. They were especially adept at integrating asanas with floor exercise routines and at incorporating postural practice into the regimen of *malla khamba,* a gymnastic apparatus used by pehlwans for developing strength and flexibility. Although national level competition was not completely established until the founding of the Yoga Federation of India in 1974, yoga was clearly conceptualised as a sport with nationalistic international aspirations by 1936 when the Vaidya brothers sent a delegation to the Berlin Olympics and a team to the Lingiad (Alter, 2007c; Ganorkar, 1951).

At approximately the same time as the establishment of HVPM, Bishnu Ghosh, younger brother of the more celebrated Yogananda Paramahansa, left Ranchi in Bihar, where he had been introduced to the practice of 'Yogoda' in his brother's Self-Realisation Fellowship, to study at Calcutta University. Under the tutelage of Professor Thakura, Ghosh began to develop a form of practise that combined Yogoda asana postures with other gymnastic techniques and forms of bodybuilding. In this environment, the idea of turning yoga into an intensely competitive sport made perfect sense, even though Yogananda Paramahansa's influence on the practice of yoga worldwide has come to highlight the path of metaphysical self-realisation rather than competitive, individual achievement. In any case, Bishnu Ghosh's nephew and student, Buddha Bose, became one of the leading figures in the development of athletically inflected postural practice in the 1930s and 1940s.[9] Bikram Choudhury, Ghosh's most well-known disciple, came to embody the aspirations of yoga as a form of competitive gymnastics and bodybuilding in the late 1960s and early 1970s. Building on this legacy, the International Yoga Sports Federation, under the leadership of Rajashree Choudhury, has systematised the rules of competition, the goal being that postural yoga will ultimately be recognised as a sport by the International Olympic Committee (IOC).[10]

THE PROBLEM AND POSSIBILITY OF THE MORTAL BODY

At least in part because of the way in which postcolonial nationalism has fetishised 'tradition', at once standardising, sanitising and then further exoticising the practice of yogsa, even as asana and pranayama have become medicalised and commercialised, one might easily conclude that yoga exemplifies the pastiche of postmodernity, where anyone can lay claim to meaning and then construct that meaning in their own image.

It is important to keep in mind that the practice of yoga, however metaphysical, has always been grounded in the materiality of the body, albeit very often in the form of the body's most subtle manifestation. As such, yoga is best understood in terms of the existential problem it defines, rather than in terms of the particular form of any specific answer provided to this problem. Thus, yoga is the articulation of a fundamental question concerning ontology, rather than an epistemological method for achieving transcendence or for doing anything else. On the level of epistemology, it is endlessly flexible.

Understood in this way, it is possible to transcend the illusion of difference, so to speak, and find, at least in terms of knowledge, historical continuity in the struggle manifest in various forms of yogic practice, as struggle relates to the problem of fundamentally never being able to transcend the material reality, and time-bound inevitability, of death as a fact of life.

If yoga is understood to be a method of doing something, be it transcendence or something much more mundane, logic immediately drags one down the rabbit hole of radical relativism, searching for the perfect manifestation of practice—the lost sage in the Himalayas, the perfect orgasm (or absolute celibacy), the elixir of enstatic immortality, the cure for cancer, the body of one colour, samadhi, or a championship gold medal in yoga gymnastics, won at a future Olympic Games when asana routines are finally certified by the IOC. Clearly, yoga cannot legitimately be all of these things at once, and so it cannot be any one of them.

But the *embodied* nature of the struggle to achieve perfection—which distinguishes yoga from a spectrum of more purely idealistic and more abstract endeavours—provides a framework for understanding how practice has taken shape historically. Thus, by subjecting transcendental idealism to the realism of a sociological critique, and by applying this critique to an examination of yoga as sport, we can see how wrestling as yoga anticipates yoga as sport in 20th-century Indian history. If the scale and scope of time and space were to be expanded, one could see just as well Patanjali's struggle with the problem of materialised magic at one point in time and, at the other, Narendra's Modi's struggle to control the meaning of modern yoga in the magical transformation of contemporary India into a nation moving into the future while trying to essentialise its past.

◆

NOTES

1. www.goatyoga.net
2. https://www.menshealth.com/sex-women/yoga-for-better-sex
3. https://prisonyoga.org/
4. See Alter (2008). http://yoggram.divyayoga.com/
5. https://www.bikramyoga.com/
6. http://bnchy.org/
7. https://www.facebook.com/events/123217815089038/
8. http://www.un.org/en/events/yogaday/
9. http://www.buddhabose.com/
10. http://www.iysf.org/

REFERENCES

Alter, Joseph S. 1993. 'The Body of One Color: Indian Wrestling, the Indian State and Utopian Somatics', *Cultural Anthropology*, 8 (1): 49–72.

———. 1994. 'Celibacy, Sexuality and the Transformation of Gender into Nationalism in North India', *Journal of Asian Studies*, 53 (1): 45–66.

———. 2000. *Gandhi's Body: Sex, Diet and the Politics of Nationalism*. Philadelphia: University of Pennsylvania Press.

———. 2004. *Yoga in Modern India: the Body between Science and Philosophy*. Princeton, N. J.: Princeton University Press.

———. 2007a. 'Yoga at the *fin de siècle*: Muscular Christianity with a "Hindu" Twist', in J. J. MacAloon (ed.), *Muscular Christianity and Colonialism*. New York: Routledge.

———. 2007b. 'Yoga and Physical Education: Swami Kuvalayananda's Nationalist Project', *Asian Medicine: Tradition and Modernity*, 3: 20–36.

———. 2007c. 'Physical Education, Sport and the Intersection and Articulation of "Modernities": Hanuman Vyayam Prasarak Mandal', *International Journal of the History of Sport*, 24 (9): 1155–70.

———. 2008. '*Yogashivir*: Performativity and the Study of Modern Yoga', in M. Singleton and J. Byrne (eds.), *Yoga in the Modern World: Contemporary, Transnational Perspectives*. London: Routledge, 36–48.

———. 2011. *Moral Materialism: Sex and Masculinity in Modern India*. New Delhi: Penguin Books.

————. 2013. 'Yoga, Bodybuilding and Wrestling: Metaphysical Fitness', in D. Diamond (ed.), *Yoga: The Art of Transformation*. Washington, DC: Smithsonian Institution, 87–95.

Atreya, Shanti Prakash. 1965. *Yog Manovigyan Ki Rup Rekha*. Moradabad: Darshan Printers.

————. 1987. 'Brahamacharya', *Bharatiya Kushti*, 24 (12): 25–52.

Diamond, Debra. 2013. *Yoga: The Art of Transformation*. Washington, DC: Smithsonian Institution.

Ganorkar, Dhundiraj D. 1951. *We go to the Lingiad*. Amravati: Hanuman Vyayam Prasarak Mandal.

Jain, Andrea R. 2015. *Selling Yoga: From Counterculture to Pop Culture*. Oxford: Oxford University Press.

Kesriya, Ramchandra. 1992. 'Hathayoga Yukt Pehlwani', *Bharatiya Kushti*, 30 (12): 35–46.

————. 1993. 'Hathayoga Yukt Pehlwani', *Bharatiya Kushti*, 31 (3): 65–82.

————. 1996. 'Hathayoga Yukt Pehlwani', *Bharatiya Kushti*, 34 (2): 35–48.

Mallinson, James and Mark Singleton. 2017. *Roots of Yoga*. London, UK: Penguin Books.

Pinch, William R. 2006. *Warrior Ascetics and Indian Empires*. New York: Cambridge University Press.

Purandare, G. N. 1992. Bharatiya Sarirk Siksha Awen Itihas. Mumbai: Majestic Prakashan.

Rajagopalan, K. 1962. *A Brief History of Physical Education in India (from Earliest Times to the End of Mughul Period)*. Delhi: Army Publishers.

Samuel, Geoffrey and Jay Johnston. 2013. *Religion and the Subtle Body in Asia and the West: Between Mind and Body*. New York: Routledge.

Sen, A. P. 2003. 'Religious Revivalism as Nationalist Discourse: Swami Vivekananda and New Hinduism in Nineteenth-Century Bengal', *Indian Economic and Social History Review,* 40 (1): 122–24.

Sen, Ronojoy. 2015. *Nation at Play: A History of Sport in India*. New York: Columbia University Press.

Sengupta, Rudraneil. 2016. *Enter the* Dangal: *Travels through India's Wrestling Landscape*. Noida, India: Harper Sport.

Singleton, Mark. 2010. *Yoga Body: The Origins of Modern Posture Practice*. Oxford: Oxford University Press.

Singleton, Mark and Jean Byrne. 2008. *Yoga in the Modern World: Contemporary Perspectives*. New York: Routledge.

Strauss, Sarah. 2005. *Positioning Yoga: Balancing Acts across Cultures*. Oxford: Berg.

Waller, David. 2011. *The Perfect Man: The Muscular Life and Times of Eugen Sandow, Victorian Strongman*. Brighton: Victorian Secrets Limited.

Whitaker, Jared. 2011. *Strong Arms and Drinking Strength: Masculinity, Violence and the Body in Ancient India*. Oxford: Oxford University Press.

White, David Gordon. 1996. *The Alchemical Body: Siddha Traditions in Medieval India*. Chicago: University of Chicago Press.

————. 2003. *Kiss of the Yogini: 'Tantric Sex' in its South Asian Contexts*. Chicago: University of Chicago Press.

————. 2009. *Sinister Yogis*. Chicago: University of Chicago Press.

————. 2014. *The Yoga Sutra of Patanjali: A Biography*. Princeton: Princeton University Press.

Yesudian, Selvarajan and Elisabeth Haich. 1949. *Sport und Yoga*. Thielle, Netherlands: E. Fankhauser.

————. 1953. *Yoga and Health*. New York: Harper.

❖❖

BODYBUILDING IN INDIA
Bollywood Bodies and Middle-class Lifestyles

MICHIEL
BAAS

INTRODUCTION

I n the last decade or so, the number of bodybuilding competitions
held at a regional, interregional and national level in India has
significantly increased. While bodybuilding has long been a
popular sport in India, until recently its visibility remained limited
and as such there was only scant mainstream awareness. This
has unequivocally changed. Often attracting large audiences,
competitions—irrespective of where or the level at which they are
held—are sponsored by popular sports clothing and nutrition
brands, and receive significant attention from mainstream
media. This paper argues that the emergence of bodybuilding
as a competitive sport in India, with an increasing number of
participants and annually held competitions, needs to be understood
within the context of the growing popularity of working out in
urban India. It cannot be denied that the Indian fitness industry has
witnessed unprecedented growth in recent years. Fitness chains,
such as internationally operating Anytime Fitness, Fitness First and
Gold's Gym, have expanded rapidly across Indian cities, while a
home-grown brand, such as Talwalkar's (in existence since 1932),
has witnessed significant growth as well. As a result, gyms have
become a ubiquitous and an indispensable presence in the Indian
urban landscape.

This paper explores the growing popularity of bodybuilding in
India in relation to the arrival of a new bodily ideal for men—mainly
lean, muscular in nature—of which it can be argued that it was
principally Bollywood that (initially) set the tone for this. Yet, as I

have argued elsewhere (2016a; 2016b: 444–56), it would be too simplistic to reduce this body to one that is merely aesthetically pleasing, glamorous or sexually attractive. The way it features in Bollywood movies, and the way such bodies are discussed in popular media in terms of maintenance and transformation is revealing for how the lean, muscular body is associated with being successful as a professional, living a cosmopolitan lifestyle and perhaps, most of all, being capable of withstanding the caprices of over-consumption. In its 'ideal-type', this body resonates with 'upper'-middle-class belonging. Ironically, this contrasts markedly with those who usually embody this ideal: fitness trainers who are employed by gyms, providing personal training to clients, and whose bodies need to come as close as possible to the ideal-type clients envision for themselves.

With the explosive growth of the Indian fitness industry, the profession of the fitness (or personal) trainer has emerged as a 'new middle-class' profession that mainly appears to offer new career opportunities to young men hailing from the lower middle classes. As a typical 'service' profession, it relies heavily on one-on-one communication with clients who seek assistance and guidance for a plethora of issues, ranging from overall health goals to the desire to emulate the latest 'bodily' trend in Indian cinema. A gap in this ostensible middle classness characterises the dichotomy between client and trainer; while the trainer's body might resonate with an upper-middle-class lifestyle, it is 'embodied' by a person belonging to the lower middle classes. In this paper, I pay specific attention to the role the body plays in middle-class belonging and how various ideals (those propelled by Bollywood[1] vs. those required for bodybuilding) also point to the complex array of notions with which the 'muscular' body is layered.

BODYBUILDING IN INDIA

Bodybuilding remains a strikingly under-researched sport, considering its connections to the fitness industry which has developed into a ubiquitous presence in cities across the globe. One of the better-known publications in the field continues to be the study by Klein (1993) that focuses on one of the most well-known gyms on the West Coast of the United States. Klein's study was interested in the gender aspect of bodybuilding which it explored in relation to issues of health, sexuality and, perhaps, most strikingly, the willingness to push bodily boundaries. His study was particularly revealing for the economic aspects of bodybuilding, the cost involved to support the bodybuilder's lifestyle, to effectuate bodily transformation, and the impossibility of combining the sport with a more regular existence in terms of a job, family, and otherwise. Monaghan (2001) partly builds on this but is more specifically focused on risk-taking behaviour, the use of drugs (anabolic steroids, growth hormones, etc.) and the idea of the perfect (bodybuilder's) body. Locks and Richardson (2012) complement these works by bringing together a diversity of scholarly work that reflects the general associations that the public at large also appears to have with bodybuilding: issues with masculinity (male bodybuilders) or femininity (female bodybuilders), drug use and other types of risk-taking behaviour, and the (understated and occasionally quite explicit) erotic and sexual dimensions of the sport and mental/psychological issues.

The key studies mentioned earlier often also draw upon the historical development of the sport. Of particular relevance here, especially concerning India, are those that have explored 'bodybuilding' in relation to colonial Empire and subsequent nation-building efforts. Chapman's (1994) study focusing on Eugen Sandow, ostensibly the first celebrated bodybuilder, is revealing for his role in propelling a fitness craze in different parts of the world. With respect to this, Watt's study of Sandow in colonial India provides a glimpse into the popular muscleman's impact on local interest in working out in the early 20th century. The tour he made, as Watt writes, 'created a physical culture "craze" in the parts of India that Sandow visited' (2017: 6). Budd's (1997) revealing study of physical culture and body politics in the age of Empire is also relevant here. What stands out from such studies[2] is how the 'muscular' body was never merely aesthetically pleasing, or found to be attractive, but also always political, made part of a religious ambition ('Christian masculinity'), and ideologically layered. My work on Indian bodybuilding takes inspiration from these studies in order to understand what fuels its emergence as a popular and competitive sport across the country.

So far Indian bodybuilding has received little to no scholarly interest other than some references in relation to Hindutva politics.[3] In general, scholarly work on sport, other than cricket, remains relatively underdeveloped in India. A notable exception here is Alter's detailed and long-term study of Indian (*pehlwani*) wrestling. In his work, we find a number of themes coming together that all relate to the (ideal-type) male body, such as questions of celibacy (1995: 109–31), sexuality and masculinity (2011), identity and ideology (1992), connections to (militant) Hinduism (1994: 557–88), as well as questions of subalternity (2000: 45–72). It is impossible to do justice to Alter's work in this limited space, but a question which immediately presents itself is: What are the connections between modern Indian bodybuilding and pehlwani wrestling, in terms of workout techniques, bodily ideals and the socio-economic backgrounds of its practitioners? While the argument can be made that, historically, Indian wrestling has provided modern bodybuilding with certain workout tools and practices that are still in use today, the connections and intersections are otherwise less pronounced. Interviews with senior bodybuilders in Delhi,[4] often now running their own gyms and no longer competing on stage, revealed that some had indeed joined an *akhara* (wrestling school) in their youth and/or their family had a historical connection with wrestling. However, such connections were hardly commonplace and heavily dependent on caste/community backgrounds. Most bodybuilders and fitness enthusiasts were quick to stress that their workout routines and diets were incompatible with the demands and requirements of modern-day bodybuilding. Ghee and milk-rich diets, preferred for pehlwani wrestlers, would not be conducive for the visibility of muscles required for a bodybuilding competition. The goal within bodybuilding is not only large muscles, but also to make sure that each muscle (group) is clearly visible. During a competition, bodybuilders will be asked to adopt various poses, flexing individual muscle(s) (groups), something that is never expected of a wrestler. For a wrestler, his muscles enable him to combat his opponent, while for a bodybuilder his very muscles are the end-goal.

COMPETITIONS ACROSS INDIA

While in the West bodybuilding as a competitive sport may no longer be as popular as it once was, in India it is clearly an emerging one. Increasingly, well-known globally competitive bodybuilders who participate in competitions, such as Mr. Olympia ('Joe Weider's

Olympia and Fitness and Performance Weekend') and Mr. Universe ('Universe Championships'), find their way to India as special guests of locally held events or to be part of new gym openings. Phil Heath, Jay Cutler and Ronnie Coleman have all visited India for this reason in recent years. While such 'names' generally perform as guest stars, in large, commercially held competitions, such as the annually held Sheru Classic, which promotes itself as an 'international fitness festival', not only have the number of locally held competitions significantly increased, but also the various local bodybuilding associations and federations. It is almost impossible to provide a coherent overview of competitions held in India, as the titles and the 'bodies' that organise them keep changing.

A long-term informant Murali Vijayakumar based in Chennai (Tamil Nadu), recently provided a detailed overview of the various competitions in which he and his 'students' had participated.[5] These ranged from Steel Man of Tamil Nadu (where he himself took third place in the under 90kg category); Mr. Tamil Nadu Amateur (in which Haresshvar Sakthivelu, whom he trains, took second place in the under 80kg category, and he himself came first in the above 85kg as well as Overall Title categories); the Open State meet (held in the town of Thiruchendur, where Sakthivelu and Vijayakumar both took first place in their respective categories); and various other competitions, such as Senior Nationals IBBF (Indian Body Builders Federation), the State Powerlifting Meet, the Open State Meet, among others. One would assume that Lakshmi Kumar, a former bodybuilder who now mainly trains aspiring ones and runs his own gym in Chennai, would provide a comparable list, but instead he listed completely different competitions. Several of his students had competed and done rather well in a recently held Mr. Chennai competition; some of them had also competed in the NABBA (National Amateur Body-Builders' Association) Mr. Tamil Nadu, including the Open Single Category State Championship and the Mr. South India Contest. A third bodybuilder, Arvind Spartacus (nickname), widely considered as one of the most promising at the moment, had similarly participated in some of the earlier mentioned competitions, but also emphasised the importance of yet another recently held competition—the Arnold Classic Asia Amateur Competition.

This overview of various competitions held annually in the greater Chennai region is reflected in a similar, equally incomplete, list that can be compiled for Delhi's National Capital Region (NCR) as well. Anoop Chauhan, a successful bodybuilder in the 65kg weight class, reported that in 2017 he had won the following competitions: Mr. Delhi, Mr. Haryana, Mr. North India and Mr. India. Himanshu Puri, based in Rohtak (some 70km west of Delhi), participated in Mr. NABBA India (held in Gurgaon), Mr. Haryana and Mr. Himachal.

Originally founded in the United Kingdom in 1950, NABBA has since become a label that is often used to impart official élan to competitions, both in India and elsewhere. However, it is certainly not the only association or 'label' active in the field. During my fieldwork in Chennai in 2015, there were three associations involved in organising various competitions in the city, ranging from Mr. Chennai, Mr. Tamil Nadu and Mr. India. Vijayakumar recently informed me that there are now at least six such associations, all with their own competitions. It reminded me of the 10 days in early 2013 when I was able to attend no less than three different Mr. Delhi competitions, all organised by different Delhi-based associations. In order to better understand where this remarkable proliferation comes from, it is important to locate this development within the larger context of the emergence of a new bodily ideal among middle-class men in urban India. In the following section, I discuss the role Bollywood has played in this, while also pointing at a divergence in terms of bodily ideals between those required for bodybuilding and those made popular by Bollywood heroes and fitness models.

BOLLYWOOD BODIES

As I have argued elsewhere (2016b: 444–56), in the last decade or so a new lean, muscular, ideal body type has emerged among middle-class Indian men, the popularity of which can be directly linked to Bollywood's strategic inclusion of this in its films over the same period. In interviews with bodybuilders, trainers and others involved in the 'industry', it is generally agreed that it was the film, *Om Shanti Om* (2007), which spurred the first significant growth in gym memberships.[6] In this film, 'super star' Shah Rukh Khan unveils his 'freshly baked abs', as it would often be referred to, for the first time on camera in the hit song, 'Dard e Disco'. From the moment Khan enters the scene, roughly 10 seconds into the song, his body is on full display and the focal point of attention. Wearing a black shirt, embellished by gold leaf, Khan is surrounded by dancing women whose hands are all over his lean, muscular body with clearly pronounced abdominal muscles. While the video is composed of various scenes, each with a different colour scheme and Bollywood theme referencing a particular 'period', the emphasis remains on his body. He is variously clad in an unbuttoned shirt, a soaked-through white vest, even bare-chested—emerging from the water, with the camera zooming in on his muscular back, abdomen and chest—or dancing suggestively as a construction worker, drenched in sweat.

Typically, the song is loaded with sexual innuendo that however never becomes very explicit, as is de rigueur in the Bollywood industry. Shah Rukh Khan revealing his 'abs', however, was considered quite radical at the time and was widely discussed in the Indian media. However, informants agree that it was the Hindi remake of the Tamil action film, *Ghajini* (2008),[7] that propelled the growth of the Indian fitness industry in India in an even more extreme manner. The swift transformation of Aamir Khan's body from that of the 'next-door neighbour' in *Taare Zameen Par* (2007)[8] to the massive, muscular physique he sported for the lead role in *Ghajini*, was to become something that the media would increasingly discuss with reference to new Bollywood releases that featured a popular male actor. John Abraham getting 'incredibly ripped' for the action film, *The Force* (2011); Farhan Akhtar's 13-month-long programme to 'become' runner Milkha Singh for the biographical sports film, *Bhaag Milkha Bhaag* (2013); or Aamir Khan's most recent transformation for the film on wrestling, *Dangal* (2016), have all been extensively discussed in the Indian media. The notion of a 'transformation' is always key to this, even to the point that Aamir Khan decided that the effect of 'this' would be greater if he first gained weight for his role as the ageing wrestler in *Dangal*, only to slim down to a leaner and muscular version of himself for the scenes depicting his character in his younger years. While he was already fit and could easily have shot his 'younger years' first, he decided to do it the other way around.

Narrations of bodily transformation have become mainstream in Indian media in recent years. Yet, while the characters played in these films may hail from various layers of society—from a 1970s junior artist in Bollywood (Shah Rukh Khan in *Om Shanti Om*); Yash, a police officer (John Abraham in *The Force*); or the lower-class son of an arms dealer in rural Gujarat (Ranveer Singh in *Goliyon Ki Raasleela Ram-Leela*)—the manner in which the actor's bodily transformation is depicted outside the film in which it was featured needs to be understood in 'middle class' terms. In the end, it is not the 'functionality' of the body in relation to the role played that is highlighted in the media, but its potential attractiveness that invokes the desire to emulate it among a gym-going clientele. The transformation that is implied then requires a highly specific workout routine, preferably with the assistance of a personal trainer (the actor's own personal trainer is often specifically named in articles), as well as advice on so-called 'clean' eating, avoiding particular foods, and thus envisioning a change in lifestyle altogether. The transformation that is 'promised', along with the one depicted in the 'hit movie of the moment' then translates into one that basically communicates a certain 'grip' or 'hold' on what could be construed as an otherwise unhealthy 'middle class' lifestyle. *Unhealthy* here signifies rampant consumerism, running the risk of various related diseases, such as diabetes and hypertension. At the same time, unhealthy also needs to be read in terms of an old-fashioned, middle-class bodily ideal, that of the 'healthy' potbelly, signifying prosperity. Obviously, this is no longer *en vogue* and desirable. Even Lord Ganesh, as an informant once slyly remarked, is increasingly depicted without his favourite sweet, and with rock-hard, six-pack abs.

BODY AND MIDDLE CLASSNESS

While it is generally recognised that films, such as *Om Shanti Om* and *Ghajini,* played a determining role in the (initial) growth of the Indian fitness industry, some trainers were also keen to point out that, to their recollection, muscular bodies had featured much earlier in Bollywood films. While it was agreed that these films did not have the same impact on gym memberships as the former did, they were, however, important for their inspiration to an 'earlier' generation of fitness enthusiasts. A stand-out film here was *Pyaar Kiya Toh Darna Kya* (1998), featuring the already immensely popular actor Salman Khan at the time. In particular, the video of one of the most popular songs, 'O O Jaane Jaana', was keenly remembered for this. In it, a bare-chested Khan drives down the beach to a make-shift stage where he arrives while an elated audience cheers him on. Subsequently, grabbing a guitar, the actor turns to the crowd and commences his song, while the focus lingers on his powerful chest and six-pack abs. It is clear, however, that while more recent videos put emphasis on the leanness and 'veininess' of the muscular bodies of its actors, this is categorically less stressed in *Pyaar Kiya Toh Darna Kya*. Also absent from the movie, as well as the concomitant marketing campaign, is the emphasis on transformation. Salman Khan's body is assumed to be his own, existing irrespective of the floundering student he depicts in this film. He is, in reality, a muscular and powerful actor, something which makes him popular in general.

With respect to this, a particular gap in class and socio-economic belonging may be deciphered that relegates Salman Khan to the working man's ranks of the hero, while Shah Rukh Khan or Farhan Akhtar could be viewed as 'middle class' heroes. It follows that in the case of the former, Salman Khan's muscles and strength are assumed to be his own, not requiring a transformation, but simply being the product of who he was always assumed to be, while in the case of the latter, this required an investment of sorts: a highly specific workout, not to mention stringent dietary interventions that would 'transform' him within a particular time frame. The emphasis on the time frame within which this was accomplished not only relates to the 'remarkable' speed of the transformation, but also appeals to the idea of a middle-class lifestyle where time is of the essence. Strikingly, competing bodybuilders would often emphasise the opposite: the bodybuilder's body was almost always understood to be the product of time, perseverance and determination. Maturity was an often employed term here to describe how 'mature', and thus developed, a particular muscular body looked. In that sense, bodybuilders were generally also much less likely to evaluate a particular muscular body based on its attractiveness, instead focusing on the way it might be received by the jurors who decided how the bodybuilder would be awarded in each particular weight category.

Bodybuilding in India remains, by and large, a labour- and lower-middle-class preoccupation. This is something which also sees itself reflected in the bodybuilder's bodily ideal in contrast with the desire of upper-middle-class clients of personal trainers. As such, the bodybuilder's body is interpreted and evaluated differently from the one that, for instance, adorns the cover of the Indian edition of *Men's Health* (published till October 2015) and other magazines that focus on men's health and fitness. For Indian fitness trainers, this poses a dilemma: while bodybuilders may have their particular interest, and competing in regularly held competitions something they desire, the 'body' that is required for it is rarely the one that upper-middle-class clients envision for themselves. While requiring a mammoth amount of determination, energy, monetary investment and time, the bodybuilder's body is layered decidedly less markedly with notions of professionalism, cosmopolitanism and, ultimately, middle classness, as compared to the ideal-type lean, muscular one made popular by Bollywood. While it cannot be denied that 'transformation' is a key ingredient in 'building' the bodybuilder's body, its references to 'lower'-middle-class belonging also makes it, crucially, one that is less marketable and, potentially, less attractive to personal training clients. Although this illustrates matters in a rather dichotomous way, as always the reality of anthropological fieldwork also reveals the grey zones that this particular paper was not able to touch upon. However, crucial to its understanding is that these 'bodies', on display as they are (constantly), are revealing for the various notions of class and socio-economic belonging that have only received scant attention so far.

CONCLUSION

It can be argued that Indian bodybuilding stands in a symbiotic relationship with the Indian fitness industry—and the lean, muscular bodily ideal on which its popularity is built—but, ultimately, they represent two separate domains where different ideal-types and interpretations of the 'muscular' body take centre stage. While bodybuilding competitions in India invariably draw a sizable audience, often in the thousands, the bodybuilder's body is not necessarily admired and revered in the way that might be the case with fitness trainers and models, whose bodies come closer to those represented in films and elsewhere in popular culture. What a bodybuilding competition does offer is a spectacle that resonates with Bollywood films in that it offers a way out of reality, or an 'improbable' interpretation of 'the real'. Obviously, while bodybuilders themselves take their competitions highly seriously, for the audience the bodies on display are hardly ever what they would like to emulate for themselves, even if they are regular gym-goers. For them, the bodybuilder's body is generally too grotesque, too much the product of extreme workout routines and diets, not to mention requiring a significant monetary investment in various supplements and drugs. As a result, a number of new bodybuilding competition initiatives have tried to break away from the association with substance abuse as well as the sole focus on the international standard for bodybuilders. Competitions, such as Musclemania and Jerai Classic, generally place stronger emphasis on health and fitness, even promoting 'natural' bodybuilding. Besides, a 'real' bodybuilding competition also includes competitions for strongmen, powerlifting, fitness models, and separate ones for women ('bikini diva'). Such developments serve to underline that the ideal-type (male) body is always under scrutiny, 'changing' and, ultimately, one that is layered with a variety of associations. The recent popularity of bodybuilding in India should be understood in the wider context of the male body as increasingly an indicator of 'urban' belonging, whether in terms of socio-economics and class or, perhaps, even more generally, the place it occupies within a rapidly changing India.

◆

NOTES

1. Although I mainly discuss Bollywood in this paper, in my research work I have also focused on other regional film industries, such as the Tamil and Kannadiga. While Bollywood has clearly been a trailblazer when it comes to these new bodily ideals, in particular, Tamil and Telugu films quickly followed suit. However, space constraints do not allow this article to discuss how the particular notion of the ideal body type and associated masculinity diverges across regional film industries.

2. I am well aware there are a significant number of other studies that discuss this, but due to space constraints I am unable to mention them here.

3. See Hansen (1996: 137–72). See also Anand Patwardhan's well-known documentary, *Ram Ke Nam* (1992; In the Name of God).

4. My research interest in bodybuilding and fitness in India goes back to 2007. Besides gathering material online as well as collecting books, magazines and films related to my research, I also conducted participant observation in a small neighbourhood gym in South Delhi (2013–2014), and interviewed fitness enthusiasts, trainers, bodybuilders and others involved in the industry across urban India, including in Bangalore, Chennai, Mumbai, Patna and Pune.

5. Indian bodybuilders usually refer to the junior/aspiring bodybuilders they coach as their 'students'. These students frequently refer to their coaches as their

teachers or gurus. It is not uncommon for younger bodybuilders to honour their trainers by touching their feet, a traditional way of paying respect.

6. I will not discuss the other hit film, *Saawariya* (2007), starring Ranbir Kapoor. In this film, Kapoor sports a lean, muscular physique, somewhat comparable to Shah Rukh Khan's. However, the film was rarely if ever remembered for it during interviews.

7. The Tamil film, *Ghajini,* was itself an adaptation of the Hollywood production, *Memento* (2000).

8. This film was rereleased as *Like Stars on Earth.*

RFERENCES

Alter, J. S. 2011. *Moral Materialism. Sex and Masculinity in Modern India.* New Delhi: Penguin.

———. 2000. 'Subaltern Bodies and Nationalist Physiques: Gama the Great and the Heroics of Indian Wrestling', *Body & Society*, 6: 45–72.

———. 1995. 'The Celibate Wrestler: Sexual Chaos, Embodied Balance and Competitive Politics in North India', *Contributions to Indian Sociology*, 29 (1–2): 109–31.

———.1994. 'Somatic Nationalism: Indian Wrestling and Militant Hinduism', *Modern Asian Studies*, 28: 3, 557–88.

———. 1992. *The Wrestler's Body: Identity and Ideology in North India.* Berkeley: University of California Press.

Baas, M. 2016a. 'The Desired Body: Bodybuilding, Fitness and Urban Space', in P. Dhall, *Queer Potli: Memories, Imaginations, Re-Imaginations of Urban Queer Spaces in India.* Mumbai: Queer Ink (e-version).

———. 2016b. 'The New Indian Male: Muscles, Masculinity and Middle-classness', in K. A. Jacobsen (ed.), *Routledge Handbook of Contemporary India.* New York: Routledge.

Budd, M. A. 1997. *The Sculpture Machine: Physical Culture and Body Politics in the Age of Empire.* London: Macmillan Press Ltd.

Chapman, D. L. 1994. *Sandow the Magnificent: Eugen Sandow and the Beginnings of Bodybuilding.* Illinois: University of Illinois Press.

Hansen, T. B. 1996. 'Recuperating Masculinity: Hindu Nationalism, Violence and the Exorcism of the Muslim "Other"', *Critique of Anthropology*, 16 (2): 137–72.

Klein, A. M. 1993. *Little Big Men: Bodybuilding Subculture and Gender Construction.* New York: State University of New York Press.

Locks, A. and N. Richardson. 2012. *Critical Readings in Bodybuilding.* London and New York: Routledge.

Monaghnan, L. F. 2001. *Bodybuilding, Drugs and Risk.* London and New York: Routledge.

Watt, C. A. 2017. 'Cultural Exchange, Appropriation and Physical Culture: Strongman Eugen Sandow in Colonial India, 1904–1905', *The International Journal of the History of Sport*, doi10.1080/09523367.2017.1283306

◆◆

RACING ON WATER
A Short History of *Vallam Kali* in Kerala

AMRITH LAL

For four months, beginning July, the rivers and lakes of the central Travancore region of Kerala turn into water stadia to host a sport unique to this region. In villages and towns that ring the waterways, people organise what is locally called *vallam kali*. Vallam is the Malayalam word for boat, while kali has a host of meanings that range from sport to performance and spectacle. But mostly it is a competitive water-sport, occasionally it signifies a ritual spectacle, a temple pageant.

◆◆◆

The river was spread out like a sheet of slate in front of me. It shimmered in the afternoon light and revealed its deep blue occasionally, when the cloud cleared. The earth smelt of rain. Out in the distance, where the river took a bend, the *chundan vallams* (snake boats) waited in their tracks. From my vantage position at the finishing point, the rowers were mere specks and the hoods of the boats loomed over them.

A mike blared out that the chundan vallam heats were about to begin. The thousands of people lined up on both banks of the river welcomed the announcement with a roar. Someone behind me gave that pulsating cheer for rowers: *Aarppoo, irroo, irroo*. The crowd picked it up and the aarppoos travelled, the crescendo rising and falling. In the distance, someone waved a white flag and blew a whistle. A roar went up from the crowd at the starting point. The oars rose and fell in unison; the race had begun, and the roar seemed to power the chundan vallams.

As the boats got closer, the oarsmen became well-defined figures and the roar turned into a deafening cheer. Dark bodies perched on the boats glistened in the sun. A single rower on the prow, behind him sat other rowers in two rows. Legs stretched out in front, body leaning forward, together they dug into the river and scooped water in perfect rhythm. The boats glided in like rattlesnakes on steroids, the steersmen standing on the stern mooring them to their tracks. Within seconds, they passed our stand and shot across the finishing line. All four chundans had done the 1.5 km stretch of the river in less than five minutes. It was a tight finish.

The announcement was lost as thousands, young and old, man and child, were up and screaming. It was one collective roar; who won, who lost, didn't matter. It was all about the race. The race was the winner. At the other end, the starting point, the next set of chundans were lining up. A drizzle had started, but no one cared. This was a celebration of life on water, after all.

I was at Mannar, a village an hour by road from Alappuzha, to watch the Mahatma Boat Race, an annual regatta held around Onam on the Pamba. It was early September and the Southwest monsoon (*Edavapathi*) was resting after pouring its heart out for days. Wherever you looked, it was green and watery. The road I took turned east from Alappuzha town, away from the coast, past endless spans of paddy fields, waterways, toddy shops and drive-in restaurants. The occasional drizzle gave a wet coating to the air and turned the road slushy.

Built in the late 1980s, the Alappuzha–Changanassery road almost floats on water as it passes through a landscape where land and water merge seamlessly. Once these were marshes, fed by the waters of Vembanad Lake and the rivers that drained into it. Centuries ago, men began to reclaim land from water. They raised dykes and drained the water to turn the mudbanks into farmland. As the road turned further east, land, though criss-crossed by rivers and canals, became the dominant feature. Nearly every village en route seemed to be hosting a boat race. Announcements about the upcoming races were visible everywhere—on flex boards, banners, posters, make-shift arches and *pandals*. They weren't really meant for tourists or outsiders, but were more of a reminder to local residents of the date and the time of the race. 'Nadinte Utsavam' (festival of the region), the announcements read. These carried photoshopped images of the organisers: For many, such engagement is a step towards establishing their credentials as local activists and worthies, a claim that may fetch them or further a career in local politics—a seat in local bodies, or, who knows, even an assembly ticket.

Past the famous Chakkulathu Kavu and the historic Niranam Church, I arrived at the site of the race, a water stadium on the northern bank of the Pamba. A narrow cut from the main road wound through the countryside, past houses, cuppolas, churches, a temple, a school, shops to the edge of the river. A grand church stood sentinel as the Pamba, half-a-mile wide, flowed serenely to the west. To the north of the church, a concrete gallery stood, the 'permanent' venue for the race. A bund had been raised and cemented for people to sit on.

The race was to begin late afternoon, but by noon the place was teeming with people. Motor boats with young men and families on the deck blared advertisements for local shops and serenaded the crowds. The occasional announcement for the participants provided the only pause as loud music and ads rent the air. On the far edge of the track, the racers were practicing. The race boats—the chundans, the stars of the show, *veppu, iruttukuthi/oadi*, country boats of different shape and size—had arrived in the morning, some from the neighbourhood, others from distant villages. The prize money wasn't much, it was more pride and prestige they rowed for. In the carnivalesque atmosphere, reputations of rowers and clubs were made and unmade. The sport, after all, was not just about winning a race, but an assertion of village pride, club pride. By evening the races would be over and the rowers would retire to their home, of course, high on spirits, with invitations in pocket for another race, another day, elsewhere. It was the Onam season and you had to race.

Shahjahan T. K., secretary of Mannar Boat Race, gave me a potted history of the event. It began half a century ago. The Mahatma (Gandhi) Trophy went to the winning chundan. Senior Congress leader and Rajya Sabha MP, P. J.Kurien, who taught at a local college for many years, has been the chairman of the organising committee of the Race for over a quarter century. The region being a stronghold of the Congress, most of the organisers had a party affiliation. Shahjahan, a local trader, had a different spin, of course. 'This is a race of people who take the morning dip in this river,' emphasising the local character of the race. 'Most of the racers are boys from Niranam and Parumala (small towns in the neighbourhoods that host many schools and colleges). Ours is a composite neighbourhood. We have the Parumala Church, the Panayannar Kavu, and this is also where Mohammed Valiyullahi Thangal was buried—the rich secular character of the region reflects in the conduct of the race as well,' Shahjahan said. And, he pointed to another interesting aspect: The races are also about the rivalry between two rich families who own boats on the two banks of the river which adds an edge to the competition. Considering the enormous interest the race generates in the neighbourhood, local politicians cannot risk absence at the Race. Shahjahan claimed that they once had 10 ministers attending the race. With the Congress in the opposition, the stars of the show were two ministers from Sri Lanka.

Later, I met Shailaj, the president of the organising committee that conducts the race, at his home in Mannar. It was an open house that afternoon with a feast laid out for visitors. Shailaj explained that preparations begin six months before the race. The rowers on the snake boats keep themselves fit for the season and arrive at the site of the race in the morning for practice laps to familiarise themselves with the river and the current. The showpiece of the Mannar race was the competition involving veppu category boats. These, he said, were owned by families in the neighbourhood. The snake boats are given ₹1.5 lakh as competition fee—there were eight snake boats racing in the 2017 season. Shailaj, who has been heading the organising committee for two decades, said the annual expenses to conduct the race came to about ₹45 lakh. The money is raised from sponsorships.

Late afternoon, the championship started with a procession of all the participating boats, 32 in all. Then the races in the category of boats rowed by women began, followed by iruttukuthi/oadi and finally, the snake boats. Veppu category boats have about 65 rowers, whereas the snake boats can take in anywhere between 90 to 120 rowers. By the time evening set in, people had lined up along the river banks and in small boats in thousands. As the names of the competing veppu boats—Shot Pulikkathra, Punnathra Vengazhi, Kottaparamban, Asha Pulikkaparambil—were announced, a roar went up from the stands. And there they were, lining up on the track, eager to impress the cheering crowd. The high point for those who didn't have any stake in the iruttukuthi battles were the snake boats. Nadubhagom, Vellamkulangara, Karichal, St. George, Pandi, some of the giants among snake boats, were on track. Late evening, the races got over. Organisers were pleading over the megaphone that it was just a race and the fight was not to be carried over from water to land. Police on speed boats kept watch on the people along the river. In the fading light, I left the river for Thiruvalla, the nearest town further east, to board a bus to Thiruvananthapuram.

◆◆◆

Water has shaped the geography and culture of the region to the south-east of Alappuzha, once the leading port town of the erstwhile Travancore kingdom and now a sleepy tourist destination. To the west of the town lies the Arabian Sea, with the Vembanad backwaters to its east. The Pamba, Manimala, Achenkovil, Meenachil and Moovattupuzha empty into the Vembanad backwaters in these parts. The silt carried by them down the Western Ghats for centuries has created the unique marshy landscape called Kuttanad. Water is an inescapable presence here and defines the nature of every aspect of human existence. Until recently, boats were the only means to travel and conduct trade. Rivers, canals and backwaters form an intricate network of water courses, which defined life in this region. The marshy land with its abundance of water helped the growth of agriculture, especially paddy. The surplus was traded and small feudatories flourished. The port of Purakkad, a few miles to the south of Alappuzha, once attracted ships from China and the Roman empire, and was the entry point to the waterways and river ports of Kuttanad. Early Christian settlements came up along the river ports and some of the oldest churches are found here. Buddhist ruins have been discovered, hinting at the existence of cosmopolitan religious communities and cultures. Many grand temples continue to stand sentinel along the rivers and waterways. Till the advent of the Travancore kingdom in the early 18th century, small kingdoms that rose from the debris of the Chera empire, which had disintegrated in the 11th century, fought for supremacy in Kuttanad. Rivers marked their boundaries. These kingdoms had inland navies to defend their political and trading interests.

The origins of the boat races of Kuttanad are hoary, but available evidence suggests that these were a product of the times when feudal principalities ruled over this region with inland navies and religious institutions having an overwhelming influence on social, economic, cultural and political life. Later, the marshes were claimed for cultivation with the blood and sweat of Dalit communities, which continue to live on the edges of the farms. When the monsoon sets in, agriculture ceases and the leisure classes get down to organising the races.

The boat races are still a seasonal sport, but the organic links of the races to local communities and cultures are now fraying. The social and economic upheavals that Kuttanad has witnessed in the past century have had an impact on the conduct of the boat races. Land reforms, the decline and outward migration of the old caste elite and the rise of the remittance economy have radically altered the nature of the races, including ownership of the boats. Feudal patronage has since been replaced by the new rich, who turned sweat into cash in the Gulf.

The races are now conducted more professionally, while increasingly being linked to the demands of the tourism economy. There is also an attempt to formalise and institutionalise different aspects of the boat race, especially its ritualistic features and cultural heritage.

State patronage, starting with the hosting of the Nehru Trophy, the premier championship that started in 1952, too has helped the expansion of the races. Vallam kali is no more limited to Kuttanad, nor is it just another ritual pageant; it is now a competitive sport with a pan-Kerala presence. The spectacle and drama in this sport, perhaps, is matched only by football. The abundant passion it generates has even found its way to cinema, an aspect only cricket in India can claim to match. At least half a dozen films centred on vallam kali have been made in Malayalam; the earliest one, named after a legendary boat, *Kavalam Chundan*, came out in 1967. Kavalam Chundan had won the Nehru Trophy multiple times in the 1950s.

It is said that the pride of Kuttanad boat races, the snake boats (chundan vallam), owe their origin to the wars between the kingdoms of Ambalappuzha (Chempakassery) and Kayamkulam in the 16th century. In his study, *Aranmulayude Samskarika Paithrukam* (Aranmula's Cultural Heritage), poet and scholar Nellickal Muraleedharan writes that the king of Ambalappuzha asked Kodupunna Venkata Narayan Asari, a master carpenter, to design a war ship that could accommodate his warriors and their weapons. The king liked the model that Asari crafted and, on his orders, the first snake boats were built. Muraleedharan writes that the Kayamkulam kingdom got custody of Asari through deceit and forced him to make snake boats for its navy. Slowly, the fine art of making snake boats spread across the principalities in and around Kuttanad. Muraleedharan marshals a variety of textual evidence to establish the claim that the snake boat was originally built as a war ship. He quotes a text, *Padappattu*, from the 17th century, which described how the snake boats of Chempakassery once defeated a Dutch armada.

The snake boat, as the name suggests, is a curious creature. Long and slender, it resembles a serpent. Its stern rises high, whereas the prow leans to virtually touch the water, almost giving it the appearance of a cobra with a raised hood. The length of the snake boat can vary from 28 to 32 metres and the larger ones accommodate over a 100 rowers. The middle portion of the boat is wide enough to store material—guns, perhaps, in the past, and now musicians, who pace the oarsmen. The art of making snake boats is a specialised craft and continues to be practised by a handful of master craftsmen. It is restricted to a few families and the secrets of the craft are handed over from one generation to the next. On the stern stands the first of five steersmen, who controls the flow of the boat and usually is the captain of the boat in races.

This is how Jacob J. Mappilacherry, who has researched the history of boat races in Kuttanad, describes the process of making the snake boat in his essay, 'A Historic Perspective of the Boat Races of Kuttanad':

> The first step in realising the dream of building a race boat is to locate the timber. Anjili (*Artocarpus hirsutus*) is the preferred wood. The right tree has to be located and selected by the master carpenter. It has to be of the right length, long enough to provide the five planks for the main part of the hull extending from below the stern to the front of the gun turret. Uma Maheswaran, the master craftsman, says he first needs to 'see' the chundan in the tree. The tree, even as it is standing, he divides and allocates to the various parts of the chundan.

Mappilacherry writes that hundreds of cubic feet of wood, about two-and-a-half quintals of iron, 40 kg of brass, and five kg of copper are used to craft a snake boat.

The longer the snake boat, the faster it is likely to be. But the math in the making of the chundan is crucial. In a way, the speed of the boat is built into it by the master carpenter when he designs the vessel. Any small error in the calculations would mean the boat would not float steadily on the water, forget speeding. The State Sports Council, according to Mappilacherry, has now regulated the maximum length of the chundan because of a trend to make them longer in pursuit of speed and success in races. Twenty-one snake boats were members of the Kerala Snake Boats and Rowers Association (KSBRA) in 2011.

So, how and when did a war vessel turn a race boat?

In Muraleedharan's view, the tradition of vallam kali dates back to 1615. Champakulam Moolam Kazhcha, according to him, marks the beginning of the vallam kali tradition. On an auspicious day (Moolam star) in the Malayalam month of Midhunam (the second half of June to the first half of August), the idol for consecration at the newly built temple of the Ambalappuzha king was carried from Champakulam, a village on the Pampa river, to Ambalappuzha accompanied by snake boats. There is a reason why the snake boats accompanied the king's entourage. The story goes that the original idol built for the temple was found to be flawed and the Ambalappuzha king instructed his minister, Parayil Menon, to steal the idol of Parthasarathi (Krishna) from the Karimkulam temple under the control of another king. Menon and his soldiers managed to row away with the idol, but were pursued by the temple guards. Ambalappuzha's soldiers took refuge with a Christian family (Mappilacherry) in Champakulam and waited out the night. The next morning, the Chempakassery king arrived and received the idol. The king and his entourage left in a procession of boats after a reception at the Kalloorkkad church. It is in memory of this event that the Moolam Kazhchavallam kali is held. Muraleedharan writes that what began as a ritual turned into a carnival some years later, and thereafter, similar snake boat processions began to be held in other parts of the region. In her essay on the Ambalappuzha temple from *Thulasi Garland*, Aswathi Thirunal Gowri Lakshmi Bayi, a member of the Travancore royalty, writes that Puradam Thampuran, the then Brahmin king of Chempakassery, started the Champakulam boat race to mark the consecration of the idol in AD 1613.

The Champakulam race continues to emphasise the ritual element and is touted as an example of communal harmony. In an essay on the Champakulam race, 'Keralathinte Kalivallangalum Champakkulam Kaliyum', Joy Joseph Kattampally points out the ritualistic aspect of the carnival and the continuing involvement of three parties in it: the Ambalapuzha temple, Kallorkkad church and Mappilassery house. The ritual in the tradition continues to this day. The Travancore king, then the *raja pramukh*, Sri Chithira Thirunal Bala Rama Varma, was the chief guest at the 1952 Moolam race. He instituted the Rajapramukhan Trophy for the winner and it was then that the race became more of a competition than a ritual and carnival.

◆◆◆

Further east of Champakulam, up the Pampa, lies the village of Aranmula. In the past, the trade on the river, mainly forest produce from the slopes of the Western Ghats, to the port of Purakkad passed through Aranmula to Champakulam. The renowned Aranmula Parthasarathi temple stands on the banks of the Pampa. The temple ramparts are to the south of the river, with the walls rising high from the river. A unique feature of this temple is its association with snake boats. The snake boats of Aranmula are called *palliyodams* (palli: temple; odam: boat) because of their links to the temple. These have a slightly different appearance from the chundans found in Kuttanad. A vallam kali involving the palliyodams is held on the consecration day of the temple, which is also believed to be the birthday of Arjuna. On the Utrattathi star in the Malayalam month of Chingam (August–September), the palliyodams, which belong to the villages that fall in the vicinity of the temple, participate in the Aranmula boat race.

In his study, 'Vallamkaliyum Vanchippattukalum', Edanadu Radhakrishnan Nair writes that the origins of the palliyodams and antiquity of the ritual are hidden in the mists of time. He says that though local lore and beliefs claim an origin that dates back over seven centuries, there is no conclusive and verifiable evidence to back this.

The origins of the Aranmula vallam kali too are buried in the mist of history, but local lore suggests a heroic tradition similar to that of the snake boats of Kuttanad. It is said that centuries ago, robbers used to target boats that carried ingredients for the famed Onam feast at the Aranmula temple. The palliyodams were launched to ensure protection to the temple boat and soon it became ritualised as a procession. Now, the palliyodams are an integral part of the temple festivities and have become both a spiritual and cultural tradition itself. Though there is hardly anything martial about the Aranmula boat procession now, it has gained in its ritual standing. It is believed that Lord Krishna, the deity of Aranmula, himself is present on the palliyodams as they move in ceremonial procession on the Utrattathi festival day.

The importance of the palliyodams to the temple's spiritual universe is evident from the fact that one of the offerings here is to organise a *vallasadya*, which is to feed the rowers of a palliyodam. There are elaborate rituals, beginning with extending the invitation to the rowers to the menu for the feast. Nair said a vallasadya would cost at least ₹70,000. The palliyoda samithi, which is a representative body of the villages that own the palliyodams, coordinates the vallasadya offering with the temple administration, providing space and utensils at the temple premises. In fact, he says, palliyodams raise the money necessary for the upkeep of the boats from offerings made for vallasadya.

Similarly, a musical tradition too has emerged from Aranmula vallam kali. Since the Aranmula race is more a carnival, the rowers throw their oars to a more slow and easy rhythm. These boat songs are called *vanchippattu*, which are mainly in praise of the deity at Aranmula. However, the rhythms and metres have now become a poetic tradition in itself, influencing even popular music.

The story goes that a poverty-stricken poet Ramapurath Varier (18th century) called on the Travancore king, Marthanda Varma, when the latter was visiting the famous temple at Vaikom. Varier's plea for help was in verse. A curious king asked him to accompany him on the royal boat when he returned to Thiruvananthapuram. The king is said to have asked the poet to compose a poem in the boat-song metre. Varier chose to narrate an episode from Bhagavatam, the story of Kuchela visiting Krishna, and wove in his plight as well. Thus was born *Kuchelavrittam Vanchippattu* (The Tale of Kuchelan), which heralded a new poetic tradition in Malayalam. Many have written, including his contemporary, the great Kunjan

Nambiar, in the vanchipattu metre—*natonnata*—but none has surpassed Varier. Critic Krishna Chaitanya writes in *A History of Malayalam Literature*, 'a rare sincerity of feeling, resulting from a complete self-identification with the main character, distinguishes Varier's poem'. High on bhakti and written in a vocabulary drawn from spoken Malayalam, it remains one of the high-points of Malayalam literature.

Vanchipattu today has found a niche independent of the boat races. Regular camps are conducted to train young people in the singing of vanchipattu. Vanchipattu is sung in two scales—in Aranmula, where the race is more ritual than competition, it is sung in a slow tempo, while in Kuttanad, where the oarsmen row to win, it is fast-paced. In any case, the metre is meant to evoke the rhythm of oars falling on the water and prodding the boat to move.

The race season begins at Champakulam, but the most competitive event is the Nehru Trophy race, held on the second Saturday of August every year. From the eponymous snake boats that have over a hundred oarsmen, to the smaller row boats, including the ones that have women as rowers, the Nehru Trophy is as much an exhibition and celebration of the boating culture of Kuttanad, though it is the least organic of all the boat races in the region. When Prime Minister Nehru visited Kerala in the 1950s, a boat race was organised for him in a part of the Vembanad backwaters on the outskirts of Alappuzha town. It is said that he was so excited by the race that he jumped on to one of the boats and later asked for the race to be institutionalised. Thus began the Nehru Trophy race, with the winner's trophy donated by Nehru himself. But it also started the transformation of the races from being an exhibition of the prowess of local talent, where villages compete, to a competitive sport that attracts money. The Nehru Trophy is telecast live on major TV channels and All India Radio has provided running commentary since the advent of the championship. Today, over a hundred boat races are held in about three months coinciding with the Onam season, watched by thousands of spectators.

◆◆◆

Some weeks ago I spoke to Baiju, a vallam kali fanatic who works in Dubai. He times his annual leave to coincide with the Nehru Trophy, where the chundan he supports competes. Baiju spoke about the changing character of the vallam kali and the Gulf remittances that seem to be triggering the change. He spoke of the Kumarakom Boat Club, which has won many a chundan, the cherished Nehru Trophy. He spoke about how expatriate Malayalis want to acquire snake boats as vanity possessions. Once the boat is acquired, the new owner wants to hold the trophy and is willing to invest any amount for it. Having bought the boat, he now wants to buy rowers. If boat clubs in the past recruited and nurtured local talent, ambitious owners now want to shop for the best rowers anywhere. Success at any cost was leading to a dilution of brand loyalty, goes the complaint. So was economics. If the seasonal expenses were limited to about ₹50,000 in the past, it now stretched to nearly ₹50 lakh. Rowers are recruited after trials and are housed and fed by the club, each rower paid daily wages of ₹2,000. On an average, a snake boat needs about 100 to 110 persons, and these men practise for about two weeks ahead of the Nehru Trophy. Since ego and vanity have no limits, people even pay to be Captain. A contribution of ₹10 lakh can fetch you the captainship of a snake boat, Baiju claimed. It pains him that the race that he first witnessed 40 years ago as an eight-year-old is slowly becoming hostage to big money. He was unsure if the races would have space for people like him as they transform into gala spectacles with money being thrown around.

It is a fear that many share. In Aranmula, there is now talk of taking out the competitive part and celebrating its ritualistic element. The Aranmula, because of it pageant nature, may retain its pull. As Edanadu Radhakrishnan Nair explained, 'Where else can you see 5,000 young men on 52 boats rowing to songs in unison with a host of other art forms?' The Nehru Trophy survives on the intense competitive spirit it generates among people. More traditional events like Aranmula, precisely because of their tradition, continue to be controlled by a caste elite, whereas the Nehru Trophy, due to its relatively new origin, has a less communal and more democratic structure.

The point is that the boat races are here to stay. The question is, how best to celebrate the past without reviving its feudal control. The challenge is also to find new rowers, train them, and perhaps, even monetise the participation in the races. The KSBRA has talked about gaining official status as an organised sport from the government so that participants can become eligible for rewards that the state offers to participants in sports like athletics and football.

Until very recently, the geography of the races was limited mostly to Kuttanad. It has started to spread to other parts of the state and is acquiring a pan-Kerala character. It may not yet command the widespread popularity of football, cricket or volleyball, but who knows, in the years to come, it may stake claim to being called the 'national sport' of Kerala. After all, its distinctiveness as a sport unique to Kerala has no challengers.

Vallam kali is not just another sport, but a wholesome cultural experience, a tradition that overlaps literature and music, bridging the folk and the classical. It is an exhibition of physical skills and prowess, no doubt, but there is also a celebration of art and craft and the primordial relationship between Man and water. It is sport as art and art as sport, an assertion of the local over the global, community over the individual, a carnival of memory.

◆

V
SPORTS ADMINISTRATION

GURU DUTT SONDHI
Indian IOC Member and Visionary of Asian Integration through Sport*

STEFAN
HUEBNER

To this day, the Olympic Games have never taken place in South Asia. One of the reasons, in addition to exploding costs, is the International Olympic Committee's (IOC's) lack of trust in Indian organisational capabilities. For example, the chairman of the organising committee of the 2010 Commonwealth Games in New Delhi was arrested for corruption.[1] Doubts concerning Indian reliability have quite a long tradition, going back to the first regional events hosted there: the Western Asiatic Games (WAG; New Delhi and Patiala, 1934) and the First Asian Games (New Delhi, 1951).[2]

Focusing on such negative perceptions leaves out the highly important contribution of Indian sports officials to the emergence of intra-Asian sports relations. Guru Dutt Sondhi (1890–1966) was the central figure in the founding of both the Western Asiatic Games and the Asian Games. Each time he proved to be a visionary of Asian cooperation and integration, first during British colonialism, and later during decolonisation and the Cold War.

Studying and discussing Sondhi's life is valuable, since it sheds light on various major events that affected the course of the 20th century. Sondhi was a member of the small British-educated Indian elite during colonialism and affected by the 'white man's burden': the claim that colonialism served not to exploit, but to 'uplift' and 'civilise' colonised peoples. He agreed on the need for a 'modernisation' process in India, which included promoting sport, but disagreed about colonialism and favoured Indian self-government. As a consequence, he also advocated Asian cooperation and integration as a means to resist Western predominance and to give India back a leading role in world affairs. Studying and discussing his activities as a sports organiser, therefore, tells us much about the impact of British colonialism on India. Moreover, it shows how the white man's burden was appropriated by Indians, and affected decolonisation and Asian cooperation.

SONDHI'S EARLY CAREER AS AN ORGANISER AND THE YMCA'S SPORTS PROGRAMME

Sondhi's main occupation was that of a university professor, not of a professional sports official. He studied first at Government College (now Government College University) in Lahore, the capital of the Punjab during British colonialism (after independence, the city became part of Pakistan). Following that, during the early 1910s, he continued his studies at the University of Cambridge's Trinity College. Sondhi eventually became a professor of economics and political science at Punjab University in Lahore and later returned to the Government College to serve as its principal. One has to assume that his British education had a strong impact on his career as a sports official. During his education he was a successful hockey player and runner. While engaging in Western sports was very common at British schools, it was not at all so in India. Most Indians who took up sports during the 1910s and 1920s belonged, like Sondhi, to the very small British-educated upper and middle class.

Sondhi's career as a sports official began in 1924, when he became Secretary of the Punjab Olympic Association. The founding in India of provincial Olympic associations and of a national one, the Indian Olympic Association (IOA), was the outcome of a design drafted by the American Young Men's Christian Association (YMCA) and its Indian supporters. American YMCA physical education directors such as John H. Gray, the son of American missionaries in India, had already, before the outbreak of the First World War, attempted to create a national sports event in India to promote amateur sports. Due to the war, this could not be realised, but another successful attempt was made in the early 1920s. The American YMCA was very important in Indian sports in the 1910s and 1920s, since its American physical education directors were well-trained experts who normally had studied physical education, and sometimes also medicine and related subjects. As is quite well known, both basketball and volleyball had been invented at the International YMCA College in Springfield, Massachusetts. Amateur

1920 Indian Olympic Delegation
Left to right, top row: Randhir Shindes, Purma Bannerjee, Kumar Navale, Phadeppa Chaugule. Middle row: Sohrab Bhoot, A. H. A. Fyzee. Seated: Sadashiv Datar, Kaikadi.
Source: *Wikipedia* at http://tinyurl.com/h2q4ncv.

sports were perceived by the YMCA as an important tool to improve public health and encourage Christian character building based on norms and values such as fair play, self-control, competition, and selection of athletes based on competence instead of family ties or skin colour. The YMCA's promotion of these values was a response to fears among Protestant social reformers that urbanisation and industrialisation in the United States had resulted in a physical degeneration of American Protestants and, because of greater anonymity in cities, a boom in vices.

Since India was one of the countries in which the highest number of non-Christians lived, it had become an important target of the American YMCA's foreign activities, including its amateur sports programme. In 1920, when the Olympic Games took place again—the Games scheduled to be held in Berlin in 1916 had been aborted because of the First World War—the YMCA and the IOC decided to cooperate in the creation of national and regional sports events in non-Western regions. One of the results was that the already planned national games for India became a reality, thanks to the YMCA, in 1924. The event is now called the National Games of India. These games served to select and train athletes for the Olympic Games, and for regional sports events in Asia. More generally, the games were seen as an instrument to make Indians familiar with Western sports and to promote participation, and the hosting of meetings on the provincial and lower levels. In 1920, the IOC also appointed Dorab Tata, a very influential British-educated Indian industrialist, as an IOC member. Tata closely cooperated with the American YMCA, and Indian teams started to participate in the Olympic Games, developments that were accompanied by the founding of the already mentioned Olympic associations.

Sondhi's early career as a sports official is important because it shows his appropriation of the white man's burden. The leadership transfer in sports affairs from Americans to Indians and the resulting attempts of Indians to 'uplift' India through sport were, after all, related to the more general question of Indian self-government and the end of British colonialism, which nationalists increasingly demanded following the First World War. The American YMCA had, for a variety of reasons, started to train Indian students as professional physical educators and was willing to grant them, if sufficiently trained, leadership positions. However, Sondhi was no YMCA trainee. Instead, YMCA physical education directors, such as John Gray, identified him as a protégé of Bhupinder Singh, the Maharaja of Patiala, a princely state that after India's independence was eventually integrated into the Punjab. This judgement was not wrong since Sondhi's plans very much depended on the Maharaja's financial contributions. Other sources of funding were scarce since governmental interest was very limited and TV broadcasting rights, another major source of income today, obviously did not yet exist. The main problem was that the YMCA and Tata had serious doubts concerning the Indian princes' interest in promoting low-cost amateur sports for the masses. This perception was encouraged by various quarrels between princes, who very often were interested in upper-class sports and supported professional athletes or teams as a means to gain prestige and entertain themselves. Such doubts on the part of the YMCA, nevertheless, did not prevent Sondhi from becoming Secretary of the IOA in 1927, when the office holder, YMCA Physical Education Director Arthur G. Noehren, returned to the United States. The following year, the Maharaja succeeded Tata as its President.

Portrait of Maharaja Bhupinder Singh of Patiala.
Source: *Wikipedia* at http://tinyurl.com/zk3ulfx.

IOC MEMBER SONDHI AND THE WESTERN ASIATIC GAMES

Sondhi now had the chance to prove—or not to prove—that he was willing and able to handle India's involvement in the Olympic movement, including the founding of a regional Asian sports event. The last point was important, since such events corresponded to pan-Asian aspirations that had emerged in the 19th century as a result of Western colonialism. Very often, pan-Asian ideas were based on claims of Asian commonalities such as common ethnicity, culture, history and an opponent or enemy in the form of the West. In the case of the YMCA, the situation had been slightly different, since its officials also identified Asian commonalities, but mostly in the sense of Asians being united in their need for American religious advice and scientific expertise. Regional Asian sports events—the YMCA had already founded one in East and South-east Asia— therefore corresponded to the perception of Western amateur sport as a rational and healthy leisure practice and a means for character building that ought to be encouraged among 'backward' Asians. However, if a regional Asian sports event was organised by Asians instead of Westerners, their supposed common ethnicity could be touted as representing a common struggle against colonialism and related claims that Asians were not ready for self-government.

India's 1936 field hockey team, captained by hockey wizard
Dhyan Chand (standing second from left), was the gold medal
winner at the 1936 Berlin Summer Olympics.
Source: *Wikipedia* at http://tinyurl.com/zsfh6r4.

The Western Asiatic Games, which Sondhi founded in
1934, mirror such pan-Asian aspirations. For several years after
he became Secretary of the IOA, Sondhi seems not to have done
anything noteworthy. However, in 1932, he attended his first IOC
meeting, having succeeded Tata as India's IOC member—an office
that is normally held for a lifetime. Soon after he attended the
meeting, Sondhi started to invite a large number of countries and
colonies situated between the Suez and the Straits of Malacca to
India. At first, he received no answer, but eventually small teams
from Afghanistan, Palestine and Ceylon arrived, while two Iranian
diplomats represented their country as delegates. All in all, the first
WAG comprised two days of competitions in both athletics (track
and field) and hockey in New Delhi, and two days of swimming in
Patiala (although only one foreign swimmer, a Palestinian, arrived in
time to participate against the Indian competitors).

Fewer than 100 athletes participated in the event. In addition
to the logistical problems, the Games also proved to be a financial
disaster since Sondhi's budget plan failed completely. The scarcity of
funding, Sondhi never having been, in contrast to YMCA officials,
trained in physical education and organisational matters, and his
full-time work as a professor certainly caused him problems. Despite
the problems, the event was a contribution to the more general
intensification of Asian cooperation since the end of the First World

War, which criticised Western colonialism and can be seen as an important step toward decolonisation. Sondhi thus demonstrated that he was a visionary of Asian integration, self-government and sportive 'modernisation'. He took away the white man's burden from Westerners and tried to 'uplift' Asia without colonial interference, though with a focus on India as the leading power. Sondhi also focused on 'Olympism'—the IOC's secular ideology of sport—instead of the YMCA's Christian interpretation, since this reduced religious resistance and facilitated Asian cooperation. It was another demonstration how he, as a member of the Indian elite, appropriated elements of the white man's burden.

The organisational deficits nevertheless meant that many of Sondhi's colleagues in India and abroad had doubts concerning his ability to put his vision into practice, meaning that not much happened for a while. A second WAG could not be held in 1938 or 1939. Problems in Afghanistan and the Arab Revolt in Palestine prevented these two member–countries from hosting the Games, while the IOA argued against organising the second meeting in India. Sondhi, moreover, had ceased to be the IOA's Secretary in 1939, depriving the potential games of a key driving force. After the

1942 Indian Olympic Association Managing Committee.
President Maharaja of Patiala is seated in the centre of the front row, and Guru Dutt Sondhi is the last seated on the right of the front row.
Source: *Wikipedia* at http://tinyurl.com/jreqboq.

The Governor of Bombay speaks at the 1950 Indian National Games
while the Maharaja of Patiala holds the umbrella.
Guru Dutt Sondhi is standing left of the Naval captain.
Source: *Wikipedia* at http://tinyurl.com/h4ack2a.

outbreak of the Second World War in September that year, which made the hosting of an event impossible, the idea remained dormant until early 1945. Sondhi then started to argue for a second WAG, but massive changes in the international situation meant that he quickly adjusted his vision of Asia peacefully growing together and Asians being educated through amateur sport.

BUILDING NEHRU'S ASIA: SONDHI AND THE ASIAN GAMES

When the most destructive war in human history had ended, large-scale decolonisation and a boom in Indian visions of Asian regional integration followed. Sometimes, such as the case with the 1947 Partition of India, the transfer of power from colonisers to colonised occurred without war—massive violence between Pakistanis and Indians notwithstanding.[3] In contrast, other decolonisation processes were characterised by wars for independence, which lasted for years in colonies such as Indonesia (1945–1949) and Indochina (1946–1954). Civil wars, such as in China (1945–1949); the suppression of Communist movements in various places; the first conflict between newly founded Israel and its Arab neighbours (1948); and big international wars, such as the Korean War (1950–1953), were further demonstrations that the end of the Second World War had hardly brought peace to Asia. Jawaharlal Nehru, independent India's first prime minister, was a prominent advocate for a more peaceful, egalitarian and interdependent world order. While he did not support the formation of a third 'power bloc' in the Cold War, such a world order necessitated Asian regional integration, meaning that the Nehru administration welcomed Sondhi's new vision of an Asian regional sports event. Political events, such as the Asian Relations Conference held in New Delhi in 1947 shortly before India's independence, had encouraged Sondhi to found an event that planned to include all Asian countries, not just those of West and South Asia. A journalist for *The Times of India* summed this up on Sondhi's death:

> It was Mr. Sondhi who conceived the idea of the Asian Games.... The Prime Minister, Mr. Nehru, supported the idea, and it was due mainly to Mr. Sondhi's untiring efforts that the Asian Games Federation was formed in 1949 and the first Asian Games were held two years later in New Delhi.[4]

Indian athletes marching through the National Stadium during the opening ceremony of the First Asian Games, held in New Delhi, India.
Source: *Wikipedia* at http://tinyurl.com/zuw2nnj.

The preparations for the new event, the Asian Games, turned into another disaster for Sondhi. His time schedule was unrealistic; East and South-east Asians, mistrustful of Indian organising competence, initially attempted to host the first event in Shanghai (prevented by the Chinese Civil War), and infrastructure construction in New Delhi took significantly longer than expected. Sondhi eventually gave up his position as head organiser and limited himself to the office of Secretary of the Asian Games Federation. The event itself, which was then organised by another Indian sports official, took place in March 1951 and was attended by 11 Asian countries, and some observers from Communist China. Reminiscent of WAG, it was marred by various organisational deficits and financial problems. The first Asian Games therefore illustrated that India was insufficiently prepared to realise the event within the time frame Sondhi had envisioned.

Despite all these problems, the hosting of the first Asian Games—taking place between the Asian Relations Conference of 1947 and the Asia–Africa Conference, hosted in the Indonesian city of Bandung in 1955—communicated the message of peaceful regional integration during a very militant time. Among others, a Japanese team took part, illustrating the country's reintegration into transnational and international organisations and networks. Another important point is that several teams had female members, which emphasised the emancipation of Asian women. Finally, despite all their problems and deficits, the first Asian Games were relevant in terms of developing a basic sports infrastructure in New Delhi, including a stadium. Designated the 'National Stadium' (now Dhyan Chand National Stadium), the building contributed to India's postcolonial nation-building process and represented a limited catching up with more 'developed' countries.

SONDHI'S LEGACY

Sondhi remained a visionary for the rest of his life: low-cost amateur sports open to everybody to serve as a democratic means for citizenship training, character building and encouraging fitness. As a consequence, he criticised the intentions of other Asian sports officials to include more expensive disciplines like yachting in the event. Sondhi also advocated against intentions to host the Asian Games in a spectacular way that was aimed at showing seemingly rapid and successful development processes though large-scale construction campaigns, since poor or small Asian countries also ought to have the option of applying to host an event.

Encouraging internationalism and peaceful Asian cooperation remained his central desire. At an Asian Games Federation meeting in October 1957, he was still affected by the 'Sputnik Shock' that about three weeks earlier had made people aware that missiles could not only transport satellites into space, but also nuclear warheads to other continents. He evoked the image of an Asia characterised by its strong spiritualism—a regularly invoked image since the 19th century, serving as a counter model to the image of a scientifically and technologically superior West on the path to self-destruction— by declaring the norms and values of amateur sport to be a modern form of spirituality. After a paean to Mohandas K. 'Mahatma' Gandhi's and Jawaharlal Nehru's love of peace, he warned his audience: 'Soul force [one of Gandhi's terms for Satyagraha or passive resistance] is the only power that can control and subjugate nuclear force.'[5] Sondhi also thought about options to discourage strong nationalism at events, such as the Asian Games and the Olympic Games, which was, among other causes, deliberately encouraged by governments of newly independent countries.

Sondhi also struggled for the enforcement of non-discrimination against Asian Games Federation member–countries, which was inspired by his internationalist and egalitarian thinking. When the Indonesian organisers of the 1962 Fourth Asian Games did not invite member–countries Taiwan and Israel to participate, claiming that these two countries were American puppets and hostile to Indonesia and its allies, Sondhi was the only openly critical delegate in the Asian Games Federation. After a few days, the situation became quite violent, as a mob of angry Indonesians started searching for him and in the process damaged the Indian embassy. Sondhi then fled Indonesia and told a reporter from *The Straits Times*, 'I was provided with police escorts ever since the controversy fired up. There were guards even at my hotel (....) Well, I am not bitter. What's past is past.'[6] Through the IOC, he later punished the Indonesian organisers by banning Indonesia from the Olympic movement. It is debatable if this decision was appropriate or too harsh, but Sondhi had shown his determination to enforce the goal of peaceful Asian integration and penalise all activities that undermined it.

Sondhi's career as a sports official was strongly influenced first by British colonialism in India, when he took away the white man's burden from the colonisers and began 'uplifting' India through sport. Later, his career was affected by the age of decolonisation that followed the Second World War, when it became easier to promote Asian cooperation as a means to challenge Asia's marginalisation. What makes him a person worthy of our attention and discussion are his creativity and humanness, which defined his vision of sport-based social improvement and peaceful Asian integration. For Sondhi, the founding of WAG and the Asian Games meant creating a counter signal, first to the division of Asia due to colonialism, and later to the very militant situation during the 1940s and early 1950s. In terms of character building and public health, he also provided important impulses through his cooperation with Indian princes, the YMCA, the IOC, and the government of independent India. Despite a series of setbacks, he did not give up his struggle to realise his vision, which emphasised his determination. Via the Asian Games, he indeed influenced Asian and Indian sport up to the present day. However, since he was a strong advocate of amateurism and low costs, one has to wonder how he would have reacted to the increasing commercialisation and professionalisation of international sport since the 1980s.

◆

ACKNOWLEDGEMENT

* A similar version of this article was published in 2016 as 'Guru Dutt Sondhi: Indian IOC Member and Visionary of Asian Integration through Sport', *Education about Asia* 21 (2): 29–34. Reprinted in the *IIC Quarterly* with the permission of the Association for Asian Studies, Inc., www.asian-studies.org/EAA

NOTES

1. For information about the 2010 Commonwealth Games in Delhi, see Majumdar and Mehta (2010); and for more general information on India, sports, and the Olympic movement, see Sen (2015); Majumdar and Mehta (2009).

2. If not otherwise stated, the text is based on Huebner (2016).

3. During World War II, there was some sporadic violence between the British and Indians.

4. 'Sondhi Dies in Sleep.' 1966. *The Times of India*. 21 November.

5. See *3rd Asian Games Bulletin* (1957; 5: 7), Tokyo, by the Organizing Committee for the 3rd Asian Games. The comment might appear slightly eccentric, but (although this played no role in 1957) it should be mentioned that China tested its first nuclear bomb during the Tokyo Olympic Games (1964), which certainly led to other statements similar to Sondhi's. On the test, see Droubie (2011).

6. 'Mr. Sondhi: "I Had to Get out Fast".' 1962. *The Straits Times*, 4 September.

REFERENCES

Droubie, Paul. 2011. 'Phoenix Arisen: Japan as Peaceful Internationalist at the 1964 Tokyo Summer Olympics', *The International Journal of the History of Sport*, 28 (16): 2309–22.

Huebner, Stefan. 2016. *Pan-Asian Sports and the Emergence of Modern Asia, 1913–1974*. Singapore: National University of Singapore Press.

Majumdar, Boria and Nalin Mehta. 2010. *Sellotape Legacy: Delhi and the Commonwealth Games*. New Delhi: HarperCollins Publishers India.

———. 2009. *Olympic, the India Story*. New Delhi: HarperCollins Publishers India.

Sen, Ronojoy. 2015. *Nation at Play: A History of Sport in India*. New York: Columbia University Press.

◆◆

SEE YOU IN COURT
The Legal Challenge Against India's Sports Bosses

SHARDA
UGRA

O ne of the most seismic shifts in global sport over the last decade had nothing to do with either athletic achievement or technological development, considerable as those were. It was to come through the surge of tumbling skeletons from the inner chambers of global sport's biggest corporations.

Financial wrongdoings, allegations of bribery over bids for mega events, kickbacks in deals and contracts related to these bids and unseemly controversies around doping were traced to the highest officials in some of the wealthiest and weightiest acronyms in sport—FIFA, IOC, IAAF.

These happen to be the bodies that run the Olympic Games (IOC: International Olympic Committee) and world football (FIFA: Fédération Internationale de Football Association). The International Association of Athletics Federations (IAAF), the organisation in charge of world athletics, found itself caught in the middle of an institutionalised doping expose (Ingle, 2016), as well as the extortion and blackmail that went with its cover-up.

Besides, smaller organisations, such as the Union Cycliste Internationale (UCI), the International Weightlifting Federation (IWF) and the Fédération Internationale de Volleyball (FIVB)—the heads of world cycling, wrestling and volleyball—were caught in controversies at the start of the new decade with accusations of financial impropriety, flaws in governance, conflicts of interest and similar issues.

Normally, India, hardly a presence in these global sports, could have considered itself immune from these rumblings. It was a good distance from these billion-dollar enterprises and their brand-marketed global events. No Indian was directly involved in the ructions that shook up these organisations over governance, accountability and transparency issues. Yet, Indian sports administration finds itself under far deeper scrutiny than it has ever been since Independence. Outside of cricket, India is a minor player in world sport but its governance, however, has collected muddy footprints over the last few decades which are now being challenged and questioned in court.

The impact of the 2010 Commonwealth Games (CWG) on Indian sport moved beyond medals won or infrastructure created. In December 2009, a case against the Indian Olympic Association (IOA) and a bunch of National Sports Federations (NSFs) had already been filed by Delhi activist–lawyer, Rahul Mehra. The CWG 2010 corruption scandal was to highlight and put into prime focus governance loopholes and administrative oversight in Indian sport. Mehra's petition arose from his 'distress and alarm' about 'the manner in which the organisations, recognised as apex bodies for their respective sports, are functioning'. However, it is possible to argue that had it not been an international-scale mega-event like the 2010 CWG at the centre of a 'scam', institutional malfeasance would have been relegated to the sports pages, and left in stasis.

While the aftershocks of the CWG scam may have subsided, over the past four years the scrutiny on India's sporting bodies has only increased. In sharp focus today is the country's richest and most powerful sporting body: the Board of Control for Cricket in India (BCCI), whose operations are being supervised by a Supreme Court-appointed Committee of Administrators.

Along with the daily skirmishes around the BCCI's internal disruptions are two documents, which, in theory, signal the possibility of a sharply focused legislative intervention relating to Indian sports governance. One is about the structure and electoral college of sports bodies, and the other about the prevention and punishment of corruption in sport. The drafts of the Sports Development Bill 2013 and the Prevention of Sporting Fraud Act 2013 are pending somewhere between the ministries of law and sports. They are brought up for air every time a piece of sports news requires a response from lawmakers, but are never implemented in practice owing to the many political and government interests prevalent in protecting the status quo.

There is now a third document—far tougher in its terms and conditions than the draft Bills, but far easier to enforce—which may be the sharpest of the demanding legalese around Indian sports governance.

The Ministry of Youth Affairs and Sport (MYAS)—outside of a few sports, the chief financiers of sport in independent India—is now in possession of the draft of a new 'Sports Code' put together to replace the 2011 version, which had already been strengthened through the legal validity given to it by the Delhi High Court in May 2014.

The most recent, updated version of this Code—its draft title reads: National Code for Good Governance in Sports 2017 (NCGGS 2017)—disqualifies ministers in the state and centre, MPs, MLAs and government servants from being involved in day-to-day sports administration (Ugra, 2017). In theory, the NCGGS 2017 can be brought into use and put into operation far more easily than the Sports Development Bill and the Prevention of Sporting Fraud Act. All it requires is an official notification from the sports ministry.

Sports Codes, whether the 2011 version or the NCGGS 2017 Code, are merely a set of guidelines which need to be followed by the NSFs under the watch of MYAS. Should they not do so, they could be censured or punished by the ministry. Whether something as radical as NCGGS 2017 will be notified by the sports ministry—and thus excise a whole layer of political control and influence out of Indian sport—remains a matter of pragmatic surmise.

SPORTS GOVERNANCE: WHY CARE?

Why must sports governance matter so much in India, especially during a period which is a transformative one for our sport? The advent of new stars, the introduction of private enterprise-backed franchise leagues, and the increasing dynamism of non-profits supporting elite athletes are its most visible developments. Issues of sports governance and the legal process surrounding this may then appear to be dampeners, a turgid recounting of the pitfalls that await any attempt to institute checks and balances in administration.

If progress is steady, even if slow, why worry?

To start with is the government's argument about NSFs taking advantage of other 'benefits' from the government—the use of the national name, the flag and other 'national' symbols. The teams the NSFs send out are said to represent the nation 'India', and use its flag. The NSFs are also beneficiaries of tax waivers and land for infrastructure at subsidised rates. This makes them private bodies which perform what are public functions.

What's more, unlike many developed countries, a large chunk of Indian Olympic sport is supported and funded by taxpayer and public money, through the sports ministry. Until the turn of the century, government funding for most NSFs—e.g., athletics, boxing, wrestling, hockey—was handed out, with no questions asked or accounts submitted. For decades, political or government heavyweights held onto high office in these NSFs, with the athletes usually at the bottom of the federation food chain.

The situation did not change despite the early advent of professionalism or India's ventures into a free-market economy in the early 1990s. With the first two decades of the new millennium almost past us, despite the changing environment around Indian sport, it appears that courts have a better chance of pushing NSFs towards professional governance standards, which can lead to improved athletic standards. The alternative, i.e., genuine self-regulation by an NSF, has yet to be sighted.

What can be argued is that the Indian example is a mere reflection of worldwide trends in resistance to governance reform across sporting bodies because of what they were and what they happen to be. These bodies are unique entities in themselves. Transparency International's *2016 Global Corruption Report: Sport* defines the fundamental contradictions that make the application of standards of accountability and good governance on these bodies particularly difficult.

Pielke (2016), professor and director of Centre for Science and Technology Policy Research at the University of Colorado, observes:

> Sports organisations sit in such an odd place in the panoply of international organisations…; they are not governmental, not inter-governmental, not corporations and not international bodies like the United Nations or World Health Organization. It is, arguably, this special, non-profit status that is at the heart of challenges to hold such bodies accountable to the same rules and norms that govern other international bodies.

This is a very unique identity, unlike commercial organisations or companies, with 'formal accountability to stakeholders (e.g., shareholders, in the case of public companies) and are often overseen by independent directors'. These bodies have protected their power, authority and control through the last century, as sport grew from the noble amateurism of the Victorian era into a professional industry over the last quarter of the 20th century. Whether international or Indian, they are resistant to independent scrutiny and internal regulation. From a neutral distance, this 'autonomy' implies that these fundamentally monopolistic bodies claim to have no duty or responsibility to follow the general governance laws of the countries where they are based or the societies with which they may engage with and benefit from.

But, across the last two decades, the eruption of scandals around allegations of bribery, favouritism and racketeering around the IOA (specifically, the 2002 Salt Lake City Winter Olympics), FIFA (over the awarding of the World Cup to Russia, 2018, and Qatar, 2022) and the IAAF (over cover-ups of state-sponsored doping) has led to two key developments, understood amongst governors of the sport, their legal departments and their fans.

(i) The first is the acceptance that governing sport has made these bodies accountable to the public, despite their technical and legal definitions as private non-profits.

(ii) The second is *to be seen* putting good governance practices into place and *be seen* as open to the idea of external, independent review. This has led to the creation of ethics/ integrity units in various international sports bodies and the establishment of an international standard that must, at least in theory, be followed by their members across the world.

In an ideal scenario, sports organisations must ensure that athletes have access to infrastructure to be involved and engaged in their sport, an adequate annual calendar of competitions to participate in, and clear 'pathways' to progress and rise in their sport. In India, the majority of sporting bodies offer very little of this—a reflection of weak governance and a lack of accountability.

The BCCI had held itself up as the exception, but the 2013 IPL (Indian Premier League) corruption scandal was to reveal its intrinsic fault lines. There is no denying that Indian cricket functions smoothly with its existing infrastructure, packed calendar of events and a clear pathway to the top. But the BCCI's inability to deal competently and professionally with an internal organisational crisis became proof that its governance and development was lopsided and preferential, and built largely around a power dynamic. It benefited those who succeeded through an electoral ecosystem of privileges and personal favours, and transgressions ignored in exchange for votes gathered.

This modus operandi was well known inside Indian cricket, but became a matter of public record only after litigation was brought to Bombay High Court, questioning the BCCI's disciplinary measures after the arrest of an IPL team owner on charges of cheating, forgery and fraud. From that single query, India's richest, most powerful and most well-connected sporting body had to face the rebuilding of its electoral college and the rewriting of its constitution. The case has set a precedent, calling all other sports bodies to account, which not even the BCCI, despite its wealth and clout, was able to evade.

THE POWER OF THE PRECEDENT

The BCCI case—in which a self-sustaining, internationally powerful, sporting NSF had its inner workings turned inside out—has also thrown into question governance failures across other NSFs in Indian sport. In December 2016, a writ petition by 28 former athletes, asking for the Lodha recommendations to be implemented across all sport in India, was admitted to the Supreme Court (Selvaraj, 2017). The petition cited 'several instances of mismanagement and corruption in various National Sports Federations which have caused the downfall of sporting activities'. The petition included the MYAS, SAI, and IOA, the parent body of every major NSF in the country.

In the past, when questioned by external authorities, Indian NSFs were often protected by international ruling bodies. External queries, particularly, regarding elections or administrative operations, are interpreted as an infringement of the 'autonomy' of an NSF and a comment is evoked about 'interference'. The possibility of punishing the member nation through suspensions or bans for having to operate under such interference can also be made. This is a means to gain leverage against the demands of external regulation and has worked in the past.

If ever an example is needed of what Indian sport and litigants fighting on its behalf are up against, it could be captured in the fate of the National Sports Development Bill 2011. Or, then again, the emergence of the National Sports Code 2011.

The timing of the radical 2011 Sports Bill, it could be argued, was most opportune. In April 2011, two of the senior-most Indian sports officials, Suresh Kalmadi and Lalit Bhanot, were arrested over the CWG corruption scandal. Yet, in August 2011, the Union Cabinet unequivocally dismissed the Bill. The Bill had mandated that NSFs limit the age and tenure of their officials, submit due accounts, exercise due rigour and transparency in the voting process, include 25 per cent sportspersons in their executive sports bodies, and be answerable to the public under the Right to Information Act. The Bill was shot down well before it could reach Parliament. Four of those in the cabinet who rejected it were also serving as heads of their respective state cricket associations in the BCCI, and one headed another NSF (Kannan and Bhaduri, 2011). Agriculture minister Sharad Pawar was president of International Cricket Council (ICC); heavy industries minister Praful Patel headed the All India Football Federation (AIFF); minister for road transport and highways C. P. Joshi, renewable energy minister Farooq Abdullah, and Vilasrao Deshmukh were presidents of their regional cricket associations in Rajasthan, Jammu & Kashmir and Mumbai, respectively.

However, the crusade of the Code continues. It was to give teeth to the sports ministry's May 2010 recall and modification of a 1975 regulation that limited the tenure of office holders in NSFs. The Code was an amalgamation of several ministry 'guidelines',[1] and was quietly pushed through and notified by the sports ministry in February 2011.

The appearance of the Code followed the Mehra PIL in the Delhi High Court, which had questioned the government's sluggishness over lapses in the operations of various NSFs, faulty electoral procedures and tenure rules. Over the next few years, the Code, for a change, was enforced by the sports ministry. In December 2012, it de-recognised the boxing and archery federations for electoral irregularities.

The same week, the IOA—the body that sends Indian athletes to the Olympics—was suspended by the IOC, its parent body. The reason? For being compelled to conduct its elections under the 2011 Code. The imposition of external regulations by the ministry was interpreted by the IOC as 'government interference in the Olympic Movement'. The suspension meant that the IOA could receive no funding from the international body, and Indian athletes could not compete under the Indian flag at Olympic events (which happened at the Sochi 2014 Winter Olympics.)

This decision by the international body did not give the IOA the leverage needed to twist MYAS' arm. One of the reasons for the ban included the IOA's decision to allow Lalit Bhanot—booked on a corruption charge—stand for office. Regardless, a day after being suspended from the Olympic movement, the IOA conducted its elections and elected Bhanot as secretary–general.

To understand the lack of accountability in Indian sport, it is also good to remember that the president of the IOA at the time was Abhay Singh Chautala. Chautala headed the boxing federation which, two days after the IOC ban on India, was suspended by the world boxing body because of 'possible manipulation' of its elections. India was readmitted to the IOC in February 2014 after Bhanot was forced to stand down, but the saga is still ongoing. Suresh Kalmadi, defeated in the 2013 election for president of the Asian Athletics Association (AAA), was appointed its 'life president' in 2015, and Bhanot was elected AAA's vice-president.

STAYING THE DISTANCE

The Supreme Court's 2013 intervention in the functioning of the BCCI has upped the ante on all other Indian sports' ruling bodies. The idea that the country's most powerful sports body could be brought to book and have its administrative and governance radically altered has changed the rules of the game.

The most recent chapter in this unrelenting tussle between the government and sporting federations is a revised Sports Code—the draft National Sports Code for Good Governance 2017. Its newest draft awaits notification by the sports ministry. Rajyavardhan Rathore, the first Olympic medallist to be sports minister, says the Code is in the process of being 'finalised', will be more 'contemporary', and that suggestions were both invited and welcome.

In reality, unlike in 2011, the Sports Code notification will not be issued until a version meets the approval of political heavyweights in power who remain involved in sports administration. In the present government, home minister Amit Shah headed the Gujarat Cricket Association (GCA), a voting member of the BCCI, till September 2019 (his son who was the GCA secretary is now the BCCI secretary); the head of Indian badminton, Himanta Biswa Sarma, is a cabinet minister in Assam; and the Wrestling Federation of India (WFI) is headed by BJP MP Brij Bhushan Sharan Singh. Across political parties, these numbers only grow larger.

A professionally functioning sporting body is fundamental to the better health of a sport, much like the choice of a coach or training programmes are needed to further the career path of an individual athlete. Yet, what is most common and revealing is that all arguments in court or on paper over sporting governance are never about what is best for Indian sport or its athletes. They always centre on age-limits, tenure restrictions and voting rights of officials. No kings ever gave up kingdoms willingly.

This perpetual tug of war over governance has always been Indian sport's tiresome background score. Achieving progress in these areas, around what should, frankly, be the bedrock of governance, has been infinitesimally slow. It is as if Indian sport, through the legal process, is forever fighting to gain inches against the powerful churn of a political machine aiming to hold onto old territory, no questions asked.

For the patriarchs who control Indian sport, however, the heat is definitely on.

◆

NOTE

1. Press Information Bureau, Government of India Ministry of Youth Affairs and Sport 2011. http://pib.nic.in/newsite/PrintRelease.aspx?relid=69503 (accessed on 27 December 2017).

REFERENCES

Ingle, Sean. 2016. 'IAAF in Crisis: A Complex Trail of Corruption that Led to the Very Top.' https://www.theguardian.com/sport/2016/jan/07/russia-doping-scandal-corruption-blackmail-athletics-iaaf (accessed on 15 December 2017).

Kannan, S. and Tushar Bhaduri. 2011. 'Cabinet Shows Red Card to Sports Bill, Maken Asked to Redraft it.' http://indiatoday.intoday.in/story/union-cabinet-halts-sports-bill-sports-minister-ajay-maken-asked-to-come-up-with-a-new-bill/1/149566. html (accessed on 27 December 2017).

Pielke Jr., Roger. 2016. 'Obstacles to Accountability in International Sports Governance.' *2016 Global Corruption Report: Sport.* UK: Routledge.

Selvaraj, Jonathan. 2017. 'SC Accepts Petition to Implement Lodha Reforms Across all Sport.' http://www.espn.in/espn/story/_/id/18536809/supreme-court-accepts-petition-implement-lodha-reforms-all-sports (accessed on 15 December 2017).

Ugra, Sharda. 2017. 'Coming Soon: A New Sports Code that Targets VIPs, Voting Lobbies.' http://www.espn.in/espn/story/_/id/20514748/coming-soon-new-sports-code-targets-vips-voting-lobbies (accessed on 15 December 2017).

◆◆

VI
SPORT
IN
FILM
AND
LITERATURE

SPORT IN INDIAN FILM

AMY J.
RANSOM

In 2001, the cricket-themed film, *Lagaan,* brought Bollywood film to the attention of international critics and audiences. Set during the British Raj, the film revisits a national history of colonial oppression, using the metaphor of sport to illustrate India's resistance, telling an underdog story of success against all odds. As Seán Crosson (2013: 2) argues, '[t]his theme of struggle, and the perceived role of sport as a means of overcoming, has been one of the most popular subjects of the sports film'. Not insignificantly, though, the villagers of Champaner, led to victory by Bhuvan (Aamir Khan), consider the British sport in relation to the local game of *gilli-danda*. Similarly, South Asian sport film appropriates Hollywood generic conventions, infusing it with locally specific themes and aesthetics. As in other modern, pluralistic nations, however, Indian sport narratives contribute to the construction of national identity built on the playing field. Conversely, some demonstrate how sport integrates diasporic South Asians into new home societies.

BOLLYWOOD'S ADAPTATION OF THE HOLLYWOOD SPORT FILM GENRE

Many Bollywood hits include sport in their plotlines, demonstrating the integral presence of athletics in South Asian daily life. Sport appears as an integral part of childhood and the maturation process, and it also signifies adult material success; for example, in *Kuch Kuch Hota Hai* (1999; dir. Karan Johar), Rahul (Shah Rukh Khan) and Anjali (Kajol) play tennis to illustrate their upper-middle-class lifestyle. Both playing and spectating sports, however, also offers less-advantaged individuals an escape from everyday cares, as seen in the documentary, *Beyond all Boundaries* (2013; dir. Sushrut Jain).

Or success on the playing field paves the way to material comfort or personal satisfaction. Beyond the numerous films in which sport plays a secondary role, this article examines the sport film *per se*, defined as 'a production in which a sport, sporting event, athlete (...), or follower of a sport (...) are prominently featured, and which depend on sport to a significant degree for their plot motivation or resolution' (Crosson, 2013: 60).

Since *Laagan*, Bollywood has produced films featuring popular stars participating in an array of team and individual sports. Since field hockey is India's official national sport, we cite first *Chak De! India* (2007; dir. Shimit Amin). Based on a 'true story', a prologue reprises the humiliation of Kabir Khan (Shah Rukh Khan), who missed a critical penalty shot against Pakistan in the World Men's Hockey Championship. In a typical Hollywood sport film plotline, the fallen hero finds redemption, however, leading an initially misfit women's team to victory. Overcoming regional differences through the leadership of their coach, these young women unite to form a team capable of success on the international field (Ransom, 2014).

The 'Bollylite' (Joshi, 2012) co-production, *Bend it Like Beckham* (2001; dir. Gurinder Chadha), was another international success, following closely on the heels of *Lagaan*, featuring a Non-Resident Indian (NRI) Punjabi girl's success in football, a sport second only to cricket in South Asian film. Indian regionalism is a sub-theme of Mumbai-produced Hindi-language films, but India's other state-based film industries have a history of sport film. Indeed, *Mohanbaganer Meye* (1976; dir. Manu Sen) may be the first of several Bengali football films, a sport which appears in Bollywood a decade later with *Hip Hip Hooray* (1984; dir. Prakash Jha), which signals sport film's cultural hybridity with its title's English-language cheer. *Saaheb* (1985; dir. Anil Ganguly), a remake of the Bengali *Saheb* (1981; dir. Bijoy Bose), explores the social tensions between family duty and individual passion for football. In many sport-themed films, 'sport is ultimately rarely the central concern' (Crosson, 2013: 60). Thus South Asian football-themed films crossover with other genres, including the romantic comedy or the personal drama. For example, *Khabi Alvida Na Kehna* (2016; dir. Karan Johar) exploits the abrupt ending of a successful career in US major-league soccer as a pretext for Dev's (Shah Rukh Khan) post-retirement existential struggles.

Among the issues addressed in sport films, political activism appears, as in *Sikander* (2013; dir. Jatinder Mohaur), and the Bengali historical soccer film, *Egaro: The Immortal XI* (2011; dir. Arun Roy), about the 1911 IFA (Indian Football Association) Shield and its impact on the Swadeshi movement. Sport films frequently construct national identity in pluralistic societies, readily lending themselves to narratives about immigrants' integration into new home states, as in *Dhan Dhana Dhan Goal* (2007; dir. Vivek Agnihotri). Starring John Abraham, it re-territorialises a diasporic South Asian community in London's Southall neighbourhood. Canada's *Breakaway* (2011; dir. Robert Lieberman) features a Sikh family's integration via the game of ice hockey.

Other sports figuring as central plot elements in Hindi films include cycling in the Aamir Khan vehicle, *Jo Jeeta Wohi Sikandar* (1992; dir. Mansoor Khan), and boxing in *Apne* (2007; dir. Anil Sharma). Boxing and kickboxing are the respective sports treated in the Tamil films, *Saala Khadoos* (2016; dir. Sudha Kongara) and *M. Kumaran s/o Mahalakshmi* (2004; dir. M. Raja). South Asian film celebrates long-distance runners, both real and fictional. *Bhaag Milkha Bhaag* (2013; dir. Rakeysh Omprakash Mehra) narrates the life of the 'Flying Sikh', long-distance runner Milkha Singh, and *Paan Singh Tomar* (2012; dir. Tigmanshu Dhulia) rehearses the story of a steeple-chase champion-turned-bandit. In the Tamil romance, *Ethir Neechal* (2013; dir. R. S. Durai Senthilkumar), the film's hero runs a marathon to prove himself. Local sports may also be featured, as in the Tamil films, *Aadukalam* (2011; dir. Vetri Maaran), about cockfighting, and *Ghilli* (2004; dir. Dharani), a love story with a kabbadi-playing hero.

CRICKET AS NATIONAL MARKER IN INDIAN SPORT FILM

Filmmakers thus adopt conventions from international sport film to tell stories that appeal to South Asian audiences, both locally on the subcontinent and across the diaspora. Tejaswini Ganti theorises this process of 'adaptation', looking at Bollywood films that adapt specific Hollywood blockbusters. This process of adaptation involves translating these films into visual and narrative formats that are 'relatable' to Indian audiences and their experiences (Ganti, 2002: 443). Given cricket's cultural significance, it represents the sport most frequently brought to South Asian screens. Thus, *Chain Kulii Ki*

Main Kulii (2007; dir. Karanjeet Saluja) transposes onto the cricket pitch elements of the US basketball film, *Like Mike* (2002; dir. John Schulz); and the romantic comedy about an extreme cricket fan, *Meerabai Not Out* (2008; dir. Chandrakant Kulkarni), borrows from the US baseball hit, *Fever Pitch* (2002; dir. Peter and Bobby Farrelly). I extrapolate this notion beyond the individual film, positing that the recent sport film explosion reveals a broader strategy of adapting entire genres from abroad to the Bollywood format. This adaptation process includes the choice of subject matter (well-known South Asian sports figures such as M. S. Dhoni, Kabir Khan, Milkha Singh and Paan Singh Tomar); familiar locations on the subcontinent (from major cities like New Delhi and Amritsar to a 'typical' village like Champaner); storylines that involve the time-tested themes of love, family duty and overcoming oppression; and, of course, integrating the spectacle of song and dance into the exegesis.

The tradition of cricket-themed films in India dates back to 1959 with Subodh Mukherjee's *Love Marriage*. Starring Dev Anand as a cricketer, it engages a modernising narrative about evolving visions of the heterosexual couple as constituted not by arrangement, but rather, as the film's title reveals, love. Since then Mumbai has produced cricket-themed films at regular intervals with at least three of these in the mid-1980s. *All Rounder* (1984; dir. Mohan Kumar), an otherwise conventional Bollywood film, tracks its orphan hero Birju's (Vinod Mehra) rise in the sport. This period saw the introduction of real-life athletes into the sport film: Sandeep Patil starred in *Kabhi Ajnabi Thé* (1985; dir. Vijay Singh); and *Cricketer* (1985; dir. Bish Mehay) included Kapil Dev in its cast. *Awwal Number* (1990; dir. Dev Anand) discourses about good sportsmanship, contrasting the egotistical aging star, Ronnie (Aditya Pancholi), with the humble rising star, Sunny, played by Aamir Khan. After the latter's success in *Laagan*, cricket film production in Mumbai rapidly accelerated to one or more films per year, including comedies like *Stumped* (2003; dir. Gaurav Pandey), *Meerabai Not Out* (2008; dir. Chandrakant Kulkarni); and *Hattrick* (2007; dir. Milan Luthria), in which cricket media personalities Gautam Bhimani and Harsha Bhogle appear as themselves. These films mock sport fans as overly obsessed with a trivial pastime which distracts them from marital duties and other responsibilities. In this sense, they draw on the sport film's 'utopian sensibility'

(Crosson, 2013: 6–8), its escapism and illusion of a more perfect life, but also uphold a dominant ideology of family values by lampooning fan behaviour as childlike. Conversely, the Tamil hit *Chennai 600028* (2007; dir. Venkat Prabhu) and its sequel (2016) focus on the positive impact of street cricket on residents of an urban neighbourhood.

Serious approaches to sport exemplify instead sport's positive impact on youth development, as with the deaf-mute title character of *Iqbal* (2005; dir. Nagesh Kukanoor) who finds an outlet for self-expression on the cricket pitch. But the theme of individual growth appears in cricket comedies like *Chain Kulii Ki Main Kulii, Ferrari Ki Sawaari* (2012; dir. Rajesh Mapuskar) and *Kai Po Ché* (2013; dir. Abishek Kapoor). *Say Salaam India: 'Let's Bring the Cup Home'* (2007; dir. Subhash Kapoor) connects sport to national identity as a group of youths from diverse backgrounds come together for a common goal. A revised take on maturation and identity appears in *Dil Bole Hadippa!* (2009; dir. Anurag Singh), in which female cricketer Veera Singh (Rani Mukherji) must cross-dress to play with male players of her calibre. The film works toward the conventional trope of building national unity while recognising India's diversity, with its Punjabi setting (Ransom, 2014).

The trope of the rise and fall of the adult sport star appears in *World Cup 2011* (2009; dir. Ravi Kapoor), which also explores the underside of cricket, including extortion and match fixing. *Victory* (2009; dir. Ajit Pal Mangat) features a large cast of real-life cricketers, both South Asian and British, appearing as themselves. Sport's ability to overcome prejudice and unite individuals from different backgrounds, seen in *Say Salaam India* and *Chak De! India*, is revisited in *Patiala House* (2011; dir. Nikhil Advani). As in a number of Indian sport films, a young NRI man faces family pressures to give up his dream of cricket playing; in this case, his father had been the victim of racial abuse and opposes his son's desire to play this 'white man's game'. Of course, 'Gattu' (Akshay Kumar) eventually overcomes his father's objections and prejudices, winning a championship for England.

AZHAR: BOLLYWOOD WITH A HOLLYWOOD SPORT VENEER

The desire to profit from the nation's passion for cricket culminated recently in two significant biopics—*Azhar* (2016; dir. Tony D'Souza) and *M. S. Dhoni: The Untold Story* (2016; dir. Neeraj Pandey)—analysed later in this article. Additionally, Sachin Tendulkar was recently immortalised in the multilingual, international docudrama, *Sachin: A Billion Dreams* (2017; dir. James Erskine). Ganti (2002) observes the conservatism of Bollywood producers afraid to lose the potential gains of the 'sure bet' by adapting an already successful hit, and the care taken to translate Hollywood films to the perceived sensibilities of South Asian audiences. *Azhar* and *M. S. Dhoni* exemplify the hybrid nature of the South Asian sport film, but they take very different strategies in their masala approach to their subject—the life of a well-known cricketer. They also suggest a greater willingness on the part of today's producers and their audiences to accept a product closer to the conventional sport film genre.

Based on the life of Hyderabad-born cricket star Mohammed Azharuddin, who led the Indian national cricket team to a number of victories in the 1990s, *Azhar* adapts the tropes of the standard sport biopic to the interests of local audiences. Its plot, involving fixed matches, has Hollywood precedents like *Eight Men Out* (1988; dir. John Sayles). The integral relationship between players, games and mass media coverage frequently appears in the sport film genre, and *Azhar* draws on this synergy via montage sequences, including newspaper headlines, viewers watching news coverage on television, press conferences, interviews, and so on. This mediatisation of the sporting world also gives the film a 'postmodern' visual aesthetic. Another device of the sport biopic is the rehearsal of the hero's landmark statistics and key events known by his fans; *Azhar* includes sequences of its subject performing in key matches, with title cards indicating significant data: the date, place, opponent and (inter)national significance of these staged matches. It references known sport stars such as Kapil Dev and Sachin Tendulkar. Furthermore, the film's sophisticated, non-chronological approach to telling its narrative through layers of flashback sequences reflects Hollywood trends. Finally, coming in at just over two hours with almost no song and dance sequences,[1] the film almost appears to fit Hollywood's standards more than Bollywood's.

Nonetheless, the film's casting, shooting, and other production choices reflect the visual conventions of Bollywood, including both the fairy-tale, prosperous world of the Bollywood set and establishing shots of not only Hyderabad and Mumbai monuments, but also of London. These not only territorialise the film's action on the subcontinent, but also reference ongoing ties with the former colonial metropole. The physical appearance of the actor reflects the character's moral standing, particularly the young hero, Azhar (Emraan Hashmi): perfectly groomed, clean-shaven, not a wrinkle in his cricket whites, an appearance reinforced by his cherubic, pale pink, clearly made-up, lips. The hero's desire to succeed in sport derives not from his own narcissistic ambition, but rather to fulfil his grandfather's dream that he 'will play 100 test matches for India'. This assertion, coupled with his grandfather's advice to 'answer with his bat' when faced with oppression, become refrains throughout flashback sequences. As opposed to the aggressive and misogynist 'hegemonic masculinity' identified with Hollywood sport heroes (Trujillo, 2000), the Bollywood film underscores Azhar's humility, his devotion to family, respect for his mother and father, and—in his courtship and first marriage—his shyness and chastity. In contrast, supporting male characters, particularly the film's antagonist, are less attractive, such as the stocky, middle-aged actor, Rajesh Sharma, who plays bookie M. K. Sharma aka 'Shawn'.

Initially, female characters appear to follow Bollywood conventions in their make-up and costuming as well, but as Azhar's story unfolds, certain transgressions of local cinematic codes occur. His first wife, Naureen (Prachi Desai), is naturally beautiful but modest, religious and respectful to her in-laws, timidly open to her new spouse's budding sexual desire. In the end she is even a faithful ex, ultimately supporting him through his trials. In stark contrast, Meera Verma (Lara Dutta), the shrewish London-based attorney, charged with defending the Cricket Association's ban on Azhar after he is charged with matchfixing, first appears in voice off, shrilly and publicly telling a man to 'shut up!'. Her aggressiveness conflicts with traditional norms for female behaviour, as does her appearance—hair bobbed and Western business clothing. Not insignificantly, her campaign to prove Azhar's guilt is explicitly linked to the trope of the 'woman scorned'; a former fan who fawned over the handsome cricket star, she wants revenge now that he has broken her heart.

Despite these images of 'good' and 'bad' femininity, the film offers a significant transgression of these conventions, reflective of Ajay Gehlawat's (2010) thesis that Bollywood film may subvert cultural norms despite critics' consistent readings of it as reflecting dominant ideology. A hinge moment occurs when Azhar meets his second wife, Sangeeta (Nargis Fakhri), the perceived temptress possibly to blame for the hero's downfall. Travelling with his team in 'London, 1996', as a title card indicates, Azhar relaxes poolside while his rakish friend Ravi (Gautam Gulati) banters about women and insinuates that he has a rendezvous with a 'Bollywood heroine'. As he asks Azhar to cover for him with his wife, an arrogant beauty strides by in sunglasses and Western dress, ostensibly the actress in question; Azhar refuses and scorns Ravi's taste, praising instead a sari-clad beauty. At this point, the hero's values reflect Bollywood conventions, rejecting the vamp in favour of the 'good Indian girl'. This image, however, is overturned a few moments later when Azhar discovers that his friend's tryst was not, after all, with the actress Sangeeta, but with the traditionally-dressed (but now morally questionable) woman. Having accused his friend of not knowing true beauty when he sees it, Azhar must now examine his own belief in appearances' ability to reflect reality.

The film engages with the unreliability of appearances beyond simply judging a woman's moral character from her dress and make-up, for the biographical narrative involves the hero's status as guilty or innocent of match fixing. Indeed, an early title card reads: 'Azhar/ love him, hate him, judge him'. From its first minutes to the film's concluding courtroom dialogue, characters repeatedly insist on uncovering the 'truth'. In the film's opening sequence, Azhar's aging teammate Manoj Prabhakar (Karanvir Sharma) accepts a police wire, asserting that 'people have a right to know about all that happens in Indian cricket', suggesting that the sting operation he is involved with will uncover the truth. Doubt is cast, though, on the righteousness of this mission as Meera Verma interrogates the bookie M. K. Sharma, who states that 'the police coerced everything out of me in the torture room'. Indeed, the film's conclusion reveals that the Cricket Association's ban was procedurally unfair, and that the sting operation behind it was based on lies. Finally, the film revisits Azhar's interactions with the bookie, revealing that he had accepted money not to pay for an expensive lifestyle with Sangeeta, but so that the villain could not buy off another player.

Azhar's moral ambiguity, cleverly sustained throughout the film via flashback and editing, suggests a swing toward more Hollywood-like narratives. A rising Bollywood tolerance for ambiguous heroes over the past decade is illustrated by the Aamir Khan vehicles—*Fanaa* (2006; dir. Kunal Kohli) and *Ghajini* (2008; dir. A. R. Murugadoss)— to cite only two examples. *Azhar* is played by Emraan Hashmi, cast as another morally ambiguous hero in the cricket sub-themed *Jannat* films (2008, 2012; dir. Kunal Deshmukh). And yet, like many sport heroes, Azhar is identified with the nation, particularly during his rise to fame. In the film's opening, he introduces himself as 'the captain of India'; this moment occurs after his fall from grace, so he revises his assertion, 'Or, shall we say, the son-in-law of India'. After the accusation and ban, he is called a traitor and burned in effigy. Although viewers know the film's outcome in advance, the film's complex structure sustains doubt about Azhar's guilt or innocence until its final moments. So while, on the one hand, the film maintains viewer sympathy for the morally ambiguous character, his vindication at its conclusion, on the other, restores him to the position of conventional hero. Thus, despite its own appearance of a moral complexity reflective of Hollywood norms, *Azhar* concludes as a very traditional Bollywood story, more about success and failure, marriage and infidelity, friendship and loyalty, than about sport.

M. S. DHONI: A 'TRUE' SPORT FILM, BOLLYWOOD STYLE

Like its own discourse on truth and illusion, then, *Azhar* uses a veneer of sophisticated narrative and visual techniques to lend itself the appearance of a more Hollywood-like sport film, when, in fact, it is not very much about cricket at all. This contrasts with the visual and narrative strategies employed by *M. S. Dhoni: The Untold Story*; although its subtitle also suggests it will reveal some hidden truth, it is actually a straightforward narrative about a straightforward, but gifted, player. It also deploys a strategy nearly reverse that of *Azhar* in its hybridisation of these two filmic styles—Hollywood sport film and Bollywood drama. Its subject matter, the life of star cricketer Mahendra Singh Dhoni who brought India victory in the 50-over format of World Cup cricket after a 28-year drought, is clearly one appealing to South Asian audiences. But its social–realist visual style holds greater international appeal than *Azhar*'s glitzy sets; its initial setting, the modest neighbourhood of the (now) state capital of Jharkhand, Ranchi, where Dhoni grew up, contrasts with *Azhar*'s privileged childhood and glamourous adult life. Indeed, what the film reveals in its 'untold story' is a different India than that found in the typical Bollywood production, with establishing shots of what were then Bihar's mines, connecting the regional capital to other peripheral areas, such as a bat factory in the Punjab. Although the hero's role is cast with attractive, charismatic actors (Sushant Singh Rajput as the adult, and actors Zeeshan and Abishek Kumar as child and youth), the viewer is struck by the worn-down appearance of his middle-aged parents. Indeed, a wig-clad Anupam Kher is nearly unrecognisable as Pan Singh Dhoni at his son's birth. Keshav Ranjan Banerjee—Dhoni's childhood cricket coach, an important adjuvant—is played by Rajesh Sharma, the same actor cast as the villain in *Azhar*. These characters all wear clothing more typical of working-class and lower-middle-class residents of an industrial town, and the Dhonis' tiny apartment reflects the cricketer's modest origins, as do his father's values.

Eschewing the glamour typical of Bollywood film, *M. S. Dhoni* nonetheless rehearses the values of mainstream India: the improvement of one's lot through education, respect for one's parents, and living a clean, moral life. As in a number of South Asian sport films, the young hero repeatedly faces his father's desire for him to study and get a good job, better than his own humble station of pump operator, instead of playing cricket: 'Sports has its own importance, but only if you study hard will you be successful.' Mahi, as Dhoni is called, respects this and faces the challenge; the dedication required to succeed—even for those with natural talent—is revealed in an early sequence in which he must juggle sitting his exams, finishing early, then rushing to the train station to attend the under-19 cricket tryouts. Although self-confident, Dhoni is always softspoken; the only time he raises his voice is when one of his friends—from whom he learns the slap-shot—drinks alcohol. His gratitude to a local supporter, the Sikh owner of a sport shop, is clear as he accepts a new cricket kit with tears in his eyes.

In contrast with *Azhar*, besides being a biography of an exemplary figure, *M. S. Dhoni* actually appears primarily to be about the sport of cricket. While it shares many of the familiar devices deployed by *Azhar*—match sequences, title cards situating the viewer in time, recitations of the star's landmark statistics, etc.—*Dhoni* engages a more detailed knowledge of the sport itself, revels in the sheer beauty of the athlete in motion, and reflects the joy that watching a star player brings to fans. This joy appears in several sequences, beginning with the sport-shop owner Param's (Surjeet Singh) dedicated support for the teenage player, as he explains to the Punjabi bat manufacturer whom he repeatedly solicits for a sponsorship despite many refusals. Param expresses his love for the game, but his lack of talent; his interest in Dhoni is that 'if he makes it big, then I'll feel like I've played, too'.[2] During a school championship game, as he performs a spectacular sequence at batting, a child rides his bicycle round town to notify people that Dhoni is ready to bat, and the schoolmistress releases the children to watch the match. Commentators, as well, begin to remember and recognise his talent at these early events. Shots of score boards, discussions of the matches, and much longer and more frequent practise and game sequences contribute to the film's homage to the sport of cricket, also bringing it beyond the three-hour mark typical of Bollywood film. Above all, the film's cricket-playing montages, in which an extra-diegetic song accompanies Dhoni's play on the field, reveal an interesting method by which the sport film can be uniquely adapted to the Bollywood format. The beauty of his body in motion, the perfect catch, and the brilliant hit readily substitute for the staged dance number, all the while maintaining the integral role that music plays in South Asian film. In this manner, *M. S. Dhoni: The Untold Story* offers an exemplary case of how the Hollywood genre of the sport film can be adapted to South Asian screens, but can also appeal to an international audience. Furthermore, it remains much truer to the sport genre than *Azhar*, as the only story it wishes to tell is that of an exemplary young Indian man who finds success and meaning by performing a sport that brings joy to others and prestige to his nation.

CONCLUSION

As this survey reveals, just as sport is an integral part of South Asian daily life, South Asian cinema has integrated the sport genre not just to the Bollywood format of Mumbai's dominant Hindi-language industry, but also figures in the repertoire of the growing state-based film industries producing films in Tamil, Bangla and other tongues. Although cricket clearly dominates Hindi film, Bangla-language film favours football, and other regional interests appear reflected, as in the popularity of kickboxing in Tamil film. While, on the one hand, the sport film reflects the cultural and linguistic diversity of the subcontinent, on the other, it is also used by filmmakers to create images of national unity and to maintain connections with NRIs abroad. And while it adopts many international genre conventions, South Asian sport film nonetheless reflects the values and interests of India's diverse population.

◆

NOTES

1. Two brief extra-diegetic song sequences play over montages of Azhar's courtships, first with Naureen and later with Sangeeta. The only actual dance number in the film is cleverly inserted into the diegesis: in an effort to save his marriage, Azhar takes Naureen to the movies, only to see Sangeeta in a tiny miniskirt singing and dancing on the big screen. The film's repetition on television underscores his inability to escape thoughts of his new love object as her media presence is everywhere.

2. Dialogue quoted from the English subtitles.

REFERENCES

Crosson, Seán. 2013. *Sport and Film*. London: Routledge.

Ganti, Tejaswini. 2007 [2002]. '"And Yet My Heart is Still Indian": The Bombay Film Industry and the (H)Indianization of Hollywood', in Julie F. Codell, *Genre, Gender, Race and World Cinema*. Oxford: Blackwell.

Gehlawat, Ajay. 2010. *Reframing Bollywood: Theories of Popular Hindi Cinema*. New Delhi: Sage.

Joshi, Priya. 2012. 'Bollylite in America', in Sara Dickey and Rajinder Dundrah (eds.), *South Asian Cinemas: Widening the Lens*. London: Routledge.

Ransom, Amy J. 2014. 'Bollywood Goes to the Stadium: Gender, National Identity and Sport Film in Hindi', *Journal of Film and Video*, 66 (4): 34–59.

Trujillo, Nick. 2000. 'Hegemonic Masculinity on the Mound: Media Representations of Nolan Ryan in American Sports Culture', in Susan Birrell and Mary G. McDonald, *Reading Sport: Critical Essays on Power and Representation*. Boston: Northeastern University Press.

◆◆

'I WON'T LET YOU DOWN'*

MOTI NANDI

TRANSLATED BY
ARUNAVA SINHA

'Play!'

A crowd of nearly 15,000 people fell silent in an instant. Even their breathing was furtive. Wimbledon semi-final on the Centre Court—Connors vs. Banerjee.

Ananda was to serve.

With calm eyes he glanced at Jimmy, crouching at the baseline like a leopard. Swaying to left and right, ready to pounce on the serve. His words were still ringing in Ananda's ears. They were standing side by side in the small dressing-room, combing their hair in front of the mirror. Arranging his flowing locks symmetrically to cover his ears, Jimmy had said, a la Muhammad Ali, 'I am the champion—just try and take my title away.'

Ananda bounced the ball on the grass. Once, twice, thrice, as he always did before serving. Jimmy hadn't dropped a single set on his way to the semi-final. Ananda had seen how he had slaughtered Tanner's 140 miles-per-hour serves in the quarter-final. The faster the serve, the better Jimmy seemed to handle it.

Ananda smiled to himself. The speed at which you run around the court, your reflexes, are all supposed to be unmatched. Let's find out.

Tossing the ball up in the air, he struck it with his racket. Bouncing at the corner where the sideline met the service line, it sped past Connors, beyond his backhand.

'Fifteen–love.'

Ananda ambled lazily to the left-hand court, as though he was playing a first-round match against a novice in a club tournament.

He served.

The ball fell on the same spot. Smoothly, but incredibly fast. Jimmy leapt to his right to somehow get his racket to it. It ballooned in the air, like a catch over the head of silly mid-on when a ball bounces suddenly from the good-length spot. Ananda had followed up his serve to the net. Jimmy was rooted to the baseline, helplessly watching the ball descend gently. Ananda volleyed it negligently to the opposite end of the court, one hand carelessly on his waist. There was a soft twang. He didn't take a second look. The point was in the bag. Strolling back to the baseline for the next serve, he caught a ball lobbed at him by the ballboy.

'Thirty–love,' came the umpire's announcement on the speaker.

Another tremendous serve. A puff of chalk dust rose from the centre line. Ace. The ball had landed on the line. A buzz rose in the stands, dying instantly. Jimmy balled his fist, looking at the line and muttering. He was swearing. Let him swear. He had no choice. How was he going to return serves like these?

'Forty–love.'

What was it that Connors had told reporters? I am getting better. I have more shots now. There's no pressure on me. Swagger. Play coolly, Ananda, keep playing coolly. The world No. 1 is on the other side of the net. Keep playing with an ice-cool head, as you planned last night. Slow the game down. Don't let Jimmy come up to the net; he'll kill you if that happens. Pin him to the baseline. The harder you hit your shots, the happier he'll be, batsmen with a wide repertoire of shots love fast pitches. Connors can play all kinds of strokes. Remember Kipling's line above the names of all the Wimbledon champions on the board? 'If you can meet with Triumph and Disaster, and treat those two imposters just the same.... If you can keep faith in yourself when everyone doubts you...'

Believe in yourself, Ananda. You can do it. You can. You have to, because...

Ananda served.

Connors had the ball on his forehand. The return arrived on Ananda's right. He hit a forehand shot down the line. Connors ran unbelievably fast, reaching the ball in a moment. A cross-court shot arrived at lightning speed to Ananda's backhand. He hit it back to the middle of the court. Connors would now hit a lethal two-handed backhand.

Which he did, and Ananda was waiting precisely where the ball arrived. As though he had known all along. He leaned forward slightly to execute his drop shot. Connors raced up and attempted a passing shot. Ananda stretched his arm out to stop the ball in its tracks and send it back over the net. Connors looked back helplessly from the net, stamping his foot on the grass like a mad bull.

'Game, Banerjee. Banerjee leads one game to love.'

Connors to serve. Ananda hit the extra balls over the net one at a time, politely and gently, the way batsmen stroked the ball back to the bowler at the nets. Connors' friend Nastase was pumping his fist in the air. Nasty was encouraging Jimmy.

Ananda glanced at the stands behind the umpire. A diminutive man, five feet seven, with his wife and two sons. He had first played here 22 years ago, even before Ananda was born. He hadn't won the championship yet. If he played Connors in the final the American would devour him. He would probably never win after this.

Their eyes met. Ananda nodded in respectful acknowledgement. Ken Rosewall tilted his head in response. A quiet smile in his eyes. Rosewall had defeated Newcombe in the other semi-final. Ananda thought he was probably about as old as one of Rosewall's sons.

Connors was about to serve...

'Fire, fire, fire!'

Ananda sat up on his bed, trying to look as far into the distance as he could through the eastern window. Some of the people from the factory were racing across the field. It appeared from the uproar that the factory was on fire.

Going up to the gate for a better look, Ananda got a scolding from Bipin-da.

'No need to come out and stare. Go into your room. A minor fire, they've put it out already.'

Ananda wasn't in the mood now that the match had been interrupted suddenly. Lying down on his bed, he looked at the clock. One-thirty in the afternoon. He took the first set 6–0, breaking Connors thrice. It was over in half a minute.

Now for the second set.

Why waste time! It was 6–1 this time. Ananda's service games had gone to deuce three times. Connors was bound to win one game at least. Such a great player—it could even be 6–2. How would it hurt Ananda to let Connors win two games? There must be plenty of Indians in London, Bengalis too. Those who had slunk out of Lord's, their heads hanging in shame, after India had folded up for 42, must be at Wimbledon today.

Third set.

1–1. 2–2. 3–3. 4–4. 4–5. Ananda was trailing.

Connors was serving. He had just played a fantastic game to break Ananda and go to 5–4. Ananda looked around. Each and every face was agog with excitement. The stands were overflowing.

'Fight, Bengali boy!'

The Bengali words, uttered in a sharp voice, cut across the Centre Court from one end to the other. Ananda glanced at the spectators.

Connors was serving. The ball stabbed at the ground and flew away.

Fifteen–love.'

Keep a cool head, Ananda. There are still many points to go before you win. Connors can fight back brilliantly. Don't relax.

Ananda was standing casually, his left hand on his hip, the racket dangling from his right, as though he was watching the game, not playing it. Connors made a V with his fingers. Victory? Ananda's lips curled in contempt.

Connors served, like a cannonball. Ananda barely got his racket to it, the ball soaring towards the stands like a catch to third-man.

'Come on, Banerjee!'

'Thirty–love.'

'Wake up, Bengali boy!'

Ananda chuckled.

'What's going on, Ananda? Steady, steady.'

'Quiet, please. Thank you.'

Nastase smashed his fist into his palm. Connors made a V again with his fingers, smirking. Ananda noticed Rosewall from the corner of his eyes, gazing at him. Such a forlorn look. Ananda's heart twisted. Don't worry. You can be sure of my entering the final. Where you'll defeat me.

Connors served. Ananda's return was a mighty forehand stroke. The ball kissed the net and the sideline.

'Thirty–fifteen.'

Connors served. An unstoppable backhand return to his left.

'Thirty–all.'

Ananda's next return of serve was magnificent. The ball just disappeared down the line, stunning 15,000 spectators. And soon afterwards, a huge cheer shook the Centre Court. Ananda had won the game. 5–5.

Winning the set would mean winning the match too. Ananda felt tired. What was the point of winning so quickly? The heat was spread across the sky like a lit-up furnace in the factory. The sun was like its open door. A strange torpor overcame Ananda.

Should I lose to Rosewall in the final? And deprive India of such a great honour? Krishnan had made it to the semi-final twice. And after him, Ananda Banerjee. Should I allow the greatest honour in the world of tennis to slip through my grasp? Six hundred million Indians would be glued to the radio with such great hope. Crowds at street corners. The boys of Netaji Park, waiting with crackers and saying loudly, 'Aando, our Aando, remember, used to be a fast-bowler, hit a batsman on the head in the nets. Such a quiet boy. Imagine him playing such fantastic tennis. Maybe he's from Bottola, but that's just like our neighbourhood.' They would be waiting impatiently to celebrate. His brother wouldn't go to work. His father would go, though, and meet clients, too. The maid would badger Bipin-da, 'What's our Aando fighting the white man for? He's so frail, you think he'll win?' And Amal—what would he be doing?

Amal alone knows why I wanted to enter the final. He also knows what the outcome will be. After all these years of tennis, Rosewall has acquired a permanent expression of anxiety and worry. His eyes have dimmed, his skin has turned flaccid and spotty. His body can no longer take the punishment that a 20-year-old can. What superhuman effort a man must have put in to ward off challenges from the best players in the world and survive for 22 years! He has won all the honours that tennis can offer—except this one. Talk about fate! Can't fate be defeated?

Six hundred million on one side, and just one person on the other. What would Krishna have done? Is Rosewall Arjun? Even if I lose this year I can win next year, or the year after. But Rosewall cannot.

Should I smash the hopes and aspirations of 600 million people for the sake of just one man? Has Amal ever considered this monstrous problem? Such a huge country, but bereft of honours, always lagging behind, trailing everyone. The world has completely forgotten that such a big country exists in the field of sport, even the people of India have forgotten that anything can be achieved. One defeat after another has broken their back, they have begun to believe they are worthless, that they cannot be fast bowlers, that they cannot be tennis champions. The entire country would stand erect again if Ananda were to win the Wimbledon. Six hundred million people, can you imagine? But instead of this, let each of them down to fulfil the desire, a mere wish, of one individual, just one individual? What should I do now? Country or self? Poor Rosewall, his quest, his willpower—will all this go waste eventually? Is the nation greater than the individual?

Ananda tossed and turned in bed, rolling from side to side.

'I want to give India something. Once, just once, this is my last chance...'

Still tossing and turning, Ananda eventually fell asleep, waking up on his own from a deep slumber a couple of hours later. Through the northern window he could see an overcast sky. There had been blazing sunshine when he fell asleep. Far away, a jet was coming in to land at Dum Dum Airport. Ananda suddenly remembered that the West Indies cricket team was due to play in India. They would trample all over an Indian team already demolished by England recently. Who would be playing for the West Indies?

The squad had not been announced yet. Only the captain had been named—Clive Lloyd. Sobers had said he hadn't retired yet, which meant he might come too. Kanhai as well. Kallicharan, Rowe, Fredericks, Boyce, Murray, Holder, Gibbs were all bound to be there. And Andy Roberts. What a team, my God! Imagine bowling against them!

Ananda's eyes began to glitter. West Indies were tearing India to shreds. People were gathered on pavements, listening to the commentary on the radio and shaking their heads in disappointment. As this vision rose before his eyes, Ananda switched on his tape-recorder, held it close to his chest, and began to whisper. 'This is All India Radio. The news, read by Barun Haldar. In today's headlines, the Indian squad for the fifth and final Test against the

West Indies at Bombay has been named. Bengal fast bowler Ananda Banerjee has been included in the 14-member squad.'

He played it back over and over again all afternoon.

◆◆◆

He was in Bombay now. His chest was bandaged heavily. The doctor had ordered him to stay in bed all day. He was taken directly from the stadium to the hospital yesterday. They had done an X-ray, found a crack in his ribs, strapped him up, and put him in a cabin.

Ananda lay there, glued to the transistor. At lunch on the second day, the West Indies were 470 for 2. Kallicharan batting on 204, Kanhai on 150. Fredericks had scored 70, someone else had made 15, the rest were extras.

Out!

Solkar had pouched Kallicharan at short-leg off Prasanna. First ball after lunch.

Who was coming in to bat? Lawrence Rowe. These commentators—hopeless. Ananda held the transistor to his ear, just like his brother. (He had visited the hospital yesterday, this morning too. The entire Team India as well.)

It was Sobers. How strange, couldn't the commentators recognise him? Pataudi had set an attacking field. New batsman. Kanhai and Sobers; 470 for 3. How much longer would they bat? They should be declaring at tea. Sobers hit his first boundary after 15 minutes, off Bedi. Thirty runs in the next 15 minutes; 101 in 80 minutes. Kanhai had made only 12 more.

Lloyd declared, having batted just a 100 minutes after lunch—620 for 3. How would it help to have India bat for 10 minutes before tea?

◆◆◆

In the afternoon Ananda visited Wankhede Stadium.

India were all out for 135 at lunch on the third day. Follow-on. Trailing by 485 runs. There were two-and-a-half days to go. Another innings defeat was looming large. There was no life in the pitch, Roberts hadn't got a single wicket. Sobers had claimed two with his googlies, Gibbs had taken six, two run-outs.

Ananda was in the hospital cabin, listening on the transistor. There were no sounds in the stadium. It was like playing in a crematorium.

The fever went down in the afternoon, only to return in the evening. The bones in his wrists, elbows, knees and ankles were all hurting. His body was wracked with pain. He didn't dare tell anyone for fear of being scolded. Trying to prove he was all right, he ate whatever Bipin-da gave him.

'Are you not well, Ananda?' asked Amal. 'Why are you panting? Your face and eyes are swollen.'

Ananda smiled.

'I'm playing against Connors right now, third set, five all. I'm very tired. Rosewall is waiting in the final for me. Meanwhile, India is following on.'

'Don't talk too much.'

'Want to hear what I did in the first over?'

'No. Rest now.'

'Fredericks smashed me all over the stadium. The spectators were taunting me. I was looking for an excuse to run away. Trying to take an impossible catch off the last ball of my over I fell on my chest. Severe injury. I'm in a hospital cabin now. I'm in the other world, Amal.'

Ananda shut his eyes. He didn't realise when Amal had moved away quietly from his spot outside the window. Ananda could see himself in the hospital now.

India were 45 for 4 at tea. Ananda switched off the transistor and put on his white flannels. The nurse wasn't here, but she could arrive any moment. His boots would make a noise, he would have to hide them. How could India lose while Ananda Banerjee was playing? A sharp pain in his chest.

He was tiptoeing out of his cabin. His boots were wrapped in a towel. The staircase at the end of the long corridor led downstairs. The place was deserted. He skipped down the stairs. The pain was worse now. Luckily, no one could see the bandage. He could borrow a bat, pads and gloves from Vishwanath or Brijesh Patel. Both were out.

'Taxi, taxi! To the stadium, where the Test Match is being played. Quick!'

India were 51 for 6. The match would end in three days. Pataudi was walking back. Clean bowled by Roberts. Just the one wicket. Very slow pitch. Not even a bowler of Roberts' pace was able to extract life from it. Still India was collapsing. Who was left? Banerjee wouldn't be batting. Prasanna, Bedi, Chandrasekhar. Abid Ali and Pataudi had left in quick succession after tea. Gavaskar was 24 not out.

Another half an hour at most. It would be over by then. Getting a bus or a taxi would be hard then. People had started streaming out of the stadium.

Pataudi was returning, taking his gloves off, his head tilted to the left. Prasanna would be going in to bat. Raising his eyes to tell him something, Pataudi stopped in surprise. His left eye popped.

'Banerjee!'

'Bad luck, Pat.'

Ananda walked past him towards the pitch.

Injured, and a bowler to boot. So Roberts bowled well outside the off stump, at medium pace. Anyone could be generous with 450 runs to spare.

Crack!

Square cut. Gibbs ducked at gully. No one saw the ball till it reached the ropes.

Sobers clapped, smiling. Kallicharan, too. They knew everyone hit reckless strokes when defeat was staring them in the face.

The next ball was straight at the stumps. Crack! Six over the bowler's head. End of the over. Gavaskar came up to chat.

'Just stay there, Sunny. Give me support, that's all. Don't take short runs because...'

Unable to translate everything into English, Ananda only put his hand on his chest and finished, '...pain.'

Gavaskar went back to his crease, looking at Ananda in surprise.

Within 15 minutes Lloyd was forced to spread out his fielders. Twenty off a Roberts over. Ananda could have taken a single, but didn't because of the pain in his chest. Twenty-six of a Gibbs over, all the three sixes over the sight screen. Sixteen off a Sobers over. Boyce was running around like a frisky water insect at cover. Lawrence

Rowe was pacing up and down like a detective at third man. Kanhai was fidgeting at slip like a wedding guest impatient to eat.

Runs were flowing like a flood at Wankhede Stadium. Kallicharan's innings was drowned. Sobers' and Kanhai's, too. Thousands of Bengalis lived in Bombay. They must be at the stadium.

'Fight, Bengali boy!'

Ananda raised his bat towards the stands.

'Kill them, Bengal tiger!'

Ananda reached 100 off the last ball of the last over of the day, late-cutting Boyce. Like Sobers, he had taken 80 minutes. It wouldn't have taken so long had it not been for the immaculate fielding and Sunny's dour defending. Gavaskar had flashed twice outside the off-stump, but had controlled himself after Ananda said, 'Steady, Sunny, steady.'

India were 160 for 6. Two days still to go. Had it not been for the police cordon at the boundary line, Ananda would have been killed by the joyous crowd. Thousands of people were jostling to speak to him. Loud sounds of celebrations. Lloyd allowed him to lead the rest off the field. All the West Indian players were clapping. Ananda stole a glance at the guest block. His brother looked grim.

No one could embrace him because of the pain. Solkar, Bedi and Abid Ali planted kisses on his cheek. The doctor couldn't make up his mind whether to be furious or not.

'Do you know the hospital has informed the police? You didn't tell anyone.'

'Why? Doesn't anyone listen to the commentary?'

'Something terrible could have happened. You're not even supposed to move.'

'You expect me to lie in bed while India loses? I'll bat tomorrow as well.'

◆

*This article is my translation from the Bengali of excerpts from *Aparajito Ananda* (Undefeated Ananda), by Moti Nandi (1984). Kolkata: Ananda Publishers.

◆◆

ABOUT THE EDITORS AND CONTRIBUTORS

JOSEPH S. ALTER teaches Anthropology at the University of Pittsburgh and has published a number of books, including *The Wrestler's Body; Knowing Dil Das; Gandhi's Body; Asian Medicine and Globalization; Yoga in Modern India; and Moral Materialism*. His research is based in South Asia, and is currently focused on the cultural history of nature cure as a globalised system of medicine, biosemiotics and social theory, and the natural history of animals in the human imagination. With a focus on ecology and natural history, Alter runs a semester-long study-abroad programme in the Indian Himalayas.

SHANAKA AMARASINGHE is a lawyer, writer and sports commentator—although not necessarily in that order—based in Colombo, Sri Lanka. He is Counsel for Sri Lanka's largest law firm Julius and Creasy by day, and by night he is the country's premier rugby commentator and analyst. Amarasinghe hosts Sri Lanka's top-rated sports chat show, 'The Score', on local radio, and is a freelance journalist who has been featured in publications such as *Wisden, The Nighwatchman* and *Cricketer*. Amarasinghe blogs at www. ballhandling101.wordpress.com and tweets @ShanakaScore.

MICHIEL BAAS is Research Fellow with the Asia Research Institute of the National University of Singapore. His research work revolves round questions of new middle-class formations and strategies of socio-economic mobility in urban India. Baas has conducted extensive research among fitness trainers and bodybuilders, as well as those working as coffee baristas in shopping malls.

KAUSIK BANDYOPADHYAY teaches History at the West Bengal State University, Barasat, India. He is also Deputy Executive Editor of *Soccer & Society*. He was Fellow of the International Olympic Museum, Lausanne, and of Maulana Abul Kalam Azad Institute of Asian Studies, Kolkata. Bandyopadhyay's areas of research interest include the social and cultural history of modern India, popular culture in South Asia, history of sport, and contemporary South Asia. His most recent publications include *Mahatma on the Pitch: Gandhi and Cricket in India*; and *Sport, Culture and Nation: Perspectives from Indian Football and South Asian Cricket*, among others.

MIHIR BOSE is an award-winning journalist and author who lives in London. He writes and broadcasts on social and historical issues as well as sport for a range of outlets, including the BBC (where he was the first Sports Editor), the *Financial Times*, *History Today*, *The Guardian*, *Daily Telegraph* and *The Sunday Times*. Bose has an honorary doctorate from Loughborough University for his outstanding contribution to journalism and the promotion of equality. The author of more than 30 books, some of his publications include *From Midnight to Glorious Morning? A Midnight's Child*; *The Indian Spy*; and the *History of Indian Cricket*. Bose has also written the only narrative history of Bollywood.

AVIJIT GHOSH is Senior Editor with *The Times of India*. He grew up in the rough and intense townships of Bihar and is addicted to cricket, football, films and music—not necessarily in that order. He writes and blogs regularly on sport. Ghosh is the author of *Bandicoots in the Moonlight* and *Up Campus, Down Campus*; and two books on film: the award-winning *Cinema Bhojpuri* and *40 Retakes*.

OMITA GOYAL has a master's degree in Sociology from the Delhi School of Economics. She is presently Chief Editor of the *IIC Quarterly*, the Journal of the India International Centre. She started her career in the voluntary sector with the Indian Social Institute, New Delhi, and then moved into academic publishing where she has spent over 35 years. She worked at Sage Publications India Private Limited, leaving as General Manager, and thereafter was a consultant for the World Bank, UNICEF, UNDP, Voluntary Health Association of India, Centre for Women's Development Studies, WHO, Institute of Social Studies, The Hague, and TERI. In 2005, she was invited by Taylor and Francis to start a social science programme under their social science and humanities imprint, Routledge, as Publishing Director. She has edited the book *Interrogating Women's Leadership and Empowerment*; and co-edited with Rajiv Kumar, *Thirty Years of SAARC: Society, Culture and Development*; with Apoorvanand, *Education at the Crossroads*; with Sujata Patel, *India's Contemporary Urban Conundrum*; with Ronojoy Sen, *South Asia's Sporting Mosaic*; and with Pratik Kanjilal, *Social Media in a Networked World*.

STEFAN HUEBNER is a historian of colonialism, modernisation and development policy. Currently, he is Research Fellow at the National University of Singapore's Asia Research Institute. In spring 2018, he will be a visiting scholar at the Harvard University Asia Center. His publications address the connections between sporting events in Asia, the muscular Christian ideals of the YMCA, anti-colonial nationalisms, pan-Asian sentiments, nation-branding-related sports infrastructure construction, and Cold War development policies. Huebner's most important contribution to the topic is: 'Pan-Asian Sports and the Emergence of Modern Asia, 1913–1974'.

NOVY KAPADIA is a versatile sports commentator and analyst in both English and Hindi for both radio and television. At present, Kapadia is a football and sports columnist with *The Asian Age*, *The Week*, *Deccan Chronicle, Sportstar* and *Economic Times,* among others. Some of his publications include *Barefoot to Boots: The Many Lives of Indian Football* and *The Football Fanatic's Essential Guide: A History of the World Cup, 1930–2014.* Kapadia has covered several international sports events, including six World Cup Football tournaments, European Football Championships, Asian Games, Commonwealth Games, Olympic Games, World Cup and Champions Trophy hockey, SAF Games and SAFF Championships.

ALI KHAN is Associate Professor of Anthropology, and Department Chair at the Department of Humanities and Social Sciences, LUMS, Lahore, Pakistan. Khan's research interests vary from labour issues to popular culture in Pakistan, focusing particularly on cinema and sport. His publications include *Representing Children: Power, Policy* *and the Discourse on Child Labour in the Football Manufacturing Industry of Pakistan.* His last two projects have resulted in co-authored and edited books on cricket (*Cricket Cauldron*) and Pakistani cinema (*Cinema and Society*). Khan has a PhD in Social Anthropology from the University of Cambridge in England.

SHAHARYAR M. KHAN is a former diplomat of the Pakistan Foreign Service and the United Nations, and twice Chairman of the Pakistan Cricket Board. Khan was educated in Cambridge and teaches Foreign Policy at LUMS, Lahore, Pakistan. His publications include: *Begums of Bhopal; The Shallow Graves of Rwanda;* and *Cricket Cauldron: The Turbulent Politics of Sport in Pakistan.* His most personal book has been the biography of his mother Princess Abida Sultaan, *Memoirs of a Rebel Princess.* Khan's most recent book, *Bhopal Connections: Vignettes of Royal Rule,* looks at the life and times of the rulers of Bhopal.

HABIBUL HAQUE KHONDKER is Professor of Sociology at Zayed University, Abu Dhabi, UAE. His research interests lie in globalisation, migration, state, civil society, social media and democracy. He has co-edited *Asia and Europe in Globalization: Continents, Regions and Nations* with Goran Therborn; and *The Middle East and the 21st Century Globalization* with Jan Nederveen Pieterse. Khondker has co-authored *Globalization: East/West* with Bryan Turner.

SANKARAN KRISHNA teaches Politics at the University of Hawai'i at Manoa in Honolulu, USA. His interests span postcolonial nationalism, South Asian studies, race and ethnicity, and critical international relations. He took his Bachelor's from Loyola College in Chennai, Master's from JNU in New Delhi and doctorate from Syracuse University in New York. Krishna's essays—on academic matters, contemporary politics, and cricket—can be accessed at: https://manoa-hawaii.academia.edu/SankaranKrish.

ABHIJEET KULKARNI began his career in journalism, covering politics and crime in the late 1990s before shifting to his primary passion, sports, just before the Athens Olympics. A former footballer, he has been concentrating more on covering Olympic sports. As a journalist, Kulkarni has been following Indian badminton very closely for over a decade now, and also during a brief stint with an NGO that identifies and nurtures sporting talent at the junior level. Kulkarni has worked for the Press Trust of India, *Hindustan Times* and *Mumbai Mirror*, and is currently Associate Editor at Scroll.in.

AMRITH LAL is Associate Editor, *The Indian Express*. He has been a journalist since 1994 and has lived and worked in Delhi, Pune and Chennai. He writes on the interface of politics and culture in Malayalam and English. Lal grew up in a village near the Kanyakumari coast, but was tutored on the myth and lore of *vallam kali* by his parents who hailed from villages in Kuttanad. Lal can be accessed at amrith.lal@gmail.com.

DUNCAN MCDUIE-RA is Professor of Development Studies at UNSW, Australia. His most recent monographs include *Northeast Migrants in Delhi: Race, Refuge and Retail*; *Debating Race in Contemporary India*; and *Borderland City in New India: Frontier to Gateway*.

SUNDEEP MISRA has covered four Olympic Games, seven hockey World Cups, two cricket World Cups, three Asian Games, three Commonwealth Games, and the 2017 London Athletics World Championship, among others. He writes for *First Post, Tehelka, Caravan, Khaleej Times, Mid-day* and *The Tribune,* and was Founder Editor-in-Chief of *Sports Illustrated, India*. He is the author of the unauthorised biography of hockey legend Dhanraj Pillay, *Forgive me Amma*; *The Best of Indian Sports Writing;* and *The Mohammed of Benares and Other Stories*. Misra was also executive producer and joint screenplay writer of the film *Prithipal Singh...A Story*.

PAYOSHNI MITRA's writings and advocacy on issues related to gender equality in sport recently led to a research project on sport, sexual harassment and gender discrimination at Jadavpur University, with support from the Ministry of Youth Affairs and Sports. She has previously worked with the Women's Sports Foundation, USA, and with the Women's Sports & Fitness Foundation, UK. She was a consultant with the Sports Authority of India (2014–2015), and with MYAS (2012–2013). Mitra is the government-appointed Advisor-cum-Mediator in the Dutee Chand case that resulted in the suspension of the controversial Hyperandrogenism Regulations at the Rio Olympics 2016.

SOUVIK NAHA is Guest Lecturer in History at West Bengal State University, and Editor of *Soccer & Society*. He has edited two books: *Global and Transnational Sport: Ambiguous Borders, Connected Domains*; and *FIFA World Cup and Beyond: Sport, Culture, Media and Governance*. Naha's research has been published in various edited volumes and peer-reviewed journals, such as *International Journal of the History of Sport, Sport in Society, Soccer & Society, Sport in History* and *Economic and Political Weekly*.

PAL PILLAI and **ALI BHARMAL**, both photographers, co-founded Focus Sports, driven purely by a passion for sport. Pillai has covered major sporting events such as cricket, soccer, field hockey, tennis, table tennis, synchronised swimming, water skiing, archery, track and field games, fencing and athletics. His work has been published in *The New York Times, Time, Newsweek, The Wall Street Journal, Sports Illustrated, National Geographic, The Guardian, Hindustan Times* and *Indian Express,* among others. Recently, his pictures of Sachin Tendulkar were used in *Playing it My way*, Tendulkar's official autobiography.

Bharmal's fascination with shape, design, colour, ratio and sequence has resulted in a profoundly visual connection with people and the world around him, reflecting in images that tell a story no words can describe but can only be felt and experienced. His journey as a sports and adventure photographer has made it possible to discover many non-core sports in India across several genres such as BMX, rock climbing, rally crossing and aerial aerobatics.

SHANTHA RANGASWAMY has various firsts to her credit in the history of Indian women's cricket. Rangaswamy was the first captain of India (1976–1984); the first captain to steer India to a Test match win (1976); the first Indian woman to have scored a century in Test cricket (1976); the first Indian sportswoman to receive the Arjuna Award (1976); and the first woman cricketer to receive the Life Time Achievement Award by the BCCI (2017). Rangaswamy has also excelled in her chosen profession of banking from where she retired as General Manager (Canara Bank).

AMY J. RANSOM is Professor of French at Central Michigan University, USA. Specialising in French–Canadian popular culture, her books include *Hockey P.Q.: Canada's Game in Quebec's Popular Culture;* and *Science Fiction from Québec: A Postcolonial Study*. Having fallen in love with Bollywood film, Ransom published 'Bollywood Goes to the Stadium: Gender, National Identity, and Sport Film in Hindi', in 2014, in the *Journal of Film and Video* (66.4), and is currently working on a study of Indian science-fiction films.

RONOJOY SEN is Senior Research Fellow at the Institute of South Asian Studies and the South Asian Studies Programme, National University of Singapore. He has worked for over a decade with leading Indian newspapers, most recently as an editor for *The Times of India*. His most recent book is *Nation at Play: A History of Sport in India* (Columbia University Press/Penguin, 2015). He is also the author of *Articles of Faith: Religion, Secularism, and the Indian Supreme Court* (Oxford University Press, 2010), and has edited several books. Sen holds a PhD in political science from the University of Chicago and read history at Presidency College, Calcutta.

SATADRU SEN was Professor of South Asian history at the City University of New York. His research interests were in the intersecting histories of the disciplined self and community in modern India, including the histories of race, childhood, punishment and citizenship. His most recent book was *Benoy Kumar Sarkar: Restoring the Nation to the World*. Sen also authored *Migrant Races: Empire, Identity and K. S. Ranjitsinhji*, and other work on the history of sport in modern India.

RUDRANEIL SENGUPTA is a writer at the business daily *Mint,* and the author of *Enter the Dangal*, a book on the history and culture of wrestling in India, published by HarperCollins. In 2015, he won the Society of Publishers of Asia (SOPA) award for excellence in reporting on human rights issues for a story on gender testing for female athletes.

IAN SIMPSON is a Sydney historian with longstanding interests in Indian and Asian histories, education and sport. His current research interests are in changes in Australian perceptions of India. As well as writing about Indian cricketers, his work has covered Indian lascars, hawkers and popular entertainers in Australia, Indian cultural influences in the early colonies, and the story of Indian food in Australia.

ARUNAVA SINHA translates classic, modern and contemporary Bengali fiction, non-fiction and poetry from India and Bangladesh into English. Forty of his translations have been published so far. He is Series Editor with the Library of Bangladesh and also curates Seagull Books' India list. Sinha is the Books Editor at Scroll.in, and teaches undergraduate students at Ashoka University.

SHARDA UGRA is Senior Editor for ESPNcricinfo.com, the world's biggest independent single-sports website, and ESPN.in, ESPN's newly-launched multisport website. A sports journalist for more than 25 years, she has also worked with *Mid-Day*, *The Hindu* and *India Today*. Ugra worked with former New Zealand captain John Wright on *Indian Summers*, memoirs of his years coaching India, and with Yuvraj Singh on *The Test of My Life*, an account of his diagnosis and recovery from cancer. In 2013, Ugra was Fellow of the Australia India Institute, University of Melbourne.

◆